For Suzanne, Peter, James, Sam, Matthew and Joanna

Nicholas Booth is a writer and broadcaster. For ten years he was a journalist, first on the the *Observer* and then *The Times*. Most recently he has worked in television and as an editorial director for online and mobile publishing. With an interest in espionage and secret warfare, he now lives between London and Cheshire, where he was born in 1964.

ZigZag

The incredible wartime
exploits of double
agent Eddie Chapman

NICHOLAS BOOTH

PORTRAIT

Visit the Portrait website!

PORTRAIT Piatkus publishes a wide range of non-fiction, including biography, history, science, music, popular culture and sport.

If you want to:
• read descriptions of our popular titles
• buy our books over the internet
• take advantage of our special offers
• enter our monthly competition
• learn more about your favourite Piatkus authors

VISIT OUR WEBSITE AT: www.portraitbooks.com

For more information go to www.eddiechapman.com

Copyright © 2007 by Nicholas Booth

First published in 2007 by **Portrait**
an imprint of
Piatkus Books Ltd
5 Windmill Street
London W1T 2JA
e-mail: info@piatkus.co.uk

The moral right of the author has been asserted

A catalogue record for this book is available from the British Library

ISBN 0 7499 5156 7
ISBN 13: 978 0 7499 5156 6

This book has been printed on paper manufactured
with respect for the environment using wood from
managed sustainable resources

Edited by Steve Gove
Text design by Paul Saunders

Data manipulation by Phoenix Photosetting, Chatham, Kent
www.phoenixphotosetting.co.uk

Printed and bound in Great Britain by
MPG Books, Bodmin, Cornwall

Author's Note

In Eddie Chapman's recollections – not to mention various MI5 and official government reports – many of the names of principal characters who appear in this book are spelled differently and inconsistently. There are notable discrepancies between Eddie's account and those of both his pre-war cronies and, particularly, his German colleagues from the war years. Moreover, many German intelligence officers used false names, though Eddie usually found out what their real ones were. Some he only knew phonetically. His wartime controller, von Gröning, for example, is referred to as Von Grunen; in some MI5 reports he is also known as 'Graumann', his 'spy name' (the name which Eddie also used to hide the fact he was British). To avoid confusion, I have changed all names in the narrative to be internally consistent. For the same reason, the Secret Intelligence Service – the British secret service – is referred to by its 'other name' of MI6.

Contents

Acknowledgments

First and foremost, it is a pleasure rather than an authorly duty to thank Betty Chapman for agreeing to collaborate with me on this book. Without her help, encouragement and unflinching honesty in discussing sometimes painful memories, this book would be a much lesser work. Her own life story is no less dramatic than that of Eddie's; she is equally brave and resourceful. Despite her ill health, Betty has borne my questions with great fortitude, stoicism and equanimity.

I am also very grateful to Carole Bell, Betty's very good friend; Carole carefully recorded Betty's clarifications and further memories without complaint. Their laughter, love and friendship, made the writing of the book an unforgettable experience.

Other members of the Chapman family were helpful in answering queries and searching out obscure pieces of information, documents and photographs. Russell Chapman bent over backwards to arrange an interview with his father, Winston. Thanks also to Suzanne Osborn and James, particularly for letting me use material from his website www.eddiechapman.com. Thanks also to Julie Cooper, David Case and Lillian Verner Bonds for sharing their memories.

Olga Daw was most helpful in providing photographs. Special thanks to Susi Paz for her help in researching the photos.

★ ★ ★

A work of this nature has required a great deal of research. To the librarians and information staff of the British Library (in both St.

Pancras and Colindale), Imperial War Museum and the UK National Archives, I offer sincere gratitude. In particular, in Kew it has been a pleasure to make a new professional relationship with James Strachan, who is now Director of Public Services and Marketing.

For their assistance in making sense of Eddie's pre-war activities, I would like to thank David Capus, Alison Clark, Andrew Dunn and Andrew Ledwidge of the Metropolitan Police.

In Jersey, Matthew Costard of the Channel Islands Historical Society and Hedley Faramus were very helpful; Dr Paul Sanders patiently provided guidance on the sometimes tangled history of how the prisons worked on Jersey. Ian Sayer was very helpful in sorting out minor discrepancies in Eric Pleasants' records.

Sabine Pusch interviewed Frau Ingeborg von Groning at short notice. Many thanks for her help in translating material from the original German. In Norway, Hans Olav Lahlum and Isa Lahlum kindly illuminated many mysteries surrounding their great aunt, Dagmar. Thanks also to David Stafford for his expert reading of the finished manuscript.

As always, I owe a particular debt of gratitude to Dominique Torode and Julian Parker, for letting me invade their spare room and for their encouragement; and to Francesca, Isabelle and Ben, thanks for letting me watch their Laurel & Hardy DVDs.

It is thanks to the extraordinary skill of Portrait that this book has been edited and published so swiftly. Alan Brooke, Editor-at-Large, not only saw the potential of this book, but provided encouragement to its author whose enthusiasm often flagged. His very fine editing suggestions – buttressed by the forensic skills of copy editor Steve Gove – have immeasurably improved the narrative. Thanks also to Alan's associates, Alison Sturgeon and Denise Dwyer, and Simon Colverson, Production Director, whose sterling efforts helped accelerate the printing of the book.

I am very grateful to my agent, Peter Cox, for guidance, friendship and his peerless skill in bringing this project to fruition. And finally, special thanks to Marka Hibbs in Pasadena, California where early portions of this book were written at the start of 2006.

The rest was completed in Cheshire where my mother uncomplainingly allowed me to invade her house with paper, chaos and (at times) choice language as I nearly drowned in the swirl of multiple drafts.

Grateful acknowledgement is made to Betty Chapman for allowing me to use copyright material that belongs to Eddie and Betty Chapman Literary Properties. These are *The Eddie Chapman Story* (1954); *Free Agent* (1955); *I Killed To Live* (1957); *Joey Boy* (1959) and *The Real Eddie Chapman Story* (1966).

Eddie's MI5 files are Crown copyright and material from them is reproduced by permission of the Controller of HMSO.

Wherever possible, I have tried to obtain permission to use material quoted or photographs used; any omissions will be corrected in subsequent editions of this book.

★ ★ ★

All photos courtesy of Eddie and Betty Chapman Literary Properties, except for the following:

p.3 Courtesy of The National Archives, *(top)* ref. ZZ/06, *(bottom)* ref. ZZ/07; p.4 Courtesy of The National Archives, *(top)* ref. KV2/458, *(bottom)* ref. ZZ-04; p.5 Courtesy of The National Archives, *(top)* ref. KV2/460 *(middle)* ref. KV2/460, *(bottom)* ref. KV2/462; p.6 *(top)* © WARNER BROS/CINEUROP/THE KOBAL COLLECTION, *(bottom)* © popperfoto.com; p.7 Courtesy of The National Archives *(top)* ref. KV2/459 *(bottom)* ref. KV2/461; p.8 © Mark Gerson, courtesy of Eddie and Betty Chapman Literary Properties, p.9 *(bottom)* © *Sunday Telegraph*

An Airman with a Suicide Pill

A GHOSTLY DARKNESS extended far across the fenlands of Cambridgeshire in the early hours of a surprisingly clement December morning. It was the week before Christmas 1942 and high above the cathedral city of Ely the familiar, though increasingly rare sound of German aircraft grew ever louder. Within moments, air raid sirens sounded. A handful of Junkers bombers had flown in over the Wash and were now heading towards Cambridge and the many factories surrounding its outskirts. A farmer and his wife were among the handful of people woken just before 2 a.m. They soon heard the stream of German aircraft heading off into the night, accompanied by the more distant sound of the ack-ack guns protecting Cambridge. Apes Hill Farm, two miles north of Littleport, would not be bombed, at least not tonight.

Mrs Martha Convine, the farmer's wife, remained awake when she heard – or thought she heard – the characteristic buzzing of a single aircraft which seemed to be flying in great circles over the farm. By the time the all clear sounded a few minutes later, it had gone. She turned over and tried to get back to sleep. Within the hour, there was frantic knocking at the front door. Martha Convine was marginally quicker out of bed than her husband. In the darkness she could make out the silhouette of a tall man standing in the doorway.

'Who is it?' she shouted through the glass.

'A British airman,' came the reply. 'I've had an accident.'

The voice was pleasant and reassuringly English. Mrs Convine opened the door and let the visitor in as her husband lit a lamp in the hallway. She was greeted by a rake-thin apparition, an affable character with a pencil-thin moustache and an infectious grin. To her horror, he was soaked in blood. This airman, whoever he was, also appeared to be extremely wet, looking more than a little sheepish in his sports coat and flannels. He said he had come down to earth by parachute.

'I need to speak to the police at once,' he implored.

Mrs Convine showed him into the lounge where, out of earshot, he used the telephone. It was only then, as she went to make a pot of tea, that the farmer's wife sensed something wasn't quite right. For a start, the man was very, very wet, as though he had been roaming around the ploughed fields for the best part of the evening. He was also clutching a large, unmarked canvas bag as though it was some sort of comforter. When she returned with the tea tray she noticed he had removed a package and left it on the chair. The visitor told her the police were on their way. She handed him a towel to help clean himself up.

Even though it was now just after three o'clock in the morning, the Convines chatted to the visitor and drank their tea. When the stranger referred to an experimental plane he had been piloting, Mrs Convine was puzzled.

'Where is this plane?' she asked.

'Across the fields.'

There was an ominous silence.

'I thought I heard a Jerry.'

'Yes,' he replied. 'That would be a cover plane for ours.'

Mrs Convine was now certain that – although very polite and obviously English – there was something not quite right about the stranger. He bore no signs of a Royal Air Force uniform nor, for that matter, flight overalls or any military insignia. He had made no attempt to contact any of the nearby air bases. A few minutes later, a couple of sergeants from nearby Littleport police station arrived on bicycles. George Convine was also a special constable and he knew them reasonably well. He showed them into the lounge where the visitor was chattering away nineteen to the dozen. Before they could ask him any questions, the man smiled and leaned forward.

'I expect the first thing you want is this.'

From inside his jacket, he handed over an automatic pistol.

'I want to get in touch with the British Secret Service,' he added.

He opened the oblong-shaped package and one of the sergeants went over to inspect it. It contained a radio transmitter, some obviously foreign chocolate and a few shirts.

'Do you have any money?' the sergeant asked.

The man leaned over again and from between his shoulders removed another small package that had been taped to his back. 'Only to be opened by your secret services,' he added mysteriously. 'It will have an interesting story to tell.' (Indeed, it did, containing a number of large denomination notes, nearly £1,000 – a tidy sum in 1942.)

The other policeman asked if he could frisk the visitor, who agreed and stood up. Nothing untoward happened until the sergeant came across a small brown pill hidden inside his trouser turn-up. 'A suicide pill,' the visitor explained helpfully.

So began the extraordinary odyssey of a suspected enemy agent whom the British authorities quickly took into custody. Given the codename Zigzag, his real name was Arnold Edward Chapman. Without a doubt he was the most remarkable spy of the Second World War. Even by the standards of the fantasists, putative playboys and incompetents who tried to spy against the Allies during that war, Eddie Chapman was unique. An ex-guardsman, a fiercely proud Geordie and, at various times, a petty criminal, a film extra, a wrestler, a self-confessed habitué of the Soho nightlife – indeed, later a nightclub owner – he had already achieved notoriety before the war as a safebreaker. Serving time in a Jersey jail when the Germans invaded, Eddie had offered to work for the enemy as a saboteur and spy. His offer had been received with alacrity.

As a result, Eddie Chapman became the only British national ever to be awarded an Iron Cross for his spying for the Third Reich. He was also the only German spy ever to parachute into Britain *twice*.

For the moment, on the morning of Thursday, 16 December 1942, the British security authorities had only a dim appreciation of who he was and what he was up to. Thanks to the reading of the German Enigma codes, a British-born parachutist who had some connection with Jersey had been expected for the best part of the month. His arrival would set alarm bells ringing throughout the corridors of power. Just whose side was Eddie Chapman on? Despite a later, unprompted declaration of unswerving loyalty to King and Crown, the British secret services were never certain whether to believe him or not. The stakes were very high. If he didn't pass muster, Eddie could be executed for having willingly collaborated with the enemy. And, as he was well aware, if he didn't make radio contact with his German controllers soon, he would risk losing his way back.

Nothing was ever quite what it seemed in this story, for Eddie Chapman was the most unlikely – and contradictory – of heroes. The man himself was not above playing off one side against the other, and, at times, deliberately pulling the leg of his more credulous chroniclers. In the years since the war, a one-dimensional portrait of Eddie Chapman has emerged: a womaniser, addicted to cheap thrills and criminal heists, fast cars and loud suits. In reality, Eddie had too much style, charm and intelligence to be a common criminal. No single label could ever describe him adequately, though many tried. Traitor? Rogue? Hero? The truth was that Eddie Chapman was one of the most astute people who ever came into contact with the intelligence world. He was always one step ahead of his captors; in war, as in peacetime, his own instinct for survival came top of the list.

When Eddie Chapman fell from the skies over Cambridgeshire in 1942, his life to date had been no less turbulent than his parachute descent to the ground. The codename Zigzag had been appropriated as MI5 thought it best described the vicissitudes of fate which had propelled him here. His fortunes and misfortunes go some way to explaining his actions and unusual view of the world. Eddie's first twenty-eight years represented a textbook case of a life that had gone wrong after much initial promise. As to why he went off the rails, his widow, Betty, says her husband attracted trouble like a magnet. 'Whenever anything went wrong, it was always Eddie they picked on,' Betty Chapman says. 'As though he was responsible for everything.'

Eddie was a generous, kind-hearted child who was proud of his roots and who, for the remainder of his life, was something of a hero for his fellow Wearsiders. When he was fifteen, he had rescued a drowning man off Roker and was awarded a certificate from the Humane Society. (At the start of the new millennium, his local paper – *Sunderland Today* – canvassed its readers for their greatest local heroes. Eddie was up there with Bryan Ferry, the Venerable Bede, BBC reporter Kate Adie and the inventor Sir Joseph Swan.)

It was the death of Eddie's mother in the mid-1930s that had propelled him towards criminality, the only way he could survive after being forced to leave the Coldstream Guards. He quickly became a part of the glamorous and shady underworld of Soho in the 1930s. Eddie knew – or claimed to his MI5 interrogators that he did – Marlene Dietrich, Ivor Novello, Noël Coward and many celebrities of stage and screen. In later years, when people wanted to film his exploits, he mixed with Alfred Hitchcock, Cary Grant, Richard Burton and Elizabeth Taylor.

'Eddie wasn't that bothered about "names",' says Betty Chapman. 'He was as comfortable with the baron as the bellboy.' (His German handler was indeed a genuine baron.)

But it was as a safebreaker that Eddie Chapman had attained notoriety. Some of his exploits had made the front pages of the *Police Gazette* and, at one time or other, most of the newspapers. The British security establishment couldn't reconcile these exploits with the breezy fellow now in their custody. He was one of the most charming people they had ever encountered.

There was something about Eddie that was irresistible. His charisma and sense of humour attracted people from all walks of life. 'One thing you'll find is that very few people had a wrong word to say about him,' says his widow. 'Most of his friends knew that he was a crook,' one MI5 handler was to report, 'but nevertheless they liked him for his manner and his personality.' Tall, thin, broad-shouldered and watchfully assessing the world with a faintly humorous disdain, Eddie was not just the archetypal lovable rogue.

Highly intelligent and a shrewd judge of character, he was a self-contained loner with a complete disregard for the petty restrictions of polite society.

'He has no scruples and will stop at nothing,' one MI5 report sniffily concluded. 'He plays for high stakes and would have the world know it.'

Because of the class prejudices of the time, the men from intelligence painted him in the worst possible light: 'reckless', 'a terrific chancer', 'a bit of a rogue', 'a cheerful ne'er-do-well', 'surprisingly sentimental' – these were some of the descriptions recorded by security officers after his incarceration in a holding centre for suspected saboteurs and spies. But there was always a grudging respect afforded him for, as one MI5 man remarked with crisp understatement, 'he loved an exciting life'.

Many in British Intelligence then – and in the years after the war – tried to portray him as little more than a common thief. 'Eddie was actually very highly educated and had a genius brain,' says one of his post-war friends, Lillian Verner Bonds. 'The intelligence people used him. They needed him, but they seemed to resent that need. If they could put him down, they would.'

This book will show the shameful way in which British Intelligence treated Eddie – both then, and in the years after the war. 'They wanted to continue to use him when it suited them,' Betty Chapman says. Immediately after the fighting, MI5 asked Eddie to lift some important papers from the Polish Embassy in London by blowing its safe. According to his friends, Eddie did so. Turning a blind eye to what was being done in their name, the authorities let him and his associates block off the traffic in Belgrave Square outside the embassy.

'The moment Eddie did anything they didn't like, they thought something up about him,' Betty Chapman says of his intelligence handlers. 'They were really wicked to him. They never at any time recognised him as doing anything worthwhile.'

They spread the false rumour that he had slept with young girls to give them venereal diseases, and portrayed him as an un-principled blackmailer. Even today, living in retirement, Betty, a spirited and alert woman of ninety, looks skyward when con-fronted with some of the more lurid claims in recently declassified official reports. 'When people say "and this happened and then this",' she laments, 'I say . . . "Don't tell me, I was there."'

Eddie was never acknowledged for his bravery, nor did he even receive a pension from the country for which he fought. Awarded the Iron Cross by the Germans, he never received any medals from the country of his birth. The human cost was great, for his health suffered for many years after the war.

With so colourful a character, perhaps it was inevitable that myths accumulated around him. Although Eddie was not above elaborating or allowing others to elaborate on his behalf, the truth was that he was far from being a 'master safebreaker'. It is clear he was simply drawn to adventure. Unlike his father and brother who were engineers of some note, Eddie was mechanically inept. 'He couldn't open the door if he got locked out,' Betty Chapman recalls.

Yet Eddie Chapman was undoubtedly one of the bravest men who fought in the war. He spent nearly three years behind enemy lines where just one mistake could have led to his arrest and execution. For unlike other double agents pitted against the Germans, Eddie worked from *inside* Occupied Europe. There was no chance he could be rescued or disappear into a safe house in neutral territory. Betty Chapman takes the long view of her husband's significance: 'Thousands and thousands of people gave their lives for this country. Eddie happened to be in the right place, at the right time, in a position to help, and had the guts to do what he had to.' This book aims to demolish the myths and tell the complete story of Eddie's wartime adventures, many details of which have never been told before or for which evidence has been fabricated.

'A lot of stuff was cooked up about Eddie,' Betty reflects. 'The more they upset him, the more he got bolshie with them and he'd say "Get lost".'

Using recently released archive material, Eddie's own letters and reminiscences, as well as first-time interviews with surviving family members and friends, this biography shows how the currents of history swept Eddie along and how – unwillingly at times, un-wittingly at others – he had little choice but to take his place in the great game of wartime espionage.

'The story of many a spy is commonplace and drab. It would not pass muster in fiction,' wrote one MI5 officer when trying, almost disbelievingly, to chronicle some of Eddie's wartime escapades. 'The story of Chapman, the spy of the German secret service [is] different. In fiction it would be rejected as improbable.' And though some of Eddie's claims – of escaping from an MI5 safe house while under guard, meeting Churchill at Chequers, sneaking undetected into the Paris headquarters of German Intelligence – may seem exaggerated, they are certainly in character. 'With Eddie,' his brother says, '*anything* was possible.'

As Betty Chapman concludes, reflecting on the events which propelled her husband into the secret war, 'It's hard to believe they're true but they really are.'

CHAPTER ONE

Genesis of a Gelly Man

'I have always liked working alone and during this time I had been doing villainy, I was never happier than when out at night prowling around like some big cat, over the walls of the side of buildings, always quietly, silently, bent on achieving some nefarious scheme. I knew that one mistake and I would plunge from off my own particular tightrope and the resulting mess would not be pleasant.'

– Eddie Chapman recalls his pre-war years

THE WORLD INTO which Arnold Edward Chapman was born was typical of his generation and class. It was one of unremitting hardship, grime and diminishing prospects. Eddie was born on 16 November 1914 in Burnup Field, County Durham, and brought up in Sunderland, the eldest of three children. Eddie's family 'belonged to the sea', for his father, Ralph, was often away from home for five years at a time on tramp steamers. 'And every time he came home,' Eddie's brother, Winston, says with a smile, 'there seemed to be a child in the offing.' For generations, the Chapmans had been masters and pilots but most recently had been marine engineers. His father was a chief engineer – 'his universe revolved around an engine', Eddie later wrote – as, in time, his younger brother was to be.

Eddie, though, inherited very little mechanical ability. His widow, Betty, says, 'It makes me laugh when I read he was a safebreaking genius. He couldn't pick a lock to save his life!'

Had Eddie not searched for adventures elsewhere, the maritime world might have provided him with gainful employment in the next few years. 'He served his time as an engineer,' Win Chapman says, 'but only for two years, then he decided he couldn't take it any more.' Eddie's younger brother, on the other hand, was happy to complete his training and eventually ended up becoming a director of the company which had originally employed him.

Eddie fondly remembered looking after his siblings (a sister, Olga, was born in 1924). He was a kind, caring boy and the rest of the family adored him, particularly his brother, seven years his junior. To the family he was always called 'Arnie' in those days to distinguish him from his father, whose full name was Ralph Edward. Even then, young Eddie was meticulous about his appearance, which probably explains why the dirt and grime from the Wearside slag heaps loomed large in his later memory. Eddie claimed he was dirty for most of his childhood and regularly dipped in the Derwent to clean himself.

His father wanted him to become an engineer but given his lack of mechanical aptitude that was hardly likely. Eddie had very little interest in school. He was a natural sportsman, though, and captained both the football and cricket teams. And he also learned how to wrestle, for his father taught the Newcastle police ju-jitsu. 'He was a tough character,' says Winston of their father, 'very tough.' By comparison, his mother, Elizabeth, was a gentle soul, an indomitable spirit to whom her eldest son was close. Although Eddie was baptised in the Church of England, according to the family his mother's lineage was Jewish. There was a sizeable, thriving Jewish community in the North-East which had been attracted to the great trading ports in the eighteenth century. 'And remember, his mother's name was Lever,' his widow says. 'Because the line comes from the mother in the Jewish faith, he could be classed as Jewish.'

★ ★ ★

Shipbuilding defined the Sunderland of Eddie Chapman's youth. Wherever you looked the towering cranes could be seen, while the relentless noise from the shipyards assaulted the senses. Great names like Swan Hunter and Vosper Thorneycroft employed thousands of local men. Sunderland had become the biggest shipbuilding centre in the country.

But by Eddie's early teens there was a growing worldwide recession, while a flood of men returning home from the Great War had swelled the labour market. Nineteen shipyards had closed by 1930; a year later, 80 per cent of nearby Jarrow's workforce was unemployed.

Economic hardship soon started to bite. Mass unemployment all around Sunderland meant that Eddie's father was forced to find work as a fitter and take a drastic pay cut. As money became tighter, his parents had to cash in insurance policies and sell off family treasures like his father's gold watch. Of particular sadness to the teenage Eddie Chapman was the day when the piano, the focal point for family singsongs, was sold.

In 1927, the Chapmans had taken on a pub called the Clipper Ship in Roker Avenue. Aged only thirteen, Eddie was regularly serving dockworkers and fishermen pints of beer. As was common in those days, no women were allowed to enter – not that they would probably want to, for the pub was small and dirty. In the company of local seamen, Eddie learned to curse like a dockhand. Money, though, remained tight. Some days he would take his sister and brother to the seaside at Roker. He had to push the pram four miles there and back as there wasn't enough money to take the tram.

The depression turned Eddie's world upside down. He left school on his fourteenth birthday and plunged into the task of making an honest living. As he would later sardonically remark, earning a *decent* honest living was never going to be easy.

To begin with, Eddie found work in the Sunderland shipyards as his father had done before him and his brother was later to do. Within a few months, though, he was made redundant. His next employment was as a motor mechanic where he often had to work until midnight. Feeling exploited, he went to a shipyard's office where an uncle worked, who helped him get a job as a wages clerk. He loathed it and left the shipyard to work for the Sunder Forge and Electric Engineering Co., where to his chagrin his wages remained static at six shillings a week.

At the time, unemployment was hitting Sunderland, in Eddie's phrase, 'like a sledgehammer'. If he was able to work one week in three in 1930, he thought himself lucky. In those days before the welfare state, the dole – unemployment benefit – lasted just six weeks. Each claimant would be means-tested and, if they were lucky, money might grudgingly be handed over. Perhaps these injustices incubated Eddie's growing contempt for the norms of society. He would later comment bitterly that the slums he saw in his native Sunderland were 'far worse than I had seen anywhere else in Europe, where the people were ill-fed and poorly clothed, and my own most lively memories of childhood had been of the cold misery of the dole'.

Luckily, he was eligible to claim some benefit, but for this he had to attend a special 'skills' school which he found a complete waste of time. Ironically, one of the skills taught was filing iron bars. 'When things were bad, Eddie was at the dole school,' says his brother Winston. 'He had one week at the dole school, one week at work, but soon got fed up with it.' Perhaps this frustration explains why Eddie ended up putting a fellow apprentice in hospital. He had learned how to box from a well-known bruiser who used to frequent the Clipper. At the dole school one day, he got into a fight; his mother made him pay the compensation for the unfortunate fellow's injuries.

In 1930, Eddie's simply stopped attending the dole school altogether. Each day he pretended he was going to the school but instead cycled to the nearby coastal sands. There he would while away his days collecting beer and lemonade bottles, which he would then sell back to the shopkeepers. While hardly lucrative, it was better than being exploited. He decided he had little need to work and was happy to bask in the summer sunshine. 'How pleasant it was to lie there, loafing, free,' Eddie would fondly recall, 'looking at the sky, feeling the soft wind, kicking the warm sand with delight.'

It was inevitable that he would be found out. One morning, a report turned up in the post concerning the progress of his apprenticeship. Eddie's frequent absences had been noted. Terror struck him as to what his parents might do next. Aged sixteen, Eddie Chapman decided to run away from home.

One night he grabbed a loaf of bread and a sixpence and cycled into the darkness. That winter of 1930 the weather was terrible, but he was attracted to the bright lights of London. Eddie pedalled as fast as he could down the Great North Road as far as Doncaster, roughly a hundred miles away. He soon fell in with a miner who was also looking for work. In the Yorkshire coalfields the miner soon found employment, but Eddie didn't. Somewhat crestfallen, he returned home early one morning. It was about 3 a.m. and, to his amazement, rather than wielding a rolling pin, his mother was sobbing with relief that he had returned – if only for the moment.

'It was no good trying to settle down,' Eddie said. 'Wandering had bitten me, and I was determined to go to London.'

Some months later came an event which passed into family – and local – legend. One sunny Sunday morning in early October 1931, Eddie and his brother were lounging on the beach at Roker when they heard a strange choking noise. 'We were sunbathing,' Winston recalls, 'we had towels on and we heard this cry for help.' About fifty yards away, out at sea, there was a man obviously in trouble. Instinctively, Eddie ran off and swam towards the drowning man. On his return, he realised an appreciative crowd had gathered – and that he was completely naked. Winston went out to him with his towel and they both managed to slip away. The drowning man, George Herring, was given artificial respiration for forty minutes and somehow survived.

'Eddie refused to say he'd saved a life,' Betty Chapman recalls, 'because he said he'd get a good hiding from his mother for not being at Sunday school.' But he was eventually hailed as a hero. Though somebody else initially claimed the credit for the rescue, Eddie himself was invited to the local town hall the following February where the Mayor of Sunderland presented him with a certificate from the Royal Humane Society. When his mother found out that both her sons had bunked off from church, she was, however, none too pleased.

Consciously trying to better himself, Eddie Chapman joined the Coldstream Guards just after his seventeenth birthday at the end of 1931. Eddie was always proud of his time in the Coldstreams, for it was one of the more illustrious regiments of the British Army. Perhaps it is no surprise that Eddie was drawn to this particular regiment. Between the wars, there had been a deliberate policy to expand the Coldstream's scope of recruitment. But the main criterion, according to his brother, was that you had to be six feet tall to join. 'I was six feet tall, lean and pretty hard,' Eddie himself later wrote, 'so getting by with a false age was easy.' By the simple expedient of forging his father's signature, he claimed he was eighteen, and was able to get in a year earlier than he should have done.

When Eddie joined the Second Battalion of I Coldstream Guards, his life became truly regimented and perhaps it was inevitable that so restless a spirit would soon kick against the system. On his first morning at Caterham Barracks as a cadet, Eddie 'slept in' after a bugle call at 6 a.m. The sergeant who came to his billet was spitting mad. 'He let out one astonished yell,' Eddie recalled. For the rest of that day Eddie found himself having to scrub the whole barrack room and stairs – alone. He didn't make the same mistake twice. On another occasion, he turned left instead of right during a drill parade. 'You constipated bleeding crab,' the sergeant shouted, 'do that again and I'll ram this bloody rifle up your arse.' The sergeant seized the weapon and banged it on Eddie's toes for good measure.

Slowly but surely, Private Chapman learned to become a guardsman. His time in the army was mainly spent at Caterham or Pirbright, with the occasional posting to either Wellington Barracks in London or Victoria Barracks in Windsor. Eddie seems to have whiled away his time playing sport. When playing handball a little too energetically one day in 1933, he smashed his kneecap, causing so much pain that he was forced to stay in bed for the best part of a month. While he recuperated, Eddie was sent to Millbank, the main military hospital in London, where his patella was found to be broken. He was given three weeks' leave, and on his return to Caterham was spotted by a sergeant who shouted at him to walk faster. Same old army, Eddie thought.

After his return from Millbank, Eddie was entered into the Guards' boxing tournament. A red-haired Irishman came at him in the first round and knocked him out cold for two hours. 'I have never been in a ring since,' Eddie said.

Within a year, he had passed through the rigours of basic military training and was entitled to wear the red tunic and bearskin of a Guardsman. His insouciant slouching had reduced sergeants on the parade grounds at Caterham to apoplectic rage. Yet spit and polish had some effect: even in later years, Eddie would remain as ramrod straight as the best career soldiers. Indeed, the rigorous training gave him self-confidence and discipline, both of which would stand him in good stead in later life. But first Guardsman Chapman was drafted to the Tower of London where he took part in the ceremony of the King's Keys. 'He guarded the Crown Jewels,' says his widow Betty, 'which I think is quite funny.'

★   ★   ★

Where did Eddie's addiction to danger come from? His surviving family agree that he had a great need for thrills and excitement. According to his widow, one of Eddie's favourite phrases was 'Never resist temptation' – usually accompanied by a knowing wink. One comment by the Security Service probably goes to the nub of the reasons. 'He is undoubtedly a man with a deep-seated liking for adventure,' MI5 would later conclude, 'and it is our view that this is more likely to be the cause, rather than the effect, of his criminal career.'

It seems unlikely that the economic climate alone fuelled Eddie's increasing waywardness. There were considerable hardships, but the Chapman children were not neglected. Even their father, despite his prolonged absences at sea, played his part. In the depths of the depression, Ralph Chapman was reduced to working as a temporary fitter where he earned just two pounds eighteen shillings a week. On that, his mother was expected to feed and clothe the whole family. But while his father was not above 'tanning the bairns' – in common with parents across the land at the time – Eddie's parents were also loving and supportive.

According to his widow, it was Eddie's own depression rather than the economic depression which explains his often manic behaviour. Braving dangerous situations was a way of exorcising his personal demons. 'Depression was not understood in those days,' Betty Chapman says. 'You were made to get on with it.'

Over the next few years, Eddie would often be overcome with waves of helplessness. Even after the war, he kept a lot to himself about the dangers he had faced and never sought counselling. In those days, people simply ignored the symptoms of depression. It is clear, too, that the death of his mother, in the tuberculosis ward of a local hospital for the poor, affected him deeply. His widow believes that this was the traumatic event that pushed him over the edge.

While at Caterham in the early summer of 1933, Eddie received a telegram informing him that his mother was ill with tuberculosis. By the time he reached Sunderland, it was clear that she didn't have long left. He rushed to the Wearmouth Consumption Hospital as quickly as he could. The memories of what he found there stayed with him until his own death: the carbolic smell, his mother's pride at seeing her eldest in his bright red tunic, her hopes for the future and then taking her dying breath in front of his eyes.

To Betty Chapman, her death turned her future husband against the norms of supposedly acceptable behaviour. His mother had had to care for his siblings and had now died in a hospital along with other impoverished people. 'If that's what society does to my mother,' Eddie later said to his wife, 'then screw society.'

The carefree life of petty villainy, with all its temporary highs and excitements, was just the sort of temptation Eddie couldn't resist. In those first years without Betty's – or anybody else's – restraining influence, anything was possible. 'When you're seventeen or eighteen, there's not a lot you can do when you go down to London,' Winston reflects. 'And he joined up with the wrong people. That's where he learned to blow up a safe and all that business.'

That summer of 1933, following his mother's death, Eddie was owed some leave. 'London was fascinating to me,' he later recalled, 'with its theatres, its air of business, the pageants and royal processions at which several times I did guard duty in the street.' So Guardsman Chapman recuperated by taking his annual leave in the capital.

One pleasant August afternoon, Eddie met a pretty girl in a café near Marble Arch. She seemed amused by his northern accent and they went back to her place for a drink. For its time, her flat was extremely luxurious. Eddie was amazed that she owned a radiogram, a divan and a cocktail cabinet. It was here, aged eighteen, that he 'ate the lotus for the first time', gallantly relating no further details save one: 'I convinced myself that I was madly in love.'

Though stationed in barracks at the Tower of London, Eddie spent the rest of the week with the girl and enjoyed himself so much that he ended up staying with her a few days beyond his official leave. Slowly it dawned on him that the girl earned her living from prostitution and was supported by several men. Horrified, he insisted he had to leave; but the girl cried and threatened suicide. In the end, she telephoned Marlborough Street police station to report him as a deserter. Private Chapman was arrested. He was sentenced to three months' solitary confinement in the glasshouse. This first imprisonment was a harbinger of those to come. His hair was sheared to the scalp and he spent his time cleaning rusty pans and buckets.

His brother provides an even more startling account of Eddie's exploits. 'Eddie disgraced the King's colours by putting a girl in the family way,' Winston claims. 'And he became the only man to break out of the glasshouse. In the early hours of the morning, there was a tap on the window. I always remember opening the window. When he got in, he fell over.' It seemed that Eddie had taken a coach up north and simply wanted to see his family.

Whatever the precise nature of his misdemeanours, Private Chapman was dismissed from the Coldstream Guards at the end of 1933. 'Discharged: Services not required' is the harsh comment on his service record. From now on, Eddie would go his own way, which was often not society's.

Eddie Chapman described his entry into the criminal under-world in the mid-1930s. 'During this period I met and mixed with all types of tricky people, racecourse crooks, touts, thieves, prostitutes and the flotsam of the nightlife of a great city.' The simple truth was that Eddie Chapman drifted. He certainly wasn't violent, or a hardened criminal, but, as with many episodes in his life, he couldn't help getting into trouble. 'In those days, you didn't have to go very far to find someone who was doing something untoward for a living,' Betty Chapman says. 'And that was how he got in with the wrong crowd.'

When he was released from the army brig, he had just three pounds in the pocket of his old suit. His jail haircut hardly helped his prospects and so, by his later admission, he was forced to do 'many things to keep from starving'. A police report mildly comments: 'From this time Chapman earned his living occasionally as an "extra" in film work, but principally by blackmail and robbery.'

The official files, of course, don't tell the whole story. What is missing is any sense of Eddie's preoccupation with enjoying himself and immersing himself with gusto in London nightlife. Eddie was drawn towards Soho when it was at its most beguiling, and night-clubs held a compelling lure for him for the rest of his life. In thirties Soho, it was inevitable that Eddie would come into contact with the crooks, petty thieves and 'whizzers' (pickpockets) who were part of the thriving underbelly of the capital. Soho was a self-contained world populated by extraordinary characters – villains like the Sabini Brothers, Billy Hill and his mob.* Soho was their 'manor', over which the police tried to exercise some control, but usually failed.

By the time Eddie left the Coldstream Guards, London was being terrorised by the 'chivs' – razor gangs – who controlled the clubs, gaming dens (or 'spielers') and street bookies; they were also running restaurants, protection rackets and illegal bookmaking scams.

---

*In later years when the press described Eddie as a career criminal, he would sometimes play up to the stereotype. In particular, his post-war association with some of the more infamous villains of the day meant he was elevated to a form of notoriety which only Sunday tabloids in the 1950s could bestow. 'I think the press played it up through the years,' Betty Chapman says quite levelly. 'They pinned on him an identity, if you like, of "the greatest safeblower of all time".'

By their standards, Eddie was hardly a master criminal. He mixed with small-time villains and ne'er-do-wells, hanging around the clubs where villainy was planned, alibis were prepared and incriminating information exchanged. Within a year of leaving the army brig, Eddie returned to a civilian jail after being arrested for his activities. His first recorded offence was on 8 January 1935 when he was 'found in an enclosed garden for an unlawful purpose'. He was fined £10 at Westminster Public Court. A month later, he had graduated to obtaining a hotel room and stealing money under false pretences. For this, he received six months' hard labour from Bow Street Magistrates.

He was then found in another enclosed garden 'for an unlawful purpose' in breach of his earlier release conditions. Another three months' hard labour was added, to run concurrently. The following year he was incarcerated for fraud, deception (forging cheques and obtaining hotel rooms by false pretences) and 'behaving in a manner likely to offend against public decency in Hyde Park'. (Presumably, he had been found *in flagrante delicto* with a woman.)

Despite these setbacks, Eddie remained undaunted. Within a couple of years, he was living life to the full with a flat in the West End, a flashy motor and more money than he knew what to do with. 'They were good times,' he would later reminisce. 'We had a suitcase full of silver and every time I went out I'd say "take a handful".' Accompanied by whichever showgirl he happened to be walking out with, Eddie would attend all the hottest dives, such as the Nest and Smoky Joe's. He was an accomplished dancer who won awards and would sometimes say he was a professional dancer. It was slightly more respectable than film extra or, indeed, petty criminal, both of which he could also claim.

One day in early 1936, Eddie turned up at the family home in Sunderland with a glamorous woman in tow. The Chapmans didn't know who she was, whether she was a girlfriend or his wife. Her name was Vera Friedberg and what everyone remembered was that she spoke in a distinct and alluring foreign accent. In fact, she had been Eddie's wife for just three weeks when she married him to gain British citizenship. 'Eddie was always willing to oblige,' laughs Betty Chapman.

Frank Owen, later Eddie's ghost writer, became aware of Vera at the time of the Spanish Civil War, on which he had reported. One day, Vera had telephoned Owen in tears, wanting to know what had happened to her lover who had been killed in the fighting. Owen lent her ten pounds for the air fare so she could travel to Spain to bury the body. In fact, he never saw her again, 'but I heard a week later that she had been squired by her living [lover]'. The name of this replacement in her affections was Eddie Chapman.

In a later interrogation by MI5, when he was asked about how the marriage had developed, Eddie was succinct: 'quite badly'. Yet he started to learn German from her, which would come in useful a few years later. When asked how he learned German so quickly, Eddie would often quip, 'Pillow talk.' Because Vera was the daughter of a German Jew who had married a Russian woman, that same MI5 report notes, 'He had not told the Germans of this Jewish connection.'

Divorce proceedings were begun well before war broke out. With his subsequent imprisonment and the declaration of hostilities, Eddie heard nothing further from her; the *decree nisi* was declared in his absence. According to a recent obituary in the *Jewish Chronicle*, Vera later married a Czech refugee called Jack Lowy – who later became a professor and world expert in the science of muscle structure – but they were divorced in 1951.

After this quick visit in 1936, Win Chapman wasn't to see his elder brother for the best part of a decade. At the time, none of the family were even aware of his criminal activities and his detention at His Majesty's pleasure.

The genteel town of Lewes, set among the undulating downs of East Sussex, has at various times been famous for its jail, its race track and the fact that Thomas Paine was born and raised there. In the late 1930s, however, Lewes was to become synonymous with violent crime and villainy thanks to an event which would have many repercussions in the world of law enforcement. Eddie was actually in the nearby jail when the notorious razor gang 'carve-up' that inspired Graham Greene's *Brighton Rock* took place at Lewes race track. On 28 April 1936, Eddie had been sentenced to nine months' hard labour. In his memoirs, he claims it was because of an act of 'road piracy' – a smash and grab raid that had gone horribly wrong; however, the official record notes it was for 'obtaining credit, goods and lodgings by fraud'. Whatever the reason, Eddie was now on his third 'stretch', which started off in Wormwood Scrubs before he was moved to Lewes a few weeks later.

The background to the battle of Lewes race track that summer was a change in the ecosystem of Soho. In the late twenties, the Sabini gang had emerged from Little Italy on the Clerkenwell Road, after which they had slashed their way to prominence. They were Sicilian, though hardly on a par with the Cosa Nostra. By the mid-thirties, the Sabinis and many other razor gangs were engaged in an escalating series of battles, fought at racecourses all over southern England.

Matters came to a head at Lewes in late June 1936 with the fiercest gang fight in three decades. The Home Secretary, Sir William Hicks, declared that the gangs must be smashed – and they were. After the Lewes carve-up, a Protection Squad was formed and, in time, so too was an Anti-Vice Squad, which would try to regulate the goings-on in and around Soho. One growth area after the demise of the race track gangs was motorised crime, usually in the form of smash and grab raids using hire cars.

The dramatic increase in car theft and the use of getaway vehicles had prompted the creation of the motorised élite force which became Eddie's eventual nemesis. The Flying Squad had come into existence in 1919 and revolutionised crime-fighting in the capital. 'A new form of street theatre had been provided by smash and grab raids, Flying Squad chases, wage snatches and robberies in which the public was able to participate by chasing or seizing criminals,' writes Donald Thomas of the years before the Second World War.

By 1938, the Flying Squad had their hands full. '[One] crime which we never got much prior news of was safeblowing,' recalled one of the leading detectives ('tophats') of the day, Inspector Ted Greeno of Scotland Yard. '[I] think I went to every job in the London area – after the safe was blown.' Around that time Fleet Street became excited by a criminal, thought to be American, who had performed a more sophisticated and brazen series of safe breaks. That he had used chewing gum to help stick the explosive into locks suggested he had started his career in the United States. This 'American' safebreaker was none other than Eddie Chapman.

Safebreakers – or 'petermen' as they were known to the trade – were often quiet craftsmen, hardened by their long stretches in prison. 'Screwing a peter', as breaking into a safe became known, required ever more ingenious skills. Eddie's singular lack of ability at anything mechanical leads Betty Chapman to think her husband could only ever be guilty by association. 'I don't think he took any active part because he would have blown himself up,' she says, suggesting that he exaggerated his own role. But Eddie later claimed that thirty-eight out of forty-five jobs he admitted to were carried out by himself alone. 'We certainly supplied Fleet Street with some exciting headlines,' he said.

Whenever he was asked about it in later years, Eddie claimed his safebreaking career had started with a chance encounter in a London nightclub with a real American gangster.

'Don't you do heists?' the gangster asked over drinks. Eddie had no idea what he meant.

Chicago's finest was succinct. 'You knock on the door and stick a fucking gun in their face.'

Then the gangster suggested another innovation: using gelignite to burst open safes. And in this way, Eddie maintained, he became a 'gelignite artiste', fuelling the legend that he was one of the greatest safebreakers in criminal history.

The facts appear to be a little more prosaic. When he was eventually released from Lewes jail at the start of 1937, Eddie sought out a friend with whom he had become acquainted inside. Jimmy Hunt was 'a cool, self-possessed, determined character' who had been doing three years for a post-office job and safebreaking. In time, Eddie christened him 'the prince of all safebreakers' and this association, more than any great ability on Eddie's part, would see his entry into the élite of the burgeoning crime wave.

'Why is the British safebreaker so good?' one magazine would later ask. 'One reason is that cracking a crib requires characteristics in which the British excel – skill, tenacity, stamina and patience.' Certainly, all four attributes were needed when Eddie went out on his first job with Jimmy Hunt at a large furrier's called Isobels in Harrogate. By his later admission, Eddie was shivering with fear and not much use. He and Jimmy parked, sawed through the bars of a grille at the back of the shop under cover of darkness, jemmied open a window and eventually came upon a wardrobe full of goodies.

'We took some beautiful mink coats off the hanger,' he later wrote, 'according to the labels their prices ranged from £350 to £450.' They then forced open the office door and inside they found a safe. Rather than blow it open, Jimmy showed Eddie how to 'pop' open the rivets at the back, one by one. After pushing the back off, they broke into the 'tin' in which they found all the money, neatly stored in bundles. It came to two hundred pounds, a considerable sum in those days.

'We finished the job and got away,' Eddie wrote. 'As we drove back to London, snow fell and it became bitterly cold.' Rather than attract attention by turning up in the small hours of the morning, they parked in a quiet country lane where they waited for daybreak. To keep warm, they removed the minks from the boot and fell fast asleep in their newly gained spoils.

Innovation on the part of the peterman was necessary by the late thirties. Locks had become more ingenious. In the pre-war years, it would be rare for a common burglar to know how to open a safe without help from a specialist. Gelignite became the preferred explosive, for – unlike, say, highly combustible nitroglycerine – it would actually leave behind a safe and a safebreaker after the explosion. So Eddie and Jimmy Hunt started to experiment with 'gelly'.

The pair decamped to Wales where they stole four hundred detonators and packets of gelignite from unattended mines. Far from prying eyes, they experimented to their hearts' content in remote woodlands. The pair tested the gelly on trees and then bought second-hand safes which they could explode to learn the best techniques. Slowly, as 1938 progressed, they developed the expertise needed to become skilled safebreakers.

To absorb the force of the explosion, each safe would have to be draped in a curtain or carpet. Most mishaps were caused by using too much gelignite, but getting the right amount to open a safe was neither a simple nor an easily repeatable calculation. It required a certain intuitive feel. Too little gelignite and the keyhole of the lock would be damaged and difficult to open; too much and both breaker and safe would be blown to smithereens.

Before the detonator was inserted into the gelignite, both would have to be reduced in size to fit into the keyhole. This required an extremely delicate operation. The safebreaker would usually crimp it with his teeth and then, once he had placed it inside the keyhole, the explosive would have to be sealed with plasticine. Sometimes the seal would be too tight, which was why Eddie and Jimmy decided to use chewing gum. They later claimed to have introduced another exotic refinement: condoms filled with gelignite and water which were knotted and gently poked into the lock so that there was no dangerous overspill of explosive.

By the time they returned to London everything was ready.

In the thirties, most safe-cracking was done by gangs. They usually included a driver, a lookout, the peterman, an assistant and any additional muscle thought necessary. Some gangs simply employed a 'gelly man' to come in, blow the safe and then leave with his share of the proceeds. The planning and execution, as well as the removal of the loot, was the responsibility of the gang. That way, they reasoned, if the peterman was caught, he could tell the police nothing.

Eddie, however, was his own man and worked only with men he knew or had chosen, like Jimmy Hunt. The gelignite would be regularly stolen from darkened, unguarded quarries. After Harrogate, their first job in London was at Edgware Road underground station where they removed a day's takings.

Their work continued apace. 'Every week we were knocking something out,' Eddie recalled. 'Every time we did a job it was on the BBC – "there's been another attack by the Gelignite Gang".' Over a two-year period, he estimated that they probably 'broke' more than fifty safes in places with readily available cash. All around Britain, cinemas, dance halls and department stores found their safes blown open.

Odeon cinemas were popular targets. After buying his ticket, Eddie would hide in the gents' toilets until the cinema closed. He would then break into the manager's office and set to work on the safe. Soon he and Jimmy became even more brazen, on one occasion smashing a hole during office hours, pretending they were water men come to repair the mains. Express Dairies were another fertile target, while Co-ops, Eddie later remarked, became his own personal money boxes. Life was 'a bit fast and furious then' as he stole and spent a small fortune.

'We used to motor down to Brighton in a drop-head Ford Sedan,' Eddie recalled. They cost £120 brand new and when they were smashed up, they went out and bought a new one. 'The one thing we had was money. If we ran out, we'd blow another safe. Sweet as that.'

Betty Farmer was one of eleven children from a quiet Shropshire village called Nene Sollers. Aged seventeen, she fell in love with the son of the local squire, but as with many teenage romances, complications arose. Most weekends, she spent time with an aunt who lived nearby. A friend of the family used to come up from London. 'And she had her eye on the son of the local squire and the married vicar had his eyes on me,' she says with a smile. 'So I thought "I have to extricate myself from this situation." '

And so, exactly as they had for her future husband, the bright lights of the capital beckoned. A couple of other aunts in Rhyl financed her to come to London where she began working in the fashion industry, rooming in Barons Court and opening a store in the North End Road where she sold – and sometimes modelled – clothes. Even then, Betty Farmer was a remarkably poised and self-possessed young woman, who turned heads.

'I met someone who had this place called the Kensington Social Club,' she recalls. 'They said "Would you like to be secretary and do the membership in your spare time?" so I said I would do it in the evening.' And that was her entrée into an establishment on Kensington Church Street, located just opposite the police station.

One night, a tall, handsome man with wavy hair and a thin moustache walked into the club. An equally tall and striking blonde presence – 'She had all the right equipment,' Eddie later said – Betty soon transfixed the man's gaze. 'I am going to marry her,' he said, in the loudest of stage whispers. Betty, pretending not to hear, turned to her companion and said, under her breath, 'A pig's ear.' And so began the great romance of Eddie and Betty Chapman.

Once they started walking out together, he took her to all his favourite West End haunts. That meant she ended up in plenty of subterranean dives. 'They were very sleazy places,' Betty reflects, 'but they were places of their time.' There was the Hell Club – with its hidden lighting that could change colour in an instant – and Smoky Joe's, the Nest, El Gaucho and the Shim Sham, all of whose owners knew Eddie well. She had no idea why he knew them so intimately, nor, for that matter, what he was up to. But slowly a courtship developed.

Eddie, two years older, was infinitely more experienced, a factor that added another dimension to the attraction. And a glamorous one, too, because at the time he was sharing a property with a recent Cambridge history graduate named Terence Young who was making his way in the film business. After wangling various jobs on film sets during the summer vacations, Terence had started his rise through the ranks of the fledgling British film industry. When Eddie first revealed to Terence that he was a crook and blew up safes for a living, the dapper graduate didn't think it was particularly reprehensible. 'Indeed,' he later told appalled security men from MI5, 'I probably thought it rather exciting.'

Both were assiduous in their appearance. Terence's style seemed to have seeped in from the dandys of Regency England. He always wore tailored suits and hand-made shirts, and later claimed that, if he could, he would change his clothes three times a day. If nothing else, their association provided Eddie with a convenient smoke-screen. The peripatic nature of the film business provided a useful alibi.

For a while, Eddie and Terence shared a cottage in Letchmore Heath in Hertfordshire. So when Eddie claimed to Betty that he was in the film business, it made a lot of sense. He was often away for long periods, and she took his explanations at face value. 'I didn't know what he was up to,' she says. 'He hid so much because he knew that I would not approve of what he did.'

Betty gladly joined in the excitements of his life. 'Eddie had the best sense of humour I'd ever come across,' she says. Laughter was what not only brought them together but kept them together.

On one occasion, he rang a man up and said: 'There's fire coming from your telephone . . . so I want you to pull your phone.

Tug it!' The man kept pulling on the wire, Eddie shouting, 'Harder' until the connection was yanked out of the wall. Another call was to a factory owner where Eddie posed as an official at the local tax office. 'You owe us £30,000,' he said. The owner protested but Eddie insisted that he come straight away and bring the money with him. 'But it's got to be in coins,' he ordered. The factory owner went scurrying round to the nearest branch of his bank to raise that sum in coins of the realm.

Another time Eddie sent round an undertaker to the house of a lord whom he had met in one of his night-time haunts. The undertaker matter-of-factly informed a horrified butler that he'd come that day to measure the master for a coffin.

★   ★   ★

Eddie and Betty's relationship was not without its trials and tribulations – especially after the war when they married – but, conversely, its strength was based on honesty. Despite his criminal tendencies, Eddie was always searingly truthful with Betty. When his MI5 files were released a few years ago, much of the subsequent press coverage focused on the subject of his 'amorous activities'. In the more lurid accounts of his life, it has been suggested that Eddie was addicted to women as much as danger.

On the subject of women, Betty is characteristically frank. 'He had six mistresses in his life. And I used to say, when he was getting towards his end, "You know, you had all those mistresses. How I wish there was one who could help me with you!" And he would just laugh.' Indeed he used to introduce her to people thus: 'This is my wife, Betty. She's lived through six mistresses, haven't you darling?' Betty would grin, saying yes through clenched teeth.

'What I found absolutely disgusting,' Betty says of his declassified MI5 personal files, 'is that they said he slept with girls and gave them some disease.' The security services were highly censorious about Eddie's pre-war activities. 'He attracted women on the fringe of London society,' its chief interrogator later noted, 'indulged in violent affairs with them and then proceeded to blackmail them by producing compromising pictures taken by an accomplice. He confessed to an experiment in sodomy.'

Betty Farmer is mentioned by name as an 'associate', a young girl of eighteen whom 'he infected with VD'. She is understandably aghast at such an accusation, denying it completely. 'Now if he was really doing that,' Betty explains with an ironic smile, 'wouldn't I have known about it?'

★   ★   ★

Far from being a master criminal, Eddie's activities often veered into the realms of the Keystone Cops. On one occasion he raided a bank, only to find that another gang had already beaten him to it. An empty safe was all that awaited him. On another occasion he stole a safe from a research establishment in Tunbridge Wells, assuming it would contain all the employees' wages. In fact his haul came to just three pounds ten shillings.

On yet another occasion, at the Swiss Cottage Odeon, he had to break open a door with a steel bar as he had forgotten to bring a jemmy. When he set the explosive, Eddie miscalculated the timing and was blown backwards through an office wall. After regaining consciousness, he stuffed all the money into a large bag and walked to the nearest tube station at dawn. He was a little disconcerted by the stares of the cleaners on their way to work. His obvious injuries and a bulging bag marked 'Property of Odeon Cinemas' were rather incriminating.

When he raided a fur store in the West End, Eddie and an accomplice entered an adjacent flat disguised as workmen from the local water board. They had to demolish two adjoining walls, both of them cheekily suggesting to the owner (a Jewish financier) that he 'cook' the amount of damage he claimed against the water board. The financier would then share the difference with them. Eventually, the owner got three months in jail for complicity in this crime. The actual perpetrators were never apprehended.

Some time in 1938, Eddie was involved in a little road piracy in and around Oxford Street. After a smash and grab raid, he and his accomplices drove off in a stolen Bentley and were chased by the cops. Close by Baker Street, they rammed into a taxi and ricocheted into a set of traffic lights. Eddie and company scarpered the scene but drew an impressive crowd in their wake. A snive – a local, small-time thief – was among them. He had the misfortune to put his hand on the bonnet of the Bentley. This fellow's fingerprints were subsequently discovered and, despite his complete innocence, he was jailed for five years. The testimony of the cab driver and one of the jeweller's assistants left no doubt. They were certain he was the guilty man.

With all this activity, it was almost inevitable that Eddie Chapman would come to the attention of Scotland Yard. Later in the spring of 1938, the Metropolitan Police tasked a special squad to hunt him down. By this time Eddie was quite visible – either out nightclubbing with Betty or making day trips down to Brighton with his ill-gotten gains – and he started to worry, like all criminals on a roll, that his run of good luck might not last. As he had more than enough money to live on, he decided to stop breaking safes for a whole year. He travelled out of harm's way to Bridport in Dorset with an accomplice.

His self-imposed retirement lasted all of six weeks.

★ ★ ★

Around this time in the late thirties, another Bentley was passing around London at the rather more sedate speed for which it was designed. On its bonnet was a blue flag which depicted a tortoise and carried the motto, 'Safe but sure'. Its chauffeured occupant was the grand old man of military intelligence, Vernon Kell, an elderly general ravaged by both heavy asthma and growing worries over the coming hostilities.

After serving five prime ministers, the director-general of MI5 knew that he – and the organisation which he had founded in 1909 – was living on borrowed time. The Security Service existed on a shoestring, recruiting through personal recommendation from well-connected gentlemen who were expected to supplement their incomes privately. Many were equally infirm and burned out, a number having come from the Indian Security Police housed next door to MI5's premises on the Cromwell Road.

When the young Dick White was sounded out about joining MI5 in 1935, he was told that the pay was poor. 'That's the bad part,' his recruiter said, 'but the good part is, it's tax free.' White would become the service's first graduate: John C. Masterman, his old tutor at Christ Church College, Oxford, had put in a good word.

Even though hostilities with Germany were seen as inevitable by 1938, the fight within MI5, so one author has written, was 'against apathy and stupidity in high places'. Chronically underfunded – and sometimes chaotically audited, too – the Security Service had tended to view the Soviet threat as overshadowing everything else, as was also the case with its sister service, the Secret Intelligence Service, MI6.

By the mid-1930s, though, the rise of Nazism had replaced the Soviets as the clear and present danger. Prompted by the rise of the British Union of Fascists, which culminated in a rally in Olympia in 1934, the focus of MI5 finally shifted to the Nazis. German rearmament had begun in earnest. The Abwehr, the intelligence arm of the Wehrmacht (the German armed forces), was also prospering, making preparations for war by running counter-intelligence operations at home and recruiting foreign agents abroad. By the outbreak of war, it numbered just under a thousand officers.

Despite its own pre-war successes – including the penetration of the German Embassy – MI5 remained a small organisation. In 1938, when Dick White was recruited, it numbered only thirty officers and just over a hundred secretaries. The following year, MI5 recruited another seven hundred and fifty new staff. They would be needed. By the time war broke out, many politicians were convinced there were upwards of twenty thousand potential enemy agents in Britain. During the summer of 1940, the agency would be overwhelmed with reports about the letting off of fireworks or farmers leaving strange shapes in fields to signal the enemy. MI5's apparent failure to deal with these and rather more rational reports, as well as the screening of foreign citizens, would lead to a drastic restructuring.

In the years to come, a whole generation of historians and solicitors from Oxford would provide the heart of the double-agent operations which were to trick the Germans so successfully. During the Second World War their work became a study in contrasts with that of the cryptographers from Bletchley Park – who mainly came from Cambridge. It was almost a grand duel within the educational establishment – Trinity College, Cambridge versus Christ Church, Oxford – as to who could better fool the Germans. And it would be Dick White who – after a visit to the Deuxième Bureau in Paris where he learned how they had succeeded in feeding false information back to the enemy – would later champion the doubling of suspected agents.

Joining him would be a career intelligence officer, Colonel Tommy Robertson – a Seaforth Highlander. He was accompanied by the best and brightest in the land, recruits like Masterman, Lord Rothschild, Herbert Hart and Arthur Koestler: White would later lament that they probably appropriated too much talent.

By 1939, they were poised to turn around the fortunes of the security service by taking deception into the realms of a true art form. And they would do it by means of unlikely recruits such as the man currently being chased around the country by the Flying Squad.

In the spring of 1939, the Metropolitan Police were finally on to Eddie Chapman. Using the name Edward Arnold, Eddie had managed to elude arrest for over three years. That he was able to live at one of the plusher addresses in the West End shows just how successful his criminal activities were. But his luck ran out that April after he 'left my flat behind Burlington Arcade and decided to pay a working visit to Scotland'.

'The detection of crime in London is not brilliant,' Eddie later remarked, 'but it is methodical and painstaking.' And these certainly were the defining characteristics of the tophat who collared him. Inspector Edward Greeno – Greeno of the Yard – was a remarkable thief-taker, remarkable both for his successes and also his tendency for 'straighteners', fights with fists. Ted Greeno was tall, heavily built – his driver considered him 'the Edward G. Robinson of the CID' – and would gather a small crowd when he asked a bystander to hold his jacket while he set about a villain who had given him some lip.

For Greeno of the Yard, getting to know criminals was part of his job 'and the best way to get to know them is to introduce them to a police station'. He was on friendly terms with all the various safe blowers, considering them to be 'like the old time jazzmen: you never knew whose outfit they were with or for how long'.

Throughout the latter part of 1938 and early 1939, Greeno was keeping tabs on Eddie Chapman and his cronies. At some point, Eddie had fallen out with Jimmy Hunt and begun a profitable partnership with George Darry, a Burmese lad who had been a bookmaker's clerk. According to Eddie, Darry 'was without nerves and made an excellent accomplice'. Despite Eddie's later claims, the contemporary official files make clear that Darry, who also sometimes used the name Anthony Latt, was the leader of the gang. Along with Tommy Lay, Freddie Sampson and George Sherrard, they used a handful of hired cars to travel around the country breaking into safes where they were least expected.

Perhaps their most remarkable escapade was the 'Grimsby Job'. Here Eddie and Darry made their way into a pawnbroker's from an empty house next door, cutting slates from the roof and making holes in all five floors before drilling through a connecting wall. Four – or possibly, six – safes (Eddie couldn't recall the exact number) were then blown open, 'the explosions being marked by a motor car being "revved up" outside'. They got away with a cool £15,000 and were never brought to justice.

But the Flying Squad soon had all the number plates of their cars, including those they had hired for 'special occasions'. In later years, Eddie couldn't help asking how Greeno kept up with him. As he makes clear in his memoirs, Greeno made it his business to know every club Eddie and his pals belonged to, 'and if they met in a Soho club, a West End restaurant or a Bayswater pub I had a man planted there, eating a meal or drinking a beer, apparently minding his own business'.

Wherever possible, Greeno would alert the local police when Eddie was in town. The problem was that it was difficult to predict which buildings would be their targets. Towards the end of 1938, the safe at an Odeon cinema in Bournemouth was blown. Four days after that, a Co-op in Leicester was raided. 'It was obvious that a mob was on tour,' Greeno recalled. 'They went up to Yorkshire, then down to Lincolnshire, then over the border to Scotland – and there they were caught.'

Eddie went to Scotland at the end of January 1939 in the company of George Darry, Tommy Lay and a driver called Hugh Anson. They'd read about a record dividend that was about to be paid out at the Co-operative store in the St Cuthbert's region of the city. Given that 'Darry's Gang' were getting a lot of heat from fellow safebreakers in London for the increase in police activity, Eddie thought a trip over the border might not be such a bad idea. They drove up to Edinburgh with golf clubs on show so that they could pretend to be visiting the Scottish links.

Eddie and friends checked into a hotel in Edinburgh and the next night made their way to the St Cuthbert's Co-op. They managed to get in via the roof but as they were trying to get out, the skylight jammed – and in a temper, Eddie smashed it. At that point, a police-man was walking past and heard the noise: the gang could see his torch flashing through the window. Doing his best to hide in the shadows, Darry managed to knock over a pile of tins.

There was a 'hellish clatter' followed by general uproar; shouts went up, whistles were blown, horns sounded and cars were revved. When reinforcements arrived the gang ran off – and nearly all of them made it. Eddie jumped over a high wall and managed to leap on to a slow-moving goods train by clinging on to the buffers. Hugh Anson, however, fell, broke his ankle and was quickly apprehended.

The others dispiritedly made their way back to the hotel. 'We settled [the] bill at 3 a.m.,' Eddie later remarked, 'a piece of honesty that did not pay off.' The police were soon on to them when they checked the most recent departures early that morning. The remaining gang got as far as Scotch Corner, where a police car headed them off the road. Eddie tried to escape into a patch of bracken but tripped over when he tried to jump a wall. He was manhandled back to the car. When the bobbies discovered dozens of sticks of gelignite in the boot, the car's occupants were hand-cuffed and returned to Edinburgh jail. Days later, Eddie was tried as Edward Edwards, 'a film extra of no fixed address'.

Their lawyer used the rivalries between the Scottish and English legal systems to good effect. To Ted Greeno's disgust, the Edinburgh magistrate was a stickler for procedure who insisted that, notwithstanding the earlier English robberies, Eddie and his cronies should stand trial in a Scottish court first. Alone of the group, Eddie, to his – and everybody else's – astonishment, was awarded a fortnight's bail.

That same night, Eddie drove out to a quarry outside Edinburgh where he stole more gelignite. Due to appear at the local assizes on 7 March, he intended using this Scottish gelignite to break into a store and a cinema in York so that he could post his companions' bail. It would be a much more successful night's work. With £600 from the York Co-op and £300 from the local Odeon, Eddie wired the money over the border to get the boys out. The next day, they congregated in Bournemouth at the Royal Bath Hotel, which they had known from an earlier raid in the seaside town. 'We have to move quickly,' Eddie told them. 'It's only a question of time before the Yard find out that we have been released.'

But it was too late: Ted Greeno was on to them already. He got word from one of his informers that one of the gang's cars had been spotted on the south coast. 'Then there was a surprise for us,' Greeno recalled. 'A cinema safe was blown, not at Bournemouth, but at York.' It took a few days for the news to trickle through, but when he was subsequently informed that Eddie's gang had checked into the Royal Bath in Bournemouth, Greeno knew that they weren't staying there to take in the sea breezes.

Overnight, there had been a break-in at the local Co-op and £470 was stolen (Eddie claimed they had raided a cinema, too). On their return to their hotel at 3 a.m., one of the gang knocked a plant off its pedestal. A number of guests were woken. The receptionist also remembered them, as did a chambermaid for whom they left a £1 tip. The police were pretty certain the money they found had come from the recent raid, a rubber band around the cash – the same as those used by Co-op cashiers – providing circumstantial evidence.

Back in London, the resourceful Greeno had traced the salesman who had hired them their cars. Though Leonard Groves denied knowing any of the gang members, Greeno found something incriminating behind a gas meter in the basement of his house in Bayswater. It was a tin wrapped in blue notepaper containing a hundred and thirty-four detonators. 'In the cupboard were sixteen more detonators in a Swan Vestas box, four packets of gelignite and twelve pieces of fuse,' Greeno later recalled. When they heard of this, the gang went their separate ways. Eddie returned to

London, checking in at the Regent Palace Hotel under a false name rather than return to his flat just around the corner. He was determined to keep a very low profile as the press were full of the details of this latest countrywide crime wave. At Smoky Joe's one night, he was told that the police were looking for him.

'A man I knew said that if we could reach Monte Carlo,' he recalled, 'he could get us on a boat for South America.'

If Betty Farmer had any sense that the little trip to the Channel Islands with her boyfriend was going to be other than a peaceful sojourn, it came on the second Sunday in February 1939. Once again, Eddie had telephoned her out of the blue. Later, while they had dinner at the Regent Palace Hotel, he had seen an advert for Jersey on the back of the hotel menu. He could fly there, he decided, before making his way south to Monte Carlo. In his usual beguiling way, he had asked her, 'How would you like to go to Jersey, then possibly the south of France?' Still unaware of his criminal activities, she had agreed.

That he didn't have a passport hardly mattered. The main thing was getting out of London. George Darry and Hugh Anson were equally keen to join him and so, on Tuesday, 7 February, they had all flown to St Helier and made their way to the plush De La Plage Hotel on the waterfront in Havre-des-Pays. Eddie and Betty checked in as 'Mr and Mrs Farmer' of Torquay.

The following Sunday, Betty was enjoying her lunch in the hotel dining room – where the other diners had been encouraged to think that Eddie and his friends were 'film people' – when all of a sudden mayhem broke out. A waiter started shaking as he poured some wine, and in an instant Eddie was aware that something was up. Sitting opposite her, facing towards the door, a look of consternation crossed his face. 'He just got up and went,' Betty says.

By the time she turned around to see what had disturbed him, a phalanx of plain-clothes policemen were rushing in. Much to the alarm of the other diners, Eddie's cronies were arrested and handcuffed in the dining room. 'I was shell-shocked,' she adds.

Eddie jumped through a window overlooking the promenade, ran up a hill and hid in an empty school. Finding a mackintosh in a cloakroom, he grabbed it to hide his clothes, which according to the police description were rather striking: yellow-spotted tie, blue sleeveless pullover, grey flannels, brown sandals and no socks. Though the Brown Hats – as the local police were known from their curious uniforms – found no signs of him in the vicinity, a man answering to Eddie's description was later spotted reading a map outside the La Croix Cemetery. The police told the local populace that caution should be exercised in his apprehension. He was, they claimed, 'dangerous'.

By nightfall, Eddie had checked into a seedy boarding house in Sand Street, claiming that he was a marine engineer. He spent an anxious night, but not nearly as anxious as Betty, who had no idea what was happening. 'She is stated to have denied all knowledge of the alleged activities of her companions,' the *Jersey Evening Post* reported the next day.

On that same day, Monday, Eddie's sidekicks Darry and Anson were taken by the Jersey police to St Helier airport, and the late afternoon flight to Southampton was delayed for half an hour to accommodate their departure. There they were met by the Bournemouth police, who had alerted their Jersey colleagues by telephone at noon the previous day. After being charged in Bournemouth, they were taken to London where they were tried not only for the burglary at the Co-op, but also for illegal possession of four detonators and two cartridges of gelignite.

The indefatigable Greeno had found these detonators hidden inside a disused chimney in Darry's house in Bayswater. (Darry insisted that his sister, with whom he shared the house, knew nothing.) When he was told that Leonard Groves, their car salesman, had confessed all, Darry was astounded. 'What a fool he must be to say he knew the parcels contained explosives,' he said. 'He has put himself in it now.'

The police, it seemed, had been on the scent, literally, of a bottle of perfume which a girl in Bournemouth had received from George Darry after dancing with her at the Royal Bath. 'The fool signed his name,' Eddie lamented, 'and the postmark did the rest.' When Ted Greeno eventually caught up with him, Darry was in possession of the same sort of lined paper that had been found in Groves's showroom. 'You seem to know everything,' Darry remarked when Greeno presented him with the incriminating evidence.

'With this gang in jail,' Ted Greeno later remarked, 'all safebreaking in Britain stopped for a while.'

★ ★ ★

Early that same Monday morning, Eddie was standing near St Helier police station when he saw a placard advertising the local paper: 'STARTLING SCENE AT JERSEY HOTEL'. When he bought a copy, he was stunned to see his own picture above a vivid account of the previous lunchtime's events. He sensed that he might not be a free man for very much longer. The owner of his lodgings, Mrs Corfield, had been highly suspicious of him. 'I did not greatly like my landlady,' he wrote, 'and was to like her still less before much longer.' Later that afternoon, she reported to the police that her lodger fitted the description of the escaped criminal.

Eddie was determined to go out in style. That Monday evening he went to a nightclub and drowned his sorrows by drinking too much champagne. Given that he had no money when he arrived, he had already decided this was his last ever chance to break open a safe. Some time the previous week, he and his chums had visited the club. As they walked in, Eddie had joked that they could open the safe that was all too visible in an office with 'a bag full of fresh air'.

Now he managed to push the safe into the basement and, using two iron bars, jemmied the back off, just as Jimmy Hunt had shown him a couple of years before. He removed the contents – various silver, copper and gold coins – before returning nonchalantly upstairs to his waiting bottle of champagne. Extremely tired – 'It had been a strenuous day' – he eventually made his way back to his lodgings. Around 2 a.m., the door burst open. 'We think you are Eddie Chapman,' said the arresting officer, 'and we think Scotland Yard wants you.' At midnight, Mrs Corfield had reported his return by telephone.

Eddie was handcuffed and thrown into Jersey jail. Because he had committed his most recent crime on the island, he was charged in the local court. When the St Helier authorities later investigated what had happened at the club, the Brown Hats found that the phone box in the hallway had been emptied and other rooms had been broken into. Now he was at the mercy of the Channel Islands' justice system. Under the gimlet eye of the police magistrate, Mr Pinel, Eddie admitted that all these activities had been his handiwork. As a contemporary newspaper report makes clear, 'the safe, badly battered, with the bottom forced out, was on a table alongside the Magistrate's desk'. Mr Pinel sentenced him to the maximum punishment – two years' imprisonment.

Eddie was determined to make one thing absolutely clear. Speaking in what the local press called 'a cultured voice', he said: 'I have a girlfriend here with me and it has been very embarrassing for her. She has been questioned by the police and she knows nothing of why we are here.' The magistrate agreed. There was nothing to keep Betty Farmer on the island, he said. She was free to go. The girlfriend herself – described in the local press report as 'an attractive blonde with blue eyes and a long page-boy bob' – was still none the wiser. When Betty heard that Eddie had been arrested – after all, it was front-page news – she sent food parcels to the prison. 'I was interviewed by the police but could not give them information on something I didn't know about,' she says.

Eddie, for all his faults, treated her with characteristic gentility, making sure she was protected from the truth of his activities. As far as Betty is concerned, she really had gone to Jersey on holiday. 'I got out as quickly as I could.' After flying home to London, she returned to Barons Court where she did her best to pick up where had left off with her life before she had met Eddie.

As for the others, Darry and Anson were charged at the Central Criminal Court in London and spent the first few years of the war in English jails. But thanks to his last-minute escape and his commission of a crime on the islands, a very different future awaited Eddie Chapman.

When Eddie later described Jersey Prison as 'old-fashioned' he was being masterly in his understatement. The jail at Gloucester Street in St Helier was positively medieval: whitewashed granite walls and a stone-flagged floor couldn't disguise the dreariness. The whole place was damp, cold and perpetually twilit. The jail was small, with more staff than prisoners. Most local criminals, it transpired, hoped for sentences of more than a couple of years as they would then serve their stretch in better surroundings on the mainland. Having been sentenced to exactly two years' imprisonment, however, there was no possibility of a return home for Eddie Chapman.

There was quite a turnover of local villains. More cosmopolitan and worldly wise than the locals, Eddie considered them small-time ne'er-do-wells; their main pastime seemed to be wife-beating. During his incarceration there was a sense of familiarity about the new arrivals, most of them repeat offenders who would appear for short intervals, sometimes just a fortnight, before they were released. Short-term men, he called them, who mostly appeared to be Irish potato diggers or Jersey natives 'in for drunkenness'.

The only distraction available to them was stone-breaking. 'I was given a small hammer and a large chunk of stone,' he would recall. 'I sat in a cell alone and broke the chunk into chips.' Reading was the only escape from the monotony of the cell. Even then, the collection of books from the library could all be read in a matter of weeks. Eddie was a voracious reader and so he repeatedly read and re-read his own particular favourite, the poems of Tennyson. Newspapers were not distributed and only snippets of information would filter through. No talking was allowed and there was very little exercise time. The guards were unsympathetic and would hover close by during the fifteen minutes a week that relatives were allowed to visit. Eddie never received Betty's food parcel. He steeled himself to endure his sentence, determined not to rock the boat or upset the warders. For at least three months.

Later that summer of 1939, the authorities relented. Acknowledged as a 'model prisoner', Eddie was given a less strenuous task after the monotony of stone-breaking: tending gardens and cleaning offices. When Mr Foster, the prison governor, had his day off, Eddie was allowed to clean the gubernatorial mansion. One day towards the end of June, he was sweeping a garden path when he came across an old airline timetable which gave him the germ of an idea. 'I reckoned with two hours clear,' he later wrote, 'I could catch the departing plane for England.'

The following Thursday, 6 July, was Mr Foster's next day off, and it became Eddie's chosen day for a daring escape. When he arrived at the mansion that morning, he noted to his immense satisfaction that the Foster family were out. That included the governor's eighteen-year-old son, Thomas, to whom Eddie bore a striking resemblance. Eddie bided his time cleaning the house while his warder, as he usually did, fell asleep outside in the pleasant summer sunshine.

Eddie went upstairs, took the lad's clothes which were conveniently laid out on his bed and calmly changed into them. To help the disguise, he borrowed a hat and a pair of spectacles. He also took an attaché case, thirty-five shillings in notes and silver, plus six pounds' worth of sixpenny pieces from the study.

In his new attire, Eddie climbed out on to the roof, jumped into a nearby courtyard and, at the nearest phone box, called the airport to book his place on the first flight out. To his consternation, the 3.30 p.m. flight had left twenty minutes before. 'You must have seen an old timetable,' added the helpful airport official. 'A pity, too, because the plane was almost empty.'

While Eddie worked out what to do next, pandemonium had broken out. The prison authorities realised too late what had happened. Eddie had last been seen at three o'clock, but by 4.45 p.m. it was clear he had escaped. All prisoners had been locked in and soon the police – with 'every available man being called in from leave and special duty', in the breathless words of the local newspaper – were on his trail. The Jersey Constabulary searched every hotel and boarding house in and around St Helier, while all outgoing boats and flights were thoroughly investigated.

In the meantime, their quarry had been blithely gathering his thoughts in a nearby café. Eddie calmly drank a coffee, bought some cigarettes and waited for darkness to descend. About the time the general alarm was sounded, he checked into the La Pulente Hotel with the attaché case purloined from the governor's residence. Some time later, the hotel owner reported that a man bearing Eddie's description had checked in at five o'clock and called a cab, but had yet to return. When the police later went up to the room, they found Mr Foster's attaché case. But that was all.

Early that Thursday evening, Eddie went to a local pub where he met a couple of girls and took them out for dinner and a dance. In particular, he got on very well with the taller of the pair, who told him that he reminded her of someone. 'You will hear of me again,' Eddie replied with a straight face.

The petty cash from the governor's mansion was hardly going to be enough to pay for Eddie's escape from the islands. Later that evening, he made his way to a couple of nearby quarries to search out some gelignite. To do this, he would need transport, and indeed, a taxi driver later recalled taking someone to the Mont Mado quarry. The driver saw his passenger chat to the quarry foreman, who when later interviewed told them that nothing untoward had happened. However, a robbery was later reported at l'Etacq Quarry where five pounds of gelignite and two hundred detonators had been stolen. The foreman here found that the 'stout steel-sheathed double doors of the main magazine' had been forced open with a crowbar. When the police investigated, it was found that there had been reports of the attempted theft of two cars that evening. It was fairly obvious who was responsible.

The second car theft was the most curious. Eddie was apparently jimmying the door open when the driver asked him what he was doing. According to the local press, Eddie struck him with a spanner; in Eddie's recollection, the driver smacked him across the back of the head. 'We had a scuffle and I threw him over a wall,' he later told MI5.

Eddie knew that he would have to run for cover. He made his way down into St Helier. 'The hue and cry had already been raised for the escaped convict who had pinched the Governor's son's suit,' the press later reported. Outside the town hall, Eddie was spotted. 'That's him!' somebody shouted. 'I bolted round the corner into the dark,' he later wrote. 'I ran towards the sea shore.' He carried on along the beach towards a locked bungalow at La Pulente. He broke in, helped himself to some food and then fell asleep. The next morning, he found that the owner's clothes were too large for him to wear. Only his hat was the right size. So by padding his stomach with a pillow, he disguised himself as an old fisherman. Friday dawned windy and squally, so the conditions might also help lessen his chances of being recognised.

Feeling hungry, he made his way to a clifftop café, where it became apparent that the word was out. 'That terrible man's escaped again,' said the waitress who served him breakfast. She brought him the papers, throughout which his details were liberally plastered. Eddie merely twinkled as he demolished bacon and eggs followed by bananas and cream.

At 11 a.m., a man answering his description was spotted sheltering from the rain at a bus stop at the top of Le Pulec Hill. Three hours later, Eddie was reported a few miles away near Plemont. 'All police engaged in the search were armed with truncheons and handcuffs,' the *Jersey Evening Post* reported, 'and had been warned to take no risks as Chapman was held to be desperate and dangerous.'

Eventually Eddie's presence at the cliff-top tea room was reported. 'He had a grey pin-striped suit and an old mac and was carrying a shrimp net,' according to the press. One holidaymaker remembered seeing someone with a shrimp net wandering along the beach at Plemont. 'Doesn't he look like the escaped prisoner?' she said to her husband.

Indeed, by the early afternoon, Eddie had made his way on to the long sandy beach on the north-western corner of the island. When he became aware that a group of people were watching him from the cliffs, he pretended to be taking part in a football game. Soon, a small crowd was making its way towards him in the rain, led by three plain-clothes police. 'Are you coming quietly?' one of them asked. Eddie loudly claimed that *he* was the policeman and that the others were attacking him. There was, he later reminisced, 'a free for all' in which several people were hurt. Eddie managed to fight his way out before a handful of uniformed police arrived to break up the mêlée. He made his way towards a cave at the foot of the cliff. At its entrance, one of the uniformed coppers shouted at him to halt. 'Your name is Chapman.'

'No it is not,' Eddie gamely replied, striking at him. According to the press, they traded punches for a few minutes – until another uniform arrived to help handcuff him. Eddie was taken to the cliff top and arrested. Under 'strong police escort', he was taken back to St Helier jail. It had been splendid holiday entertainment for the onlookers. 'We watched a fine fight,' said one. 'A first-class scrap.'

On the journey back to Gloucester Street, Eddie started laughing. 'It is a good job you didn't roll on me,' he said impishly to one of the coppers who had had to restrain him. 'I have several detonators in my pocket, besides nine sticks of gelignite.'

Eddie was once more thrown into a cell. There followed another appearance at the Royal Court for this daring escape attempt, to which the various thefts were added – those of the governor's money, his son's and the fisherman's clothes, the car and the quarry gelignite. His sentence was increased by a year. Eddie made it clear he wanted to go back to the mainland to serve the rest of his sentence, but the attorney-general refused. He was able to convince the jury 'that the prisoner would not be doing three years' – which would have seen Eddie returned to an English jail – 'but two years and one'.

Eddie was taken into solitary confinement, where he was expected to serve the next three months breaking stones all day. He refused point blank. For this, he was given another month's solitary. Once more he refused, and this time he went on hunger strike. 'If I could, I'd murder you,' he cheerfully said to Mr Foster. 'As I can't, you can murder me.' The governor relented, terrified that Eddie would die in his custody. And so his longest-serving prisoner spent the rest of the summer working in the garden.

One day, sitting in his cell, Eddie noticed a carpenter had left his tools nearby. Never one to pass up an opportunity, he decided to take the lock out of his door. Having waited to be served dinner, he set to work on the mechanism. He had been busy for some minutes when in walked the governor, the Chief Constable and a Scotland Yard detective. At that moment, the lock dropped out.

A few days later, Eddie was told by a prison guard, in an offhand way, that Britain had declared war on Germany.

Betty Farmer had no further communication with Eddie Chapman after he went through the hotel window. Back home in London, she returned to what she had been doing before Eddie entered her life: working in a clothes shop by day and acting as a social secretary in the evenings. When the Germans invaded the Channel Islands the following summer, she presumed the worst. 'I was given to believe that he had been shot.'

Eddie's contemporaries heard no more of him after he made the front page of the *Daily Express* in the summer of 1939 for his impromptu impersonation of the governor's son. Official British files on Arnold Edward Chapman ended with the German invasion and subsequent occupation. So far as his friends and family were concerned, Eddie Chapman was dead.

CHAPTER TWO

Prisoners of War

'My own term in prison was coming to an end. I had served two years and eight months of my sentence, and while I had been shut up in a cell, a war had changed the pattern of the world, altering the destiny of hundreds and millions. My own fate had not escaped the impact of these tremendous years. Nor had my own ideas remained the same. I had no money, no friends; but a plan of campaign was beginning to form in my brain.'

— **Eddie Chapman, recalling his time in Jersey jail**

THE LAST FRIDAY IN June 1940 was the finest of summer evenings in the Channel Islands. Fruit had ripened early in the fields while a large potato crop was being packed and prepared. The inhabitants of the curious crags of rock that were so much closer – both physically and culturally – to Normandy than England had been hoping that they would escape the fate of the nearer mainland. Although France itself had capitulated under the onslaught of the Nazi *Blitzkrieg*, to the islanders the fighting still seemed very far away.

'We never thought the Germans would come here,' reflected one Guernseyman. 'We realised we might be bombed from time to time but an actual invasion was unthinkable.' Everything remained as rural and serene as it always had been.

Suddenly, six Heinkel bombers appeared, racing at tree-top height, strafing indiscriminately. '*Merde*!' one islander was heard to shout. 'That bugger Göring has sent the bloody works!' Horses reared up; lorries laden with crated fruit overturned; people screamed as machine guns rattled at random from the sky. Just after a quarter to seven on that Friday evening, the war arrived in the Channel Islands. On Jersey, random bombing killed eleven people. Boats in St Helier harbour were set alight and an off-licence had its window blown out – along with much of its stock. Within minutes, Guernsey was reporting a greater number of casualties – twenty-nine dead: quayside lorries carrying tomatoes had been mistaken for military ordnance. The islanders braced themselves for the worst.

'We'd heard on the wireless how they'd come across Europe, terrifying people with the Gestapo and the atrocities in the concentration camps,' recalled one. 'We didn't imagine we would be treated any better. But, as a matter of fact, they behaved very well – at first, that is.' The Third Reich was to occupy the Channel Islands for five years, during which time the islanders' loyalty to the Crown was to be severely tested. Though the cruelty of the German forces never reached the depths attained elsewhere in Occupied Europe, as the years went on the harshness of the regime intensified. The Channel Islands were the only sovereign British territory to be ruled directly by the Nazi state.

The realities of occupation would have unforeseen consequences for many people, not least the longest-serving prisoner in Gloucester Street. 'To be bombed in a locked cell with no chance either to fight or quit is still less attractive,' Eddie Chapman would later remark.

Since Eddie's arrest and reimprisonment after his impersonation of the governor's son in the summer of 1939, there hadn't been much front-page news from the Channel Islands. When war had broken out the previous September, they had remained 'holiday' islands, advertised as a restorative destination for those who could afford the air fare. The less well off, too, continued to arrive by the boatload. Eddie, like the other prisoners, was able to catch tantalising glimpses of the nearby seashore. From their cells, during that languorously sunny summer of 1940, the prisoners could hear the cries of holidaymakers who were still arriving in numbers. Mail steamers continued to disgorge workers, newspapers and all sorts of cargo.

The certainty that peace would hold in Jersey evaporated with the shocking events of May 1940. Those with sunnier dispositions hoped that the islands were going to be left alone but the more realistic – grabbing whatever came to hand – formed a steady trickle towards the British mainland, following in the wake of the 'little boats' which had evacuated British troops from Dunkirk. By the first week of June, the German army had crossed the Seine and suddenly the war had edged perilously closer. 'If we advance much further,' a sarcastic warder said in Eddie's hearing, 'we'll be fighting in the streets of London.'

The prisoner himself was frustrated and bored. After the German breakthrough, he had asked to be sent to the front as a soldier. He was 'curtly refused'. From his cell, Eddie would pick up snippets of news from the warders, seeing the occasional headline and hearing the odd radio news report en route to the exercise yard. Rumours of impending disaster spread with the rapid march of the Germans across France. 'Everybody was giving orders,' Eddie would write. 'Nobody really knew what was going on.'

The only concrete news that June came from the mouth of His Majesty the King. On the twenty-fourth, George VI made it clear the Channel Islands were now under direct threat of attack. The King couldn't, it seemed, bring himself to make the announcement over the radio. His words were read out in the States – the local parliament – by the Jersey Bailiff, which meant very few people heard them or even knew the extent of his government's defeatism.

'For strategic reasons it has been found necessary to withdraw the armed forces from the Channel Islands,' it was announced. His Majesty was full of regret and his government was not 'unmindful' of its commitments to the islanders. Far from calming the populace, the King's words had quite the opposite effect. Clearly there was going to be no help from London; the sense of abandonment was all but complete.

Soon, the steady trickle of boats turned into an unholy scramble. Though small boats from Jersey had helped in both the evacuation from Dunkirk and, later, that from St Mâlo, 'only a few vessels could be spared to try to evacuate the population of Jersey', Eddie later wrote. Twenty-three thousand people on Jersey alone registered to leave. The local ports were bombarded with desperate requests: children got the first berths and there were reports of queues miles long. Some even jumped on the Guernsey lifeboat in an attempt to get away. The governor of the islands made a speech regretting that he, too, had to leave.

'The atmosphere in the prison was depressing and apathetic,' Eddie would write, 'and it grew still worse in these blazing June days when the truth could no longer be concealed.' A strange lethargy was felt by staff and prisoners. Half hoping there would be a direct hit, Eddie soon realised that most of the warders had scarpered. He regretted that he didn't even have the chance to appoint himself prison governor. The next day, he saw a swastika-bedecked plane fly over the island. The day after that was the last Friday in June. 'Over they came,' he remembered of the aircraft, 'the prisoners in the jail heard the bombs whistling down.' Grown men were crying for their wives and children, or for their mothers.

With very few arms available and an empty fort abandoned by its garrison, the acting governor could do little else than accept the terms of the ultimatum that came from the skies. Leaflets written in German ordering the population to remain calm drifted down like unwanted confetti. Only a handful of islanders who could read German could understand them.

Within hours, chaos reigned. Eddie realised there would have been opportunities galore had he been on the outside. As each evacuee was allowed to take only two suitcases, the extent of the abandonment was massive. 'Houses, furniture, farms, country estates were given away,' he would recall. 'Shopkeepers offered their goods free to any passers-by.' Booze was poured away, cigarettes were freely handed out; farmers even left behind six hundred cows which roamed freely, bellowing with pain because their udders were full (they were eventually shot). Another herd was congregating at the end of one runway when Luftwaffe troop transports came in to land on the following Monday morning, 1 July.

Soon white flags popped up everywhere, some simply whitened sheets draped by farmers across their hen coops and cowsheds. 'The townsfolk were terrified,' Eddie recalled, 'the streets were deserted.' But after all the petrifying publicity, the Germans seemed to be on their best behaviour. When a military band, in the first public display of the Wehrmacht's might, played 'Pack Up Your

Troubles In Your Old Kit Bag', even Eddie could relax a little. Indeed, military bands practised so often that 'it seemed', in the wry words of one chronicler, 'as if the Occupation had been devised solely to enable army musicians to practise their happy marching music'.

For the occupiers themselves, it was a pleasant interlude. Many German soldiers were keen to buy up foods and luxury items with English trademarks that could be sent home as novelty presents. Every Wehrmacht serviceman liked to have his photo taken next to a British bobby. 'The Germans are not at all bad chaps,' one of the guards said in Eddie's hearing. 'Why, they pay for everything they buy in the shops.'

In those first few weeks, all remained serene in the summer sunshine. The Luftwaffe practised stunt flights over the island, the Wehrmacht carried out exercises in preparation for the forth-coming invasion of England. Some observers saw the occupying forces in full invasion dress, singing their favourite war song, '*Wir fahren gegen England*' – 'We're marching against England'. As barges were gathered together in the French Channel ports, the subjugation of the British Isles seemed inevitable – and only a few weeks away, at most. '[The] Germans put out fantastic claims of what had been done in England,' Eddie recorded of the air attacks on the mainland that summer. 'Many of the island people believed them.'

The occupation, in Eddie's recollection, went as smoothly as a diesel train. From his perspective, the Germans 'did not need to clamp down an iron regime' and after the fright had worn off, the islanders adapted reasonably quickly. Within days, the occupying forces had taken over the various administrative buildings and imposed their will on the subdued populace. 'On the whole, they behaved pretty well,' Eddie said of the occupiers. 'All the same, it must be said that little was done to provoke them. The official attitude of the island authorities was one of complete submission.'

★ ★ ★

The Germans quickly established their headquarters at the Metropole Hotel. In their eyes, at least, military victory had established their right to rule as they saw fit. Within weeks, the *Feldkommandatur*, 'civil affairs unit', had been established. Its purview included all the business of government and law and order – including the police force, the courts and legal system and thus, the jails. All island law had to be approved by the *Feldkommandatur* and all orders emanating from it had to be registered as law.

Though its officials wore military uniforms, they were officious bureaucrats who did everything by the book, issuing rules and regulations with annoying regularity. '*Jetz geht der Papierkrieg los* (Now the paper war begins),' one said to a Jersey official soon after his arrival. He was not joking.

The local governmental bodies carried on much as before. The attorney-general – as Eddie had already found out – acted as the public prosecutor, akin to the *Procureur général* in the French system. That meant he was also in charge of the police force and ultimately received his orders from the *Feldkommandatur*. In those first few months of occupation, however, he was given a fair amount of autonomy. As Eddie was aware from the arbitrary way his jail sentence had been increased, the attorney-general could do more or less what he liked.

At the start, there was surprisingly little friction between occupiers and occupied. There were less than two dozen offences against the occupiers in the first few months of the occupation. Subversion was largely limited to the propaganda leaflets regularly dropped by the Royal Air Force. Some of the British bobbies were, however, replaced by the Wehrmacht field police, the *Feldpolizei*. Despite the officiousness of the paperwork, there were no written instructions about policing matters.*

Against this backdrop, St Helier jail was run as two halves. The attorney-general still looked after the civilian prisoners while the

---

*A myth endures that the Gestapo were regularly to be found goosestepping around the Channel Islands. Technically speaking, as part of the secret police set-up of the German state, there were no Gestapo in Jersey. There was, however, a *Geheime Feldpolizei* (GFP or Secret Field Police), a kind of 'Gestapo of the Army' which was part of the Army's *Feldpolizei*. As they were not averse to using the same methods as Himmler's men, the locals – and prisoners – would hardly know the difference.

Feldpolizei imposed sentences on German soldiers guilty of drunkenness and rowdiness (though on the British side of the jail, there were civilians who had been arrested for offences against the German authorities). So far as the prisoners were concerned, there was little change in the day-to-day running of the jail. There was no great announcement when the *Feldpolizei* came to inspect the facilities in Gloucester Street. In Eddie's recollection, the prisoners were in the stone yard, splitting logs into firewood, when one of the sentries shouted, 'Attention!' The governor walked into the yard followed by three German soldiers, the most senior being an *Oberleutnant* of the *Feldpolizei*. The prisoners stood to attention, well away from the governor, and each was asked to come forward in turn.

'What are you in for?' an interpreter asked Eddie.

'*Ich bin ein Verbrecher*,' Eddie gamely replied.

'*Ach, sie sprechen Deutsch?*' replied the *Oberleutnant*.

Eddie indicated he knew a little. 'I am in for breaking a safe open, and trying to escape.'

The officer chuckled, and Eddie decided to go for broke. 'Any chance of work?'

'Sorry,' the interpreter replied, 'not my branch.'

From the outset, Eddie was determined to make his way back to the British mainland. In his later MI5 interrogations and his reminiscences, he made clear his desire to return home – whatever the consequences. More specifically, he told MI5 that 'If I could work a bluff with the Germans, employed as a spy, I should probably be sent over here.'

'Sheer determination was going to get him out of it,' Betty Chapman says. 'He knew what would happen to him if he tried to escape.'

When Eddie was interviewed by MI5 investigators, he claimed he had confided in a fellow prisoner about working as a double agent if need be.* The fact that he had even discussed the possibility of a

---

*This revelation caused MI5 considerable anguish. Douglas Stewart, a native of Birmingham, was well known in the Channel Islands for his cognac business, and was imprisoned for black market offences. If he accidentally revealed Eddie's plans, 'he would smash up the whole business', as MI5 put it. All the Security Service's efforts to trace this businessman came to naught.

double-cross with other prisoners would, two years hence, cause a serious problem for British Intelligence.

One particular prisoner came into Eddie's life at the end of 1940 to act as a hostage to Eddie's good behaviour. Anthony Faramus was, by his own admission, a 'wild boy'. By today's standards of youthful rebellion, his litany of petty misdemeanours was innocent and typical of the pranks of the time: his transgressions included ringing church bells and running off after pressing doorbells. But Faramus was, by his own estimation, a 'public nuisance' by pre-war Jersey standards. 'He's led me a right bloody song and dance,' announced one policeman after Faramus had 'borrowed' some cars which were then left outside the local police station. For this, Faramus was given his first, month-long jail term.

When he tried to enlist in the Royal Air Force in the spring of 1940, Faramus was turned down even though he was twenty years of age. He watched the evacuation boats from St Aubin's Bay after deciding not to join the queues trying to flee ahead of the German invasion. Perhaps, as he later wrote without rancour, he should have heeded his mother's advice to get off the island before it was too late. 'You can still get on the last boat going to England,' she had told him. But, by his later admission, he only ever saw the war as a madcap adventure, which probably goes some way to explain his subsequent misfortunes.

By the time of the occupation, Faramus was working at the Miramar Hotel, one of the most luxurious on the islands. The day of the invasion itself, a Dornier 'flying pencil' raced past his bedroom so close that the pilot was treated to the naked form and jiggling breasts of a waitress with whom young Faramus had been sleeping. 'Show-off bastard!' she yelled from the window. From his perspective, the Germans' arrival was largely peaceful. 'A few bombs were dropped, which killed perhaps half a dozen or so civilians,' Faramus later recalled. 'The German aircraft machine-gunned the streets and a few people who had not the sense to take cover were killed.'

When the invaders came, it was clear that organised resistance was futile. Yet Faramus did his best to undermine the occupiers, throwing several pounds of overripe tomatoes at a portrait of Hitler, stealing a pair of German revolvers and daubing 'V for

Victory' signs on walls, as well as letting down the tyres of bicycles used by the soldiers and loosening their handlebars. Otherwise, life for him went on very much as it had done before. Though he was only earning £2 a week plus food, he was also claiming £1 extra for a non-existent dependant. 'I did not consider this minor act of false pretences to be a crime,' he would later write. By outwitting the Germans in this way, he felt that he was helping the war effort, but his minor deception was to cost him dearly.

★ ★ ★

By the autumn of 1940, when it had become clear to the Germans that the Battle of Britain had been lost, the occupation became more sinister. In time, all radio sets were confiscated and listening to the BBC became an offence. Jersey jail meanwhile remained as bleak and uncompromising as it always had been. The biggest complaint remained the food, about which Eddie had been sure to regale the new management. At the same time he had told the *Oberleutnant* that he was a safebreaker he added that prison life was monotonous, the food was terrible and he was pretty cheesed off. Wouldn't you be, he had made a point of stating, if your staple diet was potatoes, either as soup or with bread? Some of the prisoners, it seemed, had had to make do with raw potatoes. Eddie's own weight had already dropped from eleven stone seven to nine stone five.

There was silence from the *Oberleutnant*. Criticism of any kind was not looked on kindly by the occupiers. Though the prisoners were sheltered to some extent from the harsher realities, there remained certain dangers. Petty squabbles could turn nasty. When one Irish prisoner ate a meal with his hat on, it upset a German soldier who flung his hat off. After a scuffle, the Irishman was sent for a month's hard labour. A waitress in a local café, who had accompanied an order of food with a cheerful 'Four dinners for four gangsters', also got a month inside. Any complaint, no matter how trivial, ended up with the person's name added to the list of agitators.

One of the more distressing incidents concerned a group of about fifteen French students who had tried to escape from the islands. They were led by François Scorret, the son of a doctor, whom Eddie remembered as 'a dark, merry-eyed boy full of high spirits'. Their motor boat had broken down en route to England and they were subsequently captured. Imprisoned in Gloucester Street, they were at first spirited, singing and dancing, drawing caricatures of the Nazi leadership on the walls. They often jeered at the warders standing to attention whenever German officers talked to them. 'When they shouted "Attention!" to the French boys, they simply squatted,' Eddie recalled.

The following spring, this lively young leader was sentenced to death and his friends – who were only in their mid- to late teens – were each given life sentences or ten years' hard labour. The other prisoners protested at Scorret's imminent execution and were taken in to see the governor. To little avail. The next they heard was that Scorret had been executed by firing squad in the grounds of a nearby manor house. On 23 March 1941, a shocking sign appeared – *Zum Tode*, To Death – on noticeboards all around the islands. Eddie heard later that Scorret had refused to wear a blindfold and had shouted, 'Vive la France!' when the volley of shots were fired.

Wehrmacht soldiers committed for minor offences simply wouldn't obey the native warders. 'They refused to be locked up,' Eddie recalled, 'they walked about the prison doing just as they liked.' Eventually a German military guard was put in to maintain discipline. It was a source of much merriment for the other prisoners that the guard's role was to protect the warders. When the German prisoners were eventually released, their cries of '*Scheisse Englander, sie können mich am Arsch lecken*' ('Cursed Englishmen, you can kiss my arse') were no longer heard long into the night.

★   ★   ★

In many ways the occupation of the Channel Islands was seen by the Germans as a test case for the subsequent occupation of the British Isles. Further along the French coast, envious eyes looked out across the English Channel that summer of 1940 towards the cliffs of Kent. In Berlin, Operation Sea Lion was being planned. An assault on the south coast of England would be targeted on a broad swathe from Ramsgate all the way towards the Isle of Wight.

Early that summer, Hitler's military intelligence chief was called in to see the Chief of Naval Operations at the Kriegsmarine. Considered something of an inscrutable genius by the German High Command, Admiral Wilhelm Canaris had directed the Abwehr since 1935. As more than one writer has remarked, Canaris was an enigma in life, as indeed he has remained in death. The reality was that the Abwehr was badly run and, despite notable pre-war successes, often mounted operations that were doomed to failure. Nevertheless, Admiral Raedar was now asking the Abwehr to provide as much local intelligence as possible in support of the invasion. In particular, the High Command wanted Canaris to establish a new network of spies that would help the landing forces assess the local disposition of troops.

In this at least, the British defenders were well prepared. That long hot summer, 'Fifth column' fever and worry about spies reached the level of a national obsession. Despite its pre-war success and Admiral Canaris's reputation for genius, the Abwehr's attempts to spy or inveigle agents into the British Isles were disastrous. Indeed, there is much speculation that many of the broader details of Operation Sea Lion were leaked to Whitehall by the admiral himself. Whatever the truth of that, the Hamburg offices of the Abwehr came up with a series of espionage missions to support the landings which one writer on intelligence has aptly termed 'erratic, jejeune and, on several occasions, tinged with absurdity'.

Already, in May 1940, one agent had been landed to foment trouble in Ireland, carrying with him high explosives disguised as a tin of processed French peas. Hermann Görtz landed miles off course as the Luftwaffe managed to drop him in Northern Ireland, not the Republic. Görtz himself was out of shape, lost all his equipment on landing and any sense of direction after trudging across the countryside for several days. When he eventually made contact with the IRA in Dublin, it was clear the republicans were rather more interested in his money. Eventually, he was captured.

In early September, a team of four hand-picked Abwehr agents were landed by boat in the same Kentish marshlands where the Wehrmacht were to come ashore. None of them spoke English, all were hastily trained and despatched. One drew attention to himself by talking loudly in a foreign accent while another started giving orders to the locals, seemingly under the impression that the invasion had already begun. A couple of weeks later, another German agent landed by parachute – in the wilds of the Northamptonshire countryside – with his transmitter strapped to his chest. For Swedish-born Gösta Caroli (codenamed Summer by the British), the extra weight would lead to a different sort of complication. As he came to land, he was dragged forward by the heavy equipment and somehow managed to knock himself unconscious.

From the outset, MI5 was puzzled by the Abwehr's sheer incompetence. Twenty-one agents had landed in the three months until November 1940. All were captured within hours. Far from being an Aryan master race who could endlessly crank out super-spies, the Germans were unbelievably inept. As Eddie Chapman would find out on Jersey, German military intelligence worked in mysterious ways.

The first time Anthony Faramus saw Eddie Chapman, he was stuffing mattresses, one of the lesser punishments to which long-term prisoners in St Helier jail were subjected. It was towards the end of 1940, and Eddie made quite an impression on the twenty-year-old lad. 'To meet Mr Edward Chapman on the outside,' Faramus would later record, 'you would think that he was a prosperous young company director, with his expensive and well-tailored suits, snappy walking stick, brown suede shoes and cigar.' Inside, he was less well appointed in his prison fatigues, but his cheekiness and charisma were immediately apparent.

That autumn, Faramus had been asked to report to the Grand Hotel. He wasn't unduly worried but to his dismay the policeman who had often arrested him as a teenager greeted him with the words, 'You took your bloody time getting here.' It was obvious something was up. Faramus was taken to the local police station where he was charged with obtaining money – a sum of £9 – under false pretences. 'Is that the best you can do?' was all he asked. Thinking it was a joke, Faramus didn't think he would be arrested for cheating on the Germans by claiming extra money for a non-existent dependant. But he was thrown into jail, where an occurrence earlier that day took on a sinister significance.

Just that morning, Faramus had picked up some leaflets dropped by the Royal Air Force. The Wehrmacht clearly had not yet had time to hunt them all down. When one of these leaflets was found in his pocket, he was promptly handed over to the *Feldkommandatur* by the Brown Hats. Faramus spent an anxious week in a holding cell, wondering if he would be shot or even beheaded. That, the rumours circulated, was how the Germans dealt with troublemakers. When he was charged at the Royal Court, Faramus faced regular Islands justices. They showed no sympathy. What he had been told would be just one month's sentence was increased to six months – with hard labour thrown in.

By the time Tony Faramus joined him, Eddie Chapman was no longer viewed as a model prisoner. Holding out for weeks in solitary confinement for some misdemeanour or other, he subsisted on bread and water while he was singled out for petty torments from the warders. 'But,' Faramus would later write, 'Eddie was one prisoner whose spirit they were totally unable to break.' His solitary confinement wasn't entirely wasted. Having the use of grammar books, he taught himself French and German to stave off the boredom.

'That's what always amazed me about Eddie,' his brother Winston remarks. 'All he could do when we were lads was speak the Geordie language. By the end of the war, he had learned French, German and Norwegian!'

Not that there was much time for learning languages. Hard labour lived up to its name. Prisoners weren't allowed to speak and cracked stones all day. Very soon, the stone yard – where hands quickly became a mass of blisters – became their only escape from the cell. Eddie and Tony would meet each other furtively in the exercise yard. Despite the enforced silence, Faramus would catch snatches of conversation from his older companion. Though they never became close friends – the six-year age difference probably precluded it – their common sense of adversity was enough to draw them together in these most trying of circumstances. Eddie and Tony shared a natural rebelliousness.

'Eddie and I were the chief complaint-lodgers,' Faramus would later write. 'Food was our main trouble, as it generally is in most prisons.' Despite the abundance of local produce, fresh vegetables were a rarity. Faramus was able, at least, to bribe a warder with cigarettes to bring in letters from the outside – until his supply ran out. Though their sense of isolation intensified into the spring of 1941, Faramus was coming to the end of his stretch, unlike his friend. On the last day of Faramus's incarceration, Eddie happened to be having his monthly bath in the next cubicle. They made a date to meet on the outside in St Helier – whenever that might be.

At the start of 1941, events in another, rather more famous jail in which Eddie Chapman had already served time would come to have a greater effect on his future. Many spies end their careers in prison, but Eddie Chapman's later spymasters, those who ran the double-agent operations, started theirs in Wormwood Scrubs.

Because of the continued bombing of central London the previous summer, the Security Service had temporarily moved to west London's most famous jail. Conductors soon became used to perplexed military figures looking lost on the number 12 bus route. For the other passengers, there was a certain novelty in hearing the cry 'All change for MI5'. In another sense it was indeed all change. General Kell had been fired by Winston Churchill and the security services had finally been put on a war footing.

The steady stream of German agents the previous autumn buttressed a firm belief that something more could be done than just sending them to the gallows. They offered the greatest of opportunities. Hitherto, the turning of double agents had been ramshackle and uncoordinated as each agent had been handled on an *ad hoc* basis. In all previous wars, captured spies had been summarily executed as a warning to others. Now, though, a handful of the new recruits to MI5 thought that they could achieve something more useful. All subsequent German agents who arrived in the country were carefully screened, and either dismissed as unsuitable or doubled – to work against the Nazi regime. Only as a last resort were they executed (and only fourteen ever were).

MI5's response was radical, imaginative yet characteristically bureaucratic. The so-called Double Cross Committee – the Twenty Club, to its members – was a classic British compromise: a 'most secret' committee which included representatives from MI5, MI6,

the Admiralty, the War Office, the Air Ministry, Home Forces and
other interested departments. After a low-key start the previous
autumn – 'The position at the beginning was largely experimental
as no one knew very much about the working of double agents,'
said the Naval Intelligence representative, the Right Honourable
Ewen Montagu – the committee was formally convened to decide
what could and could not be fed to the Germans.

On the first Wednesday of January 1941, the Scrubs hosted the
first ever meeting of the Double Cross Committee. Its chairman was
determined to take care of the amenities, insisting that tea and buns
be served (as they would in every subsequent meeting, over two
hundred in all). John C. Masterman was not everybody's choice,
for he struck many as gaunt, humourless and incapable of coming
to a decision. But he was a dedicated committee man and a reasonable keeper of the gate in deciding what information could be
passed via the double agents.

The committee formalised how all the various arms of British
Intelligence might work together to fool the Germans by playing on
their worst fears – from Adolf Hitler downwards. Recruiting
suitable candidates for doubling was not an exact science: human
frailties and the bizarre characteristics of the agents sent by the
Germans would see to that. Eventually, the double agents themselves became part of a greater skein of intrigue in which the
Germans would be wound. And later, by the end of 1941, came the
next piece of the puzzle which would take the playing back of false
information to another level: the breaking of the Enigma code used
by the Abwehr itself.

★ ★ ★

Day-to-day survival – for prisoners or, for that matter, anyone else
on the islands – became much more difficult as 1941 progressed.
Conditions worsened because the German forces had virtually
devoured everything in sight. Jersey was normally self-sufficient,
but with the arrival of occupation troops it could no longer make
that claim. Once the Germans had garrisoned the islands, food
stocks dwindled with little chance of replenishment from the
mainland. 'There was very little food on the islands,' Eddie later

recalled. 'You couldn't buy anything because there was nothing there.' By the autumn of 1941 food rationing had become severe, and there were two meatless days a week.

Conditions were even worse in St Helier jail, though the prisoners helped each other as best they could. 'Eddie had his own source of supplies which included the prison warders,' Betty recalls, 'and that was how they managed to survive.' In fact, he was able to get supplies that even the islanders couldn't. 'Unless he was on hunger strike,' she wryly comments, 'he could always get what he wanted.' Against this background, the rise of the black market was almost inevitable. And in time, a new addition to the prison population would be in the curious position of experiencing first hand the ancient cells in Gloucester Street, the vile food and 'the absolute disregard for the human dignity and feelings of the prisoners in their charge'.

At the end of 1941, Eric Pleasants was thirty years old. A simple Norfolk lad, he had already been a boxing star, champion wrestler, circus performer and physical culture instructor. At one point, he had even been a bodyguard to the young Princesses Elizabeth and Margaret, eventually becoming a reservist on the British gymnastic team in the 1936 Olympics. A gentle giant of a man, he had the unfortunate manner of a comic-book simpleton with the physique of a fitness freak.

Born to a gamekeeper father on a Norfolk estate, Eric naturally sided with the poachers who raided the estate. The key to understanding Eric Pleasants' character came in both his strength and stubbornness – especially towards authority figures. By the time he reached his mid-teens, 'Panther' Pleasants had already established his name in the Broads as an amateur boxer and wrestler. But, rather like the young Eddie Chapman, Eric found himself in trouble when tempted by young ladies. When he got the daughter of the local squire pregnant, he was forced to head to London. Pleasants had flirted with communism but was much more motivated by a strong belief in pacifism. When war broke out, he was toying with the idea of registering as a 'conchie' (conscientious objector), for he didn't 'like firing a gun and killing people I have never seen'. First, though, he joined the Mercantile Marine, to escape to the 'grand existence of a sailor's life'.

On missing his ship home after deciding to sleep with a local Jersey girl, Pleasants was offered the chance to remain, via a scheme operated by the Peace Pledge Union,* as a non-combatant agricultural labourer. The timing was not exactly propitious for it was now May 1940. Soon, though, he made friends with John Leister, who was also conflicted over the war because of his German family and background. He too was part of the Peace Pledge Union scheme and he later became an interpreter.

Just before the occupation, Pleasants had fallen in with a group of mainly Irish potato diggers with whom he shared a barn as living quarters. With invasion looming, the labourers went to arrange their return to Eire but were refused. Their recruiters insisted there was no danger and then lied about providing a boat for them. When Pleasants remonstrated on their behalf, a punch-up ensued. The strongman ended up in Gloucester Street breaking stones in the prison yard for a fortnight.

On his release, Eric was forced into petty pilfering in order to survive. By his own admission, he and Leister hung around in 'the sort of haunts frequented by questionable characters who were either dodging the law or were about to do something to make it necessary to change the law'. As conditions deteriorated throughout 1941, Pleasants survived thanks to various black market schemes. After raiding a rabbit farm in St Brélade one night, they broke into the German bakehouse in St Helier and stole all the bread. When, as a result, their lodgings were later searched, both were jailed. So Eric Pleasants would spend another three months in jail at the end of 1941, where he made fast friends with Eddie Chapman.

By the time he arrived in Gloucester Street, he found Eddie still a rebellious spirit. Doing his daily exercise with three warders in attendance, Eddie called out a cheery greeting, despite the rigorously enforced silence. This new prisoner didn't know the cheerful chap who clearly enjoyed flouting orders. By means of

---

* A number of these non-combatants were Irish, suspected of membership of the IRA. Eddie came into contact with a lot of Irish prisoners, whose nationality interested the Abwehr (and later MI5, when Eddie told them about these potential saboteurs).

messages tapped out at the bottom of the hot water pipe, the prison bush telegraph revealed his identity.

They warmed to each other straight away. Pleasants was particularly taken with the way Eddie resisted all efforts at imposing authority and ignored all attempts to quell his spirit. As the occupation worsened, Eddie tried to get the other prisoners to protest about the filthy conditions and demand proper food. Only Pleasants joined in. The average Jersey man, he stated, had no guts.

Although Eddie was supposedly coming to the end of his sentence, there was no sign of any immediate release. 'It didn't seem right to me that a man could be detained indefinitely like that because there was no way he could be delivered to the English police,' Pleasants declared. Along with Leister, they made their way to the *Feldkommandantur* to protest that Eddie's prolonged incarceration was unjust. So far as Pleasants was concerned, the meeting 'obviously had some effect'. Eddie was released soon afterwards.

Early one morning in the first week of October 1941, Eddie Chapman was escorted to the front gate of the prison. With reluctance, the police let him walk out, if not exactly to freedom, then to the end of his jail sentence. At the prison gate, Eddie was met by a friend, a local bookie called Sandy who had also served a sentence for black market offences. He gave Eddie a £20 note and bacon and eggs, and these were soon followed by a black market job. The latter was clearly the only way of adjusting to the realities of occupation.

To obtain certain food items, even the most law-abiding citizens had to break the law and participate in the black market – if they could afford it, that is. As Eddie had noted, the rich were insulated against the hardships: they could buy in whatever luxuries they might want. The rest of the population could at least satisfy a fraction of their needs, by using the black market. Many islanders chose to become vegetarians to survive. As food supplies ran out, the black market became rife. Many realised what a great oppor- tunity it presented now that very survival was at stake.

As agreed, on his release Eddie had been reunited with Tony Faramus. Eddie had originally wanted to open a nightclub for the occupying forces. The authorities had blanched. So instead, as

Faramus knew how to cut hair and shave customers, they opened a barber's in St Helier. They advertised in German and attracted a considerable clientele. In fact, the shop was a front, as were many other hairdressers on the islands. Within a matter of days, Chapman and Faramus were doing a roaring trade on the black market. Faramus, who had spent the summer trying to avoid doing construction work for the occupiers, was delighted. The Germans were greedy and bought up, in Eddie's words, 'every ounce of coffee, tea, chocolate they could lay their hands on'.

'The barber's shop became a very handy two-way source of supply,' Betty Chapman says. 'Even the Germans found it was very useful.' Technically speaking, receiving food earmarked for the Wehrmacht was dealing in stolen goods but, so long as their superiors turned a blind eye, most soldiers were eager to participate.

'Drink could only be obtained on the black market,' Eddie would write, 'and the police were soon hand in glove with its chief operators.' The barber's was so successful that even the prison governor came in one day to look for cigarettes. For the moment, Eddie's luck held. Because he spoke German, he took care to befriend the Wehrmacht troops. Those who had recently passed through Occupied France would often bring supplies with them. Bizarrely, tea, that staple of the British Empire, was at a premium. Ten packets of cigarettes would be swapped for a pound of tea; a quarter of a pound for a bottle of good cognac brought over from the French mainland.

Thanks to the garrisoning of the island, even potatoes, the staple of the islanders' diet, were soon being rationed. It was no longer possible to buy a daily loaf of bread, just a few slices. There were acute petrol shortages and most privately owned vehicles had all but disappeared off the roads, many sequestrated by the occupiers. As petrol became ever more tightly rationed, public transport eventually evaporated and, unsurprisingly, bicycle theft increased. Cycles were exchanging hands for up to £50 a time, while even padlocks and chains could be traded at a premium.

The Germans had confiscated most bicycles and insisted that everyone drive or ride on the right-hand side of the road. Both these diktats now literally collided with Eddie Chapman. One day, riding his own cycle on the 'wrong' side of the road, he was hit by a despatch rider. 'His cycle was wrecked and I was thrown some distance,' Eddie recalled, 'but luckily got off with a few cuts and bruises.' The air turned blue to the sound of cursing – in German.

'It was rather funny,' Eddie remembered. 'After the accident, I had to write out a terrific explanation of how everything had happened.' He was reported to the Field Police and told to report to the *Kommandatur* as a matter of routine. Anybody who had had an accident was automatically detained by what the natives called the '*Feldgendarmerie*'.

For some reason, the German authorities thought he was 'a dangerous man who had brought explosives onto the Island'. Eddie appeared before eight judges, who had reason to believe he was in possession of arms, including a German rifle. This he strenuously denied. A small man who spoke good English made a point of telling him: 'Now look, we've got our eye on you, so if you try any trouble we'll make trouble too.'

'Thank you for the warning,' Eddie said, now fully aware that he would be shot if he got up to no good. He left the room feeling rather more anxious than when he entered.

The end of 1941 saw another milestone in the intelligence war. That Christmas, British Intelligence had been given its own splendid present: a chance to break into the codes used by German agents who were being trained all across Europe. On Boxing Day, the codebreakers at Bletchley Park finally cracked the Abwehr's own Enigma machines.

German military intelligence kept close tabs on all its agents around Europe. These *V-menn* (*Vertrauensmänner*, literally 'men of trust' or trusted agents) themselves did not carry their own Enigma machines. As the codebreaker (and Oxford-educated mathematician) Peter Twinn has explained, it would have been embarrassing and inconvenient for an agent 'to slip across frontiers or arrive unannounced by parachute, to be encumbered by an Enigma resembling a weighty and antiquated typewriter'.

Despite the feather-brained nature of some of its schemes, the Abwehr's officers were meticulous in recording the minutiae of their agents' training. Though many were taught sabotage skills in hermetic isolation, Berlin got to know everything about their progress. After reporting to their local headquarters, the relevant details would be forwarded by radio either to Hamburg – which was responsible for all secret activities directed against Britain – or else to the Abwehr's Berlin headquarters on the Tirpitzufer.

Radio transmissions provided MI5 with a unique window on the mysterious workings of their German counterparts. Europe, criss-crossed by extensive German radio networks, came under the scrutiny of dedicated monitoring. British Intelligence kept tabs by intercepting radio signals and trying to fix their location by cross-referencing and triangulation. At the start of the war, British radio hams had taken particular note of some inexplicable short-wave transmissions that were thought to originate from the Far East. Soon, the radio hams found that other signals were being sent on the same frequencies. Careful analysis revealed it was the Abwehr radio traffic passing from its outstations in Paris, Ankara, Lisbon and Madrid over the airwaves to Berlin. Inadvertently, they had hit the motherlode.

It became clear these signals had been encoded in a new form of Enigma. The Abwehr had its own dedicated machine which was wired up differently from those of the other armed services. Many of the hams were brought together under the auspices of the Radio Security Service (RSS) which, like Bletchley Park, eventually came under the administrative auspices of MI6. (By the start of 1942, the RSS was based at Hanslope Park, a country estate just north of Milton Keynes, not far from Bletchley.)

Eventually, a dedicated section was set up in Hut 6 at Bletchley Park specifically to decode this radio traffic. They gradually worked out how the Abwehr Enigma machine was different from those used by the Wehrmacht and decoded its settings accordingly. On 26 December 1941, they made the all-important breakthrough.

Early the next year, signals from Abwehr outstations were to reveal that its officers were checking up on an English national whose background had something to do with Jersey. In the meantime, the English national himself had taken matters into his own hands.

Three weeks after his release from jail – and after discussing matters at length with Anthony Faramus – Eddie Chapman wrote a letter to the German authorities offering his services. 'His whole theme was revenge,' Faramus would remember of its contents. 'He had no time for the English ruling classes [and] sought only a chance to get even with them.' When he heard nothing more, one morning in the winter of 1941 Eddie simply went to see Herr von Stülpnagel at the *Kommandantur*. He was stopped by a sentry but explained that what he was doing was '*geheim*' ('secret').

'I was taken up to see the Commander who wrote everything down,' Eddie recalled. When he was taken in to see this 'bull-faced' major, he didn't equivocate.

'I would like to join the German secret service.'

The major laughed and asked what qualifications he might have. Eddie handed over a choice selection of his newspaper clippings and outlined 'an appreciation of my future if the British police should get hold of me'. Von Stülpnagel then asked if he had ever been a member of the IRA. He shook his head. When Eddie added that he was simply searching for revenge, the major seemed satisfied.

He called in his secretary and after warning him that '*alles ist streng geheim*' ('everything is top secret'), he wrote down everything that Eddie told him. Eddie rose to the occasion by spinning a yarn about his criminal history, making out he was a master criminal. At the mention of the word gelignite, the major's eyes lit up. A new career in sabotage beckoned.

After a drink and a cigar, the major promised he would get in touch. Eddie was relieved. His widow reflects that he could convince the Germans that anything was better than spending a life's term in an English prison.

Despite the increasing hardships, life in Jersey for black marketeers remained easy, perhaps a little too easy for those who thrived on excitement. Eric 'Panther' Pleasants had already arranged to get Eddie a room in his boarding house, the Panama. Protected to some extent by their delightfully maternal landlady, within a few weeks of leaving prison both were up to their old tricks again. Eddie and Eric spent some time looting many of the properties abandoned in the rush to evacuate the island.

One night they came across an imposing but empty manor house which Eric had already burgled. When they found a huge safe in the cellar, Eddie could hardly contain his excitement. 'Let's swag it,' he said with infectious enthusiasm. 'Somebody might have left the family fortune behind.'

He gave Pleasants a list of the tools they would need and planned to return the following evening. All they really needed was a knife to prise open the window. Soon they were entering the cellar. The safe was an old Milner. 'They're easy,' Eddie said. 'Help me to turn it around.'

The safe weighed at least five hundredweight. Pleasants' strength came in useful. He moved the safe into position so that Eddie could work on it. It was an old safe with a thin sheet of steel riveted to the back, so he simply used a screwdriver to force the metal away from the rivet. 'Now give me that crowbar,' he said.

After a few minutes' forcing, the first rivet burst open. The rest popped easily. Ten minutes later, they carefully removed the asbestos fireproof backing. Another sheet, another virtuoso prising open and they were in. 'I was amazed at the ease with which this master craftsman opened the back,' Pleasants would recall. Both were delighted to find five hundred pounds in cash, some jewellery and a few last wills and testaments. 'Not bad, not bad,' Eddie muttered.

Pleasants wanted to leave it there and get out. But Eddie said that if the police came across the opened safe, it would be obvious who were the most likely culprits. So he replaced everything and Eric heaved the safe back into place. After they swept the floors, all looked exactly as it had done on entry. As Eddie said, with his usual cheeky smile, it wasn't a bad night's work. The pair returned to their guest house happy and rather wealthier than when they had left earlier in the evening.

In the meantime, black marketeering continued apace in St Helier. 'I doubled the price and sold the goods extremely well,' Eddie later recalled. He was soon supplying most of the St Helier pubs with black market booze. In this way, he became friendly with many of the occupying forces, often visiting one of their brothels, known as the Belle Amie. Previously a luxurious hotel called the Plaza, its highlights were specially imported French girls who appeared in a rowdy cabaret.

One night that November, Eddie was enjoying the show at the Belle Amie. Always a heavy drinker, he had blithely consumed three bottles of cognac in the company of Faramus and a German officer. They were oblivious of the time. Unfortunately for them, the ten o'clock curfew was now being strictly enforced. Just after ten, a couple of Brown Hats came over to arrest them. Eddie, much the worse for wear, got into an argument.

As they were being frogmarched outside, he recognised some of his German friends from the barber's shop. One Wehrmacht officer telephoned the *Kommandatur* and word came back that the miscreants could be taken there. The coppers were having none of it: a punch-up occurred and one of the policemen was pushed down a flight of stairs. Both Eddie and Tony had to pay £1 at the police station on their own recognisance before they were released. 'A little while later,' Eddie records, 'I was not to be so lucky.'

A few weeks after the Belle Amie incident, Chapman and Faramus were busy one morning in the salon. In Faramus's recollection, a constable walked in and told them that they were to report to the police station immediately. There they were informed that they would now come under the orders of the *Kommandatur*, allowed only to go back to their lodgings and pick up their clothes. They were then told that they would be leaving for France. Though obviously worried, Eddie remained his usual upbeat self. 'Might be a change,' he said with a grin.

The inspector who had arraigned them a few weeks before walked into the station, pretending he didn't know what had happened. As he was leaving, Eddie stuck his foot out and the inspector crashed to the floor. It would be the best laugh the pair would have for quite some time. A German guard of three was waiting for them, as Eddie prosaically recalled for MI5 two years later. '[One] day in walked the Gestapo. There was a *Hauptmann* and an *Oberleutnant* and then we were arrested and I was charged with sabotage.' They packed their bags. It was only later that they heard the full story. 'We were accused of cutting telephone communications,' Eddie explained. 'The whole story was nonsense because someone did cut telephone communications. Apparently they went to the British police [who] said that if there was any trouble, I was probably in on it.'

When he later thought about it, Eddie couldn't help wondering if this wasn't all a complicated cover story to hide his later recruitment into the German secret service. On reflection, he decided this was unlikely. At the time, though, his application to join the

Abwehr was being processed and he later found out that two groups were interested in him. 'They had all the trouble of trying to find out first if I had committed the sabotage,' he recalled, 'and then to try to get me released.'

It was a freezing, drizzling November day. Eddie and Tony were handcuffed together and driven down to the dock. Under escort, they were put on a dilapidated boat which shuddered against the waves. A number of passengers were physically sick for most of the journey. In the cold, they huddled together to keep warm. As the Channel Islands grew smaller and faded into the misty gloom, both wondered what fate might await them. There were constant rumours that those deported – whether Jews or conscientious objectors – were automatically executed in occupied territory. And for the next few hours, as they rolled in the waves, the permutations of such a horrible fate washed over them with the wintry sea spray. When they eventually arrived on French soil, they were told that they would be shot if they ever attempted to escape.

So far as Eric Pleasants was concerned, Eddie's departure was sudden but hardly unexpected. His pal in the looting business simply failed to come home one day to the Panama Hotel. Within a few days, he had heard that both Chapman and Faramus had been arrested. The Germans spread a rumour that they were behind some local sabotage, but Pleasants was shrewd enough to realise that there was probably more to the story than met the eye.*

If there was any consolation for the pair of British prisoners who arrived in Granville on that cold November morning, it was simply that the authorities didn't seem to know what was happening, still less what to do with them. Chapman and Faramus spent a day in

---

* Arrested after stealing petrol in preparation for an attempt to escape Jersey by boat, Pleasants and Leister spent the next two years interned in various prisons before offering their services to the the Britischer Frei Korps, a small unit of the SS created in conjunction with the Foreign Ministry mainly for propaganda purposes – it was never a serious military unit – targeting British renegades and fascists to fight the communist foe. With the war's end, Pleasants survived in the sewers of Berlin and then a Soviet imprisonment camp. In 1955, he returned to Britain where he collaborated with Eddie Chapman on his memoirs. Though technically guilty of treason, Pleasants had been incarcerated by both the Nazi and Stalinist regimes, and the authorities decided that he had suffered enough.

the custody of some friendly gendarmes at the local police station where they were provided with food and warmth. Just before midnight, their German guards reappeared and marched them to the local rail station.

Taken by night train in a first-class carriage – where the guards pointedly wouldn't speak to them – Eddie became aware of just how frightened Faramus was. Though he too liked adventure, he was much younger, terrified by how deeply in trouble they were. En route, kind-hearted French travellers threw in food through an open window, providing some momentary distraction. Perhaps some of this goodwill rubbed off on the guards, who temporarily at least removed their handcuffs.

They arrived in Paris at daybreak where they were taken by military truck to the industrial suburb of St Denis. Their destination was a civilian internment camp for those unfortunate US and British Empire citizens who had been left behind in the wake of the German invasion two years before. As none of their guards spoke French, Eddie translated when they kept getting lost and had to ask for directions. They spent an uncomfortable hour in solitary confinement, still uncertain what was going to happen next. Even Eddie started to fear that their fate would not be enjoyable.

Behind the scenes there had been yet another cock-up. '[A] telephone call came through,' Eddie recalled later. 'There was a terrific hullabaloo and one of [the guards] got a terrific bawling out by one German commander because we had been brought there.' Within the hour, they were taken by car under escort towards the Point de Lilas, south of the Seine. Their new home, opposite the sprawling Renault works, loomed large and terrifying with its blackened ramparts and Gothic drawbridge. Fort Romainville's menacing appearance was appropriate for a place designed to break the spirit of the resistance.

The two Englishmen were strip-searched by guards in an empty office. They still hadn't been formally charged and were shortly taken to a large, empty dormitory at one end of an old barrack-house. The hopelessness of their situation was reinforced when they saw thick barbed wire surrounding the camp. 'At each end of the building stood a guard in a tower in which two machine guns were mounted, commanding a whole view of the prison,' Eddie recalled. One bare electric light bulb provided the only heat in the echoing emptiness. The chill was soon matched by the words of a timid French voice which piped up after a light tap on the door. *'Aujourd-hui les sales vaches, les Boches, ont fusillés six hommes'* ('Today the bastard Germans shot six men').

Eddie and Tony were bewildered by the news of these executions. Would they be next? Having just reached his twenty-seventh birthday, Eddie could hardly help contemplating his own mortality.

'How would you like to be shot, Eddie?' Faramus asked.

Eddie was quiet for a while as he pondered such a grisly end.

'I don't think I'd mind so terribly as all that. I've had a pretty good life . . . I don't think I'd complain so much.'

Just before they went to sleep, they took the precaution of shaking hands and saying their goodbyes. Fully expecting to be either separated or shot, they were instead left alone in the dormitory for a couple of days. When they were eventually transferred to a smaller cell one night, they were still none the wiser. Nor were their guards, two middle-aged corporals whom they immediately christened Tweedledum and Tweedledee.

The pair later escorted them to meet the *Kommandant* in his palatial, three-storey house where a white-jacketed servant opened the door. Hauptmann Brüchenbach was short, stocky and obviously under the influence of alcohol although it was early in the morning. His owlish eyes were magnified behind thick glasses. It was clear he had no idea why they were in custody. In Faramus's later recollection, their dossiers were marked with the chilling word *'Sicherheitsgefangener'* – 'political security prisoners' – though thankfully they seemed to be held under the jurisdiction of a military tribunal.

So long as they behaved themselves, Hauptmann Brüchenbach told them, they could mix with other prisoners during the daytime. However, as they were escorted back to their cell by Tweedledum and Tweedledee, one of them – using the universal sign language of a finger inserted into a circle formed with a forefinger and thumb – made it clear that any sort of intimacy (let alone any communication) with female prisoners was strictly *verboten*.

When Eddie awoke the next morning, sunlight was streaming into the cell through a small window. He looked out on to the main courtyard of the prison. As he peered through the early morning mist, Sacré Coeur in the distance formed an unforgettable sight, ablaze in the early morning sunlight. To the left, the Eiffel Tower remained shrouded in mist. When he opened the window, Eddie was greeted by an even better sight: two pretty French girls in the cell opposite. 'Things are looking up,' he quipped to Faramus.

Their names, the girls shouted, giggling at him from their own open window, were Suzy and Paulette. Soon, using a stone attached to a lead weight, they sent across a packet of sandwiches. 'We carried on a mild flirtation for some time,' Eddie recalled. 'I began to feel that perhaps after all prison life had its consolations.'

That same morning, they were forcibly reminded of the dangers when they were taken out to work. There were 'more women than men in the camp', Eddie recalled, and mainly, it seemed, Belgian nationals. It was immediately apparent that many of them were Jewish. Curiously, their Jewishness was not the reason for their imprisonment: they were all suspected of sabotage and espionage. A number would be targeted to be turned for possible operations against the resistance. 'Periodically,' Eddie later said of the guards, 'they used to walk in and shoot one.'

Given overalls and sabots, he and Faramus joined a working party of twenty. They were soon wondering why the officer in charge held a roll call of names. A Jewish man standing next to him started trembling. '[The] first day we were there, German soldiers walked in and called out sixteen names and took them out and shot [them],' he would recall. The rest silently continued chopping wood. It transpired that these killings were reprisals for the underground having killed a German commander at Nantes.

Mindless violence was routine. A few weeks later, an Italian prisoner was shot between the eyes for merely waving at the two Britons from the courtyard. Yet despite the dangers, the two English prisoners made a determined effort to enjoy themselves as best they could. 'Life in the camp was easy,' Eddie recalled, 'not too much work and, surprisingly, plenty of amusement.'

Yet it was hardly a holiday camp. 'Things are not so good,' one of their more pessimistic fellow inmates said early on in their stay. 'The food is bad, there is not nearly enough of it, and what is worse, when you wake up in the morning, you don't know for sure whether you'll see the day out.' A typical meal was black bread, oily margarine and hard cheese. Though the soup they were served was hot, it soon became their daily preoccupation to remove maggots from the bowls. Worms, too, often appeared in the dried vegetables which accompanied other meals. To get rid of them, much of the food was repeatedly boiled to tastelessness.

Keeping warm that winter of 1941–2 became another pre-occupation. Though there were stoves in each barrack room, there was hardly any fuel. A limited amount of coal dust was however available for the authorities. Luckily for Eddie and Tony, the official supplies for their sector of the prison were just outside their door. So when Tweedledee and Tweedledum were having their lunch, Eddie would remove the floorboards to get at the coal. Later there were foraging expeditions for fuel supplies. Prisoners were led by Eddie in smashing up spare beds and pulling out rafters from the roof. The 'Englishmen's Room' gained a reputation as the warmest in the prison. In time, all the prisoners would flock there. 'I still marvel at what we got away with,' Eddie would say long after the war.

It didn't take him long to get up to his usual tricks. Despite it being made clear that any 'fraternisation' with female prisoners was an offence, the cooing entreaties of their near neighbours would prove too much for Eddie and Tony. Romainville was separated into distinct halves: one for men, the other for women. The latter was marked 'Frauen' on a floor plan they saw one day. 'About thirty women were held either as communists or espionage suspects,' he would later remember. 'The men's exercise ground was divided from the women's by a stretch of barbed wire running down the centre.' Although a locked door separated the two wings, Eddie's 'peculiar knowledge' would come in useful.

Making replica keys was an easy task, so he soon fashioned a pass key to gain entry to the women's quarters. So long as they tiptoed past the sleeping guards late at night they would rarely be caught, though most people seemed to know what was going on. Eddie was soon picking the locks of the cell doors in the immediate vicinity and making visits to the more attractive female prisoners. What some of them ruefully termed 'Hôtel de Romainville' was busy with innumerable illicit couplings. 'They soon found a way to get into the ladies' section,' Eddie's widow comments today. 'Ladies could get out of Romainville if they were pregnant. So they were very busy, he and Anthony!' As Eddie later remarked – tongue in cheek – it was his duty to get as many of the female prisoners as possible released.

Their immediate next-door neighbour, Paulette, was a fiery redhead who was always being reprimanded. She had been imprisoned for slapping a German officer who had made a pass at her. When she arrived, it seemed, she had been in the company of her fiancé, a French doctor who had subsequently been shot. As with many of the inmates, they were wanton, not knowing how long their temporary lovers might survive – if at all. ('She had "affairs" with three others,' MI5 later recorded; 'they were all unlucky. They were shot.')

Over the next few weeks, the two British prisoners were amazed at the range of nationalities they found around them. Their number included a banker with a million marks to his name, a French officer who claimed to have been with the Abwehr, two Belgian diamond merchants and an old lag from Alsace-Lorraine. Also in the camp were a former French minister in his fifties, a 'sandy-haired Jew' and someone related to the famous Colonel Dreyfus.

In addition, there was a collection of 'nondescript' prisoners of war. Their favourite was Armand Amalou, a good-looking, curly-haired Algerian with an infectious grin, who had owned a cabaret in Montmartre. Two of his girls had done something – Eddie was never able to find out exactly what – involving a pair of German officers. The camp was riddled with informants and for that reason, very few would elaborate about their supposed crimes. 'It was very difficult to find out what these people had done,' he later told MI5 investigators, 'because no one would talk.'

But during exercises and card games – as well as their various late night excursions – Eddie got to know some of the prisoners a little better. The German banker was called Kahn and claimed he had been in the British Army. He spent his time drawing portraits · of his fellow prisoners. Perhaps the most curious of these was a chubby, ruddy-faced German Swiss named Lutsch who was suspected of being a British intelligence agent. He had been expecting to be shot, but his sentence had been commuted. Lutsch had been arrested in Paris in a restaurant at the time of the occupation. 'If you ever come back to England,' he said, 'ask the British Intelligence people to inform the Swiss government of my whereabouts.'

Then there were two French engineers: one, called Ulrich, spoke English very badly and had worked at St Nazaire; another was a radio man, Le François, who had been an announcer on Radio Paris. He had refused to broadcast German propaganda, hence his incarceration, in the company of his wife. 'He was expecting to be released,' Eddie said. 'And the Germans actually gave him a date to go and work for them – that was the condition he was going to be released on.'

It wasn't every evening that a cell door was opened by a glamorous, giggling girl in a pale blue dressing gown. On one particular evening, however, that was how the lovely Paulette greeted him and Faramus. What was more, Eddie walked into the room to see a couple more girls whose modesty was barely shielded. One was dressed in what appeared to be a sheer negligée. At times like this Eddie could be forgiven for wondering if the guards had slipped something into their soup.

Even more remarkably, the girls' cell had been transformed into what looked like a chic restaurant, with *cretonne* fabric curtains, artificial flowers and dimmed lighting. And a veritable feast was on display thanks to food parcels the girls had received from their families, augmented by stolen German rations. By saving their food parcels, the female prisoners would occasionally put on amazing treats. This evening, they had managed to cook spaghetti bolognese on an illicitly acquired electric ring.

Along with the good-looking Amalou, the two Englishmen and the girls dined *à six* long into the night. They feasted on gourmet food, fine wines and cognac before, inevitably, pairing off. Tony Faramus went off with the older girl, Suzi, while Eddie went to bed with the fiery Paulette. As he later recollected, her whispered entreaty, '*Faites l'amour avec moi, cheri*,' was always too inviting to refuse. Despite the lack of privacy – blankets were used to separate the beds – the prisoners enjoyed nights of wild passion, heightened by the danger and sheer improbability of it all. Exhausted, they would make their way back to their own cells early the next morning, trying hard not to show signs of having enjoyed themselves so spectacularly.

In spite of such diversions, a sense of desperation permeated the camp. Each day dawned with gnawing uncertainty. Both Eddie and Tony lived by what they remembered as the mantra of the Romainville prisoner: 'Make hay while the moon shines, for tomorrow you may die with a German bullet in your heart.' On each of his nocturnal wanderings, Eddie's lovemaking became more desperate and less discriminating – 'I never knew which girl I was going to make love to.' The stresses and strains were like nothing he had ever experienced before.

Though he had been used to the rigours of imprisonment, this was something different. At least in British jails, there was never any danger of being shot. In Romainville nothing was quite what it seemed. The sense of danger grew with the wintry shadows. Treachery was a fact of prison life. Who could be trusted? A couple of the guards were communist sympathisers, including one called Toni who would do small favours for the inmates.

As was usually the case, the unlikeliest person turned out to be the most treacherous of all. One day, a small, shrivelled man sidled up to Eddie and asked, 'Are you English?'

'Yes,' he replied. 'What are you here for?'

'I'm from Cardiff.'

They shook hands. Over the next few weeks, it became clear that this fellow missed nothing and was a notorious stool pigeon. Known as 'The Black Devil', he was actually a Belgian called Bossuit who was also involved in the black market and always seemed to have spare money.

Bossuit claimed to know London well and his English was peppered with curious colloquialisms. Eight months before, he had helped the Belgian diamond merchants smuggle their money out of Brussels. Then he had shopped them to the police. Word soon spread about Bossuit's treachery; the merchants had obviously recognised him, although he didn't seem to know them. 'So there was quite a triangle played in the camp,' Eddie would recall. Whenever people were shot, Bossuit 'was always mixed up in it'. By the start of 1942, he had been responsible for at least half a dozen deaths.

This sinister informant, needless to say, reported on Eddie's nocturnal wanderings. A love letter from Paulette was found among his possessions, after which he was interrogated by the *Kommandant*. Though he denied the whole thing, he was sent out into the *cachot* for a couple of days' solitary confinement. He only managed to stay warm by diving into a pile of gravel which had been left behind in the corner of the cell. Paulette was not so lucky: she was kept in the punishment cells for a month on only bread and water.

Revenge would be sweet. After release from solitary, Eddie bided his time then rushed into his own barrack where a group including Bossuit were playing cards. He kicked the table over, gave the weasel a black eye and tried to throw him out of the window. The guards stepped in. For this attempted defenestration, Eddie was himself given a month's solitary. In time, a Frenchman and the Swiss-German Lutsch did the same to Bossuit. It was clear that his usefulness as an informant was over.

'Every time we saw him, we attacked him,' Eddie would recall with no little satisfaction. 'Later things got to such a pitch that the Germans removed him from the camp.'

At the end of his solitary confinement, one day at the beginning of February 1942 Eddie was invited to the *Kommandant*'s office. In a private room, he was introduced to a young man about his own age who smiled, offered him a cigarette and finally asked the question he had been waiting to hear for several months.

'You are interested in joining the German secret service?'

Tall and scholarly-looking, Walther Thomas was an anglophile. The first thing Eddie noticed was his tie, which he later revealed to be that of Southampton College. 'When you first met him, you would think he was English,' Eddie later recalled. Now, though, Herr Thomas was more interested in taking down the details of the prisoner's extraordinary life. 'He seemed amused at my escapades in the camp,' Eddie recalled, 'about which I told him freely.' Thomas had obtained Eddie's criminal records from Jersey, so when he asked for further particulars, 'there was not much point in doing anything else' than confirming his pre-war criminal career.

They talked for quite a while. 'I am very interested in you,' Thomas concluded. 'Would you be prepared to work for the Germans?'

Eddie was not aware at the time that Thomas had travelled to Jersey to investigate further the background to his arrest and suitability for becoming an agent for the Third Reich. When he had repeatedly asked if there was any chance of working against the British, he had been told the matter was in hand. Though Thomas's approach was deceptively casual, the truth was that German military intelligence had a hard time finding native English speakers to work as saboteurs. It was almost inevitable that they would call upon a native Briton who had offered to work for them.

The Abwehr, like all intelligence agencies in wartime, were confronted with a serious problem. How could they get foreign nationals to turn against their own country? And, more to the point, why would they want to work for a fascist regime? In the early days, the Abwehr chose men who were loyal to the Fatherland by birth, preferring businessmen who went on regular travels around the world. They later began to select people who could be put under pressure. In Occupied France, for example, their gaze alighted on the prisons where informers or black marketers would be recruited as possible agents.

The Abwehr had no permanent presence in the Channel Islands, but occasionally its representatives would come over either from St Mâlo, or from further afield, in Nantes. As a recent study by the Irish academic Mark Hull has noted, the Channel Islands provided a ready pool of possible recruits due to an accident of geography and language: 'The linguistic make-up of the islands also offered the Germans a unique opportunity to further their covert political and intelligence schemes via a pool of native English speakers.' By the simple expedient of youth and willingness, many offered their services.

Finding men who could qualify as *Vertrauensmanner* was never easy. When the details of an Englishman with a criminal record emerged, small wonder that officers in the Abwehr took a great deal of interest.

In the middle of February 1942, Eddie was summoned once more to the *Kommandant*'s office, to be met by a stylishly dressed woman. She made quite an impression. Her name was Frau Freusch, she worked for the German secret service and spoke English with an American accent. 'A brunette, with large brown eyes, a rosebud mouth,' Eddie recalled, 'and well-manicured hands, done with a bright nail varnish.' The memory of those extraordinary long nails remained with Eddie, as did her black lamb's wool coat with a Schiaparelli label.

She asked more or less the same questions as Herr Thomas had done a few weeks earlier. What could he do for the Germans? For the first time, sabotage was specifically mentioned. And when she asked what motivated him – money or hatred? – Eddie instantly replied, 'Money.' Given that he would still have to serve out his sentence when he got home, he quickly added that he also hated the police and the prisons.

The glamorous woman seemed satisfied, though Scotland Yard's interest in him was politely sidestepped. 'Well now,' she added, 'suppose you didn't feel like coming back to us?'

'You'd have to trust me,' Eddie replied. 'Besides, it wouldn't be all that tempting for me to stay.'

On his return to the cell, Eddie discussed matters with Tony Faramus, but exhorted him to keep quiet about his latest encounter, as Frau Freusch had told him to do. 'If they know that anyone knows, and particularly you, we will both be for it,' he said. His younger, less sophisticated cellmate was horrified. Echoing Frau Freusch's words, he wondered what would happen to him if Eddie really did not come back. 'Look Tony,' Eddie explained, 'let me play this my way. I am gambling my own life, too, don't forget.'

By his later admission, Faramus was terrified that he was going to die. Perhaps he thought to himself that he too could offer his services to the Germans. But Eddie was insistent. They wouldn't let them both become agents. And, given Faramus's youth, it would probably be too much for him.

Despite the tense nature of these discussions, the fragrant distractions of Paulette were still available. While they had both been in solitary confinement, Eddie had managed to break open the lock of his own cell – and soon, hers next door. Though their only nourishment was black bread and rancid water, they somehow continued to make love every night. 'I lost a lot of weight,' Eddie later remembered, 'but it was worth it.'

One of the sentries soon became puzzled why the lights had been left on in her cell one evening. Tweedledum and Tweedledee ransacked it for an illicit key. Luckily, all the equipment required had been smuggled in and left in a loaf of bread. Understandably, perhaps, Eddie was rather more circumspect when relating the incident to MI5. 'I got into trouble in Paris,' he said, explaining that he had got into a stand-up fight with one of the guards. 'I was given one month's bread and water every day,' he remembered. 'I had the row and there was a sort of inquiry into it.'

When Hauptmann Brüchenbach got to hear about Eddie's nocturnal activities, he was apoplectic. The *Kommandant* rushed into Eddie's cell, drawing his revolver and waving it about in rage. Even though he was spending a month in the *cachot*, Eddie's spirit remained unbound. 'I did the decent thing,' he said later, 'and still kept picking my lock to visit my sweet Paulette.' On another occasion, the *Kommandant* came into Eddie's cell early one morning, clearly very drunk. Once more, he waved his revolver and started shouting at him. Eddie treated this drunken display with disdain and told him to go ahead and shoot.

Without that pile of gravel in the corner of the *cachot*, Eddie might well have frozen to death. At times that March, it was so cold in Romainville that frost formed inside the walls of the cell. Eddie had to bury himself in the gravel to stay warm. Within days, he stank and was in need of a shave. When Eddie received yet another visitor in the company of the mysterious Herr Thomas. The visitor was introduced to him as important.

Baron Rittmeister Stefan von Gröning was a senior member of the Abwehr in France, a German royalist, 'six foot tall with a pleasant corpulence'. Eddie, who always reckoned himself a good judge of character, immediately bonded with him. The Baron, it was immediately clear, was tolerant and scholarly. 'Here in this room I met a man who was destined to become a friend, an admirer and a fellow conspirator,' Eddie would later write.

By now, it was clear he was to join the German secret service sooner rather than later. When he told Thomas and von Gröning about the *Kommandant*'s drunken threats, they laughed. He was assured that not all German officers were like that. Their message was simple: hold on, keep out of trouble and he'd be out of there in a fortnight. 'You're about to be released,' the Baron said conspiratorially. He beamed: the authorities had accepted Eddie's offer.

Then – for what Eddie sincerely hoped would be the last time – they asked him outright: 'Would you be prepared to be trained by the German secret service?'

Eddie agreed.

'What about my friend Faramus?'

'Unfortunately, we can't accept his offer,' von Gröning added. 'In times of war, we must be careful and one of you must stay.'

It was clear they wanted to hold Faramus as a hostage. By keeping him in custody, the Germans thought Eddie would be more likely to do as they bid. And when, over the next few months, Eddie tried to write to his former cellmate, the Baron would not allow it. Only later, when he was preparing to leave for England, did he get a satisfactory answer. 'Don't you worry,' von Gröning said. 'We're going to send Faramus a parcel and he'll be well looked after.'

Eddie managed to stay out of trouble for the rest of his time in Romainville. One night he was transfixed by an RAF raid on the nearby Renault factory. He couldn't help wondering if it wasn't an omen. Paris appeared 'wonderful' in the searchlights and tracer fire. The dropping of the bombs seemed to last for most of the evening and the staccato rattle of the light flak continued unabated. 'When the bombing was over,' he recalled, 'the whole city seemed to glow in the flames.'

Exactly as the Baron predicted, he was taken out of the camp a fortnight later. A contract was drawn up and signed – bizarrely, it concerned the conveyancing of tea on behalf of the German government, which served to act as a smokescreen. An order for Eddie's release was approved by the *Kommandant*, and he was allowed to collect his belongings. After dressing in his civilian clothes and shaving, he was given just five minutes to leave. (He was in such a hurry that shirts, trousers and socks were later brought for him as he had left them behind.)

Eddie said rapid goodbyes to his fellow prisoners, who thought he was being taken to another prison camp. According to Betty Chapman, who has seen a copy of it, a photograph of Eddie 'trussed up and ready to be shot' was later circulated to make the other prisoners think he was about to be executed. Most poignant of all was his shared goodbye and heartfelt offer of good luck with Anthony Faramus. 'Look me up in London after the war!' he said.

Faramus sincerely hoped his friend would succeed in his double bluff, for 'agreeing to play Eddie's game might cost me my life'.*

So it was that at six o'clock on a Friday morning in April 1942, Eddie was released from Romainville jail. Walther Thomas was waiting for him and they were whisked away in a large car. After spending a couple of nights in a luxurious Parisian hotel, Thomas offered him a gourmet meal and champagne in his suite. He asked if Eddie wanted to go out on the town, wondering if he wanted to meet some women. For once, Eddie was almost at a loss for words. 'In the prison all I've had were women and no food,' he explained. 'Here I want lots of lovely grub and no women.'

The next morning they took a first-class compartment from the Gare d'Austerlitz on a train bound for the industrial port of Nantes, smoking and – at Thomas's insistence – speaking German. When they went to the dining carriage, several German officers were present. For the first time ever, Eddie Chapman found himself having to say 'Heil Hitler'. 'Now for the first time I did this,' he would write. 'I felt a pretty big fool.' He was so hungry that he ate most of Thomas's meal too.

Despite his friendliness, the German took care to warn him not to do anything silly such as jumping out of the compartment or trying to escape. For good measure, he produced a small automatic. Eddie thought it wouldn't have been able to stun a rabbit, but with life about to become interesting, he took pains to reassure Thomas he had no intention of escaping. Thomas seemed satisfied. Their eventual destination, he explained, would be a château at St Joseph by the Loire. When they got there, all would be revealed. He insisted that Eddie would be 'looked after'.

With Teutonic efficiency, the train arrived dead on time. Eddie felt a certain amount of trepidation as they were driven to their home for the next few months. He was wondering what on earth he might have let himself in for.

---

*For Anthony Faramus, the future would involve descending 'to the most abysmal depths of humiliation and misery'. The young Jerseyman would end up in Buchenwald and Mauthausen concentration camps, losing a lung and seven ribs in the process. 'After Eddie was taken away from the hostage camp,' he told his first biographer without any apparent rancour, 'the Germans didn't really know what to do with me.'

CHAPTER THREE

___

House of Fun

'Soldiers in war never know what is going on. Vaguely they hear of wonderful battles being won, and even when they are on the retreat they hear the radio communiqué which describes it as a strategical victory. All the soldier does is to obey orders, for what reason he has no idea. He marches forward, sideways and backwards. He brings ammunition up in mule trains, or wagons, laboriously he thirsts, goes without sleep, suffers incredible hardships: then someone gives an order to blow up all the ammunition and he retreats, more ammunition is required, so he advances. He can never work it out, why so many people seem to want to die and fight over a piece of desert, which till the end of time will be valueless.'

– From *Joey Boy* (1959), Eddie Chapman's semi-autobiographical novel about wartime rogues

WHEN EDDIE CHAPMAN arrived at his new home that glorious spring afternoon in 1942, he could tell straight away that his life was about to change. After the privations of recent months, La Bretonnaire just outside the industrial port of Nantes was a revelation. It was a typical château of the Loire region, surrounded by elms, oaks and beech, even a banana tree. Sandy paths snaked around its park-like gardens. The grounds contained an orchard and many vines, some wrapping around a high wall that stopped snoopers from looking in. Clearly, the officers of the Abwehr in Nantes liked to live well and suffered few of the discomforts of war.

It came as a pleasant surprise to be greeted by the barking of a friendly Alsatian. In time, Eddie would find there were also cats, geese and squirrels. The humans were friendly, too: in the lounge, he was introduced to a couple of Germans who would, in the months ahead, teach him all he would ever need to know about the use of radio transmissions and sabotage. Even better, he was offered a three-course lunch, a 1927 Chateauneuf du Pape, coffee, a Rémy Martin and a cigar. 'I began to feel that the Germans were not all Huns,' Eddie remarked.

Further proof came when he was taken upstairs to meet the Baron, the corpulent figure whose arrival in Romainville had signalled his release. 'Glad to see you out, old man,' was all Rittmeister Stefan von Gröning said. Eddie could hardly say anything before he was offered yet another glass of excellent brandy.

In the weeks and months ahead, the safebreaker and the Baron were to bond in a way that transcended wartime necessity. At one point, the German said that he thought of Eddie as a son: '[You] know that I have no relations, and I regard you in that light.' His indulgence – as it did on this first afternoon – extended to meals and alcohol. Eddie would often be invited alone up to von Gröning's quarters where they would share many secrets.

'Life at the château was very comfortable,' MI5 would later conclude. 'They had four cars at their disposal, plenty of food, if they wanted wine, they only had to ask for it.' In fact, what Eddie really needed – and which was provided in these splendid surroundings – was rest, sunshine, fresh air and long walks. He was free to do more or less what he wanted, though he wasn't allowed to go into the nearby town unaccompanied. Within days, though, Eddie was sneaking out alone for an early morning swim in the nearby Loire. When the Baron got to hear about that, he was very concerned. Without identity papers their English visitor might well be arrested by the French police. Or he might try to escape. 'Take one of the Boys along with you,' von Gröning insisted.

The most obvious disappointment at La Bretonnaire was that there were no women, a topic which 'the Boys' – as he came to call his colleagues – would joke about. The château was monastic and while Eddie was in residence there, only one woman ever stayed the night. They would make up for it on Saturdays, which were party nights. Most of his fellow officers trooped off into the bars of Nantes – and some to the local brothels. Despite all the other temptations to which he succumbed, Betty Chapman remarks, 'That was one thing in which Eddie never had much interest.'

Prostitution was inevitable. Nantes had been a seaport since Roman times and was now an industrial town busy with the occupying forces. In Eddie's recollection, Saturday evenings usually started off at the Café de Paris, followed by less salubrious establishments. 'The place was always full of German officers and men,' Eddie recalled, 'and nearly all were accompanied by parties of girls.' Given his fascination for nightclubs, he was in his element.

After months of not knowing whether he was going to survive until the next morning, Eddie settled into his new life very quickly. Each morning, he would go for a long run with Walther Thomas or swim in the nearby Loire. The softly spoken German's principal role was to act as a companion to his English charge. Thomas was always neat and well dressed, rather like Eddie himself, though somewhat scholarly and staid. They both enjoyed music and it transpired that Thomas was an authority on folk dancing. Eddie, who often thought of himself as Scottish, thought that Scottish reels were the oldest in the world. They weren't, Thomas informed him emphatically. 'For him Germany was not the greatest nation in the world – it was the *only* nation.'

More importantly, he was in charge of Eddie's programme of training (and occasionally would work the château's wireless). It transpired he had studied in Southampton for a year under an exchange scheme in the mid-twenties. He claimed he was the best oarsman of his year, which explained why he often wore the Southampton Boating Club tie and rowing scarf.

'Now you are here,' Thomas said to him on his first day, 'we must give you a German name.' All the officers of the Nantes château used *noms de guerre*. The irony was that over the next few months, Eddie found out their real names as they often told him (such as the occasion when Thomas told him his real name was Praetorius) or he found out by gentle snooping. Eddie was permitted to share the name adopted by von Gröning, his controller, who was known as Fritz Graumann; he was thereafter almost exclusively referred to by the pet name of Fritzchen, 'little Fritz'.

Outside the château, the Boys would wear a variety of uniforms – 'some were given corporal's uniforms, some were given colonel's' – and wherever possible, they referred to their establishment as a *Dienststelle* – a government office – as opposed to an *Abwehrstelle* (a fact which MI5 found significant). The set-up of the various outstations of German military intelligence in occupied territory was complicated. La Bretonnaire specialised in Breton affairs and, though technically subordinate to the local military authority, its operations were fairly autonomous. Although the various *Stellen* were supposedly directed from Berlin, in reality each was allowed a great deal of latitude in planning and carrying out its operations. Von Gröning ran the Nantes *Dienststelle* more or less as his own personal fiefdom.

Throughout Eddie's stay, the château was exceptionally busy. 'There were constant visits from senior German officers and on each occasion Chapman was introduced to them as Fritz, his spy name,' MI5 reported. There were always people coming and going; Eddie estimated that there were up to eighteen visitors a day. He did his best to remember who they were, snooping wherever he could and recording details on scraps of paper which he managed to hide from his hosts. It was hard for him to keep tabs on all these comings and goings. He was rarely told the visitors' names, for the Boys did their best to maintain security. Von Gröning asked him not to be too nosy. 'They had instructions not to tell me anything,' Eddie later remembered.

Whenever they left the château, they often used a large Mercedes which von Gröning felt suited his stature as the head of an *Abwehrstelle*. 'When they went on car journeys,' his widow explains, 'they drew the curtains in the large limo so that he couldn't see anything.' He was told that this was for his benefit – to stop passers-by from peering in – but it was obviously the other way around. In time, the heightened security fed into his worst fears. 'I was still a lost man,' Eddie would reflect, 'living with lost men.'

This charming man: Eddie Chapman, at the height of his pre-war notoriety, always immaculately dressed and out for a good time in the nightclubs he loved.

LEFT The bairn: The only surviving photograph of Eddie as a child, showing telltale signs of being kept in his wallet for many years.

Eddie as a family man: (ABOVE) Shown with daughter Suzanne and (BELOW) on the beach with Betty and Suzanne.

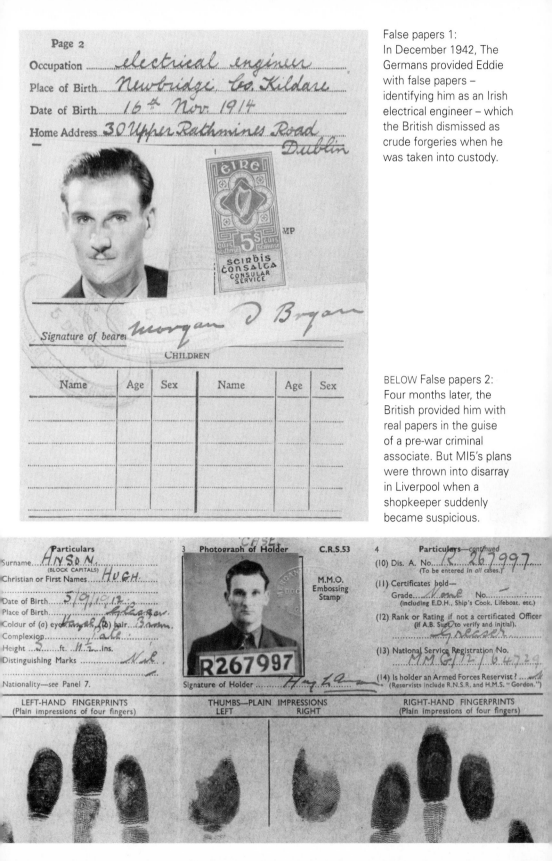

False papers 1:
In December 1942, The Germans provided Eddie with false papers – identifying him as an Irish electrical engineer – which the British dismissed as crude forgeries when he was taken into custody.

BELOW False papers 2:
Four months later, the British provided him with real papers in the guise of a pre-war criminal associate. But MI5's plans were thrown into disarray in Liverpool when a shopkeeper suddenly became suspicious.

An Amazing Transformation

A team of Royal Engineers, led by Sir John Turner, disguised de Havillands in Hatfield on the last Friday in January, 1943, to make it appear that Eddie Chapman had sabotaged the factory which built the Mosquito aircraft.

LEFT Note the dummy transformers immediately behind the 'damaged' gate.

BELOW To check on their handiwork, RAF reconnaissance planes took photographs to help Eddie lie to the Germans more convincingly.

As the spring turned into summer, Eddie learned more about the work of the château. It soon became clear that it had been created as a regional sabotage training centre. 'When the agents had any special missions to accomplish, any sabotage work, any espionage,' he later told MI5, 'then they were periodically sent out of the country.' Overall, it was a happy place and he was certainly more than pleased with his monthly 'stipend' of 12,000 francs. He gathered that the château was the property of a local cinema owner and had only been 'open' for business since February. Eddie, it seemed, was the first trainee to pass through.

'The château consisted of eight bedrooms, dining rooms, a lounge, office and kitchen,' he recalled. 'Next to the building stood a small gardener's house; this had been furnished and was given to me.' Here he could have some privacy. He got into the habit of retiring early, but not because he was tired. 'When the others had gone to bed,' he explained, 'I would dress, tiptoe down the garden and climb over the wall.' Walking around at night held a fascination for Eddie, allowing him to clear his head and gain some perspective on the dangers he faced.

The château was also a radio relay centre for the local Abwehr network – there were transmissions a few times every day – with other nearby *Stellen* in Rennes and, particularly, Angers. This regional *Abwehrstelle* further upstream along the Loire was responsible for tracking British spies in the Anjou. On one occasion when von Gröning went to Berlin for an extended trip, the head of the Angers *Stelle* temporarily took over La Bretonnaire.

Within a few weeks, a regular routine had been established. The local staff didn't arrive until 9.30 a.m., so breakfast was served about an hour earlier. After fervent 'Heil Hitlers', the Boys would eat in silence. Then von Gröning would outline the duties for the day ahead. After that, usually, Eddie went for a walk. Many of the Boys slept in during the afternoon and most evenings they all stayed in and played bridge.

There was also a French cook, two housemaids and a house-keeper. Wherever possible, Eddie spoke German or French; the natives were not to know he was an Englishman, a fact which might arouse the interest of the local resistance. (They usually called him '*Monsieur* Fritz'.) Whenever he did speak French to the domestic staff, they would often remark 'You have a very funny accent for a German.' If the French servants became aware of his Englishness, Eddie was told to say he had spent most of his life in the United States, though he had not been naturalised.

To help preserve anonymity, all mail was collected at a central sorting address, the cover being Baustelle Kersting. 'Every morning someone went through to the Wehrmacht Post Amt to collect the mail,' Eddie recalled. 'Letters came rarely and they were always official.' If especially delicate orders were received, they would be burned by von Gröning. 'He used to take it out and light a cigarette and burn the whole envelope,' Eddie recalled.

Though Eddie was no longer incarcerated behind bars – 'You are to consider yourself a free man,' von Gröning said to him on more than one occasion – the conflict of interest stirred awkward emotions within him. His mood was hardly improved when he read the British newspapers, which he was able to do roughly a fortnight after they had been published. In the first half of 1942, the war was still progressing in the Axis Powers' favour. Deep in occupied territory, it was clear that escape was out of the question.

'Von Gröning was very fussy about my visits to Nantes,' Eddie would recall. At the back of his controller's mind was the fear that Eddie might escape and somehow be inveigled back to his native land by the local resistance. So, as MI5 would later conclude, 'the Germans, after studying Chapman's record of house-breaking, safe-breaking etc., realised that they had an extremely able recruit and did their utmost to treat him in the best possible manner and keep him in good humour'.

All of them were missing their wives and families. To keep them going, an odd sort of nostalgia sprang up. In the château's impressive drawing room up went reminders of their lives before the war. Postcards, pictures and articles were stapled to the wall along with knick-knacks from home towns like Bremen, Berlin, Hamburg – and most absurdly of all, Berwick-on-Tweed.

Before long, Eddie was getting away with behaviour that would have led others directly to the firing squad. In that same grand drawing room was a large portrait of the Führer. Whenever the boys clicked their heels and saluted the portrait, their English visitor would shake his fists at it. 'For some reason,' his widow says, 'the Germans always found this gesture of Eddie's very funny.'

★ ★ ★

Eddie's capacity for humour has to be taken in context. Throughout his stay in Nantes, he was never completely certain if the Germans believed he was *bona fide*. His joking never eclipsed his natural wariness and genius for survival. In this regard, Eddie's astute reading of people's character becomes highly significant. This aspect of his personality – rarely remarked on by intelligence handlers or journalists to date – goes some way to explain his resilience in wartime. When Eddie walked into a room, his family and friends say, the room would light up. He knew how far he could go and what people would willingly believe. 'Eddie always knew how people ticked,' says Lillian Verner Bonds, a friend who became close to the Chapmans after the war. 'He was almost like a shrink, he had that ability to get under people's skin.'

As a result, Eddie was always alert to the dangers surrounding him. Wherever he went, Lillian says, he always seemed to know where the exits were. 'If there was a fire,' she adds, 'Eddie would always know how to get out.' This sizing up of his environment was essential to Eddie's long-term survival. 'Eddie was very cautious, particularly where his own security was concerned,' his widow concurs. 'He never really let his guard down.' Lillian Verner Bonds adds, 'He never showed his hand at any time, and that was probably what made him such a good agent.' Though friendly and approachable, there was part of Eddie that he always kept to himself. If – as several intelligence people on either side of the fighting seemed to think – Eddie Chapman was a chameleon, then he took care never to show his true colours.

★ ★ ★

In Baron Rittmeister Stefan von Gröning, Eddie had been provided with a benign uncle as his personal controller. Whether it was an accident that he was granted such a figure will never be known. But it was the German custom to provide each agent with a 'protector', an individual spymaster who would attempt to instil respect and personal devotion. Usually the controller was much older, hence creating the dynamic of a paternal relationship.

The controller ensured that each agent was given the right papers, good food and cigarettes, and often went with their charge to the point of departure. When the agent radioed his transmissions from enemy territory, the controller sat with the radio operator to encourage his responses. The Baron, as Eddie soon came to know him, was a most unusual man. He was not a Nazi, more a German nationalist who seemed to have been extraordinarily well educated.

He loved reproductions of good paintings, collected rare volumes and never appeared happier than when rummaging through a second-hand bookshop. He had an encyclopedic knowledge of antiques and managed to obtain quite a number of rare items for the château. 'Von Gröning sent for a lot of furnishings for Eddie's quarters in the *Dienststelle* so he wouldn't miss home,' Betty Chapman says.

The Baron was also a prodigious imbiber. Eddie – who wasn't shy of knocking it back himself – had never seen someone drink so much or, for that matter, smoke so much. His teeth were stained with nicotine. Von Gröning was probably an alcoholic yet the more he drank, the more lucid he became. An admirer of the British way of life, he would shake his head solemnly when he and Eddie were alone, expressing his lack of faith in Hitler's leadership of Germany. He took care only to make such statements when they were out of earshot of the others. The Baron had to tread very carefully.

Eddie was perplexed by tidbits which von Gröning told him about his earlier life. As they got to know each other the Baron informed him that he had only ever spent three weeks in Britain but had been to the United States several times. This puzzled Eddie as the Baron spoke with no American accent. '[He] used to astonish me by coming out with British nursery rhymes,' Eddie later told MI5. 'But apart from that he spoke absolutely without an accent and it was impossible to tell which nationality he was.' Which would doubtless have pleased von Gröning, for on another occasion he declared nationalism was a curse and that there should be a world government, something like that advocated by H.G. Wells. 'He was certainly a most unusual German,' Eddie remarked.

During the war years, Eddie wasn't sure if the Baron was married or not. As both had a fondness for animals, von Gröning showed him a picture of his Sealyham terrier. It was obvious the picture had been cut in two, probably to hide a loved one's presence. But Ingeborg, von Gröning's widow, says she didn't meet Stefan until after the war. On their twenty-fifth wedding anniversary, 11 September 1976, the couple were invited to attend the wedding of Eddie and Betty's daughter in England. 'I only ever met Eddie then and he was as charming as Stefan had always said he was,' Ingeborg von Gröning recalls.

Perhaps the most surprising aspect of the Baron's ambivalence towards the Nazi regime was the fact that his sister had adopted a Jewish child. He doted on this young girl who lived in Germany, and often sent her items of clothing. Eddie recalled seeing a letter beginning 'Lieber Onkel Stefan . . .', at which the Baron beamed. Some time later, Eddie was walking with his controller in Paris when they happened upon two little children who had been branded with Stars of David. Von Gröning was very upset. 'Don't they realise that kiddies, whatever their colour, skin or creed, are God's creatures?' the Baron asked. Von Gröning asked Eddie to go over to them and give them 2,000 francs. They would doubtless have been scared had it come from a German officer.

Eddie didn't mention this to anyone. That his own mother's family background was Jewish and that he had once been briefly married to a Russian-German of Jewish extraction were details that agent Fritzchen took great care to keep hidden from his German masters.

★ ★ ★

One obvious question presents itself. Did Stefan von Gröning know that Eddie Chapman was a double agent? According to the Baron's widow, her husband did suspect that Fritzchen was in contact with British Intelligence. Yet Frau von Gröning adds: 'Stefan always said that Eddie was exactly the sort of person you would want as an agent. Cheeky, charming and audacious.'

Betty Chapman also believes that the Baron knew Eddie was working for the British. Moreover, post-war interrogation of

Abwehr officers in France revealed there was suspicion at a higher level that Eddie was being controlled by the British. Yet von Gröning never aired any of these doubts. Their closeness seems to have precluded his raising the subject with fellow officers, particularly as he was so ambivalent about the Nazi regime.

'Why would he stay friendly with Eddie for all that time and entertain him privately?' Betty Chapman asks. 'And to do all the things like decorating his quarters, with all the stuff to remind him of home. That's not the sort of thing you'd do for anyone in the office, is it?' At the time, it seemed to Eddie that the Baron was working the system. Von Gröning was converting his money into articles of value such as those antiques. As early as 1942, it appears that the Baron knew exactly which way the fighting was going.

In many ways, von Gröning was typical of the inefficient organisation which Admiral Canaris had created and of the divided loyalties that pitched the Abwehr's officers against the Nazi state. The fact was that German military intelligence had very little understanding of the situation in Britain. Their star agent at the Nantes *Dienststelle* found himself constantly astonished. 'Up to the time of my arrival in England,' Eddie would later explain, 'they had no idea of the most elementary details of British life.' Repeatedly, he was told that people back home would be near to starvation due to the severity of rationing. The Germans didn't seem to know that cafés did not require food coupons. At almost every level – and he would meet many of its senior officers in France – the Abwehr was hopelessly credulous. In Eddie's hearing, many German intelligence officers expressed the belief that London had been totally laid waste.

The Abwehr chiefs wanted to believe what they were told, for any scoop – no matter how preposterous – would have great currency in the infighting amongst the various German intelligence agencies. He who came up with the most astonishing story was most likely to grab the Führer's ear. The truth was that the Abwehr's officers cared little for accuracy, or even the correct evaluation of information. As Sir Michael Howard records in the official British history of deception operations, most of the Abwehr's officers were too busy 'enjoying life in the oases of Lisbon, Madrid, Stockholm or Istanbul, fiddling their expenses or running currency rackets on the side'.

In occupied territory, the Nantes *Dienststelle* was no different. Far from being omniscient, the Germans were astonishingly inept in the great game of espionage. From the spring of 1942 onwards, British Intelligence produced more and more tasty morsels for its opposite numbers to believe, wrapping them up in ever more complex skeins of intrigue.

★ ★ ★

Whenever he looked back on his time at La Bretonnaire in later years, Eddie would always smile. His overriding memory was of fun. One day after he had settled in, he decided to change all the clocks and watches three to four hours ahead of the real time. 'Eddie even managed to change von Gröning's bedside clock and his pocket watch while he was sleeping,' Betty marvels. The result was spectacular. I members of the *Stelle* woke up in the middle of the night, much to Eddie's amusement, and eventually, theirs.

The Boys spent a great deal of time dealing on the black market, which was even more rife than it had been on Jersey. In particular, they bought up local butter for the Paris *Dienststelle* (at a cost of one hundred francs), taking up valuable air time to report their purchases over the radio and using official transport to carry them to the capital. There were plentiful supplies of goodies, although there was a distinct caveat. 'If you said you were a German, they just wouldn't sell you anything,' Eddie would recall of the black marketers. 'Whereas if you said you were Belgian, you could get things.'

Two of the Boys who worked in the *Stelle*, Leo and Hans, were from Alsace. They were able to converse in French with the farmers and took them into their confidence with tirades against the Boche. These weekly 'foraging expeditions' allowed them to buy much material for both the Nantes and Paris *Dienststellen*. They also bought large quantities of honey because the jars were useful for hiding explosives. 'We visited all the outlying villages and talked to the farmers,' Eddie recalled. 'They were only too willing to let us have their foodstuffs for the enormous prices we offered.' Eggs, chickens, hams and whole sheep were bought up, parcelled and sent back to relatives in Germany as presents. And this was how Eddie came to buy a pig which he christened Bobby.

'Bobby seemed to have played quite a part in Eddie's life at the *Stelle*,' his widow remarks. He let the pig loose in the garden and trained it like a dog. Everyone loved Fritzchen's pet and enjoyed watching it perform tricks such as lying on the floor and letting its tummy be tickled. Bobby would attract the attention of local people when he was taken for walks. Eddie would smile and acknowledge their presence, and onlookers would be astonished that it was not a dog but a docile pig which followed in his wake. When Eddie went swimming in the Loire, Bobby would happily wallow in the mud by the riverbank.

Eddie himself was soon bridling about being forbidden to leave the château on his own. 'This order bored me,' he later recalled. So, one Sunday afternoon, he did a bunk, jumping over the wall and walking along the riverbank. Coming upon a roadhouse, he danced, drank and flirted with *les jolies filles* for a few hours. Asking for a pre-war Johnny Walker, he and one particularly charming companion ended up drinking the whole bottle. 'And then von Gröning sent a posse looking for him,' Betty Chapman says. 'He was more worried about losing Eddie than a lost child!'

Feeling hungry, Eddie ordered dinner, at which point three members of the *Dienststelle* arrived. Obviously relieved that they had traced him, his colleagues too had a drink, then another – and another. The party ended with Eddie drunkenly driving them all home. The official car, whose occupants had been hollering the popular song '*Belle amie*', came to a screaming halt outside the château where a furious-looking Baron was waiting for them. In the event, von Gröning took it in good heart and produced three bottles of cognac from his cellar.

The drinking continued long into the night. One by one, Eddie's trio of companions left the table and were violently sick. Eddie and the Baron carried on drinking until a bottle of green chartreuse was produced. That was just too much for Eddie. 'I walked out into the cool night air and retched violently,' he recalled.

★   ★   ★

A few weeks after Eddie's arrival, he was interviewed by a senior officer from nearby Angers. It was obvious that this visitor – 'He was very, very ugly,' Eddie recalled – was checking up on him. His name was Müller and he seemed to be the head of the Angers *Abwehrstelle*. He was responsible for catching English agents and certainly looked the part of a true 'Boche' – with small, piggy eyes and a rasping voice that sounded as ugly as he looked. When he questioned Eddie, those piggy eyes never left him. Herr Müller wanted to know if Eddie would be willing to use brutality in the course of his work.

'Yes, I would,' Eddie replied in German. 'But only if it was a case of self-preservation.'

Müller subsequently visited him a couple more times, the first early in May to talk about captured radio sets and the second in early June when Eddie was feeling ill after reacting badly to some medicine. These visits made him feel uncomfortable. Later, Eddie was taken to the large *Stelle* in Angers – through which many visitors to Nantes passed – where they had lunch. They even visited the nearest branch of Lloyds Bank. He later learned that most German radio intercepts were made in Angers. The Abwehr had a dedicated section that listened out for illicit radio transmissions – from enemy agents usually known as 'black senders' – between France and the British Isles.

★ ★ ★

Before a potential saboteur could be sent overseas, he or she had to be fully trained. As a result, potential German spies were usually taught a syllabus involving Morse code, radio transmissions, the use of ciphers and invisible inks, basic counter-surveillance techniques and the recognition of aircraft types.

In the early years of the war, Abwehr spies had been despatched into enemy territory with their own transmitters. But these radios were so heavy that they were dropped separately. The ill-starred Hermann Görtz had managed to lose his in the Irish bogs in May 1940. When both agent and radio set were landed together there was the danger – as had happened to Gösta Caroli in the autumn of 1940 – that the former would be knocked unconscious by the latter. By 1942, the Abwehr had hit upon a solution: to use captured equipment brought to Occupied France by British-trained saboteurs. Around the château, Eddie was aware that there were a number of such sets – 'nine or ten', he later recalled – one of which he would be expected to use.

The purloining of British equipment extended to other areas of his work as an agent for the Third Reich. On the ground floor of the main château building, to his astonishment, was a room filled with sabotage material – gelignite and fuses, detonators and explosives. All were taken from captured British agents who had been supplied by the Special Operations Executive (SOE). 'This was a sort of store-room,' he recalled. 'I should imagine there were fifty or sixty kilos with all kinds of detonators.'

Ten days after Eddie arrived in Nantes, his course of intense radio training began. 'Radio communication was carried on by three operators in a small bedroom at the top of the house,' he recalled. 'A clothes cupboard, always kept locked when not in use, held the various wireless sets. There were sets running off the mains; also, in case of a breakdown, sets which could be run off batteries.' It was known as the Funk Radio Room, and from here all official radio communications from the *Stelle* were transmitted. Regular exchanges of information took place between Paris and Berlin, and also with stations in the south of France. Robert Keller, the dedicated radio operator for the Nantes *Stelle*, worked and slept in the room. All official messages were sent from Keller's bedroom and whenever he took a break, Walther Thomas would take over.

Neither had time to train Eddie full time so early in May 1942, a bald, plump man – a 'queer, likeable little chap' in Eddie's estimation – arrived. Maurice Schmidt was a Berliner with a high-pitched voice who always seemed to be laughing (often about his baldness, a source of much merriment to the Boys). Based in Paris, it would be his job to teach agent Fritzchen the 'black arts' of Morse code. He seemed to be in charge of all radio transmissions between Paris, Nantes and Bordeaux – and was also responsible for redirecting signals from Lisbon to *Abwehrstellen* in occupied territory.

At the start, they used a practice wireless of simple construction: it had a battery, a tapping key and headphones. Eddie was a natural. One afternoon, Schmidt checked whether his trainee 'could differentiate between the "das" and the "dits", because apparently some people can't'. As he could indeed discriminate between dots and dashes, he was pronounced a suitable candidate for further training. 'Slowly, I began to learn the radio alphabet, all the easy letters being taken first.'

In the gardener's house, Eddie could practise to his heart's content and they soon lashed up an aerial for him to practise with. 'Schmidt was a good teacher and taught me various rhythms by which I could remember the letters.' Fairly quickly, Eddie was capable of recognising eighty letters a minute, and pretty soon, a hundred and twenty.

Over the summer, Eddie visited Schmidt several times in Paris. When he returned to the château, he would practise communicating with Schmidt in the capital. Often, the operators would ask him to come upstairs and practise in the Funk Room. Each agent would be given a word just before he left, which would be the basis for the encoding of their transmissions. Using a similar, simple numerical code, Eddie would practise transmissions twice a day, sending to Paris at 10 a.m. and Bordeaux an hour later (or on the half-hour, if the circuits were busy). Though he used English or French at the start, he later sent messages in German as not all the Paris operators were bilingual.

Many messages were jocular. Eddie was allowed some leeway, often signing off with a joky greeting. His own favourite was '99 99', the symbol for 'You can kiss my arse'. A whole series of more serious 'ham chat' characters – akin to today's text-message abbreviations – were developed in case he ever got into trouble and needed to pass on messages urgently. To show that he was not under enemy control, Eddie would make sure that the first five letters in his transmission were always FFFFF.*

On what he remembered as 'a steaming June day', Eddie gained the first hints of what his mission was going to be. In the company of

---

* At various times after the war, Eddie would entertain visitors with impromptu displays of his radio tapping abilities, in much the same way as mimicking a flamboyant pianist. Towards the end of his life, Eddie would sit in the sunshine in the garden, 'and he would often be doing the da-da-da-dit hand movements', recalls Betty Chapman.

Thomas and von Gröning, he went to Paris to attend a meeting with the local Abwehr chiefs. Their destination was a well-furnished flat – with an impressive library – near rue du Bac which, it seems, had previously been the property of a Jewish man (Eddie noticed that many of the titles were in Hebrew).

When they arrived a man called Albert Schole, who had been repatriated from South Africa, served them drinks, after which the big cheeses arrived. First was a Herr Brandy, in old grey flannels and a sports coat, who seemed to be head of radio operations in Paris. 'I present my namesake,' he said affably, handing over a couple of bottles of good brandy.

Next a jolly fat man wearing a tropical suit walked in. As Eddie remembered, he 'came apparently from Berlin to have a look at me'. This was Colonel Gautier, a shrewd counter-intelligence chief who soon had them in fits of laughter as they quaffed cognac and champagne. 'He asked all kinds of odd questions,' Eddie recalled. 'Told me various jokes and spoke about various clubs in the West End.' He spoke in what Eddie considered a 'public school' accent and, it seemed, knew London well. Gautier hinted that he may have been behind some espionage in Jersey before the German occupation.

Eventually, the conversation turned to matters in hand. Was Eddie prepared to work for them? When he said he was, Eddie was told he would be sent to England on a sabotage mission. Would he mind parachuting? No, he wouldn't. It was all very amicable. Von Gröning was told that Eddie should be trained in parachute drops.

They toasted Eddie's health, and later dined excellently at the Café de Concorde. After that they spent the rest of the evening heading to one nightclub after another – 'They were always looking for new nightclubs,' Eddie's widow says – where the Germans exhorted him to join in their war songs.

This was the first of seven trips Eddie made to Paris. On this and subsequent visits, the Abwehr people were careful not to let him see too much, especially when they passed through the capital en route to somewhere else. They would always stay at the Grand Hotel – where he would check in under the name of Edward Fritz – and usually end up dining at Poccardi's restaurant on the Boulevard des Italiens, which was close by the flat where they had assembled that hot June day. He was never allowed to visit the main *Abwehrstelle* in Paris, based at the Hotel Lutétia.

When they went to meet Maurice Schmidt, they usually walked from the Grand Hotel towards the Bois de Boulogne. His radio trainer was stationed in 'a very nice house belonging to an Englishman who was interned at St Denis'. On subsequent visits, Schmidt popped by their hotel to ask questions, as well as encouraging him and pointing out mistakes in some of his messages.

That Eddie should remain word perfect – and maintain Schmidt's exacting standards – became Walther Thomas's ongoing concern in Nantes. Back at the château, Thomas would test Eddie with a stopwatch when he transmitted some of the 'black market' messages. He timed Eddie on a rolled printout on a drum that was graduated for seventy-eight letters a minute. Schmidt too would check on Eddie's accuracy and speed, as well as advising him what to do if things went wrong with his set. One day, one of the coils in his radio set burned through and an expert came up from Angers to check on it. 'Now here's an opportunity for you to go upstairs,' von Gröning said to Eddie, referring to the Funk Room. 'He will explain all the workings of the set, then if anything does go wrong, you can repair it yourself.'

In the event, the technician stayed for three days. Though Eddie watched him at work, he was none the wiser. As the radio engineer talked about the lengths of aerials and other technical information, it was all beyond him. Nearer the time of his departure, Eddie was given a transmitter for which there were problems with a switch. He ended up soldering it with a poker which, as a later MI5 report notes, was 'a method not calculated to provide a really satisfactory electrical connection'!

★　★　★

The *Stelle* was a constant hive of activity. The Germans were supporting a separatist organisation – 'La Bretagne pour les Bretons' – in an effort to foment anti-French sentiment. The proximity of Nantes to Brittany meant that it became the focus for such separatist activity. The Bretons, in one espionage writer's estimation 'an insular, suspicious, mystical and clannish people', remained equally unfathomable to the Germans, particularly the Gestapo.

One regular visitor at the *Dienststelle* was a Breton called Pierre Coussins. Eddie remembered him as a swarthy, shifty-eyed fellow, who always wore glasses and a brown suit. He was very familiar with the Boys – he gave a 'Heil Hitler' salute every time he came to visit – and, though partly of Italian descent, was among the leaders of the Breton separatists. Coussins seemed to be the publisher of a separatist magazine to which the Germans were giving encouragement. He owned flats in Jersey and was in regular contact with Stefan von Gröning.

'We met sometimes for coffee in town,' Eddie would recall. It seemed that Coussins lived in an apartment owned by an Englishman in Nantes and was undergoing training similar to Eddie's. Not that Eddie was supposed to know about it: when Coussins came in for training, he was usually sent out to have dinner or enjoy another form of entertainment. Twice a week, Coussins would turn up for target practice. He was an appalling shot.*

Eddie, on the other hand, excelled at marksmanship, particularly in shooting liqueur glasses in a row or coins in a bulls-eye from fifteen metres' distance. In fact his skill became quite a talking point. 'Every morning I did half an hour's practice with an automatic,' he recalled, 'and soon the Boys delighted in showing visitors my prowess.' (It was clear that Eddie would be expected to shoot his way out of trouble.)

One night, however, Eddie nearly got himself killed by his radio instructor. During one of his visits, after the Boys had been out on the town and were somewhat the worse for wear, a drunken Maurice Schmidt challenged him to a duel over some imagined slight. '[He] suddenly clicked his heels together and demanded satisfaction,' Eddie later wrote. Maurice insisted he do a '*fünfzehn*

---

*Eddie was certain, at one point, that the *Dienststelle* was under surveillance by the British secret service. While visiting Nantes, Eddie remembered seeing a man 'whom he had previously seen on several occasions in London', to quote an MI5 report. Tall, typically English-looking, he spoke very good French and was seen in the Café de France, as well as other haunts – but Eddie said nothing about him to the Boys.

Meter Lauf' – a fifteen-metre walk – and accused him of being a '*Feigling*' (coward) for laughing at him.

Now it was Eddie's turn to overreact. 'I drew my automatic and we both marched into the middle of the lawn,' he recalled. Von Gröning was awoken by angry noises from the garden and ordered them both to bed. Maurice, the next day, apologised profusely. They shook hands, both highly embarrassed by their behaviour the night before.

On another occasion, Eddie answered the door to two young Frenchmen, a tall gaunt kid and his silent sidekick. They asked to speak to Monsieur Graumann. When Eddie called the Baron, he was told to take a walk around the garden. Instead, he tried to listen in from the lavatory next door. 'I came back again and made a tour of the lavatory,' Eddie would recall. 'It was rather difficult to listen in on the salon.' So far as he could gather, these two youngsters were working for the Germans by penetrating the resistance. His impression was that they were being trained for sabotage missions in Britain. Eddie's own future involvement in sabotage would soon become clear.

First, though, a saboteur needed to learn the skills of sabotage. Given his pre-war predilection for blowing up safes, and despite his clumsiness, Eddie's transformation from safebreaker to saboteur was not expected to be too difficult. Yet he would need to understand all the arcane knowledge of formulae and chemical compositions. Unknown to him at the time, fifteen detonators and some fuses had been requested for him the week before his first meeting in Paris. The Abwehr high-ups wanted him to start practice straight away.

The gardener's house proved a perfect venue. The downstairs rooms were transformed, stocked with exotic compounds. 'Around the walls stood various chemicals in sealed glass bottles,' Eddie wrote, 'and on the small marble tables were scales, with bowls for pulverising crystals into powder.'

And the seclusion of the château's grounds made it ideal for blowing things up. 'The garden was quite large and when we were going to do anything we simply went out and told the gardeners to work at the other end of the garden,' he recalled. The Boys would sometimes cut down trees so that he could blow their stumps out of the ground. On one occasion, he mixed the wrong proportions and blew a trunk about fifty metres in the air. 'There was a terrific row', Eddie recalled, because it nearly killed a man in a neighbouring property. 'We went and explained to the people in the neighbourhood that we were exploding land mines.'

His principal instructor was one of the more remarkable characters at the *Stelle*, a man who, it transpired, was better paid than anyone else there. Herbert Wojch, who drove a car plastered with Breton separatist stickers, had been in Paris in the early days of the war when he had apparently killed a number of Allied officers by planting a bomb in a hotel. Small, strong and ruddy-faced, Wojch had been a boxer in his youth. In Eddie's later estimation, he was 'fresh and flashy, almost like an American', for he spoke perfect English with an American accent. Wojch was always smartly dressed and usually wore a pearl in his tie. He wore many rings and fiddled with them the whole time he was talking.

Though Wojch and Eddie never became particularly close, they were drinking buddies and enjoyed visiting bars and cafés together. Eddie learned – from some soldiers he was talking to in a bar – that the German had been in London before the war. On another occasion, Wojch himself drunkenly told Eddie that he had helped the IRA when they attempted to blow up Hammersmith Bridge in 1939. In fact, he formed the impression that Wojch had done more than just help the 'Irish Irregulars'. 'My opinion is that many of the bomb outrages which in 1939 had seemed to require a skilled saboteur were really the work of this man,' Eddie later wrote.

Shortly before the war, it appeared, Wojch had narrowly missed arrest in a nightclub raid off Leicester Square. Having escaped the police and entered Belgium on a French passport via Ostend, he was arrested, but it seems he had been released because no charges could be brought against him. Wojch had then remained in France until the German invasion, during which time he had carried out the Paris bombing. Some of the Nantes Boys marvelled at this, calling it '*ein wunderbares Eingmacht*' 'a wonderful piece of work'. For this, he had been promoted.

Wojch was a walking compendium on explosives. Under his tutelage, Eddie was taught how to make home-made explosives using materials that could be easily obtained from chemist's shops. Each day that summer he practised making thermites, various forms of dynamite and mixing different burning materials. He was told to keep everything in his head and write nothing down. Pointedly, he was not allowed to tell any of the other staff what he was up to, but Eddie had other ideas. 'I made complete lists of everything I was doing,' he recalled. 'I was told not to, but I did.' He also made notes of radio frequencies and details of visitors to the château, wondering how he might smuggle them out of the building – and, eventually, the country.

Over the summer, he gradually became expert in various types of sabotage. 'The two simplest methods of sabotage can be carried out either with a watch attached to batteries, or with acid,' he later wrote. 'An ordinary ink bottle is filled with sulphuric acid. The lid is pierced and a piece of cardboard is placed between the lid and the hole. It takes two hours to eat through the cardboard. This flows on to some specially prepared burning mixture which explodes the detonator and charge.'

Eddie was shown how to attach wires to an ordinary wristwatch to create a timer for up to twelve hours. Longer-term delays would need an alarm clock and, in time, he learned how to set them for up to fourteen days. Wojch showed him the best place to destroy a bridge, taking him around local railways to gain a better insight. He was taught how to set explosives to wreck trains by putting charges on rail lines and how to hide wiring. For the destruction of a ship, he was shown how to hide devices in attaché cases. He learned how to pack clothes to muffle an alarm clock inside a suitcase, as well as how to make a coal bomb. A piece of coal would be drilled and filled with dynamite. When shovelled into a furnace, Wojch explained, it would result in a massive explosion that would be hard to trace.

Wojch regularly went away, but never explained what he had done or where he had been. 'Whenever any of the *Dienststelle* went away I was allowed to write to them, and they invariably wrote back to me,' Eddie recalled. 'When I asked to send a letter to Wojch, I was told it was impossible.' When Herbert Wojch eventually went to

Spain, Eddie only found out because he heard some of the Boys telling him to take cigarettes with him as they were hard to come by.

★ ★ ★

Another of Eddie's Nantes cronies had also been in England before the war. Perhaps the best wireless operator at the *Stelle*, Franz Schmidt was also well informed about sabotage. By the time they were working together in the summer of 1942, it was clear he had recently spent some time in Spain. Eddie had no idea what Schmidt was doing in Iberia but many of the *Stelle*, it seemed, had spent time there, for the Abwehr had good relations with Franco's government.

Intriguingly, Schmidt had been a waiter at Frascati's restaurant in London and spoke English with a cockney accent. To Eddie's delight, in the pre-war years they had frequented some of the same clubs – Smoky Joe's, the Nest – as well as attending several tea dances. His accent was so good, apparently, that a real cockney had once said to him, 'That bleeding 'itler is going to start a war.'

The presence of both Wojch and Schmidt in pre-war London struck Eddie as significant. He was certain large-scale sabotage activities were being planned, although he had no idea what they were. 'Was it an accident that a skilled saboteur and a radio man were in London at the same time?' When he later raised these suspicions with MI5, they seemed concerned that the two saboteurs might be infiltrated into the British Isles.

Eddie formed the distinct impression that Wojch would either be sent to Britain or America. After both Wojch and Schmidt left the *Stelle* that autumn, Eddie never saw them again. He was very worried they might have already departed for England by the time he arrived there.*

★ ★ ★

* By the time Eddie landed in Britain, MI5 was aware of these two saboteurs as both their real and 'spy' names had also been revealed by Ultra, the decrypted readouts of Abwehr Enigma signals. He would later recognise a photo of Schmidt. When he subsequently remembered that both had told him that they had had to register at Vine Street police station, their alien registration forms were located in the archives.

That summer of 1942, however, the Abwehr had set its sights further afield. A group of eight agents were landed in the United States by U-boat at the end of June with the aim of sabotaging east coast factories associated with the American aircraft industry. With almost continual daylight raids by the US Army Air Force causing disruption of the Fatherland, those factories were an important strategic target for the Germans. But what was known as Operation Pastorius was betrayed by one of its saboteurs, with an eye to obtaining a reward. All eight were eventually apprehended.

A cloud of depression fell over the Nantes *Stelle* when the agents' fate became clear. As Eddie later told MI5, some of these saboteurs 'were connected with our *Dienststelle*'. Two of the eight had apparently been staying in the Grand Hotel before their departure. 'A few nights before they left by submarine for America, they were allowed a celebration in Paris,' Eddie recalled. 'When they finally landed from the U-boat in the USA, they had only been a few hours on shore before they were all arrested. They were tried, sentenced to death and some were shot.' All the Nantes-trained saboteurs – not least agent Fritz Graumann – realised a similar fate might befall them once they left occupied territory.

Against this backdrop, Stefan von Gröning promised Eddie his own mission to the United States, floating the possibility in front of him on many occasions. Indeed, von Gröning explicitly asked Eddie several times during his training if he would like to make a trip to the United States. Despite the failure of Operation Pastorius, Eddie was certain that there would be a follow-up. It was clear that the Boys in the Nantes *Stelle* knew quite a lot about what was going on in the United States and Canada. Eddie told MI5 that something was 'brewing over there'. At the château, he once overheard a conversation about sabotage which had been carried out in a Canadian port by one of their agents. 'A ship had been set on fire and this fire had spread to other vessels in the port,' he recalled. 'A wood store had also been sabotaged by either this same or another person.' Around this time, Eddie was also party to talk of '*ein gut Arbeit*' (a good piece of work) in North America.

A more immediate result of the failure of the American mission was enhanced security. Because the arrest of the saboteurs was put down to loose talk in Paris before their departure, all the Boys at the

Nantes *Dienststelle* were encouraged to tighten security precautions. 'I was told whenever I went down (to the town), never to talk,' Eddie recalled. 'And we hadn't to take women in cars.'

This latter stricture was to cause problems for Herbert Wojch. In Eddie's estimation, he was 'a flash type' who liked women and, some time that summer, he took a couple of girls to a party in a staff car. When von Gröning found out, he went ballistic. As a result, both Wojch and his sidekick, Hans Wilhelms, were transferred to another *Stelle*.

★ ★ ★

In the meantime, the bombing of Germany by both British and American aircrews continued. The Nazi High Command had found a new and pressing irritant in the form of the Mosquito, a pathfinding British bomber that was as fast as a fighter. Plans were drawn up for a sabotage operation against the factory north of London where the new aircraft was assembled, and the agent chosen for the task would be despatched in a matter of weeks.

If he didn't knock out any more teeth, that is.

CHAPTER FOUR

The Man with the Golden Teeth

'Sometimes in trying to put facts together I really thought I was going mad. Your officers probably think it incredible that a man could forget such important things, make such stupid mistakes, and miss such a golden opportunity of bringing information. I can only plead I tried so very hard.'

– The strains of trying to remember what had happened in France, from a handwritten note by Eddie Chapman, handed to his chief British interrogator at the end of 1942

EVEN BEFORE HE HIT the ground, Eddie knew there was something seriously wrong. All his previous practice jumps had gone well, but on this, his fourth low-altitude drop, the parachute had only partially opened. At the last moment, a gust of wind had picked him up, swung him like a pendulum and thrown him head first to the ground. There was a loud crack and blood spurted everywhere before Eddie felt an overwhelming sense of nausea.

When he finally stood up, he cursed his luck. He'd lost two of his teeth, which had been sheared off across the top of his mouth. The pain was excruciating and the bleeding continued for quite some time.

'He had trouble with his teeth for years afterwards,' Betty Chapman says. 'In the war years, he wore false teeth that were covered with gold.'

In many ways, parachute practice was the most dangerous phase of Eddie's training. As we have seen, the Germans had had little luck with their parachute agents but given Eddie's usual clumsiness, it is a wonder he didn't do himself more lasting damage. Yet it had all begun harmlessly enough.

His training had started with a ladder on the lawn of the château, propped against a tree, where a Luftwaffe officer named Wolfgang taught him how to avoid injury by landing and rolling without hurting himself. Wolfgang Blommers was dark, wore horn-rimmed glasses and was in Eddie's estimation 'rather good-looking'. He had known Paris before the war when he had been in the cotton business. Within a matter of days, Eddie could drop from sixteen rungs without any apparent harm. 'By this time I was very fit,' Eddie recalled of this summer. 'Every day I was trained further in radio, sabotage and jumping.'

That June, he was sent up to Paris to perform his first parachute drop from Le Bourget aerodrome. He was handed overalls and fitted with a harness that would automatically open the parachute when he jumped out of the plane. Attached to a thirty-foot rope, he would descend from a trap door beneath a Junkers bomber – from an altitude of roughly nine hundred feet.

The experience was vivid. 'The trap door opened and out I went, a dizzy dive into space,' Eddie wrote of one particular jump. 'I heard the roar of the aircraft as it passed over me, and experienced a feeling that I was going to hit its tail.' Then the parachute opened, he gained his balance and, within seconds, was delighted to be slowly descending in the summer sunshine.

Eddie was to attempt five more jumps over the next three days from ever greater altitudes. On the second day he had knocked his front teeth out. He also managed to knee himself in the chin and broke several of his back teeth. A French doctor, in a smart suite at his hotel, managed to effect some repairs. When he returned to Nantes, he was worked on further by a local dentist called Bijet who recrowned his teeth. They would continue to trouble him until August, when the various treatments were completed, having cost the Abwehr – as the Nantes *Stelle* faithfully reported to Paris – the grand sum of 9,500 francs.

These 'teething troubles' also delayed his departure by a couple of months. Eddie could only be given so many injections at a time for the pain. 'At the finish I was quite sick with having [them],' he later told MI5. 'And one day [the doctor] gave me three injections one after the other. I'd just had my parachute training and we'd been up rather high, and when I came down, I didn't feel too good.' Apparently, Eddie had inadvertently been given an overdose. He felt woozy for a few days afterwards.

★ ★ ★

While Eddie recuperated at the château, the summer of 1942 remained highly successful for the Germans. The Battle of the Atlantic was heading towards its climax in the Kriegsmarine's favour. Greater numbers of Allied ships were being sunk than could be replaced. Britain faced the possibility of being starved into submission. With Bletchley Park unable to decode a new, more secure German naval Enigma for most of the year, Allied shipping losses in the Atlantic grew alarmingly. Winston Churchill's journeys that summer to Washington, Cairo and Moscow were, Goebbels insisted, acts of increasing desperation. The British Prime Minister had been forced to grovel, cap in hand, to reluctant allies.

From Hendaye on the Spanish border of France to the North Cape of Scandinavia, Adolf Hitler ruled Europe. From Stalingrad on the Volga down towards the Elburz mountains, the Wehrmacht was advancing into the Soviet Union. After a stunning series of attacks, Rommel's forces were now gathered at the Egyptian border. One final push and North Africa would be his. Japan, too, had an empire which stretched from Burma to the Aleutians. For Eddie Chapman, it was a strange experience to be on the other side, surrounded by fervent German supporters. 'Sometimes,' he would say, 'I found it hard to control my feelings.'

One day that summer, von Gröning came clean to the agent in his charge. 'Personally,' he told Eddie, 'I think Hitler will ruin Germany. Of course, I will see that whatever happens you will be looked after.' The Führer would not, the Baron insisted, prevail. Eddie, pointing out that Hitler's forces had already taken over half the world, disagreed. With a wearying sense of fatality, the Baron said it wouldn't last.

The others, though, remained upbeat. Whenever the Boys gathered around the radio to listen to the latest news, their faces would light up, especially when the Marines' marching song '*Wir fahren gegen England*' ('We are marching against England') came on. All but von Gröning would be filled with glee and a bout of '*Sieg Heil*' would follow each claim of victory over the Allies.

Eddie's blood would run cold. 'Fearful visions of my father and brother would float through my brain as I pictured them choking in the oily water of a sinking ship,' he later wrote, 'or sliding helplessly off some lost raft in the Atlantic after days of thirst, hunger and lonely horror.'

★   ★   ★

By the middle of July, Eddie was sufficiently recovered from his parachute accident to make a trip to Berlin in the company of his minder Walther Thomas. He would be one of the few Englishmen to visit the German capital at this precarious time. As ever, though, his Abwehr masters took great care to ensure that he saw as little as possible. 'To my deep disappointment,' he later wrote, 'I did not get much of a chance of sightseeing.' The train from the Gare du Nord travelled through the night, and because of the blackout, the blinds were drawn. They arrived at a blacked-out Potsdam station around one thirty in the morning. They were met by a car which took twenty-five minutes to reach a small country house which was also completely dark.

The next morning, Eddie became aware that the house was situated deep in the Berlin suburbs, surrounded by a stone wall and woods. It was also guarded. The property seemed to be owned by a chemist and his wife whose children appeared on a photo on the mantelpiece in the living room. The couple lived well: they were attended by three female servants, as well as a gardener with whom Eddie struck up a conversation in German. When Thomas found out that he had asked this fellow where they were, he advised caution. 'If anyone realises you are British, we should both be shot without any questions being asked.' So Eddie agreed to keep quiet.

That morning he was introduced to the chemist – an 'odd chap', bent and scholarly in appearance, but also 'a dignified little man' who neither smoked nor drank. 'He was obviously a man who knew all the technical terms and explained formulae to me,' he later told MI5. '[He] gave me drawing demonstrations which Wojch hadn't given me.' But the chemist spoke only German; though he did his best, the correct English names of the profusion of chemicals he attempted to describe were beyond him.

In the extensive grounds Eddie could practise making explosives. There was a chicken run and a grass plot on which they could experiment. Inside the house, the atmosphere was relaxed and the chemist would take him into his laboratory – essentially a room filled with 'all kinds of chemical mixtures' – to demonstrate the skills needed to make a perfect explosion. 'He insisted very rigorously that I should always find the correct proportions of things,' Eddie recalled.

The chemist also tested what Eddie had been taught by the more practical Herbert Wojch. Eddie learned more about timers, acid fuses, optimum burn length and how to link explosions so they would all explode at the same time. He started fires using only acid fuses and a watch, prepared explosive coal and saw many other demonstrations. Rail sabotage remained an important part of the curriculum. Eddie was taught how to dynamite a train and how to put abrasives like sand in engines. For this, the best approach was to crack the armature of a dynamo, the wire-wound coil which carries the current.

Surprisingly, he already knew how armatures worked. 'When I was a kid, I used to test them,' he would later explain to MI5, 'I worked on them in a place called the Sunderland Forge in the north country.' And he would be taught how to blow boilers by linking and, indeed, coupling explosives together – something which would prove useful for his forthcoming sabotage mission. He was there for four days before returning to Nantes.

★ ★ ★

Later that July, Eddie made a couple more parachute drops from Le Bourget. The intention was to simulate night-time conditions, particularly concerning the 'load' – a full fifty-pound pack – which he would take with him when he was eventually despatched to Great Britain. As Eddie explained, 'the idea was to give me my first experience of jumping at night'. The first drop took place close by the airfield north-east of Paris. The second, a couple of miles from the Nantes château at St Joseph, was the highest so far – though he wasn't exactly sure of the altitude.

'The moon was up and how large the stars seemed!' Eddie recalled. 'Below me was the billowing eiderdown of the clouds: for a moment, I thought I was over the sea.' Suddenly, he was consumed by the darkness, landing on the ground far sooner than he expected. Eddie had come to earth in a meadow in which both a flak and radio location unit were based. 'He had been told that the entire staff would be advised that he was being dropped,' MI5 later recorded, 'and when he said his name was Fritz to the sentry, he was let in.' Some of his own unit drank with him in the mess, where they had been waiting for him, and then they drove him home.

What stuck in his mind, though, was the fact Stefan von Gröning had told him to bury his parachute and equipment exactly as he should do when he landed in England. Eddie formed the impression that they might try to catch him out later by pretending to drop him in England – though it would actually be France. The possibility of such a double-cross loomed large in his thoughts.

One gloriously sunny morning that August, Eddie and the Baron were sitting in the château's grounds together when von Gröning removed a bulky envelope from his pocket. It contained a contract, written in English, between Fritz Graumann and the Third Reich. Eddie read the details and was delighted to see that he would receive 100,000 Reichsmarks – or, if he preferred it, the same amount in pounds sterling, at a rate of ten pounds to the mark – for his work. It also specified what he was expected to achieve.

'My mission was to be the sabotaging of the aeroplane factory making Mosquito bombers, to wit, that of de Havilland Ltd,' Eddie recalled. 'The success of the mission would be established if I succeeded in blowing up the boiler house or destroying the electric plant.'

In addition, he was to report troop movements and target secondary aircraft factories. The continual flow of American GIs into Britain was of obvious interest to the Germans. 'We would like very much if you could manage to send some information about American troops,' von Gröning added. The Abwehr wanted to know where they congregated. Of particular interest were the corps signs displayed on American transport vehicles. 'If I could also send positions of flak artillery around London,' he recorded, 'this information would be interesting and well paid for.'

The contract was generous. While absent from France, a salary of 300 Reichsmarks a month would be paid into his account: if, for any reason, he was jailed in Britain, his fee would automatically go up to 600 Reichsmarks. He would be given £1,000 upon departure and all other incidental expenses would be reimbursed.*

If caught, Eddie was expected to keep quiet. He agreed not to divulge any of the names of people he was working for or who had trained him, the chemical formulae they had taught him or any places that were known to him. If any of this information was revealed, he would be punished by death (the fact that execution by the British would far more likely follow was glossed over).

Privately, von Gröning told Eddie that if he were caught by the British secret service, he should offer to work for them. 'As soon as you come back to France, get in touch with us,' he explained. So long as he didn't mention any details of his German training, Eddie could easily become a triple agent, carrying out jobs under the Abwehr's supervision. Eddie was more than happy with these terms. Witnessed by Walther Thomas and Franz Schmidt, he signed the six copies of the contract in his own name. The Baron told Thomas to lock them in the safe. Beaming, he said, 'If you can do this for us, you will have nothing more to worry about. Your whole future will be made when you come back. Don't worry, it

---

*In comparison, the first agent doubled by the British, Arthur Owens (codename Snow), was grudgingly given just £200. The Abwehr was notoriously parsimonious.

will be quite all right. I'll have another bottle of champagne with you.'

Yet the task ahead would not be quite as easy as it sounded. When they were drinking together on their own one night, von Gröning admitted that it was difficult to place agents into Britain. His candour extended to the overall state of German espionage in the British Isles. 'Of course, our agents are there,' he explained. 'We have them, we have the connections, but we have to be very, very careful not to take any risks.'

★   ★   ★

By the summer of 1942, British double-agent operations were delicately poised. Unknown to both Eddie and his Abwehr masters, the British Double Cross Committee had reached maturity. That summer, Colonel Tommy Robertson, who ran double-agents, stated categorically that MI5 controlled all the German agents in Britain. Meanwhile, a new officer in charge of deception had been appointed in London. Colonel John H. Bevan remarked that strategic deception needed just three essential elements: good planning, double agents and codebreaking. Under his astute leadership, deception planning would go to the very heart of Allied strategy.

Part of Johnny Bevan's success came from his intimacy with the Prime Minister. Over late night brandies, they would plot and scheme. 'Bevan and Churchill sparked each other off,' the former's deputy would write, 'and pulled out what were all the old tricks of Eton and Harrow and polished them up for the task at hand.'

From their basement in Storey's Gate, the deception planners soon became highly adept at playing on the curious beliefs of German High Command. As already noted, much of the battle between the British and German secret services was carried out over the airwaves. Thanks to the Enigma decrypts streaming in from Bletchley Park, the British could eavesdrop on what the Abwehr was reporting and thinking. As the military historian Ronald Lewin has written, those decrypts represented 'manna from heaven, the child of a radio war without parallel'.

That August, MI5 became aware that someone named Chapman was being trained in sabotage by the Germans. All summer, Bletchley Park had found tantalising references in the Abwehr radio traffic to a potential saboteur undergoing training in Brittany. Within a few days the Radio Security Service was able to listen to this agent in France practising his radio transmissions in Morse code.

With typical thoroughness, the Nantes *Stelle* reported each facet of Eddie's training programme to Paris and Berlin. The former radio hams of the RSS were thus soon able to detect the presence in Nantes of a British national codenamed Fritzchen, whose Morse call sign was 'FFF'. He had, it seemed, suffered considerable dental trouble. 'FFF seems to be a new operator,' the RSS reported. 'He is slow and makes frequent mistakes and his formation of symbols is poor.' Soon, they were aware that he 'may have some relatives or connections in the Channel Islands'.

Given that the British could no longer get hold of official files from St Helier, it was difficult for them to confirm his identity. Unfortunately, the gaze of the Security Service alighted on the wrong man. MI5 came up with the name of Robert William Chapman, aged twenty-four, a pre-war army recruit who had been posted to the Middle East. His early life had eerie parallels with Eddie's, for he, too, had been steadily going off the rails.

But further investigation by the local police in his native Barrow revealed that this Chapman's sister had on 13 August received a letter via the Red Cross. Robert Chapman was being held at Stalag Luft 3 after being captured that February. Another brother who had been in more regular contact revealed that 'he had escaped and been recaptured and because he had been punished so severely, he had gone deaf'. Given that fact – and the lack of any discernible Jersey connection – Robert William Chapman didn't seem to be their man. For the rest of the summer, the British radio listeners would be alert for any clues to FFF's identity as he practised sending rude messages through the ether.

★   ★   ★

Unaware that the British were listening to his transmissions, Eddie Chapman was rather more concerned with the charms of his local environment. The tranquillity of the Loire Valley that August would remain particularly vivid in his recollections. 'I remember the river winding lazily by, with masses of water flies skimming its surface,' he wrote, 'and small canoes and sailing boats weaving their courses across its shallow waters, while bathers dozed on its banks.'

On Tuesday, 18 August, however, the Boys of the Nantes *Dienststelle* were suddenly told to stand by. Within hours it was clear there was something major afoot. Cars were filled with fuel and ammunition, though they remained in Nantes. Planes flew over the garden all day. The tenth Panzer division moved into the area. Eddie was certain the Germans had advance knowledge of whatever was happening, for Stefan von Gröning threw an impromptu party that evening. His controller only ever did that when there was good news. But on that fateful evening there seemed to be no apparent reason for celebration.

Certainly, the next day, Wednesday, 19 August, was a busy and chaotic one at the château. The radio operators – Keller, Thomas and Schmidt – took turns in the Funk Room to take down the various incoming messages, many of which were contradictory and unclear. It appeared that the Allies had made a landing in the northern French seaport of Dieppe. By nightfall, though, it was clear that this attack had been repulsed with heavy losses – casualties ran as high as nearly 60 per cent on the Allied side. Four thousand soldiers and marines were killed, maimed or captured in just under two hours. 'This Dieppe business seems to me to be the height of folly,' von Gröning later remarked. 'The British have made a bad and stupid mistake.'

The propaganda value of the failure was profound. 'What a bloody war it was,' Eddie later wrote, 'and what a bloody mess I was in.' He got drunk, cursed and swore at his plight and, that night, cried like a baby. If he was equally unsuccessful on his return home, Eddie knew that he would be 'doomed to die the death of a traitor at the hands of my own countrymen'.

But the fiasco at Dieppe did at least provide agent Fritzchen with authentic kit and reserves. Shortly after the raid, Berlin ordered that all the material that Eddie should take with him to England had to be the real thing – that is, British. The carnage on the French coast meant there were more than enough supplies to provide him with exactly what he needed. He made a list which included suit, shoes, landing boots, wireless set, detonators, revolver, ammunition, spade, money, identity card, overalls, crash helmet and chocolate.

The Boys at the *Dienststelle* were able to obtain some of the more unusual rations carried by British troops. For weeks, they feasted on tins of salmon and treacle. A few days after the raid, von Gröning and Eddie's Luftwaffe parachute instructor, Wolfgang, motored to Dieppe to take what he might need from the survivors of the attack. Indeed, they had already augmented his equipment wherever they could. In early July, Eddie had been given a guide to London and its environs which had been found in a second-hand bookshop in Paris.

On this trip, the Germans found four wireless sets, an American Colt automatic and papers belonging to a dead soldier, a Canadian of Scottish extraction from Montreal. These included a diary and some letters, one of which, from the man's wife, made Eddie laugh. 'I hereby give my permission for my husband to smoke, drink and swear,' she had written, 'and to go out with any woman he damn well pleases and have a good time.' Along with a London hotel bill, these items were collected together and gathered in the safe, waiting to be used on his return to England.

A whole section of the Abwehr was dedicated to helping its agents get messages through in the event they couldn't make radio contact. Indeed, transmitting from within an enemy country for any length of time was dangerous. Not only could simple triangulation techniques trace an agent's whereabouts, the sight of an unauthorised aerial would alert people nearby. In wartime Britain, civilians were encouraged to become a nation of nosy parkers. Secret writing could be a useful alternative.

The most obvious means of concealment was using hidden meanings in personal or business letters. The Abwehr was also experimenting with microdots; these were, however, not particularly useful for agents in the field, who could hardly carry around the specialised equipment required without attracting attention. 'Letter drops' via neutral countries, containing messages invisible to the casual observer, were a far simpler – and safer – alternative. And so, early in September, Eddie returned to Berlin for a week to learn about yet another staple of espionage: how to make and use invisible ink.

The trip to Berlin involved the same drill as before. His handlers tried to keep him in the dark on the way to the secluded house in the Berlin suburbs. This time, though, there was something new. A tall, grey-haired old man in civilian clothes, who spoke good English, drove up in a chauffeured car and introduced himself as a chemistry specialist.

The professor's first trick was to produce 'invisible ink' within a container that looked like a matchbox. Eddie's first task was to daub this colourless ink on either side of a sheet of paper with cotton wool. The treated paper was then placed on a sheet of glass, much care being taken not to allow any part of the hand to touch the surface. A covering message – incidentally, uncoded – would be lightly written in block letters. Eddie practised with matchsticks which appeared to have specially prepared heads: one was yellow, the other white.

Once the message was completed, the paper would be examined to make sure there was no evidence it had been treated. Now it was ready for the cover message. A totally innocent letter would be written over the invisible message. The professor told Eddie always to be on the alert for tell-tale signs of treatment. 'Examine the paper closely,' he was told. 'If there is the slightest trace of irregularity, start again. Paint each letter separately with a match, remember what you have written.'

A good ink, Eddie was told, would be clear, would leave no trace. It could withstand heat, cold and sunlight. It would only ever react with the specific chemical for which it was designed. The professor was reticent about how each sheet was subsequently processed, all he would tell Eddie was that 'it had to go through three processes', and that it was 95 per cent reliable. Either pen or pencil could be used, but where a pencil could write on both sides of a sheet of 'treated' paper, messages in ink could only be written on the reverse side.

When Eddie had written out his first message with the yellow matchstick, the professor took it to another room. Eddie was alert enough to notice that the German had taken a small bottle out of his pocket. The paper came back covered in chemical solution, the letters appearing in a faint green colour.

For the rest of that week, Eddie spent the whole time practising his new-found technique. The professor seemed delighted with his progress. Though Eddie wanted to go outside the grounds of the house, once again he wasn't allowed to. And again, when they departed it was around midnight.

On his return to Nantes, Eddie took two 'operational' yellow matchsticks with him. From Nantes, he would write twice a week to the professor who, at various later stages, made three separate visits to Nantes from Berlin. Any corrections to or comments on these practice letters were then transmitted by radio. Eddie's first two efforts, it seems, were not good enough. He was told to use greater pressure. 'This he did, with little better results,' MI5 reported. 'Then he used the thicker matchstick pencil and the results were perfect.'

★   ★   ★

Eddie had only been back in Nantes a few days when his clumsiness caused yet another accident. Von Gröning had asked him to demonstrate setting an explosive for a visitor, a grey-haired doctor who had come from Paris (though Eddie believed he was based in Berlin) to ask him questions about sabotage and wireless. The doctor asked him to prepare an acid fuse, and he dutifully obliged.

'I was preparing a time fuse with acid and I put the time fuse – the acid – on the table,' he recalled. 'I put the acid in [and it] was rather loose and I broke the paper that was covering it. I only made an hour fuse,' he recalled, 'and the whole thing exploded in my face.' Eddie badly burned his right hand and singed his hair, while spraying particles of the explosive mixture all over his face. He was taken to hospital suffering from shock. His eyesight was also affected by the glare from the explosion, though he was fine after a couple of days' bed rest.

It was an occupational hazard. A fellow agent called Schindle, with whom Eddie was being trained, had already lost an eye in a bomb accident on the Russian front. Another instructor, it was rumoured, had accidentally been blown up some time before.

★ ★ ★

Events started to accelerate. At one point in the late summer, it looked as though Fritzchen's departure was imminent. Paris suddenly wanted him to develop alternative forms of communication – a Lisbon cover address and newspaper advertisements were suggested – in case his radio transmitter didn't work. At the end of August, von Gröning himself had gone to Berlin to fetch the English money Eddie would carry across the Channel.

One day, Eddie asked the Baron how he would actually be sent to Britain. It would, von Gröning explained, be done under the cover of an air raid. 'They'll probably bomb some other place inland,' he said, 'and then, while the diversion is taking place, your reconnaissance plane will go up much higher [and] you will be dropped.'

Soon, large-scale maps of England with photo enlargements were being produced for Eddie's inspection. Each of these mosaic-like maps was extremely detailed, showing an area of about five miles marked with a number of potential sites where he might be dropped. The Luftwaffe were initially keen on the Cumbrian mountains in northern England; there was little flak to worry about because of the surrounding terrain, which would allow the plane to drop him at a lower altitude. But Eddie insisted that the Lake District was too far away from London. When he was asked for his own choices, he suggested Cambridge, Torquay or somewhere in the Midlands. At this stage, it seemed likely that he would be dropped in the Home Counties, close by the capital. 'Once I am in London, it will be quite all right,' he explained.

As a consequence, some 'mission rules' were developed over the weeks ahead. His landing site should be within easy reach of London and the timing of his landing around two o'clock in the morning. He was told that he would be informed of his exact destination just before take-off. Once on the ground, he would hide, wait for dawn and then bury all evidence of his drop. The closer to London the better, and the higher the altitude from which he should make the drop, because of possible interception by nightfighters, flak or searchlights. But the choice of landing site continued to cause trouble right up to the time of his eventual departure. Eddie was insistent that he land in Norfolk, but that autumn 'Von Gröning told me that he didn't think any of these [landing sites in the Broads] could be done as they were too near London.'

The delays to his planned departure had one great advantage. By the middle of September, Eddie was more or less perfect at wireless transmission while, regardless of his damaged teeth and the effects of the acid fuse explosion, his proficiency in sabotage was improving. He carried out at least four explosions for visitors who passed through the *Dienststelle*. There was never a graduation test *per se*, just 'showings off' which culminated in target practice with a revolver and an acid fuse explosion in October.

That month von Gröning made a bet with a Major Meier, who was in charge of the security of factories in Nantes. 'His Boys', the Baron was certain, could evade the major's guards, deposit a package which represented an explosive charge and escape without detection. The guards were not told that this test was going to happen. They would be carrying live rounds when Eddie and friends broke in, so there was the danger that the saboteurs would be shot if apprehended. When Eddie successfully dropped the package without a hitch, he was delighted. 'I've got a lot of experience of getting into places,' he later told MI5.

Whenever he felt like practising with explosives, he made up the mixtures and essentially 'revised' on his own. 'I had one or two tests while I was there,' he would recall. 'For instance, a colonel came one day.' A large Mercedes turned up, apparently running out of petrol. The colonel, who Eddie remembered as a huge fellow, seemed to be a friend of von Gröning's. He had fought at Kharkov; Eddie was later informed that he had lost his life in the battle for Stalingrad. When he stayed over one evening, the Baron asked Eddie to prepare something special. 'We'll leave it to you what you do,' he said in his usual indulgent way, 'but do something good, do you see?'

During their evening meal, von Gröning nonchalantly asked his friend if he would like to see a home-made explosion. Indeed he would, said the colonel, and it should be set for two hours' time.

Using the colonel's watch as their guide, the others synchronised their own watches. Eddie would have to time the explosion to the dot of nine.

He was a little less confident than he appeared. 'It is a difficult job to time an explosion to within a minute,' he recalled. After dinner, they went out to the gardener's house and the colonel watched him prepare the timing device. Eddie took a great deal of care. In the absence of anything more suitable to blow up, he placed ten pounds of dynamite under a tree.

Just before nine, they were having drinks in the study and nervously awaiting the countdown. At the very moment the colonel announced, 'It's nine o'clock now,' there was a tremendous explosion. A number of the château's windows were blown in and the tree was nearly uprooted. Von Gröning took the cigar out of his mouth and somehow managed to refrain from patting his star agent on the head.

It was easy when you knew how, Eddie thought, while the dumbfounded colonel kept repeating, '*Mensch unde genau auf die Sekunde*' ('You got it to the exact second!'). The achievement was all the more astonishing because it had only been triggered by a small pocket watch, but it added greatly to Eddie's reputation.

That autumn, when it became clear that agent Fritzchen was about to leave Occupied France, British Intelligence began carefully preparing for his arrival. Indeed, the search for 'Agent X' – as Eddie was known at the time – started in earnest on Thursday, 1 October 1942. The whole enterprise was given the name Operation Nightcap.

From the radio traffic in France, MI5 was able to build up a reasonable picture of their quarry, for progress reports on his training were being picked up the whole time. Agent X was most likely British and 'probably from Jersey, Channel Islands', under thirty and about six feet tall. Given the accident during his training, they knew his canine teeth – 'if not more' – had been replaced by false ones. They knew he would also be carrying one or more false papers, though some might be in his real name. As for his equipment, he would bury it when he landed and most likely would be supplied with a wireless set. Other things to look out for when he was apprehended would be an address in Portugal (a postbox for him to write to), chemicals for secret writing and maps or guides to London.

Because Agent X was a native, it was probable that he might slip into the undergrowth, if not the underworld. 'We quite realise that our plans do not offer more than a 40% chance of finding our man if he keeps his head and plays his part well,' Dick White, the head of MI5's B Division – which dealt with counter-espionage – wrote in a round-robin letter distributed to all liaison staff and other agencies – particularly Home Forces – on 2 October. The problem was that if they were *too* alert, that might also create problems. They didn't want Eddie – and by extension, his Abwehr masters – to realise that they were breaking the German codes. If they formed a reception committee when he landed and this was reported back to the Germans – perhaps by Eddie himself at a later date – they would be aware that the British had cracked the Enigma code.

'In view of the secrecy attached to the search you should discuss with the Chief Constable the best cover story for the police,' White wrote as part of the standing instructions to deal with Agent X's apprehension. 'The public must not be told, even when Identity Cards are being asked for, that a parachute agent is being looked for.'

The Germans' dithering over his eventual landing site meant their net would have to be cast widely. It was unlikely that the Abwehr would announce which flight Fritzchen would come in on. An MI5 representative, Colonel Stafford, would have access to Fighter Command's operations room at Stanmore so that he could track all incoming aircraft. There he would identify which aircraft were the most likely to carry 'Agent X'. MI6 would also be alerted from radio intercepts at Bletchley Park as to which flights seemed likely to carry the potential saboteur.

When it was clear the landing had taken place, each of the Regional Security Liaison Officers – MI5's contacts with the local authorities – would get in touch with the local Chief Constable, to whom the full story would be told – save one detail. They would simply say that intelligence had come from abroad 'which we consider to be very reliable'.

From October onwards, all across Whitehall, security officials were alert for the arrival of Eddie Chapman. Their wait was almost as frustrating as it was for the man himself. Without any explanation, all traces of Agent X dried up across the airwaves. In the six weeks from 24 October to 7 December there was not one mention of him in the Abwehr's radio traffic. 'The lack of any references to Fritzchen during November suggests that his prolonged training was actually over by the end of October,' one report later surmised, 'and that he spent his last month or six weeks waiting about doing nothing.'

★   ★   ★

For Eddie Chapman, as the end of October approached and the nights were drawing in, there was still little sign of any impending exit. 'During my training, dates had been fixed several times for my departure,' he said. 'But for some reason they had always been postponed.' Eddie was fuming. His own movements were even more restricted and there were no further trips away. Most of the month was taken up with perfecting his wireless operations and obtaining further equipment, such as a crash helmet and boots. What he didn't realise at the time was that in routine radio traffic with Paris, von Gröning had pronounced Eddie 'spiritually and physically undoubtedly absolutely fit' and that any further delays would be damaging.

Unaware of this, Eddie continued with a constant litany of complaints. 'I got very jumpy waiting for the start,' he said. When his departure dates were repeatedly cancelled with no explanation, Eddie's frustration was so great that he even volunteered to fight on the Eastern Front.

Von Gröning did his best to calm him down, explaining that the Luftwaffe didn't have enough planes of the type needed for him to make a safe parachute drop. Eddie's practice drops had been made from regular bombers but these were deemed too noisy for the real drop. Moreover, because two previous agents had smashed their ankles after falling from bombers, the Luftwaffe was insistent that higher flying, dedicated parachute planes had to be made available.

By this time, the Luftwaffe's failings – 'Owing to a change in the balance of air warfare' as MI5 reported it – meant that other methods of exfiltration were being considered. The possibility was discussed of dropping Eddie by *Schnellboot* – a fast torpedo boat that could evade the Royal Navy's defences – and landing him by rubber dinghy as many other agents had done. Another suggestion was that a U-boat would drop him off in Eire, after which he would make his way to the mainland as an Irish citizen. Walther Thomas told him he was about to be smuggled over with some 'de Gaulle Frenchmen'.* None of these suggestions came to fruition.

By the end of October, there had been encouraging signs that Eddie really might be leaving at last. All around La Bretonnaire there was a spate of intense activity. His 'laboratory' in the gardener's house was dismantled and the equipment put into boxes for storage. A new selection of British ordnance seized after the abortive raid on Dieppe was made available to him. But by the start of November all that had happened was that von Gröning told Eddie he was to be measured for a uniform. No reason was given. Three days later the outfit of an under-officer arrived at the château. It fitted him perfectly when he tried it on in his quarters. 'The uniform was the usual field-green with gold trimmings around the collar,' Eddie recalled. The ever paternal Baron pronounced that he looked smarter than soldiers of the SS. There was a yellow armband with a swastika on it and a belt for an automatic pistol holder.

After the French domestic staff left, Eddie practised saluting with Walther Thomas, the cause of much amusement for the Boys. Two of them – Wolfgang and another Hans – were out running an errand in Nantes at the time. Eddie, resplendent in his new uniform, pretended to be a military policeman on their return. '*Ausweis bitte*,' ('Pass please') he said sharply as their staff car

---

*The creation of escape routes from Occupied Europe for Allied personnel – mainly highly trained airmen who were difficult to replace once they had been shot down – became an important factor in the secret war. In London, a dedicated escape and evasion service known as MI9 was set up to help downed fliers escape and evade the enemy. By the end of 1942, the Abwehr had started to inveigle into Britain agents disguised as escaped prisoners of war. Thanks to the reading of Enigma, MI5 realised that these pipelines were being infiltrated. When the Nantes *stelle* reported to Berlin about using the Free French as cover, MI9 was asked to look through its records for any Chapmans who spoke foreign languages and might have already come from Paris through its existing pipeline.

pulled up at the entrance to La Bretonnaire. Neither of them recognised him and both were visibly quaking.

'Von Gröning and the rest were doubled up with laughter,' Eddie recalled. He nipped back to the château, changed into his civvies and, by the time he had entered the dining room, the pair were talking about how they had been searched. Eddie nonchalantly handed over their control papers. 'He was stunned,' he recalled of Wolfgang, 'and it was not until I had dressed myself up again for his benefit that he believed the story.'

But now, as he would later summarise, 'the events of the war had taken a new sensational course'.

★   ★   ★

As MI5 wondered what had happened to Agent X, finally there was good news for the Allies about the progress of the fighting. In the first few days of November, Rommel and the Afrika Korps were routed at El Alamein and, just over a thousand miles away along the North African coast, Anglo-American landings at Oran, Algiers and Casablanca were successfully executed. The writing was on the wall for the Vichy government. Both battles had been underpinned by the secret war.

Tactical deception – what Churchill referred to in the House of Commons as 'a marvellous system of camouflage' – had helped win the battle at El Alamein by deceiving Rommel that the Eighth Army's attack would be sprung from the south rather than the north. Strategic deception, the intricate laying of a false trail, fooled the Germans into thinking that Torch, as the landings in Vichy territory on 8 November were known, would take place further along the Mediterranean. The surprise was complete and von Gröning, among others, was full of praise.

After the landings, Eddie saw a remarkable transformation in his controller. He appeared at breakfast resplendent in the full uniform of a cavalry major. 'The arrogance of the Prussian was stamped upon his bearing,' Eddie recalled. 'He thundered out orders and they were obeyed with much heel-clicking and saluting.'

The Boys from Nantes were being mobilised. What Eddie termed a 'tremendous outburst' now followed for those unlucky enough to be living in France. On 10 November, it was officially announced that Vichy France was to be occupied by the Reich's forces. Here was the reason Eddie had disappeared from the airwaves. 'The Germans decided to seize the non-occupied zone of France,' he recalled. 'This interlude imposed a further delay on my often-deferred journey to England.'

There were, however, no explicit instructions about what they should do with *der Englander*. The Baron happened to be in Paris on the day of the announcement and sent word that he would return. He arrived in Nantes early that afternoon, annoyed to find that some of the others had already taken the big Mercedes. So von Gröning and Eddie had to make do with the smaller one, driven by Wolfgang. 'There was not too much room because they had to fill the back of the car with tins of petrol, food and a supply of automatic weapons,' Eddie remembered.

The roads were full of military traffic, vast convoys of tankers and flak artillery units. 'Some convoys were eight kilometres long with troop transports and guns all practically brand new and modern,' he later reported. Though this delayed them, they were still ahead of the occupying troops. Eddie was dressed in his uniform to make it seem he was a private in the Marines, while the others 'had all been rigged up in a motley collection of uniforms of various ranks and services'. Most impressive was von Gröning himself in his green cavalry major's uniform and medals. 'On we went, past rumbling Panzer tanks and grinding truckloads of troops,' Eddie recalled. The impression, he thought, was intended to overwhelm the French with a sense that there were 'vast numbers' of troops available to subdue them.

From Nantes, they travelled to Limoges where they stayed in one of the best hotels, requisitioned by German troops. After saluting fellow Wehrmacht officers, Eddie felt 'unreal and strange' – the sight of some Jews waiting for deportation made him realise the full horror of his own personal war. Later that day, a major from the Angers *Dienststelle* arrived along with a mob of hefty, hatchet-faced troops. After consulting the Baron, he addressed the whole company. They had, he said, a number of jobs to do that night. A list of a dozen suspected British sympathisers was handed out, along with their addresses. They would split into two groups then go out to search for their quarry. Suspects were to be stopped and arrested. They would be shot if they resisted. Von Gröning's party took one half, the Gestapo the other.

At eleven that night, Eddie and the Boys set off in an army lorry with an array of automatic weapons. Their first target was a female doctor's apartment where a Captain le Saffre was believed to live. When they arrived, Eddie coughed, hoping to alert their man.

The door was answered by a woman in a dressing gown. Von Gröning ordered the flat to be searched. They came across a terrified teenage girl, crying uncontrollably; Eddie recalled attempting to reassure her that all would be well. Her mother, thinking she was going to be shot or raped, suddenly blurted out: 'Captain le Saffre lives in the flat above.' They reached the upstairs apartment to find the lights on and a bedroom window open. It appeared somebody had indeed made a hasty escape.

Their next suspect, they found, had been dead for two years. They had hammered at the doors of his apartment before barging in to find a pair of terrified old ladies in night caps and gowns hiding under a bed. 'When von Gröning stormed into the room and asked where the captain was,' a later MI5 report remarks, 'for some time they were literally speechless with fright.'

They had sufficiently recovered by the time Eddie left, for one of them stuck her tongue out 'with all the virulence that only enraged spinsters can muster'.

Their third raid was rather more successful. The proprietor of a small hotel was at home and he was arrested. A number of other people were also taken in for questioning that night, but the overall result was hardly worth it – a handful of people who protested their innocence and against whom no incriminating evidence was ever found. On their way back to their hotel, the Baron released three of the prisoners, including a very frightened seventeen-year-old. 'Why should I send them to a concentration camp?' he asked.

In the morning they drove on towards the south-east, skirting the Massif Central and passing through Vienne, Corrèze, Lot and Aveyron before reaching Rodez. Eddie later remembered it as 'a lovely trip'; frost hung on trees amid the beautiful scenery of mountains and ravines.

The following day – Monday, 16 November – was Eddie's twenty-eighth birthday, for which he was given the best present of all: orders to return to Paris. 'My trip to England was at last decided upon,' he recalled, 'and I was to discuss the final arrangements with the experts.'

Back at the château the *Dienststelle* threw Eddie a special party. And after dinner, von Gröning gave him a special souvenir: a gold cigarette lighter, which Betty Chapman says Eddie used for many years afterwards. The next day, he travelled to the capital. There, at the house near the Bois de Boulogne used by the Germans as a 'wireless centre', he was reacquainted with his radio instructor, Maurice Schmidt.

Together, they worked on a final plan of action. Eddie would transmit only news of vital importance once he landed in England. By the third day, he would make his first contact, revealing where he had landed. Schmidt would call first: the German call sign would always remain the same, while Eddie's would change to keep British counter-intelligence confused. There would be pre-set times in the morning and in the afternoon for their transmissions, but they would, if necessary, listen at all times. After landing, Eddie would catch the first train to London, whereupon he would disappear into the underworld. He would contact an old criminal acquaintance and offer £5,000 to him – or anyone else who offered to help. The money would be handed to him by Walther Thomas just an hour before he left the Grand Hotel on the day of his departure.

Everything was placed in rubber-fibre packing inside a watertight case seized by the Germans after being dropped to the French resistance. His wireless set and sabotage materials were wrapped tightly in an oilskin money bag, in case he fell into water. Eddie was to carry no written information about his mission. Everything was to be carried in his head.

By early December, it was clear his departure was imminent. Back in Nantes, he was shown new reconnaissance photographs of the De Havilland plant in Hatfield and reminded that it would be his main target. A week before he left, Eddie was finally told he would be leaving soon, as was abundantly clear from the radio traffic being monitored at Bletchley Park. He started to become a little demob happy. In the run-up to Christmas, there was an air of carefree excitement at the Nantes *Dienststelle*. There were plans for grand celebrations: geese were being fattened, as was Bobby, by now a chubby and contented pig. 'When the day came and Bobby was slaughtered for a feast, Eddie refused to attend,' his widow attests. 'He was physically sick at the loss of his pet pig.'

That Sunday, 13 December, Eddie, von Gröning and Thomas drove to Paris just after two o'clock with their heavy luggage. They later visited the house by the Bois de Boulogne to go through the final arrangements. 'When I thought of the uncertainty ahead, doubt assailed me,' Eddie recalled. 'Would I be treated as a traitor in England or hanged as a spy?'

★ ★ ★

The first time Oberleutnant Schlichting of the Luftwaffe heard about his latest mission across *Der Kanal* was when his commanding officer called him into his office at Buc airfield one morning in the winter of 1942. The CO looked up and barked out an order which would puzzle both Schlichting and, later, his observer.

'Have you and Charlie got civilian clothes?'

The young pilot shook his head.

'All right, buy some at the Luftwaffe's expense,' the CO replied. 'You're both off to Paris.'

The commanding officer said nothing further, save that the crew should report to the Hotel Lutétia the next day. This, they knew, was the Paris headquarters of the Abwehr. As bidden, the pilot and his observer, Charlie Ischenger, reported to the hotel where it was clear they were expected. They were introduced to a person about whom they had only been told that he was a splendid fellow and liked dogs. 'He was,' Schlichting remembered, '*sehr sympathisch*, very friendly.'

The friendliness was reciprocated. Eddie Chapman remembered the pilot wore an Iron Cross and 'was a small, thickset young man of about twenty-eight, with steady blue eyes'. It transpired that he had been one of the first Germans to land on Guernsey in July 1940. The other members of the crew were introduced as Charlie and Franz. The former, also a lieutenant, was the observer (or navigator), 'a blond youngster of nineteen, tall and extremely shy'. The radio operator, Franz, was another youngster of just eighteen.

The crew announced that they would fly towards the eastern coast of England and land Eddie as near as possible to Thetford in Norfolk. The market town was easy to reach by air after coming in from the sea over the Wash. The fenlands where he would land were relatively unpopulated and easily accessible to London by land and rail. From his various pre-war activities, Eddie also knew the area well. There was an extra advantage, the pilot added. They could also take part in a raid on Cambridge that was being planned for a couple of days' time. Thus Eddie's flight would automatically be hidden. The crew were extremely proud that this would be their fiftieth operational flight over Britain. Hitting this half-century meant they would get a week's special leave on their return.

Later that Monday afternoon, Eddie was taken out to the airport. His departure was expected some time the following evening or early on Wednesday morning. He busied himself learning how to pack his parachute and testing its integrity. It had been dyed dark brown for camouflage purposes. He was taken to the aircraft, a Junkers 88 bomber – with a curious refinement for its additional passenger. 'The only way to get out was for me to drop through the floor,' he recalled, 'which necessitated removing a machine gun and fixing a hinge door over the aperture.'

Eddie would spend the journey to England on his stomach with the dead weight of fifty pounds of parachute and supplies atop him. When told it was time to drop, he would simply press the lever next to him and drop head first. 'The hole itself was small and it was only by dint of much wriggling and squirming that I could get through it at all.'

With his departure imminent, there was an end-of-term sense of levity. On their return to Paris, Stefan von Gröning took Eddie and the Boys out that Monday evening to Poccardi's on the Boulevard des Italiens. The Baron was as effusive as ever as the chianti and champagne flowed. Over endless toasts, his controller declared that Fritzchen would be 'sorely missed' and they were sorry for having had to restrict his freedom. However, it would all be worth it. On his return, he would be allowed a new life, and would be completely free to travel around Germany – although he would have to report to Berlin first.

The question of how Eddie would make his way back to Occupied Europe had hitherto only been vaguely discussed. A scheme had been planned, the Baron had hinted, but it was to be kept secret from the others. A U-boat, possibly. Failing that, he should take a boat bound for Portugal. He would go to a contact address in Lisbon where he would say '*Joli Albert*' to a Mr de Fonseca. This gentleman would put him in contact with his German colleagues by use of a portable radio set. In Eddie's slightly drunken state, it sounded almost plausible.

Despite his prodigious intake of alcohol the night before, Eddie felt fine on Tuesday morning. Later that afternoon a final ceremony was held, one destined to appeal to his ego. He was taken to the famous George Cinq Hotel on the eponymous avenue. They were shown up to a suite where, to his slight bemusement, Eddie was introduced to a 'tall impressive figure'. Sitting behind a desk was General Gerd von Rundstedt, the German commander in France. A true *grand seigneur* of the Wehrmacht, he too seemed a little perplexed. The General politely asked about Eddie's mission and then signed his 'exit' papers to leave France. 'Again, we "*heiled*",' Eddie recalled, 'and I was led from the room.'

★ ★ ★

That Agent X was to leave that Tuesday, 15 December was now fully expected by British Intelligence. The sense of immediacy was heightened as each successive radio report to Berlin about Fritzchen was decoded at Bletchley Park. At the start of December, a further minute had been circulated that a British national would shortly attempt to land either by plane or ship.

Even at this stage, however, a certain caution remained. There had been any number of false alarms to date and, as MI5 suspected, Eddie's actual departure would have to be 'conducted with some operation by the Luftwaffe'. In mid-October, for example, all the signs – from increased practice traffic to the tenor of communications between Paris and Berlin – had been that Agent X would be leaving. A phone call at three o'clock in the morning on Saturday,

17 October from the night duty officer at MI6 headquarters suggested he may have already left. Later that Saturday morning, however, it became clear that nobody had landed unexpectedly in the British Isles.

Then came the six-week hiatus when Eddie was absent from the airwaves. 'For weeks past there have been practically no German aircraft over this country during the hours of darkness,' a review for MI5 found, 'and [on] only two occasions have German aircraft crossed the coast between sunset and sunrise.'

But by the middle of December, it was clear that something was afoot. Most significant was a passing reference in the radio traffic to a curious detail – a suicide pill, which Agent X would be expected to bring with him to Britain.

That same Tuesday evening, Eddie was travelling to the aerodrome for the last time. Both von Gröning and Thomas were in high spirits, singing along to the car radio. He was amused that although the Germans didn't know the lyrics to 'I've got a girl in Kalamazoo', it didn't stop them joining in. And then came Eddie's favourite, 'Lili Marlene'. Often he became wistful when he heard it, as indeed he did now, contemplating the dangers that would face him in the next few hours.

An hour before they had left the hotel, Eddie was handed his English money by Walther Thomas, who had deliberately left the wrapping band on. (When Eddie unpacked his money on his return, it still bore the bands of the Deutsche Bank with the *Dienststelle* markings on them.) 'I have got rather an embarrassing thing to do,' said Thomas, somewhat sheepishly. 'For every agent, we do it, but it is only a matter of form.'

Eddie was mystified.

'I hope you won't be insulted. I want to see whether you have any French tickets or anything in your clothes which could be picked up.'

Thomas looked Eddie directly in the eye. 'You don't mind?'

'No, of course not.'

Thankfully, Eddie was prepared. One evening in the Nantes château, he had gone up to the Funk Room alone where he had found some papers about the codes and frequencies of the Abwehr's control stations. He made a note of them on a scrap of paper along with names of visitors to the *Stelle*, including the

Gaullists and Bretons. 'He put it in the back of his tie,' Betty Chapman says. 'Eddie couldn't stitch anything, he couldn't stitch a button on – but he managed it.' Luckily, Eddie had been half expecting this search, so he had thrown the rest of his notes away, making a determined effort to remember all the details. 'It was rather lucky he told me,' Eddie later told MI5. 'If he had come in and searched me, he would have definitely found the stuff.'

When they arrived at the aerodrome, the Baron handed over a small brown tablet. 'Fritz, I hate to have to give you this,' he said solemnly. 'It is poison. You know if anything happens and you are caught it is better to end it quickly than be tortured.'

Eddie nodded quietly. He placed the tablet in the turn-up of his trousers. It was never mentioned again.

The full background to this curious aspect of his departure only came from British Intelligence and a rash of decrypted signals in the days immediately before his departure. Earlier that week, the Nantes *Stelle* had checked with Paris whether Eddie should be supplied with the poison tablets, 'in which case they would have to be obtained with all speed'. Paris replied that they could not obtain them so quickly, so if Fritzchen left, he would have to go without them. How quickly they were subsequently obtained is not elaborated in the files, but MI5 was not taking any chances. One official warned, 'On arrest, he should therefore immediately be searched.'

Eddie's final hours in France passed quickly. At six o'clock that evening, the colonel in charge of the airbase announced that the weather reports seemed favourable. It was neither too cloudy nor too windy. He showed Eddie a chart which revealed that at around two o'clock the next morning, the moon would be at just the right angle to illuminate his descent over eastern England. About 9 p.m., the colonel brought in an aerial photo of the Hatfield factory and discussed how best Eddie could blow it up. Around 10 p.m., Eddie was kitted in the English lounge suit that he had last worn in Jersey. He wore an overall to protect it and bandaged his knees to prepare for the landing. His money belt was strapped around his waist and he was handed a protective helmet. As a final precaution, he loaded his revolver.

Eddie desperately needed a drink. Having had no alcohol all day, he savoured the cognac he was handed. Shortly thereafter, the crew arrived and he hoped he appeared as calm and nonchalant as they appeared to be. 'On the whole he was pretty calm,' Schlichting recalled of Eddie's last few hours at the aerodrome. 'Naturally he was a bit worried about jumping with a parachute.' According to the pilot, Fritzchen now wanted to be dropped over Wisbech, near to Cambridge, so he could catch the train to London. 'He was so sure of himself,' Schlichting remembered.

In truth, Eddie was very nervous. As he was getting ready, he had felt his stomach tighten. He experienced some of the excitement he had felt when he'd gone out on pre-war safebreaking jobs. 'If you have enough guts, you can do anything you want,' he kept repeating to himself. In a short while, an expert fitted his parachute pack, which seemed a lot heavier than those used on his practice jumps. They walked together across the tarmac apron towards the ear-splitting roar of the bombers preparing for their mission. These were the cover aircraft that would perform the bombing raid over Cambridge. 'A smell of burned petrol and exhaust fumes filled the air,' Eddie recalled.

At the foot of the aircraft steps, both Thomas and von Gröning shook hands with him, wishing him all the best. Eddie was soon inside the Junkers, testing the hinge of his escape hatch door as well as his oxygen supply and the communications link. Through the headset he suddenly heard the pilot yell '*Können sie mich hören?*' ('Can you hear me?')

'*Jawohl*,' he shouted back.

And with a '*Gut! Gemütliche Reise*' ('Well! Comfortable journey') the engines were revved. Within a matter of seconds, they were airborne.

The Junkers headed out across the coast of France, up towards the Hook of Holland, arcing as far from London as it possibly could. 'Lying flat on my belly,' Eddie recalled, 'I could see nothing of what was happening in the nose of the plane where the pilot and the navigator sat.' In fact he was facing aft, crammed into a small, improvised alcove. All he could make out were the receding lights through a crack in the door hinge. Just above him was the machine gun operator – and a foot away, the machine gun itself. He was weighed down by his parachute. Six inches from his head were instruments and more were squeezed against his left side. To his right was ammunition which he prayed would not be hit by British nightfighters.

Over the engine noise, Eddie could hear the pilot and navigator discussing their altitude and speed. In the inky darkness below there were occasional pinpricks of light. Soon they were over the Channel. Eddie could make out the reflections of foam in the water. He started to feel the cold as they climbed in altitude and rubbed his legs together to stop cramp. After that he became aware of the beams of many hundreds of searchlights and little 'coloured balls' floating upwards. He realised soon enough that these were actually flak.

A tap to his head and he turned to make out the wireless operator splaying out the fingers of both hands: ten minutes. Another tap would be his cue to remove the oxygen mask and put on his crash helmet for landing. But he soon became aware of more frantic signals. At first Eddie couldn't understand what was happening. It seemed the crew had forgotten to tie the lash line of the parachute to automatically pull it open when he dropped away. 'In another few moments I should have pulled the lever and fallen to my death,' he recalled.

Oberleutnant Schlichting, it seemed, was using radio beams to find his way towards Harwich. From the conversation with his navigator, it appeared those signals had been blocked by British jamming somewhere over the North Sea. He took the plane down from 20,000 feet to try to make out the outline of the coast below. Far to the south was a ring of searchlights surrounding London. After correcting his course slightly, the pilot was certain he was on track. Suddenly, the observer's voice came over the intercom. '*Achtung! Achtung! Nachtjäger!*'

The plane yawed violently as Oberleutnant Schlichting headed for the nearest cloud bank. 'Charlie, Fritzchen has to go,' the pilot said to his navigator.

Anxious moments passed. It was now obvious Schlichting had no idea where he was. In desperation, Eddie pulled the despatch lever and started to fall. For a split second, his stomach lurched, then there was utter darkness. To his horror, Eddie was stuck in the hatch. 'I can't get out!' he screamed in German.

Above him, the pilot turned around and shouted to the wireless operator. 'For God's sake, push him out.'

Eddie was now hanging upside down, facing away from the direction of flight, and with a crackling noise in his ears, starting to feel sick. Jammed in by the weight of his equipment, he couldn't move, despite all his frantic wriggling. Suddenly he felt a good hard kick to his back and soon he was falling freely. Before he could gather his senses, he disappeared into the inky darkness below.

Catapulted through the darkened sky, Eddie could make out the swastikaed tail of the Junkers. Then he became aware of noise and fury closing in on them: the nightfighter was firing at the Junkers. For a terrible moment, he was convinced it was heading directly towards him. Would they crash into each other? And as he watched in horrified fascination, he thought that this would be the final indignity – to die having come so near to home.

CHAPTER FIVE

Hendon Calling

'ZIGZAG is himself a most absorbing person. Reckless and impetuous, moody and sentimental, ZIGZAG becomes on acquaintance an extraordinarily likeable character. It is difficult for anyone who has been associated with him for any continuous period to describe him in an unbiased and dispassionate way. Those who have been with him for any length of time will confirm that it was difficult to credit that the man had a despicable past. His crimes of burglary and fraud, his association with "moral degenerates", and his description as a "dangerous criminal" by Scotland Yard, were difficult to reconcile with his more recent behaviour.'

– From the summary of Eddie Chapman's MI5 case notes, as recorded after intense interrogations, February 1943

Everything was warmer than he'd expected it to be. For a terrible moment, Eddie Chapman wondered if the Germans had double-crossed him and landed him in France. His disorientation had started the moment he had been kicked out of the Junkers. And when he thought about it – then, and in later years – it all came back as an incessant, incoherent rush of memories, exactly akin to the experience of plummeting from the sky. Free falling was the best way of describing what had happened to him.

The parachute descent had been painful, and not just because of the kick in the back that had pushed him on his way. The oxygen mask was faulty and Eddie had bled all over his jacket and shirt. When the parachute opened, he had steadied himself, the noise had dissipated and he was soon emerging from a cloud. At one point, he wondered if he would ever make landfall, so serene was his descent.

All around him was an unearthly glow from the light of the moon and the stars. Eddie remembered looking at his watch and noting it was ten past two. He seemed to be floating and the clouds far below him looked like waves. Suddenly, another darkly paranoid thought struck him: what if he had been dropped over the sea? Moments later, he was engulfed in the shadowy darkness below the clouds. He failed to make out anything below but the countryside was in complete blackout. All at once, he became aware of a rooftop, which he just about managed to evade before landing heavily in a ploughed field. He was so surprised he wasn't prepared for the impact.

Bang! Eddie hit the ground with full force, and before he could react he was on his back, staring up at the sky. Within moments, he removed his harness and went in search of the house over which he had sailed. It turned out to be an abandoned cottage. By retracing his steps, Eddie thought he would be able to find his discarded parachute with ease. He couldn't. It took him another quarter of an hour to locate it. He took off his overalls and removed any tell-tale signs that he had fallen from the sky. As he had been trained, Eddie buried the whole lot – chute, boots and overalls – in mud close by a stream, near what he thought was a distinctive tree.

By now, his eyes had adapted to the comforting velvet of darkness. All was murky apart from the distant flak and the noise of the receding remnants of the German air raid in the distance. 'There was not a glimmer of light anywhere,' he would recall. 'The landscape was bare as a Siberian night except for that one, small, ruined house.'

And that was when he started to wonder if it wasn't all a trick. The weather seemed warmer than he had ever remembered night-time in the middle of the English winter. The conversation with Stefan von Gröning after his night drop over Nantes the previous summer continued to weigh on his mind. Had they dropped him over occupied territory to test whether he would go ahead with the mission?

Eddie had no idea where he was. It took him some time to walk through the muddy fields towards the farmhouse, stumbling through puddles of water and mud. Eventually, he climbed over a wall and shone his torch through the front door – he could make out a coat rack, an umbrella stand, and stairs. But what clinched it was what he spotted next. 'I followed the torch beam with my eyes – there was a telephone, and there, on the little table beside it, lay a British telephone book! Yes, I was really home.'

What Eddie did not appreciate at the time was just how much had gone on behind the scenes to prepare for his arrival. Operation Nightcap had been sprung and would soon successfully trap its intended target. But now in the early hours of that Thursday morning, as he shared a cup of tea with the farmer and his wife, everything had a strange, dreamlike quality. After the arrival of the local policemen came the revelation about the suicide pill. It cast a peculiar pall over the proceedings.

'Are there any more?' one of the sergeants asked.

'You'd better have a look.'

Eddie mentioned that there were some other 'items' which had been left behind in the field. Mr Convine and the other sergeant, George Hutchings, went out to find them. The remaining police-man made another call – this time to divisional headquarters in Ely. Who was he, exactly? they wanted to know. Eddie took great care to hide both his real purpose and his true identity. Unprompted, he handed over his wallet, which revealed something curious. There were two identity cards, one identifying him as George Clarke of The Grove, Hammersmith, the other as Morgan O'Brien, an Irish citizen, an electrical engineer of County Kildare. Even to the sergeant's untrained eyes, both documents looked forged. Was George Clarke his real name the policeman wanted to know. The visitor shook his head and smiled. Why, then, did he have two identity cards?

'They were given to me before I left,' was all Eddie would say.

For now, the policeman was completely baffled. The visitor continued to engage Mrs Convine in small talk, seemingly oblivious to the incriminating nature of the evidence around him. The sergeant continued to rifle through the wallet. There were two Borough of Torquay deckchair tickets, a Torquay Golf Club voucher and a YMCA hostel ticket from earlier in the summer. There was also a love letter from a girl, written on notepaper headed 'The Royal Yacht Hotel, St Helier'. The sergeant quickly scanned its contents. From the plaintive tone of her words, he felt certain its addressee had been in prison.

Mr Convine and Sergeant Hutchings returned from the fields with some overalls and a parachute. It was nearing 4 a.m. as a police car pulled up outside the farm. A pair of uniformed officers from Ely now took over. When they asked the airman for his name, Eddie cheerfully responded: 'George Clarke will do for now.'

Eddie gave a friendly cheerio to the Convines as he was taken away. That was the last they ever expected to see of him, and, as he got into the car, they were given a strict warning not to mention a word of this to anyone. The two sergeants, too, were sworn to secrecy.

On that December morning, Eddie was taken to divisional police headquarters in Ely where he was offered breakfast and then left alone in a holding cell. He was aware of whispered conversations all around him and the station seemed to be buzzing with activity. Eddie sat back and fell asleep. A couple of hours later, a major and a lieutenant from Field Security arrived in another darkened staff car. They took him with them as the sun rose over the fens. Little was said – Eddie was quite exhausted – as the car headed south towards the outskirts of the capital.

'The drive down to London was for me unforgettable,' Eddie would later remember. 'Convoys of army vehicles, uniforms of all the free nations, the dear familiar scene of London's hustle and bustle.' More than the sights, though, it was the people – and the variegated uniforms of the British and American servicemen – which made the most distinct impression. 'Something seemed to have happened to them,' Eddie wrote. 'Everyone appeared to be on friendly terms. The common threat of war somehow had welded them together.'

Though parts of the city had been badly bombed, it wasn't as bad as he feared. London was always being portrayed to the German people as a devastated wasteland, and, more significantly, 'even their own secret service believed this'. The unmarked car passed through the West End, and by 7 a.m. they had arrived at a secure holding centre located at an old school in Wandsworth.

That Thursday morning, Eddie was introduced to a policeman whom he would come to know very well in the years ahead. Chief Inspector Leonard Burt, a future Commander of Special Branch, liaised with MI5, the British Security Service, and now, in the company of an army intelligence officer, led the questioning of this latest suspected saboteur. 'Burt is a quiet man from Wiltshire,' Eddie recalled. 'I believe his shrewd blue eyes miss nothing. He laughs quietly, but the brain behind the laugh still ticks.'*

Eddie came clean. He told them that he had a criminal record but made it abundantly clear that he had been working for His Majesty the King all along. 'I'm not a traitor,' he added as nonchalantly as he could. 'There are several charges outstanding against me. If they can be dropped, I'm certain I can be of some value as an agent.'

Burt reacted as though he heard this sort of thing every day and made a few notes. 'You must be tired,' was all he said. 'We're going to take you where you can get a good night's rest.'

Eddie wasn't sure if Burt was being sarcastic or not. Outside the school, a guard detail was waiting alongside a Black Maria with blacked-out windows. The authorities were taking great care to make sure he wouldn't know where he was being taken. As Eddie was being escorted outside under cover of a blanket, one of the guards looked extremely puzzled. Chief Inspector Burt asked him why.

'I'm sure that fellow was in my Guards unit,' he said.

The Black Maria sped off into the distance, its occupant wondering what would happen next – and what his fate might be.

---

*Len Burt was famously described as the 'most formidable sleuth in England'. Close colleagues remarked that if you had twenty minutes' conversation with him, it wouldn't be until a few weeks later that it became clear what he had really wanted to know. Over the next few years, Eddie would have many dealings with Burt and formed a very high opinion of him. He noted that Burt's questions were always to the point and loaded. 'Not for him the bullying Gestapo technique,' Eddie would later write. 'He is rather like a fine chess player probing out the weaknesses of his opponent.'

It was the smell that brought it all back. Eddie had been inside more jails than he cared to remember, but here everything seemed antiseptic and peculiarly different. He could sense that there were other people around. Yet there were strange echoes and other, disconcerting noises from near and afar. In time, Eddie was pretty certain he could make out the sounds of distant horns, like boats at sea perhaps, or riverboats and tugs.

Nothing was quite as it seemed. There was something unnerving about this place.

After arriving, Eddie had been huddled under blankets out of the Black Maria. As they escorted him down a long corridor, the guards said nothing. There was no welcome, no papers to sign, no formal recognition that he was now in the custody of the British security authorities. The guards had simply marched him into an inter-rogation room where the hostility was apparent straight away.

Eddie was wheeled to attention and came to a halt, a few feet short of the raised platform on which his jailers were sitting. Three of them, unsmiling. He'd seen their sort before. The uniforms might vary, Eddie thought, but the expressions rarely did. In the middle was the man in charge, wearing a monocle and the two pips of a captain. The man stared down at him as though he had trodden in something unpleasant, then consulted a buff-coloured folder whose contents he took care to hide from view. When he spoke, he almost sneered.

'So you are Chapman,' he said, slowly and deliberately.

Eddie and the captain stared at each other. They hated each other on sight. It was a matter of honour that neither of them would blink or react first.

'Well, now you are here, you'd better behave,' he added. 'If you get tough, we can get tough.'

Eddie's face flushed with anger. He'd been up half the night and already he'd had enough of this particular game of soldiers. 'Listen, I came over here with the best of intentions. I don't like being stuck in prison. Either I am going to work for you or not, but I am not going to stay in prison.'

The captain smiled and added sarcastically, 'All in good time, all in good time.' He beckoned to two of the guard detail and said, 'Take him away and make him comfortable.'

After this terse exchange, Eddie was taken to a freezing cell somewhere along that elongated corridor. When the door clanged shut, he became aware that there was neither a mattress nor a bed frame, only a couple of tattered old blankets in the corner. It was clear that he was passing through the eye of the needle of British Intelligence.

At the time he had no idea, but he was being held in a former lunatic asylum. Perhaps it was apt that Eddie was first incarcerated where the shell-shocked and mentally ill had been held. Within a few hours, he would feel as though he was losing his sanity, and that was exactly what the British authorities had been aiming for. In psychological war, Eddie had clearly lost the first round. Soon enough, he was exhausted and slumped down onto the floor, falling into a dreamless sleep.

The sneering captain with the monocle was a former Indian policeman called Robin Stephens. Like so many who made singular contributions to the secret war, 'Tin Eye' Stephens – so named for that trademark monocle – had arrived here by accident. 'A larger than life character and even within MI5 he was considered something of an extroverted oddball,' one official historian of MI5's interrogations has written.

Stephens' fiefdom was a large, ugly Victorian pile, set apart in its own wooded grounds on Ham Common, in the well-appointed London suburb of Richmond. Latchmere House was the filter through which all suspected saboteurs and enemy agents had to pass. Known officially as Camp 020, security was rigidly maintained. Its name had been deliberately omitted from a list of camps submitted by the British government to the International Red Cross.

Once a suspected spy had arrived, he or she was stripped and searched, handed a uniform and placed in a cell alone. Captain Stephens surveyed the steady stream of subjects who came under his charge with a withering disdain. Add to that a bilious distaste for anyone not English and 'Tin Eye' was ideally suited to terrifying treacherous foreigners. The apprehension of Eddie Chapman was unusual for the fact that he was English. Given Stephens' xenophobia, it is a strange irony that he himself was half German; he insisted on being addressed by his formal title as Commandant of the Camp.

Thanks to the release of both Stephens' war diary and the individual case histories on which he worked, we now have a complete picture of what took place inside Latchmere House. His reports are masterly examples of political incorrectness. Consider the following random samples – 'both men were abnormally intelligent for Icelanders, but still not over-intelligent'; 'an odious type of Hun'. By comparison, Stephens soon came to exhibit an almost grudging admiration for his latest charge. 'The Germans came to love Chapman, but although he went cynically through all the forms, he did not reciprocate that feeling,' he wrote in a later summary. 'Chapman loved himself, loved adventure and loved his country, probably in that order.'

The Commandant was rather liked by his female staff for his courteousness and sense of humour. He was instrumental in making sure that particular attention was lavished on the staff mess, with the provision of fine wines and almost *cordon bleu* cooking. 'Tin Eye' liked the finer things in life. He had worked in various military outposts around the British Empire and was fluent in seven languages. Thanks to the old boy network – the intelligence services were well stocked with former colonial policemen – Stephens had been appointed an interrogator for MI5. At the outbreak of war, its interrogation branch was housed at the Oratory School on the Brompton Road. Here Stephens made a name for himself by haranguing British fascists and various internees whom he classed as 'treacherous, shabby nonentities' in his post-war history.

But the Oratory could only ever be a temporary measure. At the start of July 1940, 'Tin Eye' and a handful of staff moved to Latchmere House and it was here, against the backdrop of one of the capital's more attractive commons, that he would establish his name in the shadowy world of wartime intelligence.

Eddie Chapman's treatment was neither unusual nor unique. The solitude within Latchmere House was deliberate and disconcerting. Even the guards wore tennis shoes to mask the noise of their passing along the corridors. Unknown to its prisoners, bugging devices had been installed throughout an annexe of more than thirty cells. Stephens' officials were adamant that no physical intimidation should ever take place. ('Violence is taboo,' he would write, 'for not only does it produce answers to please, but it lowers the standard of information.')

None of the internees would ever meet any of their fellow inmates and, if they had landed in pairs, great care was taken to separate them. The aim was to establish guilt quickly and extract as much information as possible, leading to a swift confession. The austerity of the surroundings was deliberately designed to break the suspect.

'No chivalry. No gossip. No cigarettes . . .' Stephens would write. 'Figuratively, a spy in war should be at the points of a bayonet.'

That was exactly the sort of approach which riled Eddie. 'He would often go eyeball to eyeball,' Betty Chapman says. 'He would give as good as he got, regardless of the consequences.' At the end of 1942, those consequences were great. On this first morning of his capture, Eddie had no idea where he was or whether he might end up being shot as a traitor.

When they came for him again early on the Friday morning, Eddie was taken to a smaller room where he was quizzed relentlessly for hours. Often Captain Stephens was joined by one or more of his subordinates. After the interminable questions, Eddie later wrote, 'My head ached. I was exhausted.' They dissected the minutiae of his life story in exhausting detail: his army career; his criminal past; his family, friends and associates. And they seemed particularly interested in his activities after he had left Jersey the previous April.

Eddie recalled: 'What seemed to me to be useless information was demanded and given.' Detail after detail was asked and double-checked, a jigsaw whose outline was never clear – especially not to him. How had he been taken to the château? How many guards? What were their names? Where had he met them? And then his journeys around the Reich. Where did the equipment come from? On and on they went, his relief only coming when they took him back to his cell where he could fall into an exhausted slumber.

Eddie's resilience under examination was astonishing. It convinced his MI5 interrogators of one thing: if the tables were turned, he wouldn't crack under the pressure, not least when he returned to Occupied Europe. Then again, if he could survive a

German prison and outfox the Wehrmacht, his interrogation on Ham Common was going to be easy. After a couple of good nights' rest and the comfort of cooked English breakfasts, some of the spirit of the old Eddie Chapman returned. He started to bridle at his handling.

'I want a pardon and I want some money,' Eddie said.

The anger in Captain Stephens' eyes was plain to see. Eddie felt his own indignation rising. With an overwhelming sense that he should be treated better, he had made up his mind that if he was not out of this place by Christmas – in less than a week – he would rescind his offer to work for the British. Now it was Eddie's turn to look 'Tin Eye' straight in the monocle.

'I made an offer to the British government,' he said. 'If I am not out of here by tomorrow, forget it. Stick me on trial.'

'Don't threaten us.'

According to his widow, Eddie then threatened to go on hunger strike. 'He said he would starve himself to death if they didn't get him out of there,' Betty recalls. 'I think he convinced them that he'd have enough information for them to free him. Part of the fact was that he didn't want to die.'

Throughout all his interviews, 'Tin Eye' never let on that he and his sidekicks were being guided by decrypted progress reports of agent Fritzchen's Abwehr training. This priceless hoard allowed them to gauge the extent of Eddie's honesty by setting him traps into which he might unwittingly stumble. After four lengthy sessions, which lasted until the following Monday, it became clear that Eddie Chapman was essentially telling the truth.

Whether discussing his pre-war criminal activities (which they knew all about thanks to Scotland Yard) or what he had been doing in occupied territory (most details of which were known courtesy of Bletchley Park), Stephens and his colleagues had the satisfaction of knowing that Eddie was essentially levelling with them. Yet for all his ability to think on his feet, Eddie's interrogators found that he had a terrible grasp of continuity. Though he would astonish them with his ability to recall inconsequential details about people and places from years before, he repeatedly got dates and times out of sequence. 'A mass of information is being obtained from Chapman,' Stephens reported to his superiors. But he acknowledged that it was 'quite impossible to set all this out in logical order'.

At some point, Eddie seems to have realised it, too. Aware that he sounded confused, he laid his cards on the table that weekend by writing a handwritten note which he addressed to 'Mon Commandant'. 'My mind is such a frenzied mass of names, formulas, descriptions, places, times, explosions, radio telegraphy and parachute jumping,' he wrote, adding that 'dates, names, times are all jumbled up in my head'. Pleading nervous exhaustion, he made it clear he was doing his best to help them.

At this, Captain Stephens would doubtless have smiled with grim satisfaction. They knew more about Eddie Chapman than they would ever let on. And they were taking deliberate steps to keep it that way.

Much of Eddie's agitation stemmed from the fact that he desperately needed to make radio contact with his German controllers. If they didn't hear from him by that first weekend, the Abwehr would assume that agent Fritzchen had either been killed or captured. When British radio experts examined the transmitter he had brought with him, they were surprised. From the serial numbers, they determined it had originally been dropped into France with an MI6 agent whose fate they had never been able to ascertain. The Security Service realised that they would have to move fast to convince Eddie's Abwehr controllers that he was doing their bidding. 'Speed was [a] necessity,' Sir John Masterman, the chairman of the Double Cross Committee, would later write. 'Consequently, a quick decision had to be made and [he] was put on the air at once.'

Eddie was allowed out on Friday evening to send his first contact signal under cover of darkness. He was hidden inside an abandoned school near Latchmere House where he quickly tapped out a sample of the Morse he had learned so assiduously: 'Landed two miles north of Ely and buried gear. Took train next day with transmitter to London and later contacted friends. All OK. Fritz.'

In Eddie's later recollection, his intelligence handlers were impressed with his skill. They asked him all about his transmissions and what he had learned about the basics of cryptography. The simple code he was supposed to use to encrypt his messages was based on the word Constantinople. 'My first one was much too simple,' he recalled. 'Later, I was to be given another which I think could only have been solved after a long period.'

From the following week, Eddie was allowed to tap out cleverly doctored information over the airwaves to his German controllers. Each day, he was expected to send short contact messages at a prearranged time and on a prearranged frequency (all of which were known to the Radio Security Service (RSS)). In the meantime, he gave his captors as much information as he could remember on how the various *Abwehrstellen* in Paris, Nantes and Bordeaux stayed in radio contact with each other. Eddie could not recall all the frequencies – he had originally written them down – which were used in France. He would, he said, be able to work them out if he was shown similar transmitters to the ones he had been practising with.

His own outgoing transmissions were monitored by the RSS. Its interception staff had the satisfaction of knowing that Fritzchen's signal had been received loud and clear. 'Please send details of landing area,' came one reply early the next week. Already, the Germans were checking up on him. Over the next few days he would start assembling a fictional story about hiding out in an abandoned building (the one over which he had parachuted just before landing) and taking a train into London early that first morning of his return home.

So far as Eddie's radio transmissions were concerned, British Intelligence was in a double bind. First, MI5 didn't want Eddie to realise that for many months it had been monitoring his radio practice. Second, despite his extensive radio training, Eddie had considerable trouble making direct contact with any of the Abwehr radio stations in France. He was forced to transmit 'blind', hoping that alert Abwehr radio operators somewhere on the Continent might hear him. Though Eddie could hear his Nantes cronies coming through 'in good strength', they didn't seem to be able to hear him. 'I replied with a series of interrupting dits, then gave my call sign,' he wrote of one attempted conversation over the airwaves. 'I was disappointed they could not hear me, knowing that I was being monitored by several German stations and following my instructions, I gave my message over blind.'

Eddie became very agitated when he still couldn't make direct contact over Christmas. The tenor of desperation in his messages increased. On 23 December he transmitted 'GET MAURICE BRING YOUR SET NEARER COAST. MUST HAVE BETTER RECEPTION' – and a week later, his instructor in Paris was indeed despatched to the coast, as confirmed by Ultra. Even with this move, Eddie's transmissions were still not being acknowledged in real time, but eventually a special relay station close to the Spanish border made direct contact with him. In the same way that the Germans tracked 'black senders', Eddie suspected the British had been tracking the German agents Stefan von Gröning had assured him were at large in the United Kingdom.

'In every country at this time, skilled men sat all day at receivers,' Eddie later wrote. 'If a "black sender" was noticed other stations were warned.' He knew that the Abwehr had traced several British agents from their listening station at Rennes. There was no reason to suppose the British wouldn't be doing the same. MI5 officers acknowledged to him that they had been aware of some of his test transmissions, though they hadn't been able to understand the messages they contained. As a precaution, nothing specific was ever said to Eddie on the subject. 'The tracking down of agents in this country,' Colonel Tommy Robertson explained one day in person, 'is an extremely difficult business.' And he left it at that.

In fact, it had become a highly streamlined business. By this fourth winter of the war, the systematic deception of the Germans by double agents was extremely efficient. Thanks to the reading of the Abwehr's signals, MI5 could determine how successful its deceptions were and fine-tune them accordingly. 'By the end of 1942,' Sir John Masterman was able to conclude, 'the team of agents was distinctly stronger in all departments than it had been a year previously.'

Two of them had become stars. Juan Pujol Garcia was a Catalan with a fanatical hatred of fascism who pretended to create a network of agents in Britain. Given the codename Garbo – he was the greatest actor MI5 had come across – Pujol fabricated reports to his Abwehr controllers from no less than twenty-seven imaginary sub-agents who were regularly sending him assessments and secrets. They included a Swiss businessman based in Bootle who reported 'drunken orgies and slack morals in amusement centres' at Liverpool Docks and an enthusiastic Venezuelan in Glasgow who noted that dockers on the Clyde would 'do anything for a litre of wine'. The Abwehr, incredibly, lapped it up. Dusko Popov, codenamed Tricycle, was an equally remarkable chancer. Some writers have claimed he was a prototype for James Bond, for he too was a womanising adventurer with a penchant for expensive champagne. Travelling between Lisbon and London, Popov was provided with information to muddy the Germans' picture of British strengths and intentions.

The intense interrogations at Camp 020 were the first steps in assessing whether a captured agent could be doubled. In time, 'Tin Eye' Stephens became astonishingly adept at determining whether a captured spy could usefully be turned against his German masters. Only fourteen of the four hundred and eighty prisoners who passed through his care in five years of fighting were executed because they refused to cooperate. Roughly one hundred and twenty were handed on to Tommy Robertson and MI5's B Division for double-cross purposes. Of these, eleven – including Eddie Chapman – were doubled with great success.

Eddie's interrogation was the most important yet for the Double Cross system. As fast as the stenographers could type, transcripts were compiled, collated and distributed to other secret agencies such as SOE and MI6. This paper trail needed a label and so, within a few days, each agent was given a name that his handlers thought appropriate to his character. In bestowing the label Zigzag on Eddie Chapman, we get a measure of just how erratic MI5 felt him to be. They had certainly zigzagged through his criminal past and subsequent activities as agent Fritz Graumann of the Abwehr.

Behind the scenes, MI5 checked on all the documents he brought with him – confirming with Somerset House and other registration officials that, for example, his Irish nationality card in the name of Morgan O'Brien was a forgery, stamped by a non-existent department. In January, they were still trying to work through the many inconsistencies in his story, exacerbated by his lack of chronology.

So much information was being obtained that MI6 were worried Eddie might know too much. Zigzag might realise his interrogators had been reading German reports verbatim. They feared he would probably soon deduce from the pointed nature of their questions that the Abwehr's codes had been broken. As the organisation which disseminated the Ultra decrypts, MI6 was understandably paranoid about their security. Circulation of decrypted information was highly restricted and, even among those allowed to see it, was routinely referred to as having come 'from most secret sources'.

A report in the New Year from 'Tin Eye' Stephens himself went some way to alleviate the secret service's fears. Stephens had, he was careful to note, carefully hidden the sources from which they had obtained information about agent Fritzchen. He had told Eddie that if he had not given himself up on landing, he would not have escaped arrest as he tried to slip into the underworld. Even if he hadn't contacted them, he would have been caught.

'The British secret service was not asleep,' Tin Eye assured him. 'The paper band covering the English notes would have cost you your neck.'

Eddie had nodded blankly in agreement.

Paradoxically, his desire to be helpful – more acute after his show of bad temper at the start of his interrogation – presented them with a further dilemma. At one point, Eddie volunteered the information that over the previous summer he had been shown large-scale pictures of the Cumbrian mountains (where the Luftwaffe had been keen to drop him by parachute). Note of this fact would have been recorded in the regular radio traffic from Nantes to Paris (and presumably would have been forwarded to Berlin). The British secret service, Eddie was certain, should be able to break the codes used by the Abwehr now he had given them a possible 'crib'. His interrogators said nothing.

The RSS continued to quiz him about the Abwehr radio networks, though to be on the safe side Major Morton-Evans, who was sent to visit him, used a false name. 'We gave him the impression that our interception service was poor and that before the information he had given us, we had no idea that these services were in operation,' another MI5 radio man would record, playing down any fears that its sister service might have over the security of their 'most secret sources'.

Once Eddie had revealed his primary assignment – that he was expected to blow up the de Havilland factory – an intense debate consumed the secret agencies. How could agent Zigzag fulfil this act of sabotage to the Abwehr's satisfaction? Should he be allowed to stay in Britain, or should he return to his German masters? And just what exactly would he do if he stayed in Britain?

MI5 quickly formed the opinion that Eddie would soon disappear into the underworld if allowed to remain in London. Once a criminal, they concluded, always a criminal.

Certainly, Eddie showed no hint of remorse about his past: one of his interrogators noted with some concern that 'he does not regret his criminal activities'. It was obvious that Eddie would not want to live a law-abiding life once hostilities were over, no matter which side won. He even talked of starting a cabaret in Warsaw.

'The difficulty is that if Chapman is kept here too long he will go sour and might attempt a break,' Stephens himself noted for the files. 'On the other hand, if he is liberated I understand that not only the police but former criminal associates will immediately contact him.' Eddie's character was such that he would hardly be content to settle down and send the occasional doctored report to the Germans. His thirst for adventure meant he would have to be kept busy, for he was 'a man to whom the presence of danger is essential'. The fact Eddie had 'form', however, might come in useful. 'I think we ought to keep these things on record in case we ever want to use them,' commented an MI5 man in a handwritten comment on one of his personal files.

Under the circumstances, the Security Service decided not to say anything to the police and hoped nobody would recognise him during his stay. In time of war, the security authorities had few qualms about using blackmail. Thus far, it had only been evident on the German side, when Anthony Faramus had been made a hostage to his fortunes. When Stephens pointed out that Eddie was essentially being forced by the Germans to work for them, he did not disagree.

'As I figure it,' he confessed in one interrogation, 'with my brilliant past, I am due a stretch of something like fourteen years.'

The wartime MI5 files on Eddie Chapman now released into the UK National Archives in Kew record in exhaustive detail the Security Service's thoughts on agent Zigzag. The intelligence officers were fascinated by Eddie. But his own view of the MI5 men is equally instructive, for snobbery and class prejudice underscored much of his treatment by the Security Service. 'Tin Eye' Stephens was not alone in being disapproving. As already noted, British Intelligence tried to paint Eddie in the most unflattering light possible. Despite their best efforts, he was never a 'dangerous criminal' nor a 'blackmailer', two labels which they happily attached to him.

Many of the senior MI5 men Eddie came into contact with spent a lot of time looking down their noses at him. Betty Chapman feels that this was especially true of John C. Masterman, the chairman of the Double Cross Committee. 'Eddie wasn't from the top drawer like Masterman,' she suggests. 'He became his real bête noire. Eddie couldn't stand him.' Luckily, his contact with the former Oxford don was limited. Eddie was much happier dealing with Tommy Robertson, who actually ran double-agent operations. 'The colonel who was in charge of me was someone who I admired and could work with,' Eddie later wrote. Robertson took care to tell him that his work was valuable – and that he was an extremely brave man.

Each agent was given his own dedicated 'case officer', drawn from MI5's B Division and much more than an administrative handler. He would be responsible for the agent's domestic set-up, his general wellbeing and welfare, as well as ensuring that the messages he sent to the Germans were in character. Given the class prejudice from which Eddie suffered, there is a certain irony that the MI5 officer chosen to look after agent Zigzag was himself a working-class lad made good. Ronald Reed had grown up in a poor neighbourhood in the East End of London. When recruited into wartime MI5, he took care to refer to himself as Ronnie, rather than the more obviously proletarian Ron. From the evidence available, it is clear that Eddie and Ronnie understood each other.

Originally a radio ham who worked as an engineer at the British Broadcasting Corporation, Reed had been recruited into the Security Service to supervise the wireless transmissions of a captured German spy who was to be turned against the Germans. Commissioned as a captain, in time he became one of a small band of MI5 officers skilled at handling double agents. To some extent, his work was autonomous as action and responses were required on a daily basis. Rather than wait for approval from each fortnightly meeting of the Double Cross Committee, each individual case officer would, when required, contact a relevant service via its nominated representative. The administrative body, chaired by John Masterman, would decide at a strategic level what should be fed back to the enemy. The individual case officer looked after day-to-day concerns and supervised his chosen agent's interactions within the British security apparatus.

In the days before Christmas 1942, the interrogators at Camp 020 realised they had struck pay dirt. 'The Chapman case is perhaps one of the most fascinating we have yet handled here and gave promise of yielding a wealth of information,' Stephens was to write. 'By his courage and resourcefulness he is ideally fitted to be an agent.'

Despite his characteristic show of truculence, Eddie's more recent helpfulness was paying off. He soon became aware that his chief tormentor was unbending slightly. Two days before Christmas, Stephens actually smiled. 'Well, Chapman, good luck,' he said in his clipped tones. 'You are being released and a Merry Christmas to you.'

Finally, Eddie and Captain Stephens shook hands after 'the first kind words spoken to me since I had arrived'. Having been allowed to collect the clothes he had arrived in, at around a quarter to seven in the evening of Wednesday, 23 December Eddie was driven out, huddled under a blanket even though it was already dark. He knew better than to ask where he had been incarcerated, less still where he was being taken. The only request he made of Ronnie Reed was to give the sergeant who had brought him his meals in his cell a pound note for all his troubles.

For all his apparent cheerfulness, Stephens remained pessimistic. His final report for his superiors pulled no punches. Eddie Chapman, he declared, was going to be difficult to handle. 'We may expect tiresome brushes with the police which, even though they can be dealt with, may nevertheless compromise his position, and he will also be a potential danger and nuisance to the community in his criminal capacity.' Stephens finished his report with a curious observation, but one which would also be the assessment of others within MI5. It was clear Eddie could not remain in England and equally clear that the Germans did not want him back in France. 'They will take no steps to assist him on his return,' he declared.

The Abwehr, it seemed, had deliberately misled Fritzchen, something they did with most of their *V-menn*. Earlier on in the war, its first tranche of agents despatched to England were told, when they expressed misgivings about being caught, that the forthcoming invasion would come to their rescue. Now, Stefan von Gröning had with apparent sincerity promised Eddie a submarine and the chance of a trip to the United States. But the Abwehr radio traffic had never mentioned either of these two possibilities. 'It seems to us extraordinarily unlikely that having succeeded in recruiting and successfully despatching to England a man who was not only an expert saboteur but was also an Englishman familiar with his own country the Germans would, after a very short time, take him away,' a later MI5 report adds, 'and despatch him to a country with which he was, for all practical purposes, wholly unfamiliar.'

Under cover of the blackout, Eddie was taken by car to a house in the north London suburbs. Here he would be looked after by a pair of field security policemen. Travelling with them, Ronnie Reed emphasised that Eddie shouldn't think he was being detained against his wishes. His handlers – known to him only by their first names, Paul and Allan – were there to protect him from police inquiries, since the Security Service had thought it prudent not to issue him with documents or identity papers.

Paul Backwell and Allan Tooth had been told that their charge's name was Eddie Simpson and that he was, in Tommy Robertson's phrase, 'a dangerous criminal wanted by the police'. They were to act as chaperones: should Zigzag cut up rough, they would be allowed to restrain him. For now, though, there was much better news. They informed him he could do more or less what he wanted when he got to their destination. 'So long as one of us accompanies you, old boy,' one of them said with a smile.

Number 35 Crespigny Road was a modest late-Victorian detached house in Hendon, a comfortably middle-class area of north London. Its obscurity suited the Security Service's purposes perfectly. Rented from a Jewish army officer by MI5, it had housed two Norwegian double agents in 1941 and had, earlier that year, been Juan Pujol Garcia's home on his first trip to London. Now it would be the supposed safe house in which Eddie Chapman could hide, yet in a way that he couldn't help thinking was extraordinary. 'It was supposed to be so hush hush,' his widow recalls. 'But Eddie said that you would see all the military cars go up to the place from where they were broadcasting. Anybody could have guessed that something was going on.'

That first evening, they settled in as best they could. The next day, the minders did their own shopping and 'kept house' with a float of a fiver. They were determined to make him feel at home, for Eddie always maintained that he was his usual happy-go-lucky self. The official files paint a very different picture. He was allowed no contact either by phone or letter and very quickly he became curiously morose. His tendency to depression was aggravated over Christmas by a sense of melancholy. Within days, one of his minders reported: 'He admits to feelings of "nihilism" when he feels life is empty and that nothing really matters.'

His depression surprised them, though it was nothing new. At one point during his extended wait to leave on the other side of the Channel, Eddie had even asked his German masters if he could be sent to a concentration camp. 'If things did not go just as he planned he would go upstairs to bed and stay there for hours on end and refuse to eat,' another minder recorded. 'He never got annoyed [on] these occasions but we left him alone when he felt like this.' By his own admission, Eddie wanted a quiet life and was determined to avoid his pre-war hangouts. He often sat in his room quietly reading Tennyson, or the German novels which his handlers obtained for him.

At first, Eddie showed no signs of wanting to travel anywhere, content to listen to the wireless and talk about his various escapades. 'The effect German propaganda had had on him was enormous,' Backwell recorded. 'And it took him some time to give credence to the English news.' In particular, Eddie couldn't believe the reality of the situation on the Eastern Front – 'the news from Russia astounded him' – and they selected books that would enable him to catch up on what had really happened.

After Christmas, he started going out in the evening, even if it was only as far as the local picture house, and always in the company of his minders. The first film he saw was itself a subtle form of propaganda, Noël Coward's classic *In Which We Serve*. And for the first time in many years, he went to see a Christmas pantomime.

There was never any need for rough stuff. Eddie warmed to his guards who treated him well. All three became regulars at the Hendon Way, a local pub where Eddie was allowed to borrow money to stand his round. Given the trouble he was having in trying to make real-time radio communication, there was a strange irony that on another evening he saw a spy film at a local cinema. The sinister-looking villain carried his transmitter in a briefcase and blithely used a microphone to make instant contact with a U-boat captain. 'I wondered if the man who had made this film understood the difficulties of wireless transmission,' Eddie later wrote.

Gradually, Eddie's spirits rose as he got used to the land about which he had often been ambivalent before the war. 'To watch free men in a free country!' he would later write. 'Instead of the eternal "Heil Hitler" greeting, here was a pleasant "Good Day".'

Most afternoons he went into town with his minders to get an idea of the situation in and around the capital – including the railway termini and bombed areas – for his reports to his controllers. After one German raid, Eddie was able to report 'that an unexploded bomb had fallen at Lord's Cricket Ground, St John's Wood, and that traffic had to be diverted in that area'. He would deliberately add to the Germans' ignorance of conditions in Britain by continuing to send them carefully doctored information.

Despite his fortitude in withstanding prolonged interrogation, if Eddie demonstrated one weakness, it was women. In many of the one-dimensional portraits of his life written by the more credulous newspaper journalists, Eddie has been misrepresented as an incorrigible Lothario. Yet, as his widow points out, it was always the females who chased Eddie, not the other way round. 'And he was never a cheap flirt,' explains Lillian Verner Bonds, 'or a crude womaniser. His charm and charisma attracted female attention.'

Within a few days of arriving in Hendon, Eddie was longing for female company. Very shortly, one woman and a little girl would come to cement his readjustment to life in wartime Britain. The existence of that little girl was one of the greater surprises Eddie had faced in Jersey jail. One day – and totally unexpectedly – he had learned in a letter from a former lover that he was a father. Enclosed was a photograph of a baby girl, named Dianne Shayne. (That Eddie Chapman had sired a daughter out of wedlock is as much a surprise to his widow as it had been to him in Jersey. The fact of her mother Freda's existence only came to light with the declassification of his wartime records in 2001. 'I never knew about that,' Betty Chapman says, laughing. 'Eddie kept quiet about her. He was obviously very busy, wasn't he?') When he started talking about his daughter in the Hendon safe house, the Security Service took note.

In early 1938, Eddie had been living in Sterndale Road, Shepherds Bush, with a professional dancer called Freda White. MI5 later recorded that Eddie and Freda had lived together for eight months (immediately before he met Betty Farmer). Eventually, they tracked her down to Westcliff-on-Sea on the Essex coast, where she was working as a firewoman. Freda, it seemed, was now separated from a fellow fireman called Keith Butchart who worked in the Essex Fire Service.

There was however a certain reluctance on MI5's part to effect a reunion. As Ronnie Reed noted, Eddie 'could not easily be convinced of the necessity for great care and discretion in all matters where his presence in England might possibly leak out'. The sudden reappearance of Freda's former lover would be explained by saying he had escaped from Jersey, had been pardoned and was now about to join the Army. But, even if Eddie himelf remained discreet, it was feared that Freda might inadvertently reveal to others that she had met Eddie. If word leaked, the police might start to take an interest in his whereabouts.

Over Christmas, activity in Hendon continued apace. There were still difficulties in sending and receiving radio messages from Eddie's German controllers. Eventually, they got a reply which read: 'Thanks for message. Wish good results. OK.' One of his British field security handlers reported that Eddie continued to be 'a mine of information', and very quickly the earlier confusion turned to clarity. A steady stream of officials came up to Hendon. Sometimes MI5's Laurie Marshall stayed over; he was often regaled with Eddie's pre-war exploits, many of which the police knew nothing about. 'Visitors interrogated him at length and as he got information off his chest,' Paul Backwell reported, 'he was able to think more clearly of other episodes abroad.' Tommy Robertson had insisted his handlers listen to Eddie's suggestions. He had been treated well by the Germans and they should now do the same, if only to stop resentment from building up.

When Eddie made a successful contact transmission on Sunday, 27 December, he forgot to add the abbreviated message which made it clear that he was not under British control. 'My God, I believe I forgot the five F's,' he said afterwards. At five o'clock that same evening, he made another transmission: 'Sorry drunk over Xmas. Forgot FFFFF in last message.' He added what he later termed a boisterous 'Happy Christmas' at the end.

By now, the lack of direct radio contact was also worrying the Germans. Because Fritzchen hadn't been able to make direct contact, he had been staying on air for more than the ten minutes the Abwehr had suggested was a necessary limit. 'Irregularity, and above all, brevity are the key to [an agent's] success,' Eddie would reflect. 'Four to eight minutes for a full transmission is plenty.'

His German handlers feared he could be tracked down. A message in the Abwehr traffic revealed that they thought Eddie's prolonged contact calls – up to half an hour each time – were too dangerous. Bletchley Park recorded that the Germans thought 'they will undoubtedly get him' if such lengthy transmissions continued. This possibility preyed on Eddie's mind too. He started to ask questions about how long it would be before the British would intercept signals and track down their sender. Ronnie Reed dissembled, saying that weak signals could not be traced.

Immediately after Christmas, Eddie started to remember salient details of his radio training. 'ZIGZAG has now given us the frequencies of Paris, Nantes and Bordeaux, so that we should be in a position to intercept all the messages which go across between these three stations.'

On Boxing Day 1942, the director-general of MI5 himself sent for John Masterman, to discuss what they were going to do about the Mosquito factory. Sir David Petrie wanted his subordinates to get cracking and 'do all that we can to arrange a spectacular explosion of fire of some kind at the de Havillands works'. For the rest of Eddie's stay in Hendon, discussion would focus on what he was expected to do next.

★ ★ ★

The object on which Eddie's mission to Britain centred was one which a Luftwaffe officer had already described to him as '*ein schöne Vögel*' ('a beautiful bird'). At a time when sleek, metallic monoplanes seemed state-of-the-art, it seemed an oddly regressive step for the Royal Air Force to be flying a bomber whose airframe was made from balsa wood. Though Lord Haw Haw had crowed over the airwaves that this was because Britain was so starved of material, the Germans were secretly impressed by the swiftness of the Mosquito aircraft. The leaders of the Reich were incensed by its very existence, Hermann Göring demanding of the heads of his own aircraft industry why they hadn't brought out an aircraft made completely of wood.

In fact, that aspect of the Mosquito's construction had almost been too radical for the British Aircraft Ministry. Its officials were not convinced the Mosquito would be a worthwhile addition to the Royal Air Force. But when Geoffrey de Havilland Jr, the elder of the company's founder's sons, took the prototype to the skies in November 1940, he knew that – if only because of its speed – it would be a winner. The idea of a fast, light bomber made mostly of wood was as unorthodox as it was brilliant. Sceptical government and military leaders soon became converts as reports of the Mosquito's outstanding performance became known.

At the end of 1940, the Hatfield factory had received a contract for 150 of the fighter-bombers. In the autumn before Eddie's arrival, various Mosquitos had taken part in set-piece attacks, on one occasion dropping four bombs on the Gestapo headquarters in Oslo. The Mosquito would see wartime service as an airliner, day fighter, night fighter, intruder, photo reconnaissance aircraft, anti-shipping fighter, bomber and target tug.

The bomber that was as fast as a fighter eventually became headline news. At the end of October 1942, the *Daily Mail* let the British population in on the secret. 'Some time ago, while even the name of the new superfast bomber was still a closely guarded secret, a Mosquito crashed into the sea. High speed launches and units of the Navy rushed to the area and combed the sea for miles in order that not a single piece of wreckage should be left behind.'

The Mosquito became acknowledged as one of the safest, fastest and most versatile aircraft of the war. As a bomber, it could carry a greater load than many of the heavy bombers of the period. Because of its high speed, it was largely immune from interception. And, as the Germans had realised, all other de Havilland work had beens transferred to sub-contractors. Production of the Mosquito now dominated the Hatfield works.

Quite coincidentally, Betty Farmer had by this time become friendly with the pilot who had taken out the Mosquito prototype on its first ever test flight. At the end of 1942, Betty remained close in Eddie's affections. MI5 accordingly sought her out, but could find no trace of her after her return to Southampton from the Channel Islands in March 1939. Despite the Security Service's inability to track her down, however, Betty had been enjoying a 'happy war'. Still believing he was dead – 'Somehow it came through the grapevine that he'd been shot,' she says – she had not even attempted to find him.

Immediately after her return from St Helier, Betty had met a man in the hotel business and gone to work for him on the Isle of Man for a year. Eventually Betty returned to London and played bit parts in films, working with Laurence Olivier and Valerie Hobson. She appeared as a land girl in one film, a passenger on a Russian train in another, but there was always plenty of time to socialise. In the endless whirl of the times she was soon gravitating towards the glamorous test pilots who inhabited the same social milieu – at one point she had even rented Guy Gibson's flat in Chelsea. And she was to become close friends with another of those raffish, rather elegant pilots. This was none other than Geoffrey de Havilland, Jr.

At the close of 1942, the most serious problem concerning Betty Farmer's future husband's intended mission was, how on earth was

British Intelligence going to pretend to blow up a factory? If they didn't make some attempt at fulfilling his sabotage obligations, then the Germans would know that Eddie Chapman had been turned.

To maintain his own cover story, Eddie would have to be familiar with the site where his supposed sabotage was to take place. On Wednesday, 30 December 1942, he paid his first visit to the de Havilland factory. 'This helped to keep his mind occupied and the visit proved successful,' Paul Backwell recorded, 'and he was able to get a very good idea of the general layout.'

Accompanied by Backwell, Eddie made his way to King's Cross and St Pancras stations, the main rail connection to Hatfield, some twenty miles north of the capital. En route they noted details of lorries and troops in full kit (the kind of details that the Germans had asked him to record). When they arrived in Hatfield, Eddie and Paul asked the way to the Comet Hotel, which was close by the de Havilland plant. They took a bus which passed a short distance beyond the factory and walked back slowly, pausing now and again to talk. They made sure they took no obvious interest in the de Havilland buildings. Eddie was nevertheless able to note that roughly two dozen of the 'Wooden Wonders' were standing on the aprons of the factory airfield.

Eddie would need a good working knowledge of the layout of the works. When he had been shown RAF aerial reconnaissance photographs in Hendon, he was puzzled. 'These are quite different from the ones which I was shown before I came to this country,' he told his MI5 handlers. The greater the amount of information he could obtain first hand, the more convincing his story to the Germans would be.

Eddie and Backwell would have to note at what times the shifts changed (to enable them to work out the timing of any possible sabotage); the number, size and location of the boilers in each boiler house. They needed to know the number and type of guards (whether military or civilian), their methods of patrol and the areas they covered. And this had to be done without attracting any attention from passers-by.

'A most extensive study was made of the whole area,' Backwell later recorded. 'It is well protected in most places. Best entry is in the neighbourhood of the Comet on the main road. Defences at back of private houses not known.' They walked the length of the factory perimeter to observe all the entrances and buildings, identifying another possible entry point. They made discreet sketches of these locations, noting the types of buildings and the position of the boiler rooms and what appeared to be the fuel storage facilities. When they observed that the main entrances were guarded by police, a certain amount of frustration set in. 'Eddie would like the opportunity to scout round the area after dark, and suggests between 6 p.m. and 8 p.m.,' Backwell noted. 'It was explained he could not go alone and that discovery would upset all plans for the job.'

On that Wednesday afternoon, nobody showed them 'any overdue interest' apart from a labourer who shot them a few glances when they stopped briefly. The pair went to a nearby café, where a lieutenant colonel acknowledged them more nervously than suspiciously. Just in case there was any comeback, Backwell recorded details about him: his uniform had two service stripes on the forearm plus a Special Proficiency badge. In the event, no suspicions were ever raised.

Backwell's handwritten report of their visit was forwarded to Tommy Robertson.

That evening, Eddie wanted to transmit to his German controllers that he had seen 'Walter' – their codename for the factory, based on Walther Thomas's first name – but MI5 exercised caution. The Germans had wanted Eddie to destroy the powerhouses – they had been quite insistent on that. But it was clear that their understanding of the factory was incomplete, and it would not be possible to destroy the facilities which they had specified. MI5 would have 'to consider very carefully the camouflaging of these three objectives and possibly the demolition of one of them'.

The next day, New Year's Eve, Eddie entered a downstairs room at Crespigny Road to find his handlers listening to the radio. The announcer was discussing the execution earlier that morning at Wandsworth prison of a suspected saboteur. This was the culmination of the case of a Dutch seaman called Johannes Dronkers who had been apprehended earlier in the year, along with two others, aboard a yacht in Harwich harbour. Taken to Camp 020, he had soon become almost incoherent with hysteria. Though his testimony cleared his colleagues, the feckless Dronkers (as 'Tin Eye' Stephens characterised him) confessed he was an Abwehr spy. In November, he had been taken to the Old Bailey where he was prosecuted and sentenced to death.

The radio report deeply disturbed Eddie. He turned pale. 'He was obviously shaken,' Allan Tooth wrote, 'I had not seen him like this before.' Despite trying to maintain his usual air of carefree confidence, Eddie had little need to be reminded of how close he had come to suffering a similar fate.

CHAPTER SIX

How to Blow Up a Factory

'We then went down to Hatfield to "case" the factory. There is a large pub next door. We went in and had a drink. There were several of the de Havilland employees doing likewise, and we could hear the roar of engines starting up in the background. We swallowed our drinks, walked right round the factory, and I compared it with the photographs that I been shown before I left. We noted where the power-houses were. We also made mental notes of all obstacles to be encountered before we could climb in and decided to come down later and have a rehearsal.'

– Eddie Chapman recalls his cover story for the Germans about his supposed sabotage in Hatfield

ON SATURDAY, 2 January 1943, the safe house at Hendon was to receive a most eminent visitor. Throughout the war years, Victor Rothschild had been on the receiving end of the Germans' handiwork as a brave and resourceful dismantler of bombs. Later the recipient of the George Medal, he ran MI5's anti-sabotage section and, in that capacity, had considerable interest in what agent Fritzchen had been taught by the sabotage branch of the Abwehr. Victor, now Lord Rothschild, was about to see how useful Eddie's sabotage training had been.

Earlier that morning, Eddie, along with his field security handlers, had visited local chemists in Hendon to buy the necessary ingredients to make explosives. Almost immediately they had encountered a problem. Potassium chlorate, a weedkiller, could be obtained from gardening stores. The chemist in Berlin had explained the previous summer that its German name was *Kalium chlorat*, but Eddie – and his tutors across the Channel – had got it wrong. 'This was wrongly translated as calcium,' Paul Backwell later explained. Apparently unaware of the difference – 'suspicion was not aroused in the shop when he asked for calcium,' reported Backwell – the first shopkeeper they spoke to explained there was very little in stock. In any case, what did he want it for? 'A plant is dying and needs calcium,' Eddie explained. The shopkeeper seemed satisfied with that explanation.

They spent the rest of the morning walking around flower shops, repeatedly asking for the mythical calcium. 'My gosh, you've got a nerve haven't you?' Lord Rothschild exclaimed when Eddie related this story just a few hours later.

But the authorities were taking no chances: because their agent had asked for the chemicals in their foreign names, they wanted to make sure there were no 'abnormal purchase' records registered, as would be expected in wartime. Thankfully, there didn't seem to be any. The MI5 files show that a Mrs Barton was later sent to Crespigny Road to help – 'his German is fluent and satisfactory', she reported – followed by a copy of the comprehensive *Muret Sanders German-English Dictionary*.

The house in Crespigny Road was soon a hive of activity as Eddie demonstrated the tricks of the sabotage trade, including how to create wristwatch timers and acid delay fuses. As they talked, an acid fuse merrily fizzed away in an ashtray. Rothschild interviewed Eddie for many hours, and it is clear from the transcripts of their conversation that his Lordship believed that Eddie was some sort of criminal mastermind. Eddie happily described exploding trees with his improvised bombs, as well as breaking into the guarded factory on the outskirts of Nantes. 'I've had quite a little experience of getting into places,' Eddie told Rothschild with a perfectly straight face. He went on to explain what else he had learned in the château. 'I was taught to make my own gelignite,' he told Rothschild, 'my own dynamite, and they taught me to make my own burning material and fuses and my own electric detonators.'

Some of these exploits provided the germ of an idea for the eventual sabotage of the Mosquito factory. Given his survey of the de Havilland factory two days earlier, Rothschild wanted to know what he'd been told about how he should blow it up. The Abwehr had shown him aerial photographs and suggested that maximum damage could be achieved by attacking the machine room, which contained the electrical generators or boilers. They had wanted him to blow the generators with high explosives. Eddie had been instructed that he should put the explosives on top of the boiler – the middle one – so it would appear as though the explosion had taken the other two with it. 'But when I saw the photographs shown me here,' Eddie explained, 'I didn't recognise it.'

Furthermore, the Hatfield job had been identified as only one of many possible activities for agent Fritzchen to carry out. The Germans had permitted him a certain amount of latitude. He could identify his own targets and 'if I had nothing else to do, nuisance work', such as placing attaché cases filled with explosive in station locker rooms, just as the IRA had done before the war.

The interview was drawing to its close. But Eddie still had time to wax lyrical about one particular piece of equipment he had been shown. He described how to drill a six-inch hole in a piece of coal, plugging the explosive and detonator in, much as he had done in his safebreaking days. It would be sealed up with plasticine, then covered in bootblack and coal dust. When pressed, Eddie said he hadn't practised this for himself in Nantes, but had gained the impression from both Herbert Wojch and the professor in Berlin that it would be easy to make a coal bomb.

Rothschild was at his most charming when he gently suggested: 'I wondered if some time you'd care to have a shot at it?' Eddie couldn't help but agree.

'And I've brought you the coal if you'd like to do an explosion one day with it,' his Lordship added.

Over the next week or so, Eddie started to put his sabotage theory into practice. 'We experimented on a small scale with different types of explosives,' Backwell recorded, 'burning mixtures and time bomb mechanisms.' Eddie's normal restlessness surfaced fairly quickly. He complained that if he was allowed to write everything down, he would learn it all so much quicker. By the end of the month, though, he had virtually completed the tasks set by Rohschild, who seemed pleased with his progress.

By the second week of the new year, Eddie's minders were regularly taking him into central London, primarily to record details that would be reported back to France, such as bomb damage and the insignia on troops' uniforms. On his first visit an air of new-found confidence had been apparent after the great victory at El Alamein, when church bells had been allowed to ring out for the first time since the outbreak of war. Yet, after four years away, Eddie found the capital a strange and unnerving place. The deprivations of wartime had transformed London into a very different city from the vibrant and carefree metropolis in which he had thrived before the war. When Eddie first went into cafés, for example, he treated his food coupons like tickets, throwing them away at every available opportunity until it was gently pointed out that this would draw attention to him.

The Security Service still feared that the pre-war criminal would find it all too much and disappear into the underworld. They needn't have worried: without his guards, Eddie seemed lost. One night he was 'pale and shaking' when they were delayed by a few minutes after they had agreed to meet him in the lobby of a bar. On another occasion, in Princes' restaurant, Eddie was even recognised by a 'face', an underworld crony from before the war. He had the presence of mind to speak in fluent French, protesting a case of *l'identité mixe*. It cannot have helped his equanimity that this former associate kept watching him for the rest of the evening.

In time, he was allowed to buy clothes and visit pubs in an attempt to regain his confidence. Up to this point, he had shown little interest in chatting up women but soon something of the old Eddie resurfaced. One day on New Bond Street, he picked up a girl and disappeared. 'Luckily there was a pub just opposite the flat he went to with the girl,' Backwell recorded for the files. 'He promised to meet me there in about half an hour.'

In later years, when Eddie Chapman's wartime adventures were first discussed publicly, a pervasive myth soon sprang up: that he only became a double agent for the money. His supposedly mercenary nature has been much commented on. It is instructive, therefore, to examine what was actually being written at the time.

'Though anxious to get as much money as he can from the Germans,' his handler Allan Tooth wrote, 'he does not seem very interested in the financial side of the undertaking.' Betty Chapman explains that during his time in Nantes, Eddie had gone down to the vaults of the château with von Gröning. 'Fritz, get what you want,' his controller had said when showing him the large amounts of money on display. 'Eddie could have taken a hundred thousand pounds,' Betty says, 'and von Gröning couldn't have cared less.'

Now, in early 1943, MI5 realised that a small financial inducement might help keep Eddie sweet. He wanted to pay the money he had brought with him from France to Freda and his daughter in the event of his death while serving his country. To another MI5 man Eddie talked about the ultimate risk ('If his betrayal of the Germans is discovered, he will pay with his life') and how valuable his continuing mission would be. Eventually, MI5 allowed him to keep the money, Laurie Marshall agreeing that an extra £350 should be added to a war bond for Eddie.

And then there was the money he would receive from the Germans when he returned to France. 'If it is not possible for you to get the money out of the country,' Eddie wrote in a handwritten note, 'then I hope when the Allies enter Germany, they will make the Germans pay up.' They also discussed another ingenious method for continuing payments for his daughter. In Nantes, Eddie knew of a Swiss watchmaker who was allowed to visit his native land to procure spare parts. He might act as a willing courier for any money Eddie might accrue in France. This could then be forwarded from Switzerland to pay Freda directly.

Behind the scenes, there had been considerable debate within MI5 as to whether Eddie should be allowed to return to the Germans at all. Zigzag himself was keen to return. But all other double agents under British control were based in neutral countries; there was always the possibility that they could be smuggled out via the local embassy. If Eddie's cover was exposed at any point once he returned to Occupied Europe, he would be taken to Berlin and interrogated by the Gestapo. One word out of place would prove to be fatal.

Yet remaining in London could prove equally dangerous: Eddie would go stir crazy if he was constantly chaperoned and locked up in the Hendon safe house. The Security Service's concern, though, was not motivated by any philanthropic interest in agent Zigzag's wellbeing. They were afraid that if Eddie started associating with his old criminal associates, he would start bragging about his clandestine activities. Claiming that he was a double agent who had been on a one-man crusade against the Nazis was just the sort of blustering that could bring the whole of the Double Cross system down. All the best efforts of British Intelligence might be lost over a drink in an underworld dive or a boast whispered between the sheets.

At the start of the new year, something approaching consensus had been reached about Eddie's future. 'In our opinion, Chapman should be used to the fullest extent. This means that, in view of the importance the Germans evidently attach to [this], he should be sent back to France when his mission in this country has been completed.' Eddie would have to be note perfect.

Eddie would have to be note perfect on his return to Occupied Europe. To make sure he could convincingly recount his elaborate cover story, he first needed to see in daylight where he had landed by parachute. So on Saturday, 16 January – exactly a month after his arrival – Eddie once more turned up in the fields near Littleport in the company of his handlers, Allan and Paul. Alan would record that 'a number of incidents took place' which did not help maintain security.

They drove up to the fens in the morning. Arriving in the village at 11 a.m., it was quite cold and they were hungry. Although most of the local pubs were closed, one called the Marquis of Grundy was open. They ate lunch and had a drink. Backwell added that they subsequently bought some chips at noon from a fish and chip shop. After sharing these among themselves, they asked their way to Wisbech and walked towards Apes Hall Farm. 'Farmers and labourers accepted our presence normally and greeted us casually,' Tooth recorded.

In an effort to get all the details right, they trudged across the wet fields, crossing a deep cutting and a stream (though Eddie wasn't sure this was the one near to which he had buried his parachute). Eventually they came across the spot where Eddie believed he had landed. After wandering around for a while, however, they were soon lost. Eddie was puzzled for, in Backwell's phrase, 'he could not single out the building he had almost landed on'. What he thought was a burned-out cottage was actually an outhouse, close by the Apes Hill Farm. Even today, three men traipsing across muddy fields would attract attention; in wartime England, such behaviour could lead to immediate arrest. George Convine, the farmer in whose living room Eddie had spent his first hours at home, spotted them.

Mr Convine came over and was delighted to see Eddie once again. He was amiable, but obviously curious as to what they were all doing. 'Passed time of the day, told him we were having a look to see what place looked like in daylight,' Backwell noted for the record. 'Asked him not to mention seeing us to anyone.'

After this short, casual conversation, Eddie and his handlers walked back towards Littleport on the main road. About a mile later, they were picked up by the two sergeants who had come to apprehend Eddie a month before. Mr Convine, it transpired, had done his special constable duty and called them as a precaution. Walking along and chatting in what was described as a friendly manner, it seemed funny to Backwell 'that Eddie, wanted by the police, should be in such circumstances'.

As casually as they could, Backwell and Tooth explained they were examining the area in daylight. The policemen were quite insistent that the information they had obtained from Eddie in the small hours of 16 December had gone no further. At the time, his handlers had another worry. They suspected that one of the sergeants knew about Eddie's criminal past (for he had discussed his time in the Coldstream Guards with the police official who had 'clocked' Eddie when he was taken into custody). Both sergeants stated that nobody in Littleport had suspected a thing.

This casual encounter provided much useful information about the area. More than that, though, despite the constant fears about maintaining security, it was clear that the episode of the airman's mysterious arrival in the middle of the night had been completely hushed up.

Back in Hendon, Eddie's real-time radio connections remained infuriatingly difficult. A couple of days before the visit to Littleport, his instructor Maurice had told him over the air not to be discouraged. Fritzchen should continue to keep sending 'blind' messages as reception would shortly improve. When there was no noticeable change early the following week, Eddie sent a message addressed to von Gröning which outlined his disgust. 'The whole thing seems a hopeless bungle,' he telegraphed. In fact, no satisfactory two-way communication was made until Sunday, 24 January. No reference to his petulance was ever made.

Eddie's emotions were still up and down. The enormity of what he was doing had begun to hit him and soon he was obsessing about how he would never be able to live a normal life after the war. Perhaps because of his criminal past, he claimed on several occasions that he was 'a man without a country'. He obviously needed cheering up and so, on the Thursday following his trip to Littleport, he was greeted enthusiastically one morning by one of his handlers: 'I have a surprise for you,' he said. 'We are dining tomorrow night at the Savoy. An old friend of yours who's now a captain in the Guards. He'll be pleased to see you.'

Eddie thought no more of this curious invitation until they walked into the dining room overlooking the Thames. From a distance, he spotted an equally elegant gentleman grinning with pleasure. For the first time since he had returned home, Eddie Chapman could relax. The return of his former flatmate, Terence Young, into his life would prove to be cathartic. 'From that day my life changed,' Eddie later said. 'Mentally, I felt a great relief.'

During his first interrogation at Latchmere House, Eddie had mentioned in passing that before the war he used to play football with a Cambridge half blue who, at the time, was establishing himself in the film industry. And, Eddie seemed to recall, Terence Young's father had been a governor of Shanghai. Here, at last, was somebody of whom his MI5 handlers might approve. One of them recorded, 'if it is considered advisable, we could safely permit him to meet'. Making contact with Young, who was now serving in one of the smarter regiments, would also have the benefit of allowing the Security Service to get a better idea of Eddie's pre-war activities.

At the start of 1943, Young was a captain commanding a tank with the Welsh Guards Armoured Test Division. He was on manoeuvres near Catterick in Yorkshire when he was suddenly called to London by MI5. 'I was petrified,' he recalled. 'I thought I was going to be court-martialled.'

When it became clear the reason was Eddie Chapman, Young had to smile. The Guards captain was met at the War Office by a couple of spooks who could hardly believe that someone of his social standing would associate with a ne'er-do-well like Eddie. 'We used to play squash together,' Young told them. 'He played very badly. I'd have dinner with him from time to time.'

The MI5 men were puzzled. They pointedly asked him if he was in the habit of hanging out with criminals. 'Not particularly,' Young replied smoothly. 'Let me put it this way. I'd rather trust Eddie Chapman than a lot of officers in the Brigade of Guards.' There was an embarrassed silence. According to the files, Young vouched for Eddie's character in the following terms: 'He's an extraordinary fellow. You could give him the most difficult of missions knowing that he would carry it out.' And then he smiled. 'Eddie would never betray the official who sent him but I think it's highly probable that he would rob him, too.'

Terence Young wondered why MI5 had bothered to bring him all the way down to London for an exchange which could quite easily have been carried out over the telephone. He was asked to remain in London for another week. 'I had a marvellous time living it up in a luxury hotel,' Young recalled many years later.

A few days later, Captain Ronnie Reed returned with a plan. Would Young meet Eddie Chapman to see if he was telling the truth about his adventures since his incarceration in Jersey prison? The last time he'd heard of his old mucker was when he'd made headline news in the *Daily Express* after his recapture on the beach in July 1939. Young agreed. It would be great to catch up with him, he added. That Thursday evening, Young and his Norwegian-born wife quietly awaited the arrival of Eddie Chapman at the Savoy.

'He was brought in with three of the most obvious dicks* I've

---

* At this time, the word 'dick' was a disparaging description of the more lugubrious sort of policeman, not the insult it has latterly become.

ever seen,' Young recalled with a chuckle, 'complete with bowler hats, raincoats and big feet.' The MI5 men, led by Captain Reed, were astounded to see Mrs Young but said nothing.

The two old friends were delighted to see each other. As the wine flowed and food was served, the conversation became very animated. The conduct of the war was high on the agenda. Terence repeatedly said he was utterly confident of Allied victory, a statement which Eddie found too complacent. Putting forward the controversial views that had been instilled during his year in Nantes – of Hitler's 'idealism' as well as the strength and efficiency of the German soldier – he drew a rather startled remark from Mrs Young. (Later, the MI5 men asked Eddie to refrain from making such comments in public.)

Throughout the meal, Eddie was back to his usual tricks, ordering magnums of champagne which, given their scarcity in wartime London, cost a small fortune. 'He sent supplies over to the detectives who were placed at strategic intervals in the restaurant,' Young recalled. 'When the bill came in it was for £140. The Chief Inspector didn't have enough money to pay it back. He had to stay there while somebody went back to Scotland Yard to get the cashier out of bed and get the money.'

On the way back to Crespigny Road, Eddie said he was happy to have seen his old friend. 'At the same time he was very disappointed in Young himself as he had changed so much in the last few years,' his handlers recorded. 'He was artificial – success seemed to have gone to his head.' And that was the last Terence saw of Eddie during the hostilities. He was none the wiser as to why his old housemate was being chaperoned by the Security Service but assumed it was connected to some sort of secret mission. He knew better than to ask them outright.

★ ★ ★

In the closed world of wartime intelligence, the old boy network had many advantages. There was always someone who knew somebody who could help sort out a problem, no matter how mind-boggling or obscure it may at first have appeared. And in this regard, perhaps the most exotic member of the Double

Cross Committee was the man known by the nickname 'Conky Bill'.

Thanks to his large, slightly crooked nose, that was how Sir John Turner was known in the corridors of power. Sir John was a dominant personality, well known for having, in the words of one official report, 'almost single-handedly created a remarkable hoax'. During the Battle of Britain, he had built dummy bombers and dressed dummy airfields to deceive the Luftwaffe. For this, he had called upon a cast of former film technicians whose expertise was in dressing movie sets that were always at the mercy of the weather. Come rain or shine, their wartime dummies, too, would have to pass muster. What became known as Colonel Turner's Department was based at the Sound City Film Studios in Shepperton.

To date, their work had been connected with airfields and aircraft. During the summer of 1940 – when resources were at a premium – Turner's department had created five hundred decoy targets during the Battle of Britain to confuse the enemy. These crude devices consisted of rows of parallel flares which looked like emergency landing strips. Located close to real airfields, they drew the attentions of German pilots who were keen to drop their bombs before heading for home. After this initial success, Sir John's technicians developed what were known as Q Sites, where airfields were simulated by rows of lights along with chevrons strategically placed on satellite fields. They were of particular value when the Luftwaffe changed tactics to concentrate on night bombing.

As the war progressed, Turner would develop camouflage and decoys on behalf of the Air Ministry wherever it was required. Sir John, who was always referred to as Colonel Turner, carried no RAF rank although he did command his own flight of aircraft in Hendon for surveillance purposes. That way, he could examine his handiwork from the air. Turner was knighted for his work in the summer of 1940 and his contributions were noted where they mattered most: the world of wartime intelligence.

Early in 1941, Sir John was invited to join a working committee involved in the systematic deception of the Germans. His work for the Double Cross Committee became ever more important and, now, at the start of 1943, came the strangest request of all.

His mission: to make it appear as if a factory had been blown up, without alerting the suspicions of either the employees or the enemy.

On Wednesday, 13 January, Sir John accompanied Tommy Robertson and Ronnie Reed to the Hatfield plant. The de Havilland security chief showed them round, relieved, no doubt, that any sabotage was merely to be simulated. The main boiler house – from which half the factory's power was generated – was at the centre of the plant. This was potentially a major problem. 'Conky Bill' pointed out that if they erected camouflage over that, 'a pinpoint would be gratuitously given to the Germans enabling them to bomb the works'. After the whole site had been inspected, a smaller building fairly close to the centre was identified as a better target.

Sir John needed to consider the matter more fully and planned to return the next day. Colonel Robertson consulted with the Home Forces to see what back-up might be necessary. In the event, Fighter Command was alerted to allow any German reconnaissance flights through. To be doubly certain, the RAF made its own inspection and submitted photos to Sir John's experts in the Air Ministry for scrutiny. By the weekend, a plan had evolved.

On 16 January, the same Saturday that Eddie had visited Littleport, Sir John came to MI5 to discuss how he and his experts could blow up the 'transformer building'. In outline, two of its four mains transformers would be dressed to make it appear as though they had been destroyed. Another building next to the swimming pool should also be dressed to make it look as though it contained a further large sub-station; that would explain why the factory was still drawing power supplies. In addition, further aerial photographs would be shown to Eddie to give him a better idea of what they had been trying to achieve.

Sir John wanted the 'sabotage' to be undertaken on a night when the moon rose at around seven o'clock in the evening, 'so that the explosive charges could notionally be placed in position in darkness and the camouflage erected in the moonlight'. That would give his men enough time to dress the factory overnight. All he would need, Turner had said, was three or four days' notice. Colonel Robertson agreed to give him a week to prepare. Moon charts were consulted and the last Friday in the month was eventually chosen as the optimum date for agent Fritzchen to pretend to blow up the factory.

Eddie's role in the planned destruction was secondary. Though he would claim to the Germans that he was in the vicinity, he would actually be safely tucked up in bed in Hendon. For the rest of his time at Crespigny Road, Eddie became word perfect in recalling the details of the supposed explosion, learning and revising his cover story. By the last week of January, he was becoming bored. The constant presence of his field security and MI5 minders was becoming irksome. 'Wherever I went one of my three shadows always accompanied me,' he recalled. 'Finally, I rebelled.'

One night, around ten o'clock, Eddie pretended to turn in early. When he was certain that everyone else was asleep, he shimmied down a drainpipe, jumped over the walls and calmly walked towards Hendon station where he grabbed a taxi. 'Take me to Barnes,' he declared.

He had decided to make an impromptu visit to Jimmy Hunt, the man who before the war had taught him the art of ripping the backs off safes. Jimmy, he had been told, was serving in the Royal Air Force. 'Now he was going to be part of my cover story to the Germans,' Eddie wrote. 'The intelligence people had kindly supplied me with details of his whereabouts and what he was assumed to be doing. I wanted to see him for myself.'

When Eddie arrived at the address in south-west London, Jimmy's wife answered the door. 'God, where did you spring from?' she gasped, and the usually cool and self-possessed Jimmy reacted similarly. They sat in the lounge drinking whisky, where Eddie told him of his own secret plan: there were great riches to be made by duping the Germans. On several occasions, the Abwehr had suggested that Eddie might want to bring one of his criminal cronies with him. Jimmy Hunt could hardly believe what he was hearing. 'I think you're potty,' he said at length. 'If that bleedin' Gestapo think you've doubled on them, they'll chop you into little pieces and feed them to their pet wolfhounds.'

Eddie, for all his impetuousness, was never one to push things too far. He knocked back the drink, thanked the Hunts profusely

and took a cab back to Hendon. After shimmying back up the
drainpipe, he had the satisfaction of knowing he had not been
missed. In any case, he could never have persuaded his handlers to
let him head back to Europe with Jimmy Hunt. When he raised the
topic of having a companion, his MI5 handlers made it clear it was
'unwise and dangerous' for others to join him.

By now, the preparations for blowing up de Havillands were far
advanced. It was clear that the aftermath of the notional explosion
had to be carefully managed, too. John C. Masterman was
despatched to visit the editor of *The Times*. On Wednesday, 27
January, he asked Robert Barrington-Ward if he would be willing to
place a story about the sabotage. The editor, though sympathetic,
thought that printing a bogus notice was a bad idea for the paper of
record. Later that same Wednesday, Barrington-Ward called
Masterman at MI5 to say 'the answer is regrettably no', and they
both agreed that their meeting had never taken place.

Two days later, however, the editor of the *Daily Express* was
successfully prevailed upon to do as the spooks wished. A short
paragraph – written by Masterman – would appear in the following Tuesday's paper. Everything was now ready.

On Thursday, 28 January, Eddie sent a message to his controllers
that he would attempt to sabotage 'Walter' the next evening,
adding that his objective would be the sub-station not the power
plant. The following morning – the day of the planned explosion –
Eddie and Ronnie Reed were driven up to Hatfield by Jock
Horsfall, MI5's driver, to make a final reconnaissance of the de
Havilland plant.

During their visit, it became clear to all of them that the real
boiler houses would have been too difficult to dress. What Sir John
Turner had called the 'notional sub-station' did at least have the
advantage of being close by a gated entrance to the factory that was
secured by a padlock. This would be an ideal entry point – Eddie
could claim to have broken the lock and then replaced it with an
identical one. The agent professed himself satisfied. Now he would
have to devote himself not just to learning the details of the
supposed destruction of the factory, but of all the other places he
had visited. 'Wherever possible ZIGZAG has travelled to the
objectives and locations which he will mention on return and has

seen the districts in which his crimes are supposed to have been committed,' MI5 would later record.

The last Friday in January 1943 was cold, damp and – even allowing for wartime blackout restrictions – very, very dark by late afternoon. In the 'inky blackness' enveloping the de Havilland factory, a handful of figures made their way into its compound unnoticed by the workforce. Their number included pre-war set designers and stage dressers from the Old Vic theatre. At their head were a handful of Royal Engineers, briefed and trained by 'Conky Bill' Turner.

They spread out a large relief canvas to cover the entire roof of the transformer building. The canvas was painted to represent the damage supposedly been wrought by Eddie's sabotage. Papier mâché dummies were brought in resembling the broken fragments of the generator. 'Four replicas of the sub-transformers had been constructed of wood,' says the MI5 report. 'Two of these were lying on their side in the real sub-station as if they had been blown from their positions.' Chipped bricks, battered blocks of concrete, smashed furniture and other props were strewn all around. Walls were skilfully blackened and tarpaulins raised as though positioned to stop the rain coming in.

Colonel Turner's men were finished by eleven o'clock that Friday evening. When MI5 later checked in and around Hatfield – sending a field security policeman to the pubs and cafés nearby – 'no rumours of sabotage were heard.'

Early the next morning, Colonel Tommy Robertson and Ronnie Reed returned to the plant in the company of Sir John Turner himself. All three visitors declared the results 'excellent'. Within a couple of days, Colonel Turner had ordered a reconnaissance flight which revealed what looked like gaping holes in the roof of the sub-stations through which pieces of the generator could clearly be seen. To observers from the air the whole area looked completely and convincingly wrecked.

On this cold but bright Saturday morning, one of the factory workers, who was in charge of a small boiler house, had arrived for work in a 'state of great excitement' because he thought his machinery had been hit by a bomb. By then, Eddie had already sent a message across the Channel to say that 'Walter' had been 'blown' in two places. As a result, he added, it was now a matter of some urgency that he return to the Continent before he came to the attention of the police.

That Saturday morning, Eddie's morale was on the rise, but it had nothing to do with the Hatfield job. Much to his amazement, the Security Service had done what he had requested and traced 'Freda and the child'. By the end of January, Freda White and her four-year-old daughter, Dianne Shayne, were coming to stay in Hendon. Allan Tooth reported that 'now Freda is coming to London, he has lost interest in other women and in going to the West End'. After lodging for a few days at the nearby Brent Bridge Hotel, Freda and her daughter moved into the house in Crespigny Road over the weekend, where they were to stay for a couple of weeks before returning home to the Essex coast. Eddie's spirits soared.

'Since he has seen Freda and the child,' a handwritten note records, 'E has been in very good spirits and says that his whole outlook towards the future has changed.' When asked about his post-war plans 'he wondered if perhaps he could not remain in his present work after the war, as it would fulfil his need for excitement'. In a note on the covering letter to Tommy Robertson, 'What a man!' is written in the margin by hand.

Remarkably, they were able to hide from Freda much of Eddie's secret activities. Sometimes, they even let them both go to the local pub on their own. If they all went out – as they did to Maxim's in the West End one night – Freda accepted the presence of his handlers but said nothing. Eddie simply told her that he had escaped from Jersey and the authorities had dropped all charges against him. He was now being 'protected' because of an unspecified underworld threat.

Yet the most curious aspect of this cosy domesticity was that Freda stayed in the same room in which Eddie made his radio transmissions. To keep her in the dark, Allan and Paul had to choreograph an almost split-second routine. Freda would have to be up, dressed and downstairs before Eddie started transmitting at 9.45 a.m. The tapping of the keyboard could be heard in the stairwell. 'Freda must have got very used to strange things happening,' Paul Backwell wrote, 'but she never asked any questions.'

The last Saturday of the month also dawned bright and crisp in the German capital. The date, 30 January 1943, marked exactly a decade since Adolf Hitler had come to power and the anniversary was to be celebrated with a speech by Reichsmarschall Hermann Göring. Just before 11 a.m., Göring arrived to address a large assembly of officers in the Hall of Honour at the Air Ministry building on Berlin's Wilhelmstrasse to deliver a peroration about the Sixth Army at Stalingrad, about whose fate rumours were swirling around the Reich.

Berlin Radio was scheduled to carry the speech live. At the precise moment when Göring was making his way towards the stage, without warning or explanation the radio station suddenly went off the air. Three RAF Mosquito bombers of 105 Squadron had swept low over the German capital. Their pilots had already gained a reputation for pinpoint accuracy and they hit the radio transmitters exactly on cue. That afternoon, the broadcast authorities tried again. There were, however, further delays, culminating in a second wave of Mosquito attacks which threw the capital into chaos.

Eventually, the Propaganda Minister, Josef Goebbels, took to the airwaves at 4 p.m. with a speech purportedly written by Adolf Hitler himself. The Führer, Goebbels solemnly declared, was too involved in the crisis on the Eastern Front to address his people directly. Listeners were stunned. It was the first time Hitler had failed to publicly celebrate the anniversary of his accession to power.

Given the events in Hatfield the night before, there was a certain irony in this first ever daylight raid by Mosquitos on Berlin. The Führer had been growing increasingly incensed at the embarrassments inflicted by the planes on the Third Reich. The disruption of his anniversary was the final straw. Neither the Luftwaffe nor the anti-aircraft defences had been able to shoot any of the aircraft down. Something, the Führer had been demanding, must be done.

And, with excellent timing, the spymasters of the Abwehr could finally report something had been done. Thanks to a message forwarded from France, Admiral Canaris's associates could now report to the Nazi leadership that the Mosquitos' days were numbered. Agent Fritzchen had been as good as his word. The

ABOVE Dagmar Lahlum, Eddie's Norwegian girlfriend, at the house in Grafsin where she lived with Eddie at the end of 1943.

LEFT Johnny Holst, one of his German handlers, asleep at the house. Looks were deceptive: Eddie considered him one of the most dangerous men in the German secret service.

BELOW Eddie, eating breakfast. These photographs were developed by MI5 in July 1944 when Eddie brought the camera – containing these test shots – back to England.

Smoke and Mirrors

The mythical Eddie Chapman as portrayed in film and in newspapers.

ABOVE In 1967, Gert Frobe (left) played a German controller in the film *Triple Cross*, while Christopher Plummer (right) valiantly plays Eddie Chapman despite being badly let down by the script.

LEFT Oberleutnant Fritz Graumann on His Majesty's Secret Service? A post-war shot of Eddie hamming it up for the press; in reality, he was never a member of the SS and always felt foolish when he had to wear a German uniform.

First look: Within hours of his apprehension on 16 December 1942, MI5 took their first photographs of 'the airman with the suicide pill' who had landed in the middle of the night.

Infernal machine: The coal bomb provided by the Germans in Lisbon in March 1943, for Eddie to sabotage the *City of Lancaster*.

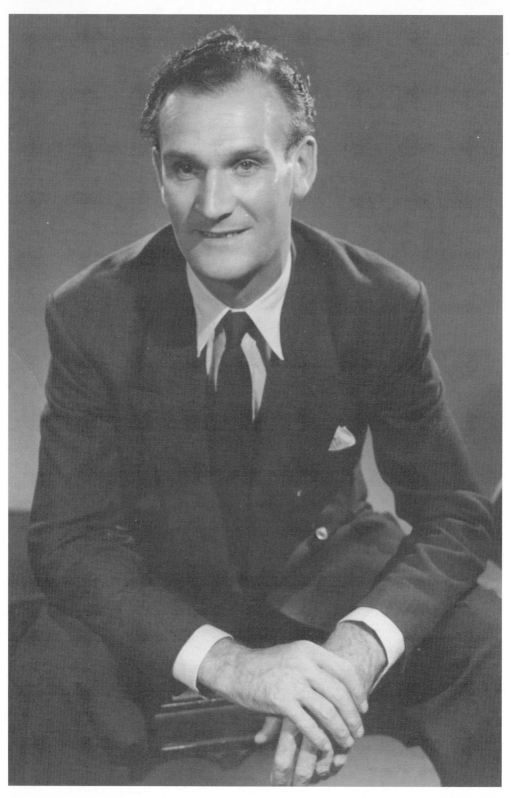

Survivor: Eddie, immediately after the war, gave no signs of the effects of his wartime secret service.

following Wednesday, 3 February, they sent him a congratulatory message.

Confirmation that an act of sabotage had taken place also came from British press reports. The Nazi intelligence services kept a keen eye on the London newspapers, which were shipped to the Reich via Lisbon or Madrid. In the 5 a.m. edition of the *Daily Express* on Monday, 1 February, a brief note had appeared about Saturday's events. 'Investigations are being made into the case of an explosion at a factory on the outskirts of London,' the report said. 'It is understood that the damage was slight and there was no loss of life.'

This seemed to satisfy Eddie's controllers, and a follow-up article went some way to helping maintain the fiction. The *Evening Standard* on Tuesday, 2 February carried a brief note headed 'Gelignite Inquiries'. It revealed that a man had been 'questioned at Shepherd's Bush police station last night in connection with the possession of gelignite'.

Most readers, however, would have found their attention drawn to a larger picture and a banner headline at the top of the same page: 'Here are the Mosquito men who bombed Berlin on Speech Day'. It was a heartening tale about the weekend's remarkable raids into the very heart of the Nazi empire. 'Twice within five hours, in the broad light of day, the RAF sent its twin-engine Mosquitos to Berlin on Saturday,' the London evening paper breathlessly reported. 'And these are some of the men who held up Göring's speech and spoiled the Nazi anniversary.'

Few readers would have suspected that the two stories were related.

February saw more detailed preparations for Eddie's return to Occupied Europe. The newly released MI5 files show the exhaustive planning that went on. Nothing was left to chance: dates, times, places were learned and relearned. There would be three options for getting him back to occupied territory: he could travel as a seaman, either directly or via Ireland, or else he could take a U-boat, though as MI5 had already concluded, 'we think that it is a reasonable certainty that all attempts to persuade them to despatch a U-boat would fail'.

To prepare for Eddie's return, a series of detailed questions about the Abwehr's operations were asked – and in such a way that if he ever revealed them to the Germans, there would be no hint that the British were reading their Enigma codes. The questionnaire went on for four pages, taking in details like Walther Thomas's boating college tie (presumably in case he ever came over on a sabotage mission). Eddie was asked to commit it all to memory.

The Security Service also went to a great deal of trouble to provide Eddie with details about the Hatfield explosions. Lord Rothschild double-checked with SOE on the amount of explosive required to cause them. Eddie was questioned at length by MI5's own sabotage investigators to make sure his story didn't appear flawed. Sometimes, he was grilled under the influence of alcohol. 'Fortunately, I think I have a hard head and I passed with reasonable ease the questions fired at me,' he recalled. 'Would I do so when the Gestapo had me? Doubts more than once assailed me, but I shook them off.' (According to Betty Chapman, her future husband was beaten with sticks to test his resilience, but there is no mention of 'rough stuff' in the files.)

Eddie's interrogators were concerned about any inconsistencies in his story. If he used two aerials in making his radio transmissions, how would they not have been seen? (He used the reserve one, which was smaller.) How did he and Jimmy Hunt know the explosions had taken place if they had returned straight away? And on it went, the MI5 men merely recording that his performance during this time was 'satisfactory'.

'On Zigzag's return to France we may assume that he will be interrogated at length about conditions of life in this country and about his movements in connection with the sabotaging of de Havillands,' they wrote. His handlers were now fairly certain that they could rely on Eddie's ingenuity to provide telling details and amusing vignettes which would add to their realism. They did have to take into consideration his character: 'He is by nature impetuous and reckless and under interrogation is extremely vague when questioned about the dates and times when they had occurred.' But Eddie was not easily rattled. On 8 February, Ronnie Reed recorded: 'I do not believe that he will experience any real difficulty in persuading them that he carried out his mission to their satisfaction.' For the rest of the month, he continued to perfect the story on which his life would depend.

Two months hence, in a Paris apartment, Eddie was to undergo the first of many extensive debriefings by the Abwehr. For the rest of the year, his German colleagues repeatedly asked him to retell his exploits in England, alert for any logical inconsistencies. For the rest of his life, Eddie was grateful that his 'cover story' had been rehearsed so many times.

Claiming that he was now lying low in the capital, Eddie soon became aware that his German masters had lied to him, much as MI5 had predicted. Breaking its promises was typical of how the Abwehr treated its agents. They were usually paid late or sometimes not at all; requests for help were mysteriously never received; and more than a few were left hanging in the most dangerous circumstances imaginable. Despite the promises that they would do their best to assist his return, Eddie was curtly informed during a routine radio transmission on Monday, 8 February that it would be impossible to pick him up by submarine. Agent Fritzchen would, they insisted, have to make his way back to Lisbon in the 'normal way' as a passenger.

To some extent, the Security Service was relieved. Despite the inherent difficulties – Zigzag was, after all, technically speaking, a felon on the loose – arranging Eddie's passage to Lisbon presented the least problematic option. If Zigzag remained in England, he might well be expected to carry out further acts of sabotage. MI5 would arrange for him to obtain the correct papers; if he went as a stowaway, Eddie might be arrested on landing. 'It would be a disaster if you managed to get arrested by the [Portuguese] police,' Tommy Robertson said. Travel documents would have to be obtained at least three weeks before his departure and it was decided that Eddie should – 'by begging, borrowing or stealing' – get hold of a National Registration Identity Card.

Zigzag's security handlers realised that because of the 'smoothness' of his work to date, 'some upset' should be introduced into his reports to the Germans. In the aftermath of the sabotage, Eddie would explain to the boys in Nantes that friction had developed between him and his pre-war crony. After Jimmy Hunt had subsequently been arrested, Eddie would claim that he was scared because there was a considerable 'hue and cry' for Jimmy's accomplice. One morning, he transmitted a series of letter Ps in his ham chat, to let the operators on the other side of the Channel know that the police were in the vicinity. The Germans would conclude that after his supposed arrest, Hunt had talked. Because of this, Eddie would then have had to close down his transmissions far quicker than he had wanted.

To explain how he had left the country, Eddie would tell the Germans that he had tried to get his seaman's papers from Franny Daniels, one of his old underworld acquaintances ('who was concerned with shipping circles in peace time'), who had told him all he would need were civilian documents to register. Via Jimmy Hunt, Eddie would claim, he obtained the relevant paperwork from their pre-war driver, Hugh Anson, for £100. Daniels would then make contact with his friends in Liverpool so that Eddie could set sail for Portugal on the first available boat.

By the Wednesday of that second week in February, Agent Fritzchen was telling the Germans that it was too dangerous for him to continue. In one of his last messages, sent on Saturday, 13 February – exactly two weeks after the explosion – he added: 'Jimmy arrested. See *Evening Standard* February 12th Front Page. Closing transmitter at once. Will try to get to Lisbon.' He would tell his Abwehr handlers that he had buried the wireless in the garden in Hendon.

The continuing lack of radio contact worked in both directions. Once Eddie returned to 'the other side', MI5 wanted to make sure that it could keep in contact with him. It would be too dangerous for agent Zigzag to carry a transmitter, though they presumed the Germans would be happy for Eddie to keep up his radio training.

So, as he had done when practising in Nantes, MI5 encouraged him to continue sending 'silly or joking messages' when he returned to occupied territory. Via innocuous-looking ham chat Eddie could thus send messages to his British handlers. He could alert the British radio monitors to his presence by always signing off 'FFF' or 'FRITZ' even if the Abwehr changed his call sign. If the phrase 'QLF' appeared in his ham chat, it meant the Germans were satisfied; '99' would mean they were suspicious. 'On no other occasions would he use these expressions than to indicate to us the arranged information,' Ronnie Reed recorded.

If he was involved in further sabotage missions, MI5 would obviously wish to be alerted where he was being sent. 'While I was learning the art of transmitting in Germany, I had often at the end of transmission fooled about with the Morse key and sent a series of ha ha ha he he he hi hi hi,' he later wrote. 'We now worked out a combination of these and other seemingly harmless jocularities into a fully comprehensive code.' They agreed that if he was going to Berlin, he would sign off 'HI HA HU'; Paris, 'HA HU HI'; Angers, 'HU HI HA'; and the United States, 'HE HE HE'.

Yet MI5 might want to send messages to Eddie. Agent Fritzchen would presumably still be allowed by his German handlers to look at the English papers and listen to the radio. Eddie himself came up with the idea that on the Tuesday or Thursday after sending a message in his ham chat, confirmation should come from the English press that it had been received in London. It was eventually agreed that the following should be placed in the personal columns of *The Times*: 'Mrs West thanks the anonymous donor of the gift of £11'. As Ronnie Reed explained: 'The second figure of the amount of sterling designated indicates the number of the message i.e. £11 = message No. 1, £12 = message No. 2.'

And a back-up – missing from the official files – is provided by Betty Chapman. Victor Sylvester was a popular bandleader during the war years and MI5 had arranged for him to play a certain song if they needed to confirm receipt of a message. 'Victor Sylvester would play "I've Got a Girl in Kalamazoo",' Betty says, 'and Eddie would then know that they had received the message.'

And in case the Germans did see through his cover story, his MI5 handlers concocted a final twist, which in Ronnie Reed's phrase 'he might possibly get away with'. Eddie would explain that although he had been arrested by the British, he had continued to transmit without the five Fs, which indicated that he was under British control. When the British had become aware of this, Eddie would claim, he had been forced to add them in subsequent transmissions. His forgetfulness on the day after Christmas would add some credibility to such a claim.

Eddie would claim that the Security Service had taken Freda

White hostage as a form of insurance. In the words of Ronnie Reed's report, 'should he ever reveal that he had been caught by us and turned around we should shoot this woman'. Reed thought it highly unlikely that the Germans would believe such a claim, but it seemed prudent to have some bluff ready to hand.

The question remained: would the Germans believe this increasingly complex story?

With his enforced radio silence, MI5 remained worried that Eddie might become complacent or bored. His handlers had realised early on that he had to be treated very carefully. They had already pegged him as vain and egotistical; and now they were only too well aware of his moodiness. Throughout his stay, Eddie came up with ever more ingenious plans to prove his worth. And the many contemporaneous official reports are highly revealing about a question that was to puzzle many people in the years to come: whose side was Eddie really on?

'Discussing patriotism, a subject which he himself brought up, he said he wondered what it was that had made him leave Germany to come over here,' his handler Allan Tooth recorded. 'In Germany, he could have lived well, both now and after the war. In spite of being much impressed by German propaganda and by his favourable treatment, [he] is proud to be British and wants us to win the war.'

At Christmas, he had suggested that he should be allowed to take half a dozen British saboteurs with him back to occupied territory to pay 'the Gestapo in their own coin'. In France, he explained, he could direct these saboteurs to blow up various facilities, including the Nantes *Stelle*. He might use the pretext of visiting Stefan von Gröning's quarters with a large bottle of cognac as a present, the bottle itself holding enough explosives to destroy the room. 'There are many targets which could be attacked and I can give fairly good schemes for attacking them,' Eddie wrote. But his MI5 handlers were opposed to such schemes. British Intelligence did not want to sanction what could turn out to be a suicide mission. Putting Eddie into contact with other agents might increase the likelihood of the arrest of them all.

'I consider you far too valuable to risk any such link-ups,' was how Ronnie Reed diplomatically put it to him.

Yet Eddie had an even more audacious plan. In the last few weeks of his stay in Hendon, he referred more than once to a mysterious mission which he wanted to undertake in Berlin. Eventually, in the living room in Crespigny Road, he revealed all to senior MI5 officers, including Colonel Tommy Robertson.

In front of the Boys at Nantes, Eddie claimed, he had taken care to give the 'Heil Hitler' salute and make complimentary remarks about the Führer. If his sabotage mission in Britain was successful, Stefan von Gröning had said, he would be happy to reward Eddie by taking him personally to Berlin. There he would be placed in the front row at one of Hitler's showpiece speeches. It would, the Baron said, be too dangerous to introduce him personally to the Führer. No matter, Eddie had replied, for what he realised – as he now explained to his British handlers – was that it would afford a great opportunity to assassinate Adolf Hitler.

Eddie – in his usual breezy manner – was not sure exactly how it could be achieved, but his knowledge of explosives and incendiaries would come in useful. One of the MI5 men suggested that it might be more difficult than that. It would also inevitably lead to his immediate liquidation.

Eddie smiled. 'Ah, but what a way out!'

Perhaps this was the most revealing part of his whole confession to the British Security Service. Eddie's need for adventure was matched only by a desire to make his mark on history: not fame for its own sake, but the kind of infamy that could only come from the ultimate sacrifice. It was something that MI5 recognised in its final summary of his stay in Britain:

When describing his criminal experiences, ZIGZAG has always played on the amount of publicity which he has obtained in the daily press and has always been very proud of this. He believes that he is now a man without a country who cannot come back to Great Britain and lead a normal life, firstly because his past would make it impossible and secondly because he does not want to, and yet he realises that his future in the occupied countries would always be extremely uncertain. Furthermore, I believe that he has a considerable amount of loyalty towards Great Britain and these sentiments all serve to make him want to take 'the big way out'. He can think of no better way of leaving this life than by obtaining world press reports and a place in the pages of history.

Though he never got the chance to assassinate Adolf Hitler, Eddie always maintained that he did meet Winston Churchill in the winter of 1943. Perhaps it isn't such a ludicrous claim, for the Prime Minister had an almost schoolboy fascination for espionage. Churchill's personal interest had already transformed the craft of intelligence from the obscure practice of a handful of well-connected establishment figures to perhaps the greatest success of the Second World War. He was also drawn to mavericks and buccaneers.

According to Betty Chapman, Churchill sent for Eddie personally to go to Chequers some time after he had carried out the Hatfield job. Indeed, we know from MI5 files that 'the P.M.' was 'very interested' in the case. So it is not beyond the realms of possibility that he wanted to hear from the man himself what agent Zigzag had been up to.

In Betty's account, the Prime Minister was sitting up in bed when Eddie arrived. 'What's your drink?' he asked.

'Brandy,' Eddie replied.

Churchill rang a bell attached to a rope and after a while a butler appeared. 'I want you to go down to the cellar and bring some Napoleon brandy,' he instructed him. Messrs Chapman and Churchill spent the rest of the evening emptying the bottle, doubtless coming up with ways for Eddie to win the war.

Despite calculating all the various permutations of his cover, many MI5 officers remained worried about Eddie Chapman's impending departure. After two years of pulling the wool over German eyes, even the more optimistic members of the Double Cross Committee felt the existence of double-cross operations might eventually be compromised. Now, as Eddie was preparing for his departure, the dangers were intensifying.

Eddie was about to set sail during the most dangerous month of the war so far as the Battle of the Atlantic was concerned. By March 1943, Hitler's U-boats had come perilously close to cutting off supplies from the United States, without which Britain would be starved into submission. When he finally departed for Lisbon, the course that Eddie would have to navigate would be no less perilous than that of the convoy he was about to join. Agent Zigzag would be living on his wits and having to face terrors even greater than the prospect of drowning after a U-boat attack.

CHAPTER SEVEN

Voyage to Lisbon

'Elaborate arrangements were discussed for my return to the Germans and also the part I was to play for Britain in the event of my story being accepted, that I had successfully carried out the mission they had sent me on . . . Armed with my seaman's book and in company with one of our Intelligence boys, we dressed as seamen and with a Lüger in my belt, travelled up to Liverpool. Heavy convoys sailed from here to all parts of the world but we had to find a ship that was going to Lisbon . . .'

– Eddie Chapman recalls how he returned to the Continent

ON THE SUNNY MORNING of Friday, 5 March 1943 a convoy of ships steamed out of Liverpool, heading west towards the region beyond Iceland which sailors called 'torpedo alley'. The ships were soon making their way through the choppy sub-Arctic currents to the north and west of Ireland: some would head towards North America while others would peel off towards the ports of West Africa. One ship in particular, the *City of Lancaster*, a pre-war steamer converted for the needs of convoy supplies, would first head for Lisbon and then sail around Gibraltar into the Mediterranean. Within days, all would come under threat of both long-range Luftwaffe reconnaissance aircraft and U-boat packs. The crews of the convoy knew only too well what was in store for them.

The convoy was to suffer the fate of so many that spring as the Battle of the Atlantic reached its climax. Within just a week, seven of its ships had been sent to the bottom of the ocean. Heading in the opposite direction, another twenty-three ships would be lost after leaving the eastern seaboard of the United States. For once, the Nazi propaganda was justified. When the U-boat crews later referred to it as 'the Month of the Thunderbolt', there were few on the Allied side who would disagree.

Somewhere within the sub-aquatic depths of the *City of Lancaster* lay Assistant Steward Hugh Anson. Tall, thin and rakish-looking with a pencil-thin moustache, he wasn't feeling in the best of health. This was his maiden voyage and he was suffering terribly from nerves and nausea. As he got used to the Atlantic swells the sickness passed, but the nervousness remained. It wasn't because he feared the inevitability of attack or the horrors of drowning. The simple fact was that Hugh Anson was living a lie.

His papers were false, his cover story an elaborate mixture of verifiable fact and fiction; and somewhere in his possession was an illicitly obtained Lüger and a clip of spare bullets that he hoped would keep him out of trouble. Anson was also carrying a tranche of secret information on shipping manifests and diagrams of ordnance written in invisible ink. If discovered, they would lead to his arrest.

Eddie Chapman was returning to his German paymasters in the guise of a pre-war criminal associate whom he had last seen in Jersey four years before. Now, as the convoy headed towards the freezing waters of the mid-Atlantic, his sense of isolation increased. Alone in his bunk, Eddie feared he would be found out. Though he wasn't aware of it at the time, many of his crewmates had already formed the impression that there was something not quite right about him. They were harder to deceive than the Germans. But Eddie's temporary identity as an assistant steward would have to pass muster until they docked in the Portuguese capital in a few days' time. If the *City of Lancaster* made it that far.

★ ★ ★

It says much for Eddie Chapman's strength of character that not only had he overcome the lassitude which had gripped him over the winter but had persevered with his double life at all. The Abwehr had effectively abandoned him, but Eddie's criminal past had come to his rescue.

When a man was released from prison, he was given three weeks in which he could join one of the armed services. Few questions were asked so long as the miscreant subsequently behaved. The scheme had been extended to the Merchant Navy, for whom both Eddie's father and brother were working. It made sense to follow his family's example.

A *civvy ship to Lisbon*. Eddie could bluff his way on board by saying he had just been released from jail. Imprisonment would explain his amnesia about many of the pivotal events of the war. Impersonating a criminal sidekick would also show the degree of ingenuity the Germans had come to expect of their star agent.

What was more, it would help British Intelligence out of a dilemma. MI5 couldn't provide Eddie with a passport in his real name. Nor could he – like the other double agents who worked under British control in Iberia – simply take the regular seaplane service from the south coast to Lisbon. If the Germans bothered to check, they would find that Eddie had been entirely self-reliant in returning to the fold. The footprints of British Intelligence were nowhere to be found.

When Eddie outlined the idea to his MI5 handlers, they agreed. With the providence that smiled on agent Zigzag from time to time, it seemed that 'one of the boys' had just been released from prison. Hugh Anson had last been with Eddie when the police swooped on the dining room at the hotel in the Channel Islands in early 1939. Anson was better known to the police as a wheelman – the term 'getaway driver' was not then in common usage – but Eddie knew he could easily assume Anson's identity. After sharing so many adventures, they knew each other's background extremely well. It would be a simple matter for the Security Service to have an identity card made up in the name of Hugh Anson, along with the Seaman's Book without which the port authorities would not let him sail. When the time came, Eddie would say that he was 'just out of the nick' and claim that he wanted to go straight. The Merchant Navy, he felt certain, would welcome him with open arms.

Although it was irregular, the Double Cross Committee could see the wisdom of this approach. Eddie's handler, Captain Ronnie Reed, wrote to his superiors in early February, 'To the enemy he would say that, through his underworld connections, he had bought some civilian documents, got a friend to fix him with a berth on a Lisbon ship and used his false civilian papers to register in the normal way as a seaman, thus obtaining genuine seaman's documents.' In his last week in London, Eddie spent a few days in the East End Shipping Offices to start the paperwork trail. On his last day at the MI5 safe house in Hendon, he sent his final message to his German controllers via the radio transmitter hidden in the loft: 'Closing transmission. Too dangerous to work. Am returning via Lisbon. Fritz.' There was never any acknowledgement, nor any apparent concern on the German side as to how agent Fritzchen was going to make his way back.

Just getting Eddie on board a ship had been fraught with danger. The Saturday before, 29 February 1943, he had made his way to Liverpool by train from Euston station in the company of Ronnie Reed and Allan Tooth. Their presence would help iron out any problems he might face with dockside officials.

As they were on an official mission, his handlers didn't scrimp. Reed and Tooth checked into the Adelphi, then the most majestic of Liverpool's hotels. Eddie, to maintain the fiction that he was still associating with his old underworld cronies, stayed around the corner in a less glamorous establishment. Over dinner that Saturday evening, they decided on a plan. Thanks to preparatory work by MI5, Eddie, in the guise of Hugh Anson, had already obtained a genuine personalised ration book and clothing book as well as the warden's card required by all householders. Now he had obtained a hotel registration card for his stay in Liverpool. All this paperwork would, it was hoped, convince even the most officious bureaucrat. Eddie would later inform his German controllers that he had bought these documents on the black market. Yet he still needed a cover story to explain his arrival on Merseyside.

Eddie would maintain that he had been in Lewes Prison for the last five years. Released on a ticket of leave, he had come to Liverpool after being offered a job through the good offices of the Prisoners' Aid Society. There were three options for possible employment – fireman, greaser or ordinary seaman. Eddie didn't think he could 'put up a sufficiently good show as a fireman' but his handlers managed to persuade him otherwise.

Now came the hardest part of assuming Hugh Anson's identity. Obtaining a selection card from the wartime Board of Trade would not be easy. Eddie would have to take pot luck in being chosen at random from a 'pool' of available seamen. If he was unlucky, he might end up waiting around for weeks. Each selection card had a counterfoil that had to be signed and cross-referenced by the shipping authorities. If there was any hint of subterfuge, Eddie's impersonation of Hugh Anson would be over before it had begun. After some debate, it was decided to take a blank card and forge the details.

Early on Monday morning, Eddie went down to the docks. He was accompanied by a genuine dockyard official who had been let in on the real identity of 'Hugh Anson' and had signed the Official Secrets Act. Eddie was thus expertly guided through the correct departments to register for work, find clothing coupons and obtain the right gear to become a fireman. But then an extraordinary complication occurred.

When Eddie went to purchase his fireman's equipment from a dockside supplier that afternoon, the owner asked him a number of pointed questions, insistent that he knew the name Anson. Moreover, Eddie thought the man was aware of his real identity. This had always been a possibility, for in the guise of 'Edward Arnold' and 'Edward Edwards', Eddie had been a well-known pre-war 'face'. He had appeared in several newspapers – including the front page of the *Daily Express* – thanks to the notoriety of his safebreaking exploits. Eddie was convinced he had managed to bluff his way through. If the shopkeeper did his civic duty, his cover could be blown.

'This gave rise to some speculation as to whether the real Hugh Anson was in Liverpool or was, in fact at sea,' the official MI5 report of this event records. 'It was considered necessary to try and find out immediately the exact whereabouts of the real Hugh Anson.' The next morning, Reed and Tooth made an urgent trip to Preston, about an hour's drive away. This had been Anson's last known whereabouts after committing a minor offence in July 1941.

The local police records showed that Anson had been dismissed from the Bury Corporation two months after that. He had then worked for a time in a laundry in the same town. By the spring of 1943, the records revealed, Anson had been serving at an RAF airfield in Yorkshire for six or eight months. If nothing else, there was some consolation that the real Anson was now far away from any of his criminal cronies.

To avoid arousing the shopkeeper's interest any further, Eddie's handlers decided on a new tack. 'Hugh Anson' would become a caterer and ask to be taken aboard ship as an assistant steward. He would swap his fireman's uniform for a caterer's at another shop. This change of career required a new selection card; this the MI5 men stole. 'Though morally incorrect, [it] was practically the more suitable' is the explanation in Ronnie Reed's subsequent report to his superiors. That Tuesday night, Eddie was having a good laugh about their duplicity in a dockside pub called the Flying Dutchman when the dock official who had been so helpful joined them. Doubtless any chief steward, he remarked to Eddie, would be delighted with another helping hand.

'Not another bloody assistant steward,' said the clerk who would have to countersign Hugh Anson's selection card early the next morning. For a moment, Eddie wondered if he had been rumbled. By the evening, though, he was sufficiently recovered to return to type. Reed and Tooth discreetly followed him from a distance, wanting to make sure he got back safely to his hotel. 'Some sort of feminine intuition however told [us] to investigate,' Ronnie Reed later wrote. 'And sure enough ZIGZAG was in the bar with a prostitute.' Eddie hadn't seen his handlers arrive, so they returned to the Adelphi. One of them called Eddie's hotel by telephone from the lobby. All had gone well, he said, making no mention of this liaison.

'He did not wish to dine with us as he was "busy",' Reed added in his official report, 'but [he] would come over to the hotel at 9 p.m.' After spending the evening in the Adelphi dining room, Reed and Tooth returned to the MI5 man's room to find their troublesome charge reclining on the bed. They were astonished. Eddie had already ordered a room service dinner and had consumed a number of bottles of beer. In his inimitable fashion, agent Zigzag was determined to enjoy his last few days in his homeland at the expense of His Majesty's government.

Thursday was going to be crucial for Eddie's cover story. Behind-the-scenes prompting by the dockyard official had paid dividends with the Ellerman Line. Three of its ships would be leaving for Lisbon on the next morning's tide. Captain Kearon of the *City of Lancaster* was also told that Assistant Steward Hugh Anson wasn't who he said he was. That was a calculated risk, but, given that Kearon had already been awarded the Order of the British Empire for his services to shipping, hardly a grave one. After Kearon had signed the Official Secrets Act, Ronnie Reed revealed that 'Hugh Anson' was on a mission – he didn't say what – and would jump ship in Lisbon. Kearon was asked to keep quiet about it and report him as a deserter once they landed in Portugal. Eddie had already made it clear that this should happen only after he had made contact with the Germans.

Some time that morning, Eddie was introduced to the captain in a dockside office. The sympathetic skipper seemed 'rather too kind' in Eddie's estimation and 'would possibly be too helpful during the voyage'. He feared that if he were to receive preferential treatment, it would give the game away. Nevertheless, he entrusted the kindly captain with the secret notes in invisible ink he had been making. For safekeeping, they were kept in an envelope marked 'On His Majesty's Service'. Captain Kearon agreed to hand them back to him on arrival in Lisbon.

Eddie spent his final night in England quietly at his hotel, preoccupied with the thought that he might not be returning home for quite some time, perhaps not at all. It was with a great sense of relief that Ronnie Reed reported early the next day that 'ZIGZAG is now on board ship and we are awaiting any further developments.'

When Eddie boarded the *City of Lancaster* early the next morning, his heart sank. He wasn't prepared for a filthy, small 'seagoing tramp of perhaps a thousand tons'. Everything seemed to be smothered in dust, including the hatches and berths. The chief steward told him that his job would be laying tables, lugging victuals and cooking the bacon and eggs for breakfast. The only onboard entertainment, he added with a smile, would be watching fights.

Given that the ship's company of about thirty men were tough and predominantly of Liverpool-Irish extraction, Eddie thought punch-ups would be inevitable. After boxing training as a youth and later bouts in the Coldstream Guards, he was certain he could look after himself. Once they set sail, Eddie was soon making friends with what he termed the 'cockney' gunners with whom he berthed. Throughout the voyage, he was extremely popular because of his generosity with the large bundle of cash provided to him by MI5. As a result, 'Hugh Anson', with his gold cigarette case and gold watch, was regarded as a little flash. To explain his apparent wealth, Eddie spread the story that he was a high-class burglar.

'His behaviour has borne out his contention that he was a bad lad,' a post-voyage report by MI5 concluded. 'Several members of the crew were impressed with his good education and the gunlayer summed up the general opinion that he was a man of good family gone wrong.' The chief steward, though, was not so impressed. 'Anson was seasick for most of the time,' he told security investigators. 'And quite useless at his job.'

Later that afternoon, the *City of Lancaster* joined fifty or so other ships that would form a transatlantic convoy off the north-westerly approaches to Scotland. They were protected by an escort of four destroyers and three or four corvettes. After his initial queasiness, Eddie soon got used to the monotony of the voyage. He would be up at 6 a.m. to serve tea and then breakfast at eight. He would scrub the dining area to prepare for lunch, which was served on the dot of one o'clock. Then he would help clear up and wash the plates. His afternoons were largely free. On his first night, having made his way down to his berth, Eddie put on his pyjamas. The chief gunner pointed out that if they were torpedoed, his cotton pyjamas wouldn't provide much warmth.

By their second day at sea, the ships were steaming towards Iceland and out into the Atlantic. By the third day, the sea became much rougher and Eddie developed a 'nausea' headache. The gunners gave him some sound advice. 'Eat as much grub as you can,' he was told. He soon found this to be an excellent remedy. The rest of that week passed by uneventfully. To bide his time,

Eddie wrote an autobiographical poem which provides an insight into his current preoccupations:

> Stripey at the table sits
> Rolling cigs and making cracks
> Calming his man, using his wits
> He'll live to give many smacks
> To drink much beer, sleep with many girls
> To watch as life a'bye whirls
> Happy go lucky, come what may
> Three cheers for stripey hip hip hooray

The tedium was rudely shattered at around 3 p.m. on Saturday, 13 March. Eddie was awoken by gunfire. Against the cloudy sky, he saw the outline of a Heinkel bomber flying towards the *City of Lancaster*. In horror, he watched it release a huge bomb which just missed a nearby cargo boat. There was a terrific explosion, but none of the ships were damaged.

Eddie hoped that would be an end to it for the rest of the voyage. The faces of the crew at breakfast told a different story. They all knew that the Heinkel would have reported the convoy's position to any nearby U-boats. For the rest of the day, a sense of doom pervaded the *City of Lancaster*. That evening, Eddie joined his gunner friends on deck to pass the time. For some reason, he was powerfully reminded of his native Sunderland and his family.

Later that Saturday night Eddie turned in, knowing full well what might happen. At around two o'clock the next morning it did.

Eddie was awakened by a violent explosion. In the panic, he put his boots on the wrong feet and couldn't get his lifejacket on properly. As he was running around in the darkness, another explosion rocked the ship. He made his way up to the deck, where he beheld a sight 'which will remain forever indelibly fixed in the memory'. Just a few hundred yards away a tanker and two merchant ships were on fire and the whole convoy was silhouetted by the flickering of their flames. Very soon, there was another huge explosion and the *City of Lancaster* seemed to jump out of the sea. Its sister ship, just a hundred yards to port, disappeared under the waves. Soon it was clear that the munitions ship which had

narrowly avoided the earlier Heinkel attack had now suffered a
direct hit.

Eddie was overcome by anger and helplessness. He could hear
shouts from the water. The convoy was illuminated by the
profusion of exploding shells. 'We spoke in frightened whispers,' he
later recalled, 'stunned by the horror of the catastrophe.'

There were no further attacks that morning. At dawn, Eddie
went down to the galley to make tea and assess the damage. There
were broken windows and, in the distance, he could make out a
large freighter that was slowly sinking. By mid-morning, the ships
had reformed into the patterns of a convoy and were continuing on
their way. Just before noon, the *City of Lancaster* – along with the
Algerian and the *Baron Napier* – separated and made their way
south, towards the coast of Portugal.

On Tuesday evening, Eddie's spirits rose as the lights of Lisbon
came into view. He had already promised the gunners a good time
when they reached dry land. Following the U-boat attacks, Eddie
had confided in them that life at sea was not for him. After the
horrors he'd just witnessed, they could hardly blame him; he was
genuinely shocked by the carnage he had seen. Swearing the
gunners to secrecy, Eddie shared £10 between the eight of them to
bribe them into keeping quiet. They would be free to share his kit,
he said; he wouldn't be coming back.

At the same time that Eddie was heading towards Portugal, his
brother was making a routine trip across the Atlantic as a merchant
seaman. Winston Chapman's boat was the *Atlantic City*, a 10,000-
ton cargo ship which regularly sailed out of the Clyde towards the
eastern seaboard. 'We landed in Brooklyn after carrying general
cargo,' he recalls of his whereabouts that March. 'I actually knew
the ship that Eddie was on.'

The hardest part of Eddie's enforced isolation in Hendon had
been that MI5 hadn't allowed him to make contact with his family.
During his darker hours in Nantes, Eddie had been preoccupied
with what might have happened to them. 'I knew that possibly both
my father and brother would be back in the Merchant Navy as
engineers,' he wrote. On many occasions, he had 'shuddered to
think of their fate' when German radio broadcast how many tonnes
of Allied shipping had been destroyed.

When he had discussed Winston with Ronnie Reed, Eddie suggested that he might be in Libya ('presumed to be in the army') as he was of military age ('said to be 21 or 22', MI5 recorded). Eddie had asked his case officer to trace his brother but that would prove difficult. Without knowing his rank and unit, MI5 might waste a lot of time, as they had done the year before when they had traced the 'wrong' Chapman from the Abwehr signals. Just before Eddie had left Hendon, he had suggested if they ever did trace Winston that he should be told to listen out for Eddie's radio communications on his return to occupied territory. Gently, it was pointed out to him that this was a non-starter.

Lisbon beckoned. Not subject to the strict blackout of wartime London, the Portuguese capital was awash with lights, colour and the heady atmosphere of carefree living. 'There was a seeming surfeit of goodies and all remarkably cheap,' one MI6 man who was stationed there later recalled. By 1943, Lisbon was, like Madrid, a crucible of intrigue, rife with agents, adventurers and informers. The supposedly neutral Salazar government was inclined towards the Fascist cause, which made it difficult for British Intelligence to operate unobserved. The Portuguese secret police, the PVDE, had been well trained by the Gestapo. British citizens were always being approached or hassled by its officials.

As a result, the crew of the *City of Lancaster* were treated to a lecture by a security officer on how they should behave ashore. They should avoid coming to the attention of the secret police at all costs. 'Pay no attention,' Eddie said to one of the gunners when the lecture ended. 'That's just a load of bullshit.'

On Tuesday, 16 March, the *City of Lancaster* made an attempt to berth alongside Santos Quay but was unable to dock. The next day it docked successfully and the crew were allowed out on shore leave. Straight away, Eddie and four of his gunner friends rushed over to what he termed a 'foul place', a bar called the English Café close to the docks. It was exactly the sort of dive the security officer had tried to warn them about, for it seems to have been little more than a brothel.

Within minutes of their arrival, he was getting on famously with a slim, dark girl dressed in black. A waitress in her mid-twenties, her name, she said in halting English, was Anita. (By the end of that day, as later reported by MI5 investigators, Eddie 'informed all the ship that he was sleeping with the woman'.) Later that afternoon, Eddie said he had business to attend to. When challenged, he claimed he wanted to catch up with one of his friends with whom he had robbed cinemas in pre-war London. 'If I find him, I'm well away,' Eddie explained. When another of the gunners asked him what he was going to do, Eddie glared at him. 'No names, no packdrill.'

Eddie took a cab to rua Sao Mamede, exactly as he had been instructed by Stefan von Gröning three months before. Assistant Steward Hugh Anson would now be transformed back into Oberleutnant Fritz Graumann, alias Fritzchen, star agent of the Abwehr. Eddie presumed that he would be swiftly despatched to Berlin, where a hero's welcome and his promised fee of 100,000 Reichsmarks would await.

The street was in a working-class area of the city. A small girl answered the door. As instructed, Eddie asked to speak to a Senhor de Fonseca. He tried English, then French and finally German. The girl was none the wiser. Eventually, her mother let him into an almost empty flat. Eddie wrote the name de Fonseca on a piece of paper. Using sign language, she indicated that nobody of that name was present. She did, however, write down a telephone number. Eddie looked around and saw there was no phone anywhere to be seen. He recalled that he had passed a nearby café in the cab and took the little girl with him. He found a payphone near the bar and his spirits rose slightly when his call was answered in French.

'I have only one thing to say,' Eddie said. '*Joli Albert.*' This was the contact codeword which had been agreed with Stefan von Gröning.

There was a long, embarrassed silence. *Le monsieur* on the other end of the phone obviously did not understand. Angrily, Eddie told him to take a cab and come to the house on rua Sao Mamede in an hour's time. He bought an aperitif for himself and a lemonade for the little girl. Exasperated, he was consumed by darker thoughts. Was he being watched? Or set up? Was that one-sided phone call tapped? German Intelligence hadn't exactly distinguished itself: first, they hadn't provided him with a submarine and now there was a contact who didn't seem to exist, as well as a codeword that didn't mean anything.

Eddie and the little girl returned to the house and a short while later a 'good-looking Latin type' appeared at the front door. Senhor de Fonseca was accompanied by a short, fat man whom it transpired was a German Swiss. Eddie repeated the codeword, adding that he was anxious to return to Germany. He asked for advice as to how he should now proceed. '*Es tut mir leid*,' ('I am sorry') said Senhor de Fonseca, shrugging.

The two men maintained that they did not know what he was talking about, nor why he was using such a strange codeword. Astounded, Eddie suggested they forget all about it. The German Embassy was now his only hope. For security reasons, MI6 had moved some of its operations to its own separate building and Eddie presumed the Abwehr had done the same, but he didn't know where. Despite the risks, he decided to hail a cab and make his way to the embassy. Both the Germans and the British took care to keep a close watch on each other's embassies, while informers loitered outside in the hope of picking up tips or spotting people and passed on their information to the highest bidder.

The cab made its way through the rush-hour traffic into the fashionable district of Lapa, following the course of the River Tagus. It was early evening when Eddie arrived at the embassy buildings on rua do Pau Bandeira and, as he expected, their wrought-iron gates were already closed. As the embassy obviously wouldn't reopen until the morning, Eddie decided to return to the English Café to carry on drinking with his shipmates. When the taxi pulled up outside the café, he asked the driver to stand in the shadows outside for a few minutes. That way, Eddie reasoned, his gunner friends would think he really did have a friend in Lisbon.

Eddie carried on drinking, the alcohol numbing his anxieties. Not for the first time since he had been recruited into the secret war, he wondered how he was going to get out of this mess, spending a nervous night in the company of Anita in her room at the cheap brothel hotel. He was disturbed by the thought of what might happen if he couldn't make contact with the Abwehr or, worse, how the British security apparatus might react. Eddie was haunted by how he might end up in no man's land, possibly arrested by the local police.

Perhaps he shouldn't have been surprised. The Lisbon *Stelle* was infamous for its indolence even within so slothful an organisation as the Abwehr. 'There really was everything you could imagine,' recalled one senior official of the debauchery that went on there during the war years. 'We hardly had time to sleep.' Thankfully, Eddie did.

On Wednesday morning, Eddie made his way to the embassy as soon as the sun was up. He walked the two miles before breakfast with grim-faced determination, oblivious to the colourful shops and the springtime flowers. His greatest fear was that the Germans would think he was an agent provocateur.

'I want to speak to someone important because I have secret business to attend to,' Eddie said to the security guard when he arrived. None of the staff had yet arrived so he was told to wait in a chair in the reception area. A few minutes later a well-dressed man appeared. When Eddie told him that he was a member of the German secret service, he was given an address on rua Borges Canara. Finally, here was somewhere he might be expected.

The embassy had obviously called on ahead, for there was a scar-faced thug waiting outside when Eddie arrived. Rather than bandy around the useless codeword, he said nothing. The tough told him to go and wait on the corner of the street. A few moments later, a Fiat drew up from which a middle-aged, thickset man introduced himself as Herr Braun.

'You are Fritz?' he asked, squinting into the sunshine.

Eddie nodded tentatively.

'You need not speak until we are back at my flat.'

Without a further word, Eddie jumped in. Perhaps ten minutes later, they arrived at a luxurious apartment overlooking the river. From the medical certificates lining the hallway, it was apparent that Herr Braun was a doctor.* After settling into the plush upholstery, Eddie was offered a brandy and a cigar. Apologising for his unkempt appearance, he told Braun the story of his escape from Britain. The

---

* By the time of Eddie's later return to the United Kingdom, MI5 was certain that Braun's real name was Baumann, the chief of the Abwehr II sabotage section in Lisbon since 1942. According to the MI5 files, his other aliases were Blau and Bodo.

German smiled and said little apart from asking him to remain on board the *City of Lancaster* for the foreseeable future.

Eddie couldn't help thinking that this might be a little dangerous. As an incentive, Braun handed him five hundred escudos (roughly £500) and drank to agent Fritzchen's health.

That same evening, Eddie obligingly returned to the ship where he was glad of the chance to relate the farce of the last couple of days to Captain Kearon. Knowing he could talk freely with the captain, Eddie couldn't help putting in a little dig which would get back to his MI5 handlers. 'Their organisation works just the same as it does in London,' Eddie said, drawing an unflattering parallel between his German and British handlers. 'No doubt Ronnie will be pleased to hear that!'

For the rest of that week, Eddie came and went as he pleased. When he wanted to go ashore, he borrowed his gunner friends' yellow shore leave passes. When not spending time in the English Café with Anita, he would return to the *City of Lancaster* to sober up. By the weekend, Captain Kearon informed him that the other two ships of the Ellerman Line would be leaving for Freetown: his own would shortly be going on to Gibraltar and the ancient Moorish port of Huelva.

Eddie was alarmed. Would his ship leave before he had had time to make good his desertion? If the security officer aboard the *City of Lancaster* thought Eddie had jumped ship, the Portuguese police would soon be on to him. He had no false papers as a back-up and MI5 had warned him to be careful. Equally puzzling, why were the Germans apparently in no particular hurry for him to leave? Had he been compromised? Did they want him to twist in the wind?

Luckily Eddie had already arranged to return to Herr Braun's apartment the next evening. That Sunday he was introduced to two other German nationals, a good-looking blond doctor and a courier who spent his time shuttling between Berlin and Lisbon. Eddie regaled them with his activities in London and the hazardous voyage by sea. He took care to make a few pointed references to the lack of help along the way. Their smiling acquiescence didn't fool him. They were obviously Abwehr security men alert for inconsistencies, errors or admissions.

What Eddie didn't know at the time was that the details of his story were radioed that night to the Abwehr's headquarters on the Tirpitzufer in Berlin. Bletchley Park was now so efficient at un-buttoning the Abwehr's Enigma traffic that the Double Cross Committee in London had the satisfaction of reading the decrypted reports even before they reached the desks of their German counterparts. As a result, British Intelligence was alerted to some-thing very curious indeed.

Sometime that Sunday evening, Bletchley Park decrypted a signal from the Portuguese capital to Berlin which appeared 'to indicate that ZIGZAG was planning with the Germans to commit an act of sabotage against the ship in which he had travelled to Lisbon'. Such an act would prove beyond any doubt Eddie Chapman's loyalty to his German masters. As an incentive, Braun informed him that he would be handsomely rewarded for this additional act of sabotage. (Permission had to be expressly granted by Admiral Canaris as such an act contravened Abwehr policy in neutral countries.) In Eddie's later recollection, Braun asked him outright if he would be prepared to sabotage the *City of Lancaster*. But according to the relevant security files (only released in 2001), it seems clear that Fritzchen himself offered to blow the ship up.

Early on Monday morning, the phones started to ring all over Whitehall, from Hut Six at Bletchley to the offices behind Admiralty Arch where members of the Naval Intelligence Division were arriving for work. As the organisation responsible for the safety and security of British maritime vessels, they now had a serious problem on their hands.

In the Honourable Ewen Montagu, RNVR, the establishment had produced a dedicated secret servant who was prone to neither rash actions nor impetuous behaviour. Montagu was the son of a Jewish banking baron, a graduate of Harvard and Trinity College, Cambridge, and reputed to be the greatest fly fisherman in Britain. Working alongside Ian Fleming in Room 39 of the Admiralty, Commander Montagu was Naval Intelligence's representative on the Double Cross Committee.

Montagu now liaised with the other secret agencies to gauge the seriousness of the situation in Lisbon. A rogue agent wanting to blow up a civilian ship was a problem with many permutations, none of them attractive. If Eddie carried it out and lives were lost, there would have to be an inquiry. Routine police questioning would reveal that Anson wasn't who he said he was. Even if the British tried to remove the bomb, the crew – and any informants – would be alerted to the fact that they were being shadowed by 'spooks'. In so intrigue-ridden a city as Lisbon, rumours of this intelligence interest would undoubtedly get back to the Germans.

In London, there followed a day of anxious meetings. A great deal was at stake. If the security services overreacted, the Germans would become aware not only that the British were capable of reading their most secret communications but also that Eddie Chapman was in their employ. Ultra and the Double Cross system, the two shining successes of British wartime intelligence, might easily be compromised.

Montagu contacted Zigzag's case officer at MI5, Ronnie Reed. 'It was clear that whatever view we took of ZIGZAG's character and patriotism,' Reed would write of this day, 'we could not run the risk of taking it for granted that he would not, in fact, commit the sabotage.' The phone lines were still burning late that Monday evening when Reed was ordered to make his way to the Portuguese capital. It was felt that Eddie Chapman would be honest with his case officer as to what exactly he had been asked to do by the Germans.

Unaware of the turmoil he was causing, Eddie Chapman had spent most of that Monday with Anita before returning to meet Herr Braun and his companions. On the evening of Monday, 22 March, Eddie was handed two lumps of coal about six inches square. Very few onlookers would have realised that these beautifully made 'infernal machines' were explosive.

In one sense, Eddie was glad. There was always a difficulty in using explosive coal, for each lump would have to match exactly the other pieces of coal among which it was going to be hidden. There are differences in grain between, say, Welsh and Newcastle coal – and Eddie had enough childhood memories of the latter to be aware of the difference. Bidding goodbye to the Germans, Eddie placed the pieces of coal in a bag and returned to Anita at the brothel hotel.

Early the next morning, he took one piece of 'coal' aboard the *City of Lancaster*, a cursory police inspection at the docks having failed to pick anything up. One detail absent from both the files and Eddie's memoirs is exactly where he had hidden the coal. 'He carried it aboard between his legs,' Betty Chapman reveals. 'Eddie said, on many occasions, "I could have lost it all."'

Once on board ship, he spoke to his gunner friends and told them he was going to do 'some work' in the coalroom. In fact, he went straight to see Captain Kearon. The kindly Irishman showed little sign of alarm as Eddie showed him his piece of explosive coal and asked where the best place was to keep it out of harm's way. 'Where's the last place to put it so it won't get burned for a few days?'

Later that afternoon, a Sunderland flying boat came in to land a few miles away along the River Tagus. Captain Ronnie Reed already had an inkling of how Eddie might attempt to sabotage the ship. He had spoken to Lord Rothschild, who remembered that Eddie had explained in great detail how to make one of these 'infernal machines'. 'You take a piece of coal and you drill it,' Eddie had informed his Lordship. 'You fill the coal full of dynamite with a detonator inside, then you place it on a heap near the boiler, so that when the lump is shovelled in with the rest of the coal it explodes.'

Eddie was now trying his very best to make sure that this didn't happen. He accompanied Captain Kearon down to the coal bunker and, after crawling over most of the main coal supplies, placed his 'infernal machine' in the side pocket of the coalhouse. Kearon nodded solemnly when Eddie told him it would detonate only when it came in close proximity to a heat source. The safebreaker stood up and looked around the grimy coalroom. 'I reckon it would blow the bottom out of the boilers,' Eddie said. That, they both knew, would be enough to disable the vessel.

They shook hands and the captain went back to his office. Eddie went off to retrieve his belongings. He intended to leave and never return, certain that he would – as had been confirmed by Herr Braun – be flown out of the country later that afternoon.

But then what MI5 called a 'worrying incident' took place.

When Eddie reached his bunk one of the assistant stewards, a bruiser by the name of O'Connor, was fast asleep in his berth. Annoyed, Eddie woke the man up. Without a word, O'Connor grabbed Eddie by the lapels and headbutted him. Blood spraying all over his face and clothes, Eddie was knocked to the ground before recovering sufficiently to reach out and hit O'Connor with an empty bottle of whisky. His assailant stayed down.

'My face was now a terrible mess,' Eddie recalled. 'I had a swollen eye which was rapidly discolouring, one of my teeth had been knocked out and my nose was bleeding.'

The fight had attracted a small crowd of onlookers and an anxious crewman advised him to see a doctor. Eddie left the scene, as if to do so. He made his way ashore, called Herr Braun and told him he'd had an accident, then took a cab over to the apartment, his face still bleeding. As Braun patched up Eddie's injuries, bathing his swollen face and bandaging it up as best he could, he seemed more concerned about whether or not Eddie had planted the coal in the ship's bunker. 'Yes,' Eddie said. 'And I hope the bloody ship goes up with a bang and blows that damned sailor to smithereens!'

After a couple of glasses of brandy, Eddie said he felt a little better. A while later the courier who had been present on Sunday evening reappeared. He looked horrified at the extent of Eddie's injuries. Braun ordered him to get a passport made up in the name of a Norwegian-German seaman, telling him he wanted Eddie in Madrid that same evening where he would be met by a representative of the Abwehr. 'Tell him our man Fritz will be bandaged,' the doctor said in Eddie's hearing.

With his face still throbbing, Eddie only hoped that they would finally recognise the strange codeword *Joli Albert* and acknowledge that he was working for the Germans.

Back at the docks, it didn't take long for word to spread that Hugh Anson had deserted. Captain Kearon called the port authorities to make sure that the assistant steward's name was added to the watch list of deserters.

Early the next day, Ronnie Reed was settling into the office of the assistant financial attaché at the British Embassy. Captain Ralph Jarvis had been a pre-war merchant banker who now worked under diplomatic cover as the local MI6 station chief.* A former member of the counter-intelligence section (where had worked alongside a rising star called Kim Philby), Jarvis now gave Reed a 'disquieting report'. Eddie Chapman, it seemed from the calls he'd already made, had been behaving in a most alarming fashion aboard the *City of Lancaster*. 'He's been involved in a number of fights,' Jarvis said. 'This morning he seems to have had a knife duel with one of the assistant stewards.' This fellow, the MI6 man said, was now in a Lisbon hospital. Far from keeping a low profile, Eddie had drawn attention to himself in the worst possible way.

Jarvis went off to make more phone calls and left Reed to work out what they should do. The desertion did at least give them an excuse to go aboard the *City of Lancaster* where, posing as maritime officials, they could ask questions of the crew.

After further calls to the port authorities, Reed and Jarvis arrived at the docks within the hour. They started with Captain Kearon, about whom Reed had formed a favourable impression during their dealings in Liverpool. The captain told them that Eddie had behaved 'magnificently' and more than lived up to his reputation as a jailbird. 'He was very realistic,' Kearon said of Eddie's acting out his cover story. As for the fight, Kearon seemed to think it was premeditated. Eddie had mentioned it in the coal bunker, he said, and had created the disturbance to give him the excuse to disappear.

Reed and Jarvis then went down to the berth and talked to each of the gunners individually. Despite his bad behaviour, most of the crew remained highly sympathetic towards Assistant Steward

---

*In the early years of the war, there had been much infighting as to who was responsible for agents recruited overseas who then later worked out of the British Isles. MI6 was responsible for all overseas intelligence but there was always a great deal of overlap with MI5 when it came to the work of double agents in overseas territory. The previous summer, for example, Ronnie Reed had been handling a number of Icelandic double agents in Reykjavik, his presence confirmed by a number of telegrams addressed to him there as an officer of the Security Service. Later these Icelandic double agents were handed over to an MI6 officer whose cover at the embassy was as a commercial assistant to the Ministry of War Transport.

Anson. Showing admirable loyalty to their friend, none of them could suggest where he might have disappeared to. 'Try a bar,' one of the gunners quipped.

That night, Reed called at the British Seamen's Institute down by the docks. By chance, both the skipper of the *Algeciras* and the second officer of the *City of Lancaster* were propping up the bar. Clubs like this, the second officer said in Reed's hearing, were necessary to let their crews let off steam. Look what had happened earlier aboard his own ship. Feigning mild interest, Reed was told about the ne'er-do-well who had just got into a fight and subsequently deserted.

Ronnie Reed did eventually make contact with Eddie in Lisbon, although this detail is absent from the MI5 files. In a reminiscence recorded just before his death in 1995, Reed recalled that both he and an MI6 man – presumably Jarvis – had met Eddie, both together and separately, in an effort to dissuade him from sabotaging the *City of Lancaster*. Indeed, the MI6 man had pressurised Eddie quite heavily. Eddie was in a terrible quandary. For all he knew, the MI6 man might well have been a German plant: such were the dangers of being a double agent in neutral territory. He claimed he didn't know what Jarvis was talking about.

'Ronnie, am I glad to see you,' Eddie said when his MI5 handler turned up. 'I've had this chap breathing down my neck. I simply don't know how to deal with him.'

Reed was most insistent. 'Eddie, you must not blow up that freighter,' he said. 'It will substantially affect the war effort!'

Eddie smiled as he thought of an even more obvious solution. He handed Reed the piece of coal. 'You take it.'

'No bloody fear,' Reed replied. 'I'm not handling that. You can keep it yourself and simply chuck it overboard when it's safe to do so!'

In the meantime, some of Eddie Chapman's gunner friends feared that he might be lying unconscious somewhere in the city. Given the severity of his beating and his propensity for boozing, it did not seem so far-fetched a possibility. One, Raymond Richards, tried all the hospitals he could think of. Later, he sought information from Anita, Eddie's companion from the English Café. Eddie had been sleeping with her each night and then heading back to the *City of Lancaster* every morning. Surely she would know something? All Anita would say is that he had flown back to England.

The next day, Ronnie Reed became aware of Anita's existence. When they eventually spoke, Anita wouldn't even confirm where Eddie had spent his nights. A while later she told a still anxious Ray Richards that Eddie had gone to a hospital. The gunner was never able to ascertain which one.

Not that it would have mattered, for by now Hugh Anson, alias Fritz Graumann, né Arnold Edward Chapman, had left the country. The only consolation, so far as British Intelligence was concerned, was that Eddie's gunner friends obviously believed his cover story – that, as he had hinted to them on their arrival, he had vanished into the night to resume his carefree life of crime.

A far graver concern now consumed British Intelligence. What should they do with the bomb that Eddie had left behind? Should they let the ship go down? Or should they retrieve the piece of coal and bring it home? Could it be smuggled in via the diplomatic bag? When consulted in London, Lord Rothschild urged caution. If there was an acid fuse trigger, there was no telling what even a slight change in air pressure might do to the internal workings of the 'infernal machine'. The bomb had been primed by someone else, and MI5 had no idea when it was set to explode.

For that reason alone, the piece of coal could not be brought back on a commercial flight. It would, in Ronnie Reed's masterly understated phrase, be unfortunate 'for the plane, the political consequences and myself'. A number of BOAC seaplanes which flew between Britain and the Iberian peninsula had recently sustained damage 'and this could happen again, attracting unnecessary attention'. But if they just threw the coal overboard, the Germans would want to know how and, more importantly, why the *City of Lancaster* had not blown up.

Behind the scenes in London, frantic meetings continued well into the last week of March. There were earnest contributions from all branches of the intelligence establishment, all of which were routed to Ronnie Reed and Ralph Jarvis via the Lisbon embassy. Elaborate plans for a deception – given the codename Operation Damp Squib by Lord Rothschild – were developed to make it appear as though the bomb had been detonated. 'If the coal is not found,' Ewen Montagu later warned, 'there must either be an explosion or ZIGZAG is blown.'

The MI5 files show there was a considerable debate as to what should happen next.

'Reed will not be bringing the coal,' Jarvis reported back to London on Saturday, 27 March. 'Captain of *City of Lancaster* will take it with him to Gibraltar.'* Captain Kearon himself agreed to keep his eye on the piece of explosive coal in the reserve coal store. In due course, the *City of Lancaster* made its way to Huelva before returning to Gibraltar in mid-April, where it anchored half a mile off the coast.

Some in British Intelligence wanted the bomb to be 'discovered' there, because the Germans had a sabotage centre in Algeciras across the bay. This proximity would explain why the crew would be alert to any such sabotage attempts. Replacing Eddie's device with a less powerful bomb was another option. This would be deliberately detonated, making it appear that some sort of explosion had, in fact, taken place. The fear was that word of the switch would leak among the crew. For similar reasons, another idea in Operation Damp Squib – of doing a similar substitution in Glasgow and exploding a less powerful bomb – was cancelled because 'this coincidence was so unlikely as to arouse very considerable suspicion of it'.

It was decided not to explode anything on board the ship. Ultimately, any sort of explosion would either not deceive the crew or be too dangerous for their physical wellbeing. More to the point, if this was done in Glasgow, the crew would wonder why it hadn't happened sooner.

In the second week of April, the *City of Lancaster* drew up at its berth in the Scottish port of Greenock, along the Clyde to the west

---

*In the event, the coal bomb was removed from the ship on 15th April in Gibraltar and examined in detail by X-ray fluorescence. 'Detonator clearly seen, NO time fuse.' The detonator was removed and then the piece of coal was couriered by air to London. 'Coal sent by air,' a cable reads from 18th April. 'Should be delivered Admiralty at 1600 hours today.' Lord Rothschild marvelled at how quickly the operation was done.

of Glasgow. Three MI5 officials posing as customs officers – one of them Ronnie Reed, who had flown home from Lisbon the week before – came aboard. Speed was of the essence for the men who had sailed from Spain would quickly be replaced by a relief crew. These security people would explain that they had heard that a stowaway might have attempted to get aboard when the ship had been moored off Gibraltar. When they started to ask if anything strange taken place, the MI5 men would hear about the desertion of Hugh Anson. Explaining that one of the crew had told them that he had been seen in the coal bunkers, his belongings would also be examined. Something 'incriminating', they would explain, had been found in the lining of one of his shirts. One of the MI5 men would return with the 'infernal machine' for, as the files relate, he was 'very dirty and smothered with coal dust and had moved about half a ton of coal before finding it'. If German sub-agents subsequently quizzed the crew on their next trip to Iberia ('probably in most cases from intoxicated seamen' in John Masterman's characteristically prissy phrase), they would realise something curious had happened – but in such a way that would not implicate Eddie.

As news of the discovery spread among the crew, the chief engineer revealed his suspicion that the device had been put aboard at Huelva. Moreover, to MI5's consternation, some of the crew felt sure the bomb had been planted since their arrival in Greenock. But Captain Kearon insisted that it had been placed aboard in Lisbon, and that was the message that went out. Thankfully, no suspicions were raised about the operation with its supposed perpetrator. The *City of Lancaster* set sail once more and, in the meantime, Eddie Chapman was recognised by the Germans as a resourceful and ingenious hero who had not only blown up a factory but probably an enemy ship to boot.

After the successful completion of Operation Damp Squib a mystery endures. What happened to the other piece of coal? Eddie told Captain Kearon that he had hidden it on top of a wardrobe in the room he was sharing with Anita. After the fight with the steward, he simply left it behind. When Eddie later returned to Britain, MI5 officials were still curious about its fate. 'He does not remember the address of the house in which he abandoned the other piece of coal,' Reed reported to his superiors, 'and for all he knows it may still be there.'

A note in the MI5 files from Duff Cooper, an intimate of Winston Churchill's, reveals that he had spoken about Zigzag's return to the Prime Minister. 'The P.M. is most interested in this case and wants to be informed of any further developments,' Cooper writes in an undated, handwritten note which was collected in Eddie's personal file. Nothing else is minuted, but this fact, like so much other circumstantial evidence, suggests that Eddie Chapman's claims of drinking with the Prime Minister out at Chequers are not as outrageous as they first might sound.

Herr Braun was true to his word. A passport in the name of Olaf Kristiansson, a Norwegian sailor, was presented to Eddie – stamped and in order – shortly before he left the doctor's apartment. He had time to borrow a suit of clothes and an overcoat before accompanying the doctor to the airport.

It seemed likely when he arrived that the elements would conspire to keep him in Portugal. 'The weather was vile,' Eddie remembered. 'A strong wind was blowing and rain fell heavily.' When Braun spoke with the pilot, he refused to take off as the weather was so bad. But the Germans wanted Eddie out of the country as soon as possible. Given his facial injuries, somebody, somewhere would remember him. If the port authorities learned of his whereabouts, he might be arrested for desertion. After forcing the pilot to sign a note saying that Herr Braun would take responsibility for what happened, he reluctantly agreed.

Only half a dozen passengers were brave enough to tempt fate and the flight was extremely bumpy. 'The rain slashed across the windows and drove through the plane itself,' Eddie recalled, 'and two of the passengers were violently sick.' For the next few hours, the plane braved the skies – it 'bumped and lurched and battled with the wind for several hours' – before coming down, unscathed, in Madrid.

After he passed through customs, a local Abwehr representative – a small, rosy-cheeked man – walked up to Eddie and spoke to him in Spanish. Finally, the codeword *Joli Albert* worked.

'A car took us to the Hotel Florida, where a suite had been reserved for me,' Eddie recalled. Exhausted, he just wanted to rest.

Because of his appearance, his Abwehr minders decided they had better not tempt fate for a few days – Eddie's facial injuries were quite memorable – by heading out into the city. Eddie and his contact dined sumptuously in the hotel suite. 'Sucking-pig was the main item,' Eddie recalled, 'and it was washed down by three bottles of brandy.' He felt he had truly earned such a meal and promptly fell fast asleep.

The next day, Eddie was horrified when he looked in the mirror. The lingering effects of his fist-fight had swollen his eye grotesquely. The bruise was blue, with yellow and red streaks. For security's sake, talks with the local Abwehr men over the next five days took place 'in this hotel room, in the hotel lounge or cafés', as a later MI5 report makes clear. When Eddie was eventually allowed out for a haircut, the barber smiled and mimicked the motions of a boxer.

Eddie was treated extremely well by the Germans in Madrid. One day, a fat man from the embassy turned up and gave him one of the first of what Eddie later termed 'my interminable series of interviews'. He found the embassy man easy to convince, apart from one telling detail: that British civilians didn't need ration books in restaurants. All the Abwehr representatives he came into contact with could never quite believe that this was so.

While in Spain, Eddie took the opportunity to obtain as many luxuries as possible. Compared to Lisbon, the Spanish capital was much less well appointed. Everywhere he went, Eddie recalled being followed by dirty children, pointing out his bruises. 'The people of Madrid seemed poor and dejected,' he recalled, 'many went barefoot and in rags.' The Madrid shops, however, were well stocked, though the prices were exorbitant, too high for most Spaniards to afford. Flush from his recent payment for the attempted sabotage of the *City of Lancaster*, Eddie bought clothes, tea and coffee, which he knew would come in useful as presents for the Boys back in Nantes.

All the Germans he met in Iberia seemed to be connected with Branch II of the Abwehr, responsible for sabotage, and were permanently stationed there. As MI5 later recorded: 'He was not given the names of his companions and, in fact, when not absolutely essential, the Germans usually abstained from making themselves known by name.' They made several visits to the hotel over the next few days, quizzing him about events in Britain. He was taken to the funeral of the German ambassador and had a fine view of the procession, in which General Franco himself walked behind the cortège.

On his sixth day in Madrid, a courier arrived from Lisbon. Eddie was to travel with him that night by train to the French border in a first-class sleeping compartment. The courier, he remembered, had ten sacks of mail, all of which bore the diplomatic seal. Both of them expected to be picked up by German officials at Hendaye, just before the border. But their train was late and when they got off, to their dismay, no car awaited them. After waiting around for what seemed like hours, the courier went off to make some anguished telephone calls. Eddie was amused that he had now been left in charge of the diplomatic bag. 'There I sat, on the frontier of Fascist Spain and Nazi Europe,' he later wrote, 'guarding the secret diplomatic mail of the Germans!'

Their car finally appeared a couple of hours later. Eddie and the courier were driven over the bridge which separated France and Spain. Within moments, Eddie became aware of the profusion of Wehrmacht uniforms. His stomach tightened, for now he would be on his own, inside Occupied Europe, with only his cover story to protect him.

Early the next morning, Eddie and the courier took another train, this time to Paris. En route he once again became the centre of attention as he blithely ate a banana from a bunch that he had bought in Madrid. His fellow passengers were astonished. When they pulled into a station, a group of kids congregated on the railway platform to marvel at this rarely seen delicacy. With typical generosity, Eddie handed each of them a banana from the bunch. As they approached Paris, the corridor filled with women and children. Eddie continued to get friendly glances from *les jolies femmes* – but not, he sighed, because of his overwhelming attractiveness. He wished he had brought with him a ton of bananas; he would have taken the French capital by storm.

When the train pulled into the Gare d'Austerlitz, a familiar bespectacled face was waiting in the crowd. It was Wolfgang, his parachute trainer from the Luftwaffe, who had failed to recognise Eddie when he had dressed up in a military uniform the previous

November. Now, as he scanned the faces along the platform, Wolfgang didn't recognise him again. Suddenly, he realised it was *der Englander*.

'Fritz!' Wolfgang shouted. 'What on earth have you done to your eyes?'

Accompanied by Albert Schole, they drove towards the luxury apartment in rue de Luynes where, the previous summer, Eddie had agreed to be trained on a sabotage mission. The Germans started asking him questions but he managed to stall them, insisting that he would reveal all when Stefan von Gröning came to see them.

There was an embarrassed silence. It seemed his original controller had been banished to the Eastern Front. Eddie was horrified, for he would now be without his greatest protector.

Advised by Schole that he should not work for the large Abwehr station in Paris, Eddie was well aware that in Nantes he had been a big fish in a small pond; in Paris, he would never have so much influence. 'At the Paris *Dienststelle* he had not felt comfortable,' MI5 would later report. 'The personnel was [sic] unknown to him and they had even made difficulties when he asked for an advance against the reward due him for his work in England.' And he realised too that he would have some leverage about his future if he said he would only reveal details about his recent activities to von Gröning personally. 'If I withheld certain information from the Paris Bureau,' Eddie later explained, 'and refused to work with anyone but von Gröning he would most certainly be brought back.'

After a bath at the apartment, Eddie went on the offensive. The German government, he stated, owed him 200,000 Reichsmarks. In his usual charming and insouciant manner, he told Wolfgang and Albert that he would take an advance of 20,000 francs. With this, he would take them both out for a 'swell' dinner. After suffering the Abwehr's characteristic parsimony – with both money and the truth – he wanted to see how far they could be pushed. That way, he could gauge how useful he was to them. In the event, they grudgingly handed him 10,000 francs – equivalent to 1,000 Reichsmarks – which was more than enough to enjoy themselves.

They started the evening at the legendary Maxim's where Eddie found the cost of the meal 'stupendous'. Thanks to the black market, it seemed that the price of food had soared by 300 per cent in the time he had been away. Next, they took in a musical show at a club called Scheherazade (after the war, this was to become a favourite with Eddie and his wife; even today Betty says it 'was very special to me').

The evening passed in an alcoholic haze. It was clear the Boys were now off duty and, far from trying to prise secrets from their English comrade, they would willingly conspire with him to bring back their 'favourite uncle'. Over a bottle of champagne, Schole explained what had happened to the Baron. Von Gröning, it seemed, had quarrelled over policy with Colonel Waag, chief of the Paris *Abwehrstelle*. As Waag happened to be a nephew of Admiral Canaris's wife, it was inevitable who would win out. The Baron's prodigious alcoholic consumption had become the excuse to fire him. 'I pondered carefully over this development because I regarded the old boy as a valuable friend,' Eddie wrote. 'My contract had been signed personally with him, not with the German government.'

Thankfully, both Wolfgang and Albert liked the easy-going Baron. They were chafing against the petty restrictions – as they saw them – introduced in the wake of his departure. Schole told him Colonel Waag wanted to handle Fritzchen's case personally and would give him all he needed 'within reason'. He wanted Eddie to write to the authorities in Berlin to complain that the Baron was incapable and incompetent. But Eddie absolutely refused to criticise von Gröning. Even in his drunken state, he made it abundantly clear that he would only ever work with the Baron.

If von Gröning returned, Eddie said, he would demand of Berlin that both his current drinking companions should also continue to work with him. Wolfgang and Albert both agreed to help. 'It was incredible how everyone [tried] to curry favour with his superiors,' Eddie marvelled. By tying himself to von Gröning's coat-tails, Eddie would be able to play the system exactly as he – and the others – wanted.

They proceeded to spend what Eddie later remembered as the best night he had spent since joining the German secret service. After leaving Scheherazade, they took in the Lido ('more of a cabaret', Betty Chapman recalls) and Suzy Solidor's Fashionable Club, which the occupying forces seldom visited. Another half-dozen bottles of champagne later, they left the club at four o'clock in the morning. He slept in late, hoping to sleep off the mammoth hangover as he prepared to relate his cover story.

Wolfgang and a typist from the Hotel Lutétia came into Eddie's apartment to start recording the exact details of his exploits in Britain. He considered this first interview very friendly, but he knew that there was much at stake. Despite his matiness with his immediate Abwehr colleagues, they weren't fools. Wolfgang – and the others who later read the finished report – would be alert to any inconsistencies. Indeed, testing his cover story was to be a prolonged and painfully slow process. The Abwehr's approach was to get him to tell the story over and over again. That way, they could tease out subtle differences and ask more searching questions than he would ever have been able to prepare for. 'Considerable interest in Chapman was shown by various people in Paris,' MI5 would later report.

Over the next day and a half Eddie would face 'the searching inquiries of the German secret service with infinite resource'. As this was the later conclusion of his interrogator on the other side of the Channel, 'Tin Eye' Stephens, it was praise indeed. After having spent months learning the details of his cover, Eddie thought he was word perfect. Yet the most innocuous details continued to amaze the Germans. 'When I told them of my visit to the buffet at Liverpool Street Station,' he recalled, 'they were astounded and refused to believe that I had obtained a meal without giving up coupons.'

After arriving in central London, Eddie claimed, he had left messages at various clubs for Jimmy Hunt, whom he eventually found living with a woman he had never met before. Jimmy was surprised – but obviously delighted – to be reunited with his partner in pre-war crime. (At one point it had been intended that they would recruit Freddie Sampson and Tommy Lay – the old Jersey gang – to help him with his mission. Eventually, MI5 decided that Jimmy Hunt alone should be invoked, 'in name only', to make the narrative simpler.)

Having met Jimmy in a pub ('Hello, bastard-face' was his greeting), Eddie had hidden at a cover address in Sackville Street, near Piccadilly. Jimmy reckoned that this bolthole wasn't safe, as the police had been chasing him, and was about to rent a house in

Hendon, bringing the rental period forward to accommodate his friend. (In his explanation to the Abwehr, Eddie substituted Beaufort Road, where Jimmy's supposed rental property was located, for Crespigny Road.)

In his memoirs, Eddie says, he later told the Germans that they had spent a couple of evenings 'plotting and planning'. Jimmy Hunt, he claimed, was pretending to run an electrical business based in a north Kensington mews house. Jimmy seemed keen to join in with his sabotage activities. (For Eddie, the lock-up would have been strangely familiar for, as MI5 noted, 'on inspecting it, he realised that it was here that the safes which they used to steal from the United Dairies and Co-operative Wholesale stores were taken and broken up'. This neatly buttressed the earlier details he had given the Germans about his pre-war escapades in the 'gelly gang'.)

The crucial details concerned the last Friday in January. Eddie claimed that both of them had gone up to the de Havilland plant at the start of the new year to carry out reconnaissance (much as Eddie and Paul Backwell had actually done on 30 December). They discovered that the factory's main power house was too brightly lit for any attempted sabotage. People were in and out of it the whole time. As a result, they came up with the back-up plan of destroying the transformers, which would 'completely ruin the output of the whole factory'.

Because of his legitimate work as an electrical contractor, Hunt had had no problem finding petrol. In any case, he was able to forge petrol coupons fairly easily. A few nights after they had visited Hatfield – again as suggested by MI5 – he and Jimmy had gone to a quarry in Sevenoaks where 'there were several hundred sticks of gelignite and a couple of hundred detonators'. They then made up a wristwatch detonator in two separate bombs which were wired into attaché cases.

On the actual day of the sabotage, Eddie explained, he and Jimmy had returned to Hatfield at 6 p.m. By then, the factory was already shrouded in darkness. Their arrival coincided with a shift change so they climbed over the perimeter fence in overalls belonging to employees. They soon parted. Eddie made his way to one of the transformer houses, jumped its wall and entered without being noticed. With a fuse already set, he left a case under

one transformer while Jimmy did the same at the other. 'We then
went back to the car, drove two miles from the factory, stopped
the engine and waited for results.'

Wolfgang was more interested in the details of the sabotage.
As well as detailing his work at the de Havilland factory – and
why they had to change their plans in blowing up a different
powerhouse – Eddie also had to draw a diagram and explain
how the explosions had taken place. A key point in MI5's cover
story was that the explosions were not simultaneous. 'Jimmy
Hunt and ZIGZAG would, therefore, have heard two explosions
within a few minutes and would have realised that both of their
explosive charges had been successful,' Ronnie Reed recorded
for the files.

Eddie claimed to the Germans that three days later he had
gatecrashed a staff dance for a contractor to de Havilland's which,
by a happy coincidence, had taken place at one of their local pubs
in Hendon. Here he had talked to a woman called Wendy
Hammond whom Freda genuinely seems to have met at the
Hendon Way pub. Wendy explained there was an 'awful mess' at
the main Hatfield factory. The authorities, Wendy claimed, were
trying to hush it up. It was exactly what the Boys of the Nantes
Abwehrstelle wanted to hear.

Eddie then related how he boarded the *City of Lancaster* as a
steward and what he'd done to sabotage the ship. He regaled them
with his more recent adventures in Iberia. Wherever possible, he
got in subtle digs about having to return on a merchant ship and
not a U-boat. When they were finished, the document was nearly
forty pages long. Its contents were read back to him and he signed
it. Having passed the first act, he could afford to relax a little.

The next day, Wolfgang announced conspiratorially that 'some
of his friends' were coming to see them. Eddie was understandably nervous: this was the standard approach by the Abwehr
which always left him with a tight feeling in his stomach. The
'friends' might not necessarily be friendly: their visit could mean
anything from a celebration to a forced march to a concentration
camp.

In fact, they turned out to be Wolfgang's colleagues from the
Luftwaffe, who had witnessed Oberleutnant Fritz Graumann's near

demise at the hands of a British nightfighter. Both the colonel in charge of the airfield and a couple of the aircrew who had flown Eddie to England – the pilot and the wireless operator – were delighted to make his reacquaintance.

'Fritz! It's grand to see you back again!' the colonel enthused. 'A fine job of work you have done!'

He continued in this effusive vein for the rest of the afternoon as they sat around a large table, fascinated by Eddie's adventures in England. Oberleutnant Schlichting would have another reason to remember his return. 'He unpacked a couple of parcels he had brought with him,' he recalled long after the war. To his delight, they contained chocolate and coffee – 'real bean coffee, a rarity in those days'.

They were soon joined by an army officer – a small man, also in civilian clothes – who asked him fifty or more technical questions. He seemed happy with the answers. 'The general atmosphere during these talks was friendly,' MI5 later recorded. 'Chapman is of the opinion that his visitors were all from the Paris *Dienststelle*.'

The Luftwaffe crew recalled the inelegant circumstances of his departure from their aircraft. The wireless man revealed that as he was stuck in the hinged door, as Eddie had suspected, he had kicked him as hard as possible in the back. 'I was scared,' Eddie told them. 'My head was stuck in the slipstream and I could see the clouds rushing by. I thought, "God, I'm over the sea. They're going to drop me in the drink." I dived through the clouds, but then found myself coming down over a house. I missed it and I hid the parachute in some woods.' To their evident professional pride, he had landed 'right on the nose' of where he was supposed to. When he finally reached London, Eddie told them, he had slipped back into the underworld.

His mood darkened when he explained how he had made his way to Lisbon on the *City of Lancaster*. 'It was a terrible trip,' he explained. 'Half the ships in the convoy were sunk.' When he was done, they had some coffee and, saluting him as they prepared to depart, the crew invited him to dine at their mess. As they left the apartment, in Schlichting's recollection, one of his Abwehr handlers could hardly control his excitement. 'Isn't Fritzchen just a great little fellow?' the man said.

Eddie Chapman's insistence that he be reunited with Stefan von Gröning paid off. Early the following week, he was told that he was finally going to meet the Baron. Clearly, the chronicle of his work in England had been believed; the *Abwehr* would hardly accede to his demands if there was any doubt about his exploits in Britain. On the first Sunday in April, Eddie and Wolfgang took a train to Berlin. This time, there was none of the secrecy which had marked his earlier visits. They shared their own first-class compartment, with strict orders not to let anyone else in.

With each stop en route to Berlin, the already crowded train filled further. Eddie and Wolfgang's civilian clothes made them highly conspicuous. A number of military officers tried to join them, but Wolfgang kicked them out of the carriage. An increasing number of senior officers, standing in the corridor, glared at them, particularly when Eddie poured himself a generous cognac. At one point, an officious SS major had to be evicted by the transport police despite his threats of reporting them both to Himmler personally. Even a woman and child who got on at Metz weren't allowed in. Wolfgang was certain he would suffer punishment if he disobeyed his orders.

At around nine o'clock that evening, they were met at Potsdamer station in Berlin by car. They were taken to the Hotel Petite Stephanie in the Kurfürstendamm by a *Wehrmacht* Hauptmann who took care not to reveal his name. 'During my short stay in Berlin I was not able to see much,' Eddie would recall, 'but the bombing did not appear to have had any great effect.'

After checking in at the hotel, they were met by someone who was obviously a big cheese at the *Fuchsbau* – the fox's lair, as the Abwehr headquarters at the Tirpitzufer was known – who questioned Eddie again about his adventures in England. The questions seemed, in Eddie's recollection, deceptively casual. At one point, the German asked about the explosives used in the Hatfield job. But when Eddie explained how the batteries had been taped with adhesive tape inside the case with drawing pins on the right-hand side, his suspicions were aroused. Eddie had previously said they were on the left. 'His eyes glinted disagreeably,' Eddie remembered, aware that he had made a mistake, 'I felt hot.'

For a horrible moment, he thought he might have been rumbled.

Calmly, he went on to explain that he meant the left-hand side. The senior man – whose name he never learned – seemed satisfied.

Later that day, Wolfgang was beaming. Without any ceremony, Eddie was handed papers, a Reich passport in the name of Fritz Graumann, and a military pass (Ausweis) which identified him as an *Oberleutnant* domiciled in Berlin but born to German parents in New York. They would shortly be going to meet 'the old man who had been recalled from the Eastern Front'.

The next morning, they travelled out to the airport at Tempelhof, which also seemed relatively unscathed by bombs. Just after ten o'clock, Eddie – along with sixteen other passengers – boarded a small Lufthansa airliner bound for Oslo. During a scheduled fuel stop in Copenhagen, Eddie soon came to understand why the Germans referred to Denmark as 'the Promised Land'. Having feasted on bacon, eggs and cheese – followed by 'several pastries with cream' – he rejoined the plane, looking forward to what he would soon come to consider his own promised land.

CHAPTER EIGHT

The Oslo Connection

'What a change of scene! Below lay ranges of rocky hills cut by deep fjords, carrying in their still waters the reflections of endless conifer forests. Snow still clung to some of the hill crests, and it was cold in the plane. We glided up Oslo fjord, passing over the U-boat pens and reservoirs which the Germans had built.'

– Eddie Chapman's vivid recollection of his arrival in Norway

NORWAY WAS THE LAST place Eddie Chapman had thought he would end up after his return to Occupied Europe. After breakfasting in Berlin and lunching in Copenhagen, he arrived in Oslo just in time for dinner one April evening in 1943. Not that he felt like eating after a worrisome horseshoe-shaped descent to the ground. The airport in the Norwegian capital, Eddie reflected, 'must be one of the most difficult in the world on which to land'. No sooner had he passed through the customs barrier than he made out a familiar figure among the crowd. It was the large and ruddy-faced countenance of Stefan von Gröning.

'Thank God you are back, Fritz!' his controller shouted, visibly moved.

On many occasions, von Gröning said that Eddie had saved his life. Without star agent Fritzchen's insistence that he be reunited with his personal controller, the corpulent Baron might still have been serving on the Eastern Front. It was an indication of Fritzchen's stock after the Hatfield factory job; the Germans really did believe he had blown up the Mosquito factory. Indeed, his controller was 'very enthusiastic about his success'. As they headed into the city, he blamed the various trials of Eddie's return on Colonel Waag in Paris. 'But do not worry about these things, for you are now going to receive the money I promised you.'

Eddie was fêted by some of his former colleagues from the Nantes *Stelle*, who had also been allowed to join him. Agent Fritzchen could more or less now have whatever he wanted. At first they wanted him to be 'looked after' by a member of the local Oslo *Abwehrstelle*. Eddie said no. He wanted to work with people he trusted and with whom he was familiar. It was also in their interest to bask in Eddie's reflected glory. His friends from Nantes were hardly likely to quiz him too closely for inconsistencies in the story of his exploits in England.

They drove to von Gröning's comfortable flat near the Royal Palace, a building guarded by the followers of the Norwegian fascist politician Vidkun Quisling. (The term quisling came to describe all collaborators and traitors in Occupied Europe.) Also with them was a cheerful, chubby fellow with a wide grin who – like Eddie's controller – was fond of a drink. Yet looks were deceptive, for 'Kapitain' Johnny Holst, as Eddie soon started to call him, was 'one of the most dangerous men in the German secret service'.

After discussing his adventures in Britain, Eddie made it clear that all he needed was an extended holiday. Both Abwehr men agreed: he deserved it. 'Johnny here will show you around,' von Gröning said.

Over the next few weeks, that was exactly what happened. Eddie went drinking and sailing with Johnny Holst. It was obvious that Holst was there to keep an eye on him, but they got on reasonably well. Though only holding the rank of *Feldwebel* (sergeant), Holst was an important member of the Oslo *Stelle*. He spoke both Norwegian and Danish. He had spent time in Copenhagen, where in recent months, he told Eddie, a policy of 'reprisal sabotage' involving 'apparently senseless outbreaks' of violence had been pursued by the German authorities against Danish patriots.

Before the war, Johnny had been a seagoing master. His merchantman had been in a South American port when war broke out and had made its way back through hazardous Atlantic waters, avoiding various Royal Navy vessels, but before reaching Germany it had run out of fuel. The crew had made use of anything that burned, including the wood from decks and doors ripped out of their frames. Johnny and the crew were awarded the Iron Cross when they arrived in Bremen.

That night, Eddie was taken to his hotel in Slemdahl, a modest establishment called the Fossheim. After unpacking, they went to a restaurant exclusively reserved for quislings and German forces – it had been renamed the Löwenbrau – and crowded with troops. The third floor was marked 'Civilians Only'; no uniforms were allowed, an antidote to the ritualistic clicking of heels which accompanied the arrival of senior officers on the lower floors. 'It was always easy to spot Germans in any restaurant in Occupied Europe,' Eddie wrote. 'They were all so badly dressed.'

And here, as they would do on many occasions in Oslo, Eddie and his companions got wildly drunk. Some hours later, after two of his new colleagues came to blows over a girl who was secretary to the head of the Abwehr in Norway at a flat in Skillebekk, Eddie found himself wandering around the darkened streets of Oslo in the early hours of the morning, befuddled and disorientated by drink. Eventually, he fell asleep on a park bench. Too late, he realised he couldn't recall where his hotel was.

'Strange,' he thought when he had sobered up. 'Here I am, an Englishman in the centre of the Nazi-held Norwegian capital and not even a damned German policeman to help me find my whereabouts.'

The Norwegian shiftworkers – and bleary-eyed members of the security establishment – ignored him. 'Many curious glances were thrown at me,' Eddie remembered, 'but nobody bothered to ask questions.' Thankfully Stefan von Gröning had given him his phone number. Eddie called the Baron, who informed him of the name of his hotel. Eddie took the first train to Slemdahl. As he sat disconsolately on the train that morning, Eddie was already aware that in Oslo, as someone allied to the Germans, 'a wall of hatred rose against you'. He was glad to be able to sleep off the hangover in his hotel room.

Norway holds a special place in the secret war as the focus for many Allied feints, ruses and stratagems. These deliberately played upon Adolf Hitler's obsession about its strategic importance. He had once read an essay by a German admiral, Walter Wegener, on naval strategy where he had explained that the Kaiser had lost the First World War because the Royal Navy had pinned the Kriegsmarine down in the German Bight. Only by seizing Norwegian ports, Wegener had argued, could the German Navy be in a position to disrupt Britain's mercantile marine.

Many on the Allied side thought they had been on the receiving end of a German deception plan at the start of the war. It came in the form of a letter handed in to the British Embassy in the Norwegian capital in November 1939. What became known as 'The Oslo Letter' detailed a wealth of technical details about German weaponry: new torpedoes, radars, navigation systems for bombers that would use radio beams, and most worrying of all, something called the *Aggregatprogram* which seemed to be centred near Usedom in the Baltic. The literal translation of this work at Usedom was 'rocket programme', a notion that seemed a little far-fetched at the time. But it soon became clear that these original weapons of mass destruction did exist from aerial reconnaissance.

Now, however, in 1943 and early 1944, Norway was to become the focus for the secret war in the months before D-Day. To deflect the attention of the German General Staff away from Normandy, a number of ingenious deception operations were to be mounted in the country with the help of the new cadre of double agents who had landed in Britain. Among their number were the two native Norwegians who, two years before Eddie Chapman lived there, had been looked after by the Security Service at the same Hendon safe house in Crespigny Road. They and other Nordic double agents would become part of the much wider Allied deception operation that swung into gear in the autumn of 1943.

The star agent himself soon settled into his new life in Occupied Norway. Eddie's controller told him that he should enjoy himself and so they spent a leisurely fortnight completing the draft of yet another report for Berlin. A week or so after his arrival, Stefan von Gröning took Eddie to the railway station to meet another old pal from the Nantes *Dienststelle*. Walther Thomas, in the field uniform of the Wehrmacht, looked grimy and tired. The German was most put out to have been sent to the frozen north – but not because of the cold. 'My life belongs to my country,' he complained. 'I think I could serve it better in battle against the Reds than by working in this service.'

Together, Eddie and Walther moved into a more upmarket hotel called Forbunds in the Tullingsgate. Eddie was forced to repeat the details of his activities in his native land, his questioners still alert for inconsistencies. Distraction was provided only by watching a parade through central Oslo to celebrate Adolf Hitler's fifty-fourth birthday. Cheered on by fellow Germans, the procession was greeted by sullen resentment from the Norwegians.

The Baron explained that Eddie would not be rewarded until the latest report had been fully digested by his superiors in Berlin. On his return from a visit to the capital a few days later, von Gröning announced that agent Fritzchen had been singled out for a great honour by the high-ups in the Abwehr. 'Fritz,' he beamed, 'they have decided to award you one hundred thousand marks.' Apparently Eddie's latest version of events had been accepted.

There was an ominous pause.

'It is not enough,' Eddie complained. 'They promised me two hundred thousand marks.'

Privately, Eddie was elated at the offer, but he took care to keep a poker face, pretending to accept the remuneration with bad grace. Telling him that it was still a lot of money, von Gröning added that during his stay in Norway he would effectively act as Eddie's broker. If Eddie wanted any money, he would take it from his account and hand it over. The Baron, with a solemn expression, stood up to his full height. To Eddie's absolute amazement, he then handed over an Iron Cross.

'It was sent to our *Dienststelle* to be awarded to the member who had shown the most outstanding zeal and success during the year,' the German said. 'And after consultation with the chiefs here, you are the choice!'

Eddie tried not to laugh out loud. Not bad, he told himself, for his work at Hatfield. Oberleutnant Fritz Graumann was now immeasurably richer than when he had woken up that morning.

And he was also the proud owner of a medal for his exceptional bravery.* Eddie was struck by a bizarre thought.

'If I stay with this mob long enough,' he couldn't help wondering, 'I might end up a Reichsmarschall.'

The atmosphere in Norway, in its third year of occupation, felt very different from that of France where German hegemony had been accepted with such apparent docility. In the Nantes château, Eddie had been largely isolated from the realities of the war – and the terrors of occupation – but in Oslo, he was most definitely not. 'Though German cruelties in Norway never approached the scale of their atrocities in Poland and Russia, they laid the land under a real terror,' Eddie wrote. 'In return, came sabotage and murder from the Norwegian side, provoking more reprisals.'

Oslo was full of troops on their way to or from the Russian front. Rationing was severe and soon Eddie grew used to the permanent reek of the fish on which the natives seemed to subsist. Even in the classier restaurants, fish was all that seemed to be available. An atmosphere of absolute hatred was palpable. 'People of all classes and from all walks of life almost openly defied the Germans,' he recalled. 'They dismissed with contempt every kind of social cooperation or even civility.' On one occasion Eddie happened to be on a tram when a German soldier got on. A group of Norwegians stood up and made a point of sitting on another bench.

One day, a mysterious fire started at the Forbunds hotel. 'A loud explosion was heard, and going out to discover what had happened, Chapman found that the top floor was in flames,' was how MI5 later succinctly reported these events. The man in whose

---

* Was it an actual Iron Cross? Mystery surrounds what the medal was and what later happened to it. 'It certainly looked like an Iron Cross when I saw it,' Betty Chapman says. If so, Eddie was the first Englishman to have received it since the Franco-Prussian War in 1870. Formally speaking, the Iron Cross was only ever given to military personnel. There is some speculation that the medal Eddie was given was the War Merit Cross 2nd Class (*Kriegsverdienstkreuz*). According to Nicholas Reed, Ronnie Reed's eldest son, Eddie later gave the medal to his MI5 case officer for safekeeping. The Reed family didn't even know where it had come from. 'That was the sort of thing which Eddie would do,' says Betty Chapman. 'He didn't care.'

room the fire had started swore blind that he had not left a burning cigarette behind. Delighted Norwegian onlookers gathered as German officers rushed out in the confusion.

The fire brigade eventually arrived and sprayed water everywhere – everywhere except the fire, that is. Eddie's room looked, in his graphic phrase, as though 'something like a Niagara had come directly in through the windows'. The fire was stopped only, in the words of a later report to MI5, 'after they had partly demolished the building'.

For these first few weeks, Walther Thomas was stationed with Eddie round the clock. Eddie soon bridled and complained. To his absolute amazement he was given complete freedom. In the time he had been away, it seemed the Abwehr had made him a German citizen; he was now to be treated and saluted as a Wehrmacht officer.

The Baron told him that he would receive a monthly stipend on top of his fee for the successful sabotage in Hatfield. There would thus be plenty of money for the sweeter pleasures in life. Eddie had a sneaking suspicion that the Germans wanted him to spend as much as possible so he would have to undertake another sabotage mission to replenish his funds. For now, though, he just wanted to rest and recuperate. 'I've been lucky and I don't want to tempt fate,' he said one evening over dinner. 'I'd rather stay here and spend my money. Perhaps I may even find myself a wife.'

★   ★   ★

'Here, in German-occupied Norway, I was respected, among friends and comrades,' Eddie wrote. Despite the seeming trust they had placed in him, Eddie was constantly being questioned about his work in Britain. His various Abwehr cronies seemed to be working on the principle that a double agent would always remember the truth but never be able to repeat lies convincingly. One day, a man with grey hair, who spoke good English with an American accent, turned up to chat to him. Identifying himself as Herr Koenig, he seemed to be in charge of another agent who was about to be sent to England. He not only asked Eddie details of where he had hidden his radio transmitter but requested of him a safe contact and address (Eddie proffered the name Milly Blackworth at the Eagle Club in Gerard Street, whom he knew had passed away a few years before).

The probing went on for days. This smiling controller with grey hair – who Eddie later learned was a psychologist – even got him drunk to test the reliability of his story. For his own part, Eddie thought he had hoodwinked the enemy. But at the end of their final session, Koenig declared: 'You are not absolutely sincere.'

'I know I am not,' Eddie said, savouring the ambiguity. 'Do you expect me to be?'

Nothing more was said about this meeting. As a later MI5 report states, 'From [von Gröning] afterwards, Chapman heard that the interview had been successful and that the doctor was quite satisfied with the answers and information he had received.'

As in France, Eddie and the Boys were determined to have fun. The Ritz restaurant, near Karl Johannes Gate, became a regular haunt. One day, Eddie found himself seated next to an attractive girl in her early twenties. He waited patiently for an opportunity to engage her in conversation. Unlike the uniformly dowdy Germans, Norwegian women were elegant and attractive. When this beautiful girl reached inside her handbag for a cigarette, Eddie went to light it for her. She stiffened and shook her head.

'I am not German,' Eddie said gently. 'I am French.'

On hearing this, she relaxed a little. When he related that he was a French journalist doing a report on her country, she unbent even further. Her name was Dagmar Lahlum, she was twenty years of age and was dining with a friend. Like most of her fellow Norwegians, she hated the occupiers. Eddie invited her for dinner that evening, but she declined. With his usual determination, he eventually persuaded her to join him. Shortly thereafter, Dagmar became his 'constant companion' and then, 'in due course', in the anodyne words of a British security report, 'Chapman got to know Dagmar intimately.'

In fact, Eddie became besotted with the luminously beautiful Norwegian girl with dark eyes and straw-coloured hair. Dagmar remembered Eddie as a kindly and charming fellow, always smiling. And he was fiercely protective of her. At one of their regular drinking haunts, he beat up a legionnaire for some slight aimed at her. He obtained the release of a close friend of hers who had been rounded up by the Gestapo during a student demonstration. He even provoked an argument with a German soldier and a Wehrmacht officer in the street.

After hearing about this incident, his Abwehr colleagues asked him to tone down his behaviour. Norway, they pointed out, was a difficult enough territory to control without him adding to their problems. Eddie had to keep his feelings to himself when he saw at first hand the battle of the population against the quislings and the Gestapo.

By the early summer, Dagmar was living with Eddie on a yacht, a Swedish yarl he had purchased with the proceeds from the Mosquito job. Though married, she was separated from her older husband. The danger – if not sheer improbability – of the situation drew them closer together.

Eddie would have been quite happy to sail the yacht with Dagmar and take an extended holiday from his activities as a saboteur for the Abwehr. But Stefan von Gröning insisted that he keep up to speed with his Morse. Two or three times a week, Eddie went with Walther Thomas to meet a pair of radio instructors. To begin with, he practised in the flat in Skillebekk where the drunken brawl over the secretary had taken place on his first night in the country. After an initial run through, the captain in charge of radio training declared that Fritzchen was a little rusty, but perfectly competent at using his transmitter.

Eddie was never allowed to visit the *Abwehrstelle* in Oslo. Johnny Holst took him to what appeared to be the local radio transmission office at 78c Drammensveien. For a short period, Fritzchen acted as the chief radio operator for the despatch of messages between France and Norway. He and the unknown operators in France often added rude sign-offs – his favourite was still '99 99', which stood for 'Kiss my arse'. Eddie sometimes sent the sign-off 'FRITZ' as agreed with MI5 in London, so they would recognise it was him.

Because he always took care to bring booze to the radio office, Eddie soon became popular with the dozen or so operators whom the Germans were also training. A trio of other instructors were teaching Morse to some Norwegians and Icelanders. 'It was intended to use these quislings in intelligence work,' Eddie wrote.

One of the more exotic trainees, a Finn married to a German girl, was known as 'Johann the Devil'. MI5 described Johann as a 'rather extraordinary character, champion ski-er and parachutist, whose ruthlessness and adventures clearly fascinated Zigzag'. Johann regaled Eddie with stories of how he was once trapped behind Soviet lines in Arctic conditions. 'He and his small group of four men had travelled hundreds of miles on skis,' Eddie marvelled, 'living entirely off the land, fishing, hunting and stealing.' At one point, they were surrounded by the Red Army and had to fight their way out.

By comparison, Eddie's own adventures in Norway were rather tame. At some point, he was taken to the sabotage training centre in Grafsin. After four months at the Forbunds Hotel, Eddie moved across the street to number 8 Kappellveien, with Dagmar and Johnny Holst. The property had belonged to a Jewish hairdresser named Feldmann whose fate Eddie was never able to determine.* 'The house stood in its own garden, surrounded by trees of pears, apples and plums,' he remembered.

Under Holst's direction, this latest course of sabotage training was lax: Johnny often cancelled classes when he felt like it, never following a set timetable. Eddie considered him 'jittery', perhaps because of his heavy drinking. 'Whilst he attended the Oslo sabotage school, he was strictly an observer and had nothing whatever to do with the curriculum,' MI5 later reported of Eddie's time there. '[He] learned nothing new in sabotage', though he was 'regarded as an expert and was often asked to give advice as a result of his exploits'.

Sometimes spies were taught individually, at other times in groups. On one occasion, it led to a farcical set of circumstances when the house was visited by potential saboteurs. To maintain security, each successive agent arrived at an allotted time; agents already present would be hustled into different rooms, so they wouldn't see each other. The same pantomime occurred when they left. Eddie thought that this was very funny.

---

*According to information obtained from the Norwegian Resistance Museum, Feldmann and his wife were murdered by their Norwegian guides when they tried to escape to Sweden in late 1942.

Though Johnny Holst wanted to demonstrate some explosions, von Gröning was against it. Instead, Eddie learned about newer, more advanced ways of causing explosions with limpets, magnetic clams, detonators – including a new process he had not been aware of, involving explosive pellets dried in a muslin sleeve. Quite how this was going to be used was never made clear. For now, Eddie was determined to continue enjoying his indefinite, well-paid holiday. His major preoccupation was to spend time with Dagmar, with whom he had fallen helplessly in love.

Much of that summer of 1943 was spent sailing up and down the Oslo fjord, originally in the company of Johnny Holst. Eventually, Eddie and Dagmar were allowed to sail together on their own. As they made their way along the fjord, Eddie took care to make notes on all the U-boat pens and military targets along its coastal reaches. Early one beautiful morning, when the fjord appeared like glass, he was preparing the yarl to sail. On a nearby quayside, a car pulled up with three Germans and a Japanese admiral inside, followed by some senior marine officers.

A phalanx of press photographers followed in their wake. When this party boarded a waiting boat, it started to sink. Somebody had drilled holes in the floor of the boat. Eddie was transfixed. 'Violent voices were raised on all sides, angry fingers were jabbed in the direction of the boat,' Eddie recalled. Only the bemedelled and bespectacled Japanese admiral seemed to find it funny.

At times, his life with his Norwegian girlfriend was positively idyllic. 'Every day Dagmar and I were sailing,' Eddie recalled of that summer of 1943. 'We made love; swam in the nude.' Dagmar, too, fondly remembered her time with him, though in the words of her great nephew, Hans Olav Lahlum, 'she led a very quiet life and didn't have much contact with the family' in the years after the war. Indeed, she drew a veil over her time with Eddie Chapman.

'At the time of her death at Christmas 1999, the family was completely unaware of her relations with him,' Hans Olav says. 'We only learned after her death that she not only had an affair with him during the war, she even visited him in England.'

According to Betty Chapman, Dagmar actually became pregnant by Eddie during the war years. (The surviving members of Dagmar's family know nothing about this, hardly surprising as she kept quiet about much of her past. Her pre-war marriage was also something of a taboo, 'For nobody within the family even knows the first name of her husband,' says Hans Olav Lahlum.)

When Eddie learned about the pregnancy, he had no idea what to do. He suspected it could severely affect his standing with his Abwehr colleagues; because theirs was such a small community, word would soon get out that this British renegade had got a local girl 'into trouble'. The result would lead to many unpleasant consequences, none of them particularly appealing. Both the Norwegians and the German occupiers would be unsympathetic.

'So Eddie really didn't know what to do and neither did Dagmar,' adds Betty Chapman. Abortions were restricted so Eddie turned for help to Stefan von Gröning. 'And he arranged for Dagmar to have a termination,' Betty says. 'Turning to him was natural, because they were very close.'

Eddie himself never spoke of this matter, though he obviously enjoyed the time in Oslo best of all his wartime experiences. 'A lot of water has flowed under the bridge since last we met,' Eddie wrote to Stefan in November 1974, 'but I often think of you with affection, remembering some of our delightful times together, and, of course, the unforgettable experience of Norway. Do you remember Dagmar, I suppose she is married now? I wonder what happened to my little sailing yarl?'

★ ★ ★

One day in early July Stefan von Gröning informed Eddie that their superiors wanted to see him in person. Agent Fritzchen's reputation had preceded him. So they flew to Berlin to attend what they thought would be an important conference. This time, Eddie was trusted sufficiently to be allowed to see the capital in daylight. They landed at Tempelhof after stopping in Copenhagen, arriving in the German capital before dark and in the immediate aftermath of an American air raid which had not stopped the early evening traffic. Eddie was booked into a luxurious hotel.

Next day, taking care to appear as smart as possible, Eddie and the Baron were taken to a flat off the Kurfürstendamm. MI5 would later report that 'great interest' was shown in him, with many detailed questions being thrown at him. As ever, the Germans were not introduced by name. Seated around a long table were an elderly colonel – sporting an Iron Cross – and a pair of other people, one on either side of him. Given pride of place on the table was a half-empty bottle of cognac; and when the colonel spoke, it was clear that he was slightly the worse for wear. After toasting Eddie's good work in England, he said: 'Have a drink, Fritz.'

The colonel's first question concerned what sabotage might cause most damage to the British war machine. Eddie stiffly suggested that it was 'his employers' who should decide on these objectives. Stifling an urge to laugh at this 'silly old burbler', he responded in kind when they pressed him further.

'Well, why not blow up the Houses of Parliament?' he said straight-faced. 'Or bump off Winston Churchill?'

The colonel said that they weren't interested in political assassinations, rather factories or aerodromes. Eddie explained the difficulties of getting into manufacturing plants. There followed a discussion about trying to target machinery which could only be replaced from America.

Two bottles of brandy later, Eddie was completely baffled. Why had they flown all the way here for a conference that had achieved precisely nothing? Outside, von Gröning was livid. 'My God, Fritz! And with men like that in our service, we expect to win the war?'

For the rest of their stay, they explored Berlin. The shops were empty, though an illusion of plenty was created by the full display cabinets. When they returned to the Metropolitan Hotel's restaurant for dinner it became apparent why the Germans were obsessed with rationing in London. 'Everything was rationed,' Eddie recalled, 'there was just enough food on a coupon card to satisfy one's hunger.' There were already two meatless days each week, so Eddie asked what else was on the menu. The waiter beamed as he announced the special.

'Salt fish.'

They groaned.

On their first night, they visited a variety show at the Winter Garden. Afterwards, they wandered around the city taking in the sights. Eddie walked with Walther Thomas to the Olympic Sports Palace, now used by the Wehrmacht as a storage depot and training ground. Both the building and the monuments nearby were showing signs of dilapidation. 'It reminded me of the Nazi regime, once so proud, haughty and new,' Eddie wrote. 'Now it was visibly falling apart, and soon would be in ruins.' Though everything remained upbeat on the surface, the façade of Nazi Germany was beginning to crumble.

The next day, they returned to Tempelhof for their departure. There they chanced upon an Abwehr man who had been present at the earlier meeting. He was reading a book called *The English Secret Service* by a French author. Over coffee, he explained the workings of Britain's intelligence agencies, much to Eddie's silent amusement. He then turned to von Gröning. 'If I had my way,' he said portentously, 'I would make Fritz here the chief of our service.'

Eddie's controller nodded in agreement.

In the event, they weren't able to leave that day because their aeroplane had broken down. They spent Eddie's last night watching a circus, as good a metaphor as any for the way in which star agent Fritzchen had wasted a few days at the behest of his Abwehr masters.

German military intelligence had already demonstrated far greater incompetence that year. At the conclusion of Operation Damp Squib, Commander Ewen Montagu of the Naval Intelligence Division had focused his attentions on Operation Mincemeat, better known as the ruse of The Man Who Never Was and perhaps the most famous covert operation of the war. After the Allies' victories in the desert, its aim was to make it appear as though Allied forces would next attack Greece and Sardinia rather than their actual target, Sicily.

In a briefing paper, Montagu had written: 'Why shouldn't we get a body, disguise it as a staff officer and give him really high level papers which will show clearly that we are going to attack somewhere (other than Sicily)?' The plan was audacious but breathtakingly simple. In April 1943 the recently deceased corpse of what appeared to be a British marine was washed ashore in Spain, a briefcase chained to his hand. When the body, identified as 'Major

Martin', was examined by a doctor in Huelva, the local Abwehr agent copied the contents of the briefcase, including a letter from Lord Mountbatten. He swiftly despatched them to Berlin. Major Martin, it seemed, was an expert in the deployment of landing craft. 'Let me have him back, please, as soon as the assault is over,' Mountbatten's fake letter read. 'He might bring some sardines back with him . . .'

That was the neatest touch of all. The Germans were now certain Sardinia would be the target. Hitler's general staff swallowed Mincemeat whole and the invasion of Sicily in July 1943 came as a total surprise.

Having failed to foresee the invasion of Sicily, the Abwehr again demonstrated its incompetence that July by its failure to predict Mussolini's subsequent downfall and the resultant surrender of Italy. And the Abwehr also failed to predict the defection of Italy to the Allies – unlike the *Sicherheitsdienst* (SD), the intelligence-gathering arm of the SS. In the wake of this and other intelligence failures – notably the Torch landings in North Africa the previous year – Admiral Canaris's fate was sealed.

That summer, Germany itself began suffering 'terrible ravages', as Eddie put it. The Allied air campaign reached a climax with the massed raids on Hamburg at the end of July. 'The horrors of bombing attacks were brought home to me personally by several friends who had lost their homes,' he noted. Their number included Johnny Holst, who was home in Hamburg when he witnessed first hand the effects of incendiary bombs. Entire streets curled up like tissue paper, and he lost his own house in the raging fire. In time, other members of the Oslo *Stelle* too lost their homes and, Eddie remarked, as 'they lived in widely separated parts of Germany, I gained a fair idea of the magnitude of the Allied attack'.

Yet Nazi propaganda remained as sure-footed as it always had done. As regards the Eastern Front, newspapers and radio broadcasts still claimed that most of the Sixth Army had escaped at Stalingrad. Whenever the arch-nationalist Walther Thomas pointed out a decorated war hero, Eddie would tease him that within a short while, the man would be a frozen corpse on the Eastern Front.

'Better death for one's ideals than sitting here doing damn all.'*

By the late summer of 1943, the war was tilting in the Allies' favour. The last great German offensive on the Eastern Front at Kursk – the largest tank battle in history – had failed in July. Eddie sensed there was a feeling of impending doom, 'a falling market in Hitler's stock'.

On his return to Oslo, Eddie was still determined to enjoy the sweeter things in life, particularly after the matter of his girlfriend's pregnancy had been attended to. 'I had made enough money,' he recalled, 'now I only wished to lead a life of pleasure for a while.' Dagmar herself was rather more preoccupied by a lawsuit over the return of some money from her estranged husband. Eddie told her not to worry. 'I've got plenty of money,' he said.

When she repeatedly refused to accept any help, Eddie told her how he had come by the money. It had come from the Germans, he said. For once, he was being totally serious when he continued: 'I am putting my life in your hands.' He was, he explained, working for the British secret service.

If Dagmar let slip to the Germans that Eddie had double-crossed them, it would have disastrous consequences. Not only would it let the Abwehr know that Fritzchen was deceiving them, it would call into question the reliability of all their other *V-menn* abroad. One word out of place and the whole edifice of the Double Cross Committee would come tumbling down. After a number of near misses, British Intelligence already felt that double agents were living on borrowed time. Nobody, though, had envisaged that the weakest link might be a Norwegian girl living on a yacht with a pre-war safebreaker.

When MI5 later heard about Eddie's indiscretion, they were aghast. Nerves were stretched tight because the double agents were

---

*Thomas seemed to fall out of favour with his colleagues, eventually being asked by the chief of the *Abwehrstelle* in Oslo to return to Berlin. The former school-teacher later toured Germany giving lessons in sword dances and reels. Von Gröning was disgusted that his former deputy hadn't found more useful work. Eddie received a letter from Thomas which contained a photograph of him performing a sword dance. He had to laugh. Of all the Boys in the *Stelle*, Eddie thought that Thomas would not rest until 'gun in hand, he had defeated the savage Russians or the decadent British'.

about to play a crucial role in deceiving the Germans about the forthcoming landings in Normandy. Sir John Masterman would write of the situation in 1943, 'From our point of view, the chief cause of satisfaction was that the agents survived with un-diminished prestige ready for the more important operations of the future.'

Across the North Sea – in a London now full of British and American armed forces – all had gone quiet so far as agent Zigzag was concerned. After the excitements of Operation Damp Squib there was little for British Intelligence to report about the activities of Eddie Chapman.*

That September, though, the British sustained a shock when a trial run for the deceptions which would surround D-Day fell flat. Known as Cockade, the operation involved the instigation of rumours about an impending landing in the Pas de Calais. One of these, given the codename Tindall, suggested that an attack on Stavanger, by air and sea, was to take place in September 1943; within days, word would reach the Germans that the attack had been 'cancelled' to release forces for a later, larger assault at the Pas de Calais. However, it was patently not believed by the Germans. With the Allies' return to Europe imminent, the Double Cross Committee knew they had little time to get everything right. Worse, with German suspicions raised, they would now be alert for other ruses. The position of double agents was becoming increasingly vulnerable, and yet they would be vital in fooling the Germans that the Normandy landings were nothing more than a feint for the real landings in the Pas de Calais.

Eddie Chapman was convinced he had done no wrong in telling Dagmar Lahlum he was a double agent. The girl herself seems to have taken his revelation in her stride: all she said was that she had suspected Eddie was British all along, as his accent was decidedly curious. When he said that he would soon be going off on another mission, she readily agreed to keep in contact with him.

---

* Apart from a brief mention about a cover address in Lisbon in December 1943, Fritzchen's name does not seem to have been mentioned in any of the Abwehr's subsequent radio traffic. There is also no evidence – despite the elaborate sign-offs agreed with Eddie – that any messages were ever picked up by the Radio Security Service.

That was where further danger lay. Dagmar would still be looked after by the German secret service at the flat in Kappellveien and continue to draw a spousal stipend, the 600 kroner a month provided by the Abwehr for agent Fritzchen. She and Eddie took the precaution of agreeing on a plan in case he couldn't return. If anyone needed to contact her on his behalf, they would greet her by her full name, Dagmar Mohne Hansen Lahlum. Eddie asked her to keep her eyes open for any other information that might be of use to the British.

Yet just how dangerous a game he was playing had already become clear that summer. As they strolled hand in hand through Oslo in early July 1943, Dagmar popped into a tobacconist's. When she returned to Eddie, she told him that the Allies had invaded Sicily. As this fact had yet to be broadcast by the Germans, it was clear that she had some contact with the resistance. And that meant there was a danger that she might accidentally let slip the double game that Eddie was playing. 'It appears, therefore, that Dagmar is in contact with the Norwegian Underground movement,' one of his MI5 case officers would later write, 'and at the same time, has the confidence of a British secret service agent and is at present being maintained by the German secret service.'

Dagmar said nothing of this to her family, who are amazed to learn of her wartime double life. 'Dagmar did have a reputation of being on friendly terms with the Germans during the war,' her great nephew, Hans Olav Lahlum, says. 'That was definitely an unpleasant reputation to have in Norway for many years after the war. It remains a mystery why she never did anything to tell the true story about her war efforts.'

Eddie himself now came under suspicion of being a spy. One night in the Löwenbräu, an older, flashily dressed woman asked if she could sit next to him. She soon expressed puzzlement at his accent.

Eddie decided to play along with her. 'Yes, I am a German,' he explained, 'but I was born in America.' He had already recognised her as a well-known *agent provocateur* known as 'Frau Arna' who frequented all the best hotels and cafés. She tried to trap him into criticising German policy. Eddie did not react in any way, for it was clear what she was up to.

The next night, he returned to the same bar where he dined with one of the few Gestapo people he ever met. Sturmbannführer Alex Etling was responsible for sending out the vehicles used to arrest suspected saboteurs and despatch Norwegian officers for internment. Eddie later remarked that he was 'a sufficiently agreeable fellow, even if he was a Nazi thug'. During the course of their meal, Etling was called over by some of his fellow officers, who were dining in the company of the glaring Frau Arna. 'She has reported you to my bureau on suspicion of being a British spy!' Etling said when he returned to the table.

They both roared with laughter.

The next night, Frau Arna came over, even more hatchet-faced. 'I still think you are an English spy,' she spat.

Eddie had had enough. He called in the military policeman on guard at the door and had her arrested. A number of his fellow diners were obviously pleased. 'Several came across to my table,' Eddie recalled, 'and expressed their indignation at such a slanderous accusation being levelled against me.' When informed the next day about what had happened, Stefan von Gröning said Eddie should leave the matter to him. Eddie never saw her again or learned what her fate might have been.

As in France, the constant fear for the *Abwehrstelle* was that the Norwegian resistance might act when they realised that Eddie was actually British and was working for the Germans. Von Gröning was insistent that Eddie should always carry his Lüger with him. 'Perhaps the British secret service may trace you up here,' he said, 'and we certainly don't want to lose you.' Eddie feigned ignorance, but he was well aware what might happen if the resistance became interested. If either he or Dagmar were assassinated, it would work against the Allies. Details of the secret life of Fritz Graumann would come to light, at a moment that would cause maximum damage for the Double Cross Committee.

The capture of Sicily and Mussolini's subsequent fall seemed to stiffen the resolve of the *Abwehrstelle* in Norway. In September, insistent that he should take on another sabotage mission as soon as possible, the Baron suggested that Eddie should return to Britain forthwith. When von Gröning said he would be paid the same as last time, Eddie replied that this wasn't going to be nearly enough.

'I want at least five hundred thousand marks or fifty thousand pounds,' he coolly declared.

Berlin had even sent contracts which Eddie was expected to sign. As a later MI5 report states, Eddie 'refused to do so, however, saying that he had enough money and that he did not consider the proposition of sufficient importance'. There was general disbelief and anger from the Germans. With the Abwehr coming under increasing pressure after its repeated failures, all of them – the Baron, Holst and the soon-to-depart Walther Thomas – were horrified because their own standing would be damaged by agent Fritzchen's recalcitrance. The Baron went so far as to stop funding Eddie's payments. 'I will see you in hell before I sign a contract which does not suit me,' he told von Gröning in response. He said he would be prepared to go to a concentration camp rather than sign a contract whose terms he didn't agree with.

The Baron headed to Berlin to take soundings, returning, as Eddie put it, 'in good spirits and with particulars of a new mission'. A few days later, his money supply was restarted and nothing was ever said about the matter again. The resumption of friendly relations with his corpulent controller was complete when von Gröning stood up drunkenly one evening, shouting, 'Fritz, you are the only bastard who understands me! And the only one capable of drinking with me!' before falling flat on his face. Mammoth drinking sessions were usually prompted by the Boys, and Eddie invariably ended up paying out of his own pocket. He was soon wise to what they were doing. The quicker he squandered his funds, the sooner he would need to go on another mission to replenish them.

Later that autumn, further orders came from Berlin. Eddie was invited to meet the head of the Oslo *Stelle*, a Captain von Bonin, at a plush place in the Munthessgate across from Frogner Park. Disconcerted by a portrait of the man himself, with 'piercing blue eyes, bald head and thin, weak chin', that hung in the lounge, Eddie was informed of his next mission. 'The Germans were still wanting details of the British system for detecting U-boats,' MI5 would later report, 'and there would be a large reward for Chapman if he could obtain these details.'

Von Bonin produced a contract – identical to the earlier one apart from the sum of money detailed at the end – and announced:

'We are now prepared to offer you five hundred thousand marks if you will undertake and successfully carry out a mission for us.'

As the summer of 1943 turned to autumn, there was a subtle change in the air. The Norwegians picked up on the altered atmosphere; indeed, many became openly hostile. 'Rumours of landings by the Allies were always running through the population,' Eddie recalled of this time in Oslo. 'The Germans feared that if one took place there would be a general uprising.'

Across the North Sea, plans were afoot to keep the Germans looking in the wrong direction – towards Norway and not Normandy. The British deception planners, led by Colonel Johnny Bevan, had come up with some of the most complex strategic deceptions ever attempted. Their aim was to keep twenty-seven Wehrmacht divisions garrisoned in Norway at the time of the Normandy invasion. Using double agents and simulating activity by false radio reports, they made it appear that a powerful force of Allied ships and soldiers would soon be making its way towards Norway.

'It never took much to make Hitler believe in a threat to Norway,' Sir Michael Howard, the official historian of deception operations, has written. As a later intelligence summary prepared for the Führer makes clear, all the evidence indicated another determined attack on Norway that autumn. The German Supreme Command believed – as the Allied deception staff wanted them to – that there were would be four to six divisions involved.

For the remainder of 1943, the pressure by the Allies remained relentless. There were repeated commando raids all along the Norwegian coast as well as attacks by Mosquito bombers on coastal radar stations. There were hints of forces marshalling in Scotland, of ports clogged with landing craft. Double agents reported all sorts of suspicious activity north of the border, being aimed across the North Sea. The result was that the Führer continued to pour money, men and weapons into Norway. Nearly half a million troops were to remain on station there, along with ninety thousand naval and sixty thousand Luftwaffe personnel. None of them would be available to repel the Allied assault forces when they came ashore on Normandy's beaches.

Throughout his stay in Norway, Eddie was free to explore the beautiful countryside. The Oslo *Stelle* actively encouraged him to record the stunning vistas on film. 'To increase the usefulness of my work,' he recalled, 'the Germans decided to teach me photography.' For this a photographer called Rotkagal – 'a funny little chap with shrewd tired eyes' – became his instructor. A pre-war manager of the Leica factories, he was apparently a landscape photographer of some note. But now his task was to record on film suspected sabotage and acts of violence. Eddie, thinking about his post-war prospects, was delighted to become a snapper.

'Rotkagal taught me rapidly the rudiments of camera work, how to hold and focus the instrument,' Eddie wrote, 'and how to read the light meter.'

He was encouraged to photograph 'living beings' – animals and people – and even to attempt portraiture. Many of his subjects were those who happened to be on hand in and around the wooden house at number 8 Kappellveien. Curiously, British Intelligence got to know what the house and both Johnny Holst and Dagmar looked like. 'Eddie bought a camera in Oslo and took some pictures,' his widow recalls, 'and he forgot to take the film out before he left.' When he subsequently brought the camera with him to Britain in June 1944, the film was developed by MI5, and the German saboteur and Eddie's Norwegian girlfriend were revealed relaxing around the house. But there was a far more serious purpose behind this activity: the photography of documents, a skill which might come in useful for his next mission.

On 16 November, Eddie's twenty-ninth birthday coincided with an escalation in the violence of the Nazi occupation. That Tuesday, von Gröning had held a party in his flat where he presented Eddie with a Van Gogh reproduction. A birthday cake was also presented and all the Boys got wildly drunk. Eddie became terribly homesick, particularly when they all started singing Auld Lang Syne.

On his way home to his apartment the next morning, Eddie noticed excited crowds in the square in front of the university. A teenage youth suddenly shot past him, followed by several Gestapo guards. The crowd were delighted when the boy managed to evade them. He dodged in and out of the trees until one of the Germans drew a pistol and threatened to fire, whereupon the youth surrendered.

As he walked on, Eddie estimated there were about a thousand people gathered together, surrounded by guards. 'From time to time, a Norwegian would be dragged out of the crowd of spectators watching the commotion,' he remembered. He saw a Gestapo officer smash a knuckle-dustered fist into the face of an old man who had failed to understand an order. Blood poured from a wound as he was shoved into the heaving crowd. Eddie was momentarily stunned, then found himself being pushed forward.

'You seem rather too interested in this,' a harsh voice said into his ear. Eddie turned round to face a young corporal who pushed him towards the crowds. Eddie treated him to a choice selection of invective. This attracted the attention of a nearby officer who came over to investigate. When Eddie took out his *Ausweis*, the corporal found himself on the receiving end of further abuse. 'Make sure, you stupid swine,' the senior officer yelled, 'that next time it is a *verdammter* Norwegian that you are arresting.'

The officer then explained to Eddie the cause of the uproar. The university was a hotbed of resistance activity to which increasingly brazen acts of resistance – including sabotage – had been traced back. In 1941, when the rector refused to kowtow to German demands, he had been sent to a concentration camp and replaced with a collaborator. By the end of November 1943, the arrest of a number of students and lecturers was ordered after a group of communist saboteurs set fire to the university.

On the morning after the fire, the university was closed when all male students and lecturers were rounded up to be sent to a camp in Germany. It was this operation into which Eddie had unwittingly stumbled. 'All day long the arrests went on,' Eddie recalled. 'The Gestapo seized anyone and everyone they pleased. Late into the night, lorries laden with human cargo for the concentration camps thundered out of Oslo.'

When neutral Sweden made strong protests, the Germans realised they had gone too far. Eventually, they released most of the internees. But the cycle of reprisals continued, and as Eddie recorded, many 'took advantage of this atmosphere of violence to settle private scores'.

Eddie's own memory of the violence contained a curious twist. The shooting of a German soldier after visiting a local brothel was investigated by von Gröning and the *Abwehrstelle*. Eddie joined them. It was a depressing experience. The women, in Eddie's recollection, 'were the typical products of any third-class French brothel – old, tired and worn out'. During an interview, the girl with whom the soldier had spent his last night recalled a quarrel among his friends. She gave the Baron their names. Von Gröning sent the military police to arrest them; all three confessed that they had shot their comrade in cold blood and were court-martialled.

An argument could be made that the Battle of the Atlantic was the most important of the war, certainly so far as British survival is concerned. After their huge losses at the start of the year – when ships were being sunk faster than they could be replaced – the battle had turned in the Allies' favour after heavy U-boat losses in March 1943. Partly this was brought about by a change in tactics, but mainly it was the result of technological developments on the Allied side. So in December 1943, the Baron and Johnny Holst accompanied Eddie to Trondheim in the company of Fritz Stube, a lawyer from Bremen and a recent recruit to the *Stelle*. It was here, in a naval base hewn out of a cliff face to protect it from attacks by Mosquito bombers, that Eddie was to be instructed about his next mission.

After driving directly to the local *Kommandatur*, they stayed at the Hotel Norge for three nights, making daily trips to the *Nordseestelle* close by the harbour. From here U-boat operations were directed. They were met by two captains and a lieutenant in a cramped office containing a large desk, its walls covered by maps on which a variety of coloured flags had been pinned.

The senior man was a submarine officer whom Eddie recalled as 'a bald, ugly fellow with a huge wart on his nose'. Eddie was quizzed at length; they seemed highly suspicious of him. Indeed, the ugly submariner kept staring at him, apparently certain that he had seen him somewhere before. Despite their antipathy, however, it was clear these Abwehr marine specialists were in desperate need of Eddie's help. German submariners were not just baffled – they were terrified. One captain had recently told the story of being attacked even though the Atlantic above him was covered in thick fog.

The briefing soon became highly technical. Among the subjects discussed were 'parabolic reflectors', rebounding rays, detonators, infra-red rays and heat signatures. 'Most of this data appeared on the syllabus which had been sent to von Gröning from Berlin,' a later MI5 report records. 'The technicians at Trondheim certainly made it clear to Chapman that they were extremely worried about our methods of U-boat detection.' It had been observed that before U-boats were attacked, their crews heard a secondary detonation which they thought was related to improved Allied tracking of their submarines. (In fact, it was the firing of depth charges transmitted through the hull and water.) There was talk of 'red glows' seen beneath Sunderland flying boats, and of 'invisible rays'. The Abwehr had also received reports of a curious weapon called a 'Hedgehog' which was supposedly towed between two ships along a cable to help track submerged vessels. By the use of mysterious rays – infra-red or invisible, they weren't sure – it could sense where a U-boat was submerged.

The Germans seemed worried that the British were using 'radio location' devices. He was asked to be particularly alert for aerials and short rods on ships so these experts could calculate the frequency of their transmissions. But long before this point, Eddie's eyes had glazed over. 'As the discussion continued interminably,' he would recall, 'I became certain of one thing: the Germans had no positive plan for combating the menace to their U-boats.'

At the end of 1943, Eddie was told that his next mission would start in March the following year. After he had carried out his next sabotage operation in Britain, he was told that this time the Luftwaffe would help him. They would expect him to steal a boat from a North Sea port and, 'after wirelessing his position to the Germans, he would be met by five or six Luftwaffe seaplanes'.

Unlike his father and brother, Eddie had little experience of ocean sailing. A few days after the Trondheim visit, he was taken to Bergen harbour where Johnny Holst gave him instruction on a large blue yacht. The Bergen harbourmaster also gave him 'three lessons in the use of a compass on a small fishing cutter'. By this time, Johnny Holst was now living with two potential saboteurs whom Eddie subsequently met back in Olso at the Löwenbräu and the Ritz café. He took them to be Norwegian but they were actually Icelanders. Their despatch – just a few weeks before Eddie himself

– would go some way to solving the riddle of his whereabouts so far as the British were concerned.

Years later, Dagmar recalled that Eddie's departure happened with haste. 'As far as I remember, you left Oslo some days before my 21st birthday, 48 years ago – incredible!' she wrote in March 1992. And Dagmar thought she would never see – or hear from – him again.

By the start of 1944, MI5 was wondering what exactly had happened to agent Zigzag. With the Prime Minister interested in the case, it was most uncomfortable to report that enquiries concerning his whereabouts were continuing to draw a blank. So far as British Intelligence was concerned, Eddie seemed to have disappeared off the face of the earth. To their dismay, he had not been mentioned for several months in Abwehr contact reports or routine radio transmissions. Some within MI5 feared the worst. Had he been compromised? Or tortured? Or even killed?

By now, there was an air of expectancy across Scandinavia. The military focus shifted towards the sea lanes that would make Iceland strategically significant. Hitler's naval adjutant had written that 'whoever has Iceland controls the entrances and exits from the Atlantic'. At the start of the new year, wireless traffic all around Scandinavia – as far apart as Iceland, the Faroes and Bear Island – suddenly increased in volume. Ships sailed from Scapa Flow all along the Norwegian coast, while Russian submarines were spotted off the coast of Petsamo.

To play upon the Führer's fears, Icelandic agents were employed by MI6 to feed misinformation. Deliberately muddying the picture, they reported that many troop ships were making use of Icelandic ports as the British ones were full. These were all part of the deceptions surrounding D-Day.

One of the most crucial contributions to the secret war was the deliberate confusing of meteorological conditions. The Allies wanted to ensure that accurate weather forecasts were denied the Germans in the days and hours before the Normandy invasion. Kriegsmarine weather ships were sunk, land-based weather stations destroyed and the US Coast Guard repeatedly repelled enemy combatants who tried to establish weather stations around Greenland.

With the retreat of the U-boats, the Germans had little hard information about weather conditions out in the Atlantic where storms formed.* To remedy this, the Third Reich embarked on attempts to land spies in Iceland, one of whose tasks would be to report local meteorological conditions to Berlin. To this end, the Abwehr had tried to land two separate groups of agents on to the Icelandic ice floes at the end of April. And as late as 5 May 1944 – only a month before the original date for the Normandy landing – they made a final attempt with a further trio of spies who were expected to report on the concentrations of troops believed to be massing for an invasion of Norway.

Some time that Friday evening, a seal hunter reported to the local authorities that he had spied a trio of strangers scrambling ashore. Taken into captivity in Reykjavik, the team consisted of two native Icelanders and a German who declared that he was the leader of the expedition 'for a German shipping institution'. The pair of young Icelanders had been forced to work for the Germans and been trained in sabotage in Norway. Hjalti Bjornsson and Sigurdur Juliusson were flown to London after their capture, but weren't separated, much to the annoyance of 'Tin Eye' Stephens. After arriving at Latchmere House, they were 'word perfect in a story that was moderately shy even of the half truth', to quote Stephens directly. Eventually, they confessed to what they were really up to.

The most notable aspect of Bjornsson and Juliusson's interrogation was their description of sabotage training in Oslo. One of their instructors, they recalled, was known as Fritz but they weren't sure of his nationality. He spoke German with a pronounced English accent. He had two gold teeth on the upper right-hand side of his mouth, wore a pepper-and-salt summer suit and had, in their recollection, 'a rather loud and high-pitched voice'. According to the Icelanders, this instructor had been showered with money

---

* To confuse the picture even further, many of the double agents who had landed in Britain were transmitting false weather reports, an enterprise which had started with the appropriately named Snow (Arthur Owens), the first agent to be turned against the Germans in 1939. All the other agents currently in Britain at the start of 1944 were feeding incorrect information about atmospheric pressure and other physical parameters whenever they could.

which he had spent lavishly. As to what he might do next, they weren't sure. In March – as, years later, Dagmar was to confirm – he had suddenly disappeared from the *Stelle* in Oslo. They had no idea where he had gone.

The two gold teeth clinched it. It had to be Eddie Chapman.

As for Eddie himself, his own return to Britain was imminent. Its timing, however, depended on something else: the invasion of Europe, expected to happen any day now. Like the thousands of troops massing all around the coast of southern England, all Eddie Chapman really wanted to know was when – and where – he would be allowed to return to the land from which he came.

CHAPTER NINE

The Long Goodbye

'The German cause received a fillip a little later in June when the news came of the first use by Hitler of his long-vaunted secret weapon . . . The German propaganda machine worked full blast on these weapons, telling of the colossal damage caused, and claiming that everything within two hundred yards of an explosion had been wiped out. London was in flames, according to Goebbels, and traffic was everywhere disrupted. I was impressed and worried. I wondered if it could be true.'

– Eddie Chapman's recollection of how the V-1 'doodlebugs' were reported in Occupied Europe

WHEN THE LUFTHANSA AIRLINER dropped through the clouds, Berlin was a revelation. It was March 1944 and the toll of constant air raids was immediately apparent. As the capital came into view, an old Wehrmacht colonel, seated next to Eddie Chapman, captured it best: '*Das sind die Ruinen von Pompeii*' ('Those are the the ruins of Pompeii'). The aircraft was now descending into Tempelhof, and the contrast with Eddie's visit the previous summer couldn't have been starker. At first, he didn't recognise the bomb-strewn city below, transfixed by the desolation which 'was the result of the terrible hammering inflicted by thousands of Allied bombers by day and night'.

As the plane taxied to the stand, an air raid siren sounded almost immediately. The passengers sprinted with their luggage the hundred yards or so to the nearest shelter. With standing room only, they waited for over an hour until the all clear sounded. As he made his way to a waiting staff car, Eddie noticed how even the airport had changed. 'Everywhere was havoc,' he recalled. 'Hangars were burned out, offices wrecked beyond repair.' The trail of destruction increased with the ride into the city. The streets were piled high with wreckage: 'There were literally mountains of rubble, and no attempt was being made to repair the damage,' was how MI5 would record his observations. 'The effect of the block-busters was so terrific that the Germans merely cleared the streets of rubble, cordoned off the affected areas and made no effort to excavate the ruins or the bodies of persons buried underneath. The whole city reeked of fire.'

All along the Friedrichstrasse, Eddie was delighted to see strewn haphazardly among the wreckage several safes which had crashed through walls from bomb-damaged buildings. As he later remarked, Berliners might have defied the blockbusters but not the lockbusters – like him and his pre-war criminal pals – who would have loved the chance to burgle them. 'Sometimes four or five of these would be piled up together among the blackened debris,' he would later write. 'I surveyed them, nostalgically and regretfully.'

As they approached the Metropole Hotel, Eddie recalled, 'it stood out like an island in a sea of rubble'. By now it was clear that time was running out for the Nazi regime. 'The course of the war, in all its enormity, will reach its critical point during this year,' Adolf Hitler had written on the first day of 1944. The Allied return to Europe had become the foremost topic in the minds of leaders on both sides of the Channel. For the Führer and his High Command, second-guessing Allied intentions became a matter of great urgency. 'Everything suggests that the enemy, at the latest in the spring but perhaps even earlier, will move to attack the western front of Europe,' he had written a couple of months earlier.

The Führer was nothing if not prescient. That spring, the land-ings *were* imminent, planned for the start of June when the tides and moon would be right. To support them, the intensity of the secret war would be increased all around the boundaries of the Third Reich. To keep the German High Command guessing, confusion would be deliberately sown about the exact location of the landings. The deception plan known as Operation Fortitude, whose opening notes had been played in Norway, would consume all the Allied secret agencies, reaching its climax that spring. Nothing like it – in either scale or ambition – had ever been attempted before.

In the labyrinthine stratagems being used to cloak Allied intentions, the role of double agents would become critical. The plans were so intricate that even the most optimistic feared that this veritable orchestra of deception could come crashing down before the first night. The musical analogy was one which MI5's counter-espionage staff often used. In various parts of the British Isles, fifteen primary agents were still working, seven with transmitters – the latter of which were seen as 'first violins'. Throughout the world, there were also, in the words of another British secret servant, 'musicians and choristers' attuned to the grander, global scores of deception. Each would come in on cue, in staccato bursts, playing to the prejudices of the Germans.

Because he was stationed in Occupied Europe, Eddie Chapman could not take part in these endeavours in the prelude to D-Day. Throughout 1943, though, the Führer's boasts about weapons of vengeance had become ever more strident. Eddie's new role would be to help combat the menace of the doodlebugs, whose own launch would come any day now.

The D-Day landings were unrepeatable. If they failed, then everything else would fail. The sometimes fragile grand alliance between the British and Americans would rupture. Even worse, Hitler's scientists and engineers would have time to complete the 'wonder weapons' by which the Nazi leadership set such great store: jet aircraft which could outrun Allied bombers, long-range submarines which could effectively blockade the British Isles.

The wait for the wonder weapons had been long and tortuous. Though the existence of the 'rocket programme' had been widely derided by many in British Intelligence, evidence was now incontrovertible. Careful reading of Ultra decrypts and fragmentary evidence from resistance workers had made it clear that there were, in fact, two programmes. One seemed to be a 'pilotless aircraft' run by the Luftwaffe, a prototype of which had crashed and been photographed by a Danish naval officer. When the photographs were forwarded to London there was great scepticism, as some experts believed that only solid propellants would have sufficient power to propel a rocket-powered aircraft. Known as the FZG-76 – the letters stood for *Flakzielgerät* (anti-aircraft gun aiming device) to deliberately confuse the enemy – it was designed for mass production, easily constructed from plywood and metal sheeting. Later renamed by Josef Goebbels the more apocalyptic *Vergeltungswaffe-1* (reprisal weapon 1), it became, in effect, the world's first cruise missile.

The second programme, a true ballistic missile project run by the German Army, was even more fantastic. A first test in March 1942 had ended in failure, but six months later, a prototype of this missile – later named the V-2 – reached an astonishing altitude of eighty kilometres. That remarkable success led the general in charge of the Peenemünde facility to exclaim, 'Today, the spaceship was born!'

Enigma decrypts showed just how close their launch was and how many were coming off the production line. The threat of these missiles creating havoc in the assembly areas for the Normandy invasion had to be taken seriously. The race that had started with the Oslo Letter was moving to a conclusion as the Germans prepared to head off any breach of *Festung Europa*.

If the D-Day invasion failed, the launch sites for the V-1s would not be overrun. The cumulative firing of these missiles, later joined by the V-2s of Peenemünde, would see 'London levelled to the ground and Britain forced to capitulate,' Hitler had prophesied. As the Allied military planners prepared for the embarkation of troops towards Normandy, they were aware that the race was on between the landings and the launchings – D-Day and the buzzbombs.

★   ★   ★

Berlin was depressing. From the boards of thick compressed paper wedged into the hotel windows to the advice against unpacking because of the constant air raids, Eddie became conscious of an air of resigned fatalism. 'A peculiar tension could be felt throughout the hotel,' he wrote, 'everyone appeared grim and anxious.' When he went for a drink in von Gröning's room, he was introduced to a Luftwaffe pilot who had been shot down by the RAF. The pilot reminisced with grim humour about reconnaissance flights over London in the Blitz just four years earlier. 'It burned well though Berlin burns better!'

That summer, bombing of German cities had become a round-the-clock exercise. Von Gröning informed Eddie that the Abwehr thought that certain airfields were being used for specific targets. For example, all RAF bombing runs from Cambridge might be aimed at Hamburg while those from Bedford were directed towards Berlin. 'The Germans wanted to know the exact schedules of each station,' he records. 'They proposed to supply me with a simple wireless set and, once in England, I was to instruct accomplices there in its use.' The plan was for him to recruit sub-agents to visit each airfield and, using a simple code, alert the Abwehr to which city was going to be attacked when the bombers trundled down the runways.

After falling into a fitful sleep, Eddie was awoken by the alarm a few minutes before midnight. Putting on his dressing gown, he looked out into the corridor: hotel staff were running up and down the corridor, waking guests by shouting, '*Alarm!*' ('Alert!') Accompanied by staff from the Japanese Embassy carrying boxes of secret papers, he rushed along with von Gröning and Stube towards a shelter below the Winter Garden. Many years later, Eddie could still remember the hushed voices, white faces and commentary from a wireless about the progress of the raid – right up to dawn.

The following morning, there was another telling indication of the state of the war. Even though he had been issued with a double supply of food coupons, there was hardly enough for a decent breakfast: a bitter cup of ersatz coffee, skimmed milk and one lump of sugar, two white rolls, a slice of black bread and a tiny pat of butter. Food was scarce, as were clothes, cigarettes and alcohol. 'There was no black market as the penalty of death sufficed to keep even the most hardy exploiters in subjection,' Eddie would recall.

Later that morning, a major from the Luftwaffe arrived in a car to take him to the vast Air Ministry building on Leipzigerstrasse. En route, Eddie saw that both the Kaiserhof Hotel – reputedly the Führer's favourite – and the Bank of Berlin had been virtually destroyed. But the Air Ministry building itself, shored up with

tensile concrete, remained implacable, surrounded by heavily
armed guards. They headed up to the fifth floor where he was introduced to some technical experts: two majors and a captain, the
captain remained in the room to brief him.

In English, he explained why the Luftwaffe was losing so many
aircraft. 'It's all done by radio location. The British have installed
in their home-based fighters a device which enables them to locate
our nightfighters and bombers with the greatest of ease.'(It was
clear that the Germans thought this was some sort of radar device.)

For some reason, the Germans thought these fighters could not
leave British airspace, though one had been engaged over the
Channel and had crashed in France. A secretary brought in a
partially reconstructed radio location device – they were deliberately
destroyed on landing by explosives. 'If you can get us one of these,'
the captain said, 'you will be very well rewarded.'

'He was informed that, although various parts of the mechanism
had been captured,' an MI5 report says, 'it was impossible to
reconstruct them completely, as the parts were so badly smashed.'
The Luftwaffe did not know where these devices were being built
and so, by theft or bribery, they wanted Eddie to determine where
the components were being assembled. (In fact, these parts had
been rescued from crashed Mosquitos, whose factory he had supposedly destroyed just over a year earlier.) In particular, they were
puzzled by a square-shaped valve. No reward 'would be too great'
if he could find out more.

While in Berlin for those ten days, he spent at least a week at the
Luftwaffe *Ministerium*. One day, he was introduced to a Herr
Weiss, a civilian in scruffy clothes who primed him for yet another
mission. 'As you probably know,' Weiss began, 'both sides are
experimenting with remote-controlled aircraft.' Showing him
photographs of some unlikely-looking machines, Weiss explained
some were fuel-controlled, others by radio. If he came across them,
Eddie should try to find out how they were propelled. The next day,
Weiss gave him a lecture about rocketry and asked him to find out
if the British had such weapons.

What stuck in Eddie's mind, however, was how terribly fed up
ordinary Berliners were by this time. One night, he and his
intelligence handlers went to the Winter Palace where they saw a

variety show. It had to be finished by 9 p.m., like most entertainments in the capital. Everybody seemed exhausted, 'a pathetic resignation' etched upon their faces. 'They were near the end,' Eddie reported, 'and for all that most of them cared it could come at any time.'

The end had finally come for the Abwehr. Canaris's men had failed to predict the Allied landings at Anzio in January 1944 and, after a wave of defections of officers around the world, the Admiral was summarily fired by the Führer himself.* Within days, most of Canaris's senior associates were also dismissed and the Abwehr itself was merged with the SD. As with most activities in Nazi Germany, the amalgamation was messy and protracted. In the next few months, the bureaucratic complexities – the merging of files, furniture, people and procedures, not to mention another greater preoccupation, jockeying for position – would take precedence, reaching their greatest intensity in May, just days before the planned invasion of Normandy.

Nowhere was the chaos more keenly felt than in the Hotel Lutétia on Boulevard Raspail in Paris. In the weeks before D-Day, the headquarters of the Abwehr in France had been in turmoil thanks to the takeover. What Eddie did not appreciate at the time was that most of the people in the hotel were on alert for signs of the Allied invasion that spring. A dedicated radio section led by Colonel Oskar Reile, a Prussian of the old school who was chief of the Abwehr's counter-espionage service in France, was paying particular attention to the ether. Thanks to the infiltration of some resistance cells, certain of the Allies' codes were known. By now Reile's men were aware that an army group was forming in the Dover region.

These signals were, however, another part of the campaign of deception surrounding the D-Day landings. General George Patton, who the Germans already knew was in Britain, appeared to

---

* Wilhelm Canaris was allowed to keep his rank while effectively being kept under house arrest in a castle near to Frankfurt. Given a makeweight job of directing economic warfare against the Allies, Canaris spent most of his time pottering around and playing with his dogs. Implicated in the 20 July Bomb Plot, Canaris was executed just days before the end of the war.

be in command of an army known as the First US Army Group (FUSAG) which was to land in the Pas de Calais. Dummy landing craft were spotted, beaches in the Pas de Calais had been softened up by bombing and lines of communication in the area had been destroyed.

False radio messages made it appear as though there were 150,000 men ready to move under Patton's command. News about the troops was leaked to the press, while vicars fulminated about the moral collapse in East Anglia brought about by the American soldiers and their prophylactic remedies. By May, the forces of FUSAG had supposedly been assembled from dummy tanks; four hundred dummy landing ships were filling up ports and rivers all along the south and south-eastern coast of the British Isles.

The sheer strength of Allied air superiority meant there were few aerial investigations by the Germans. The Luftwaffe's lack of reconnaissance at this time was – in the phrase of more than one historian – as much a miracle as the destruction of the Spanish armada in 1588. By the time D-Day dawned, the Nazi intelligence services were not only looking the wrong way, they weren't looking at all.

If there was any doubt that the Germans were losing the war, proof came on Eddie Chapman's return train journey to France. On Monday, 20 March he travelled from the Potsdamer station to the Gare de l'Est in Paris. Their journey was an eye-opener: compared to the precision of Eddie's earlier travels in 1942, the effects of near constant Allied bombing were evident. The train timetables were in shambles, with trains frequently up to twelve hours late.

A kaleidoscope of destruction passed by: damaged stations, platforms and bombed-out trains. The carriages were impossibly crowded and the journey was repeatedly delayed. 'The train was crammed with soldiers, sailors and airmen,' Eddie recalled. 'The corridors were impassable, for men lay on the floors between the legs of others who leaned upright. The smell of this sweating humanity was unbearable.' Passengers sat on top of each other; some had even squeezed into the luggage racks. After a long delay at Aachen, they did not arrive in the French capital until the following evening at 10.30 p.m. They were dirty, dishevelled and very tired.

Worse, there was no official car waiting for them. Stefan von Gröning was not best pleased. He made an irritable telephone call, losing his temper when some of the accompanying officers started making a joke of the situation. 'Do you think it is funny being stranded here like this? The whole trip seems to be regarded as some huge, idiotic joke!' Then, with what Eddie termed 'fine old Prussian wrath', he bellowed: 'This is war – bloody war!' An argument developed, in full view of the bored French railway porters.

When their car finally arrived they made their way to the Ambassador Hotel on Boulevard Haussmann in stony silence. Eddie shared a room with Fritz Stube, thankful for the peace and quiet.

All was forgotten by the next morning. While von Gröning went to the *Abwehrstelle* at the Hotel Lutétia, Eddie showed his travelling companions the sights of Paris. After the deprivations of Berlin, they seemed magical. 'There was a vast difference in the social climate between the two cities,' Betty Chapman reflects. 'Eddie was always a Paris man.' And small wonder, for along the Champs-Elysées, 'the champagne of spring was in the air'. Eddie, as might be expected, enjoyed himself watching the beautiful and fashionable women.

These would be the salad days, before frustrations set in as he waited to return home. 'During the following three months,' MI5 would later comment, 'Chapman did no work but was in daily expectation of news from the Luftwaffe branch that a "plane was ready for him".' Eddie killed the time as best he could in aimless people-watching, enjoying himself in the evenings when there were always excitements to be had. 'They were always looking for new nightclubs,' Betty Chapman says of her future husband and his controller, 'and they would go to gay bars, lesbian bars and nude bars.'

That spring, Paris was a babel of many different nationalities. Eddie saw Cossacks, Japanese and even Frenchmen in the green uniform of the Wehrmacht, 'followed by the curses of their fellow countrymen'. There were also members of the *Legión Azul* ('Blue Legion') of Spanish fascists who had fought on the Eastern Front. They had, it seems, some of Eddie's entrepreneurial spirit, for their uniforms would attain a good price on the black market.

By now, illicit trading was a matter of routine, despite the supposed penalties. Eddie decided he needed some new clothes, as he suspected he might be in the French capital for some time. 'The Germans had organised a black market for themselves,' he recalled, 'which one could only use on production of a military pass.' Using his *Ausweis* he was able to buy some good pre-war English cloth. A girl called Lilli whom he had met at the Lido cabaret one evening took him to a tailor in Romainville, of all places. As he passed the austere jail in which he had spent the first few weeks of 1942, Eddie had a 'shaky feeling' and couldn't help wondering what had happened to all his old pals.

Eddie was introduced to a Norwegian tailor who spoke English. Overjoyed to meet an Englishman, he asked Eddie if he know Golders Green. As this was one of the primary Jewish neighbourhoods in London – and a suburb where he himself had raided an Odeon cinema – it was a hint that the tailor was an orthodox Jew. It was confirmed when the tailor showed him some photographs of his son at a wedding ceremony, a *Kiddushin*. Eddie warned him not to show these photographs to strangers. The tailor just laughed. 'Sir, you are a friend,' he said, 'I am sure.'

★　★　★

By the spring of 1944, the Luftwaffe had virtually been swept from the skies thanks to overwhelming Allied air superiority. With fighters now capable of escorting US Army Air Force bombers beyond the Rhine, even the Luftwaffe's home defence forces had been steadily destroyed. It lost nearly seventeen hundred fighter pilots in the first four months of the year, replacing them with unskilled youths. Eddie, waiting in Paris, became aware of this when he met his youthful Luftwaffe liaison officer. The youngster – only about twenty-four, yet already sporting an Iron Cross – made it clear there were no aircraft available. 'It's not going to be easy this time,' he said of Eddie's mission, 'since the British nightfighters are bringing down an unpleasantly high percentage of aircraft.'

There was no longer any pretence at aiming for mastery of the air over the Channel. More recently, Eddie was told, agents were having to be inveigled into Britain by sea.

The Berlin newspapers 'were full of secret weapon hints, and of threats of the fearful vengeance which was to be inflicted on

England'. The civilian expert, Weiss, who had talked of remote-controlled aircraft, had asked him point blank: 'Is our threat of a secret weapon being taken seriously in England?' Indeed, it was, although at the time Eddie didn't know that. Enigma decrypts were revealing that the vengeance weapons programme was marching ahead rapidly.

After an air raid the previous autumn on the rocket facility in Peenemünde, production of the V-2 rocket had been transferred to an impregnable underground factory in the Harz mountains. The most immediate threat, however, came from the V-1 doodlebugs which by then were being rolled off the production line in great numbers. Juan Pujol Garcia (Garbo) and Dusko Popov (Tricycle) were already providing important clues about the vengeance weapons. 'The first hint received through these channels came [in] September [1943],' records Sir Michael Howard, 'when Tricycle was warned by the Abwehr against continuing to live in London, since this was likely to become a target for rockets sited on the French coast.'

The Double Cross Committee was emboldened to use Garbo to find out more. He wrote to a Madrid controller that his wife had been perturbed by press reports about an enormous rocket gun which was to be used for reprisal shellings of the British capital. Should he, Garbo enquired, evacuate his family? He offered to make daily reports as to where these projectiles had landed in order to correct any inbuilt aiming errors. At first, Garbo's control told him not to worry, but just before Christmas he too was warned to move as far from the capital as possible.

By the spring of 1944, 'ski sites' – so named because of the long ramp needed to launch the missiles – had been identified all over northern France by Allied photo reconnaissance flights. In April, Bletchley Park decrypted Hitler's orders to establish an operations centre close to Amiens. It was apparent that the onslaught would be directed from this region. Though many ski sites came under aerial bombardment as well as sabotage attack from the local resistance, they couldn't all be destroyed.

These sites were clustered all around the Pas de Calais, which the Germans believed was the target for the forthcoming invasion. From their own reading of the Enigma decrypts, the Allies had known for a while that the Germans had assumed that the Pas de

Calais would be the logical place for the attack. If they landed there, the Allies could effectively cut German forces in half and make a quick push towards the Reich. It also represented the shortest sea crossing (which was why FUSAG's embarkation point was supposedly based in Dover) and the shortest possible journey time into the industrial heartland of the Ruhr.

The Normandy landings would thus be portrayed to the Germans as a feint intended to draw in Wehrmacht reserves. The Allies did not want the Germans to be tipped off from inadvertent patterns of bombing so the coastal defences in the Pas de Calais were attacked equally, and sometimes twice as heavily as those in Normandy. In those last few weeks before D-Day, as the final notes of the chorus of deception were played – against a backdrop of double agents, dummy signals and false tanks, rumours and leaked information – one British deception officer shook his head ruefully at their complexity. 'I can't believe we will ever get away with this,' he said.

For the first couple of weeks of his stay in Paris, von Gröning had gone to the Luftwaffe headquarters at the Hotel Scribe each morning. He would return distraught, his face drawn. Over Easter at the start of April, however, the Baron came into his room early one morning, barely able to contain his excitement. 'Fritz, you are off tonight, conditions permitting,' he almost shouted. 'We are going today to an airport just outside Paris.'

After carefully packing Eddie's equipment, they set off to a cleverly camouflaged airfield close by Le Bourget. Eddie was met by two commanding officers, both holders of the Iron Cross. One was a major, greying and preternaturally older, who after fifty kills to his name was tired of the fighting. The other was a captain who reminded Eddie of a boxer who had, he claimed, lost his plane that very week over the Channel. After testing Eddie's kit, they went to the officers' mess. 'We sat down to a meal of good food and when it was over,' he recalled, 'the commandant asked me whether I would like to hear some music.'

They spent a surreal evening singing Anglo-American hits like 'Swanee' and 'Yankee Doodle' in broken English. Eddie was amazed that they were allowed to learn the words to these songs. 'We are the Luftwaffe,' the major declared indignantly. 'We are not naughty children to be told what we may or may not do. My men like dance music; we are lonely out here and I have given them permission to listen to foreign broadcasts.'

Throughout the evening, weather reports were brought in. All seemed to be set fair. Just before midnight, Eddie was getting into his overalls and having a last good luck toast with von Gröning when a subaltern entered, saluted smartly and handed a message to the commandant.

'Sorry, Fritz,' he announced sadly. 'You are not going tonight.'

Eddie took off his overalls and they headed back to Paris in silence.

The squadron was needed to attack shipping in Portsmouth. Eddie thought it likely that the German air force had almost run out of fuel and aircraft. The next day there was much speculation that there would soon be a landing in France. Von Gröning told Eddie that when he eventually did get to London, his immediate priority would be to find out when and where the landing would take place. And as if to reinforce this, Eddie was asked to take some equipment to a fellow *V-mann* who had managed to ingratiate himself with the most feared general on the Allied side. But for Eddie – as with most of the troops on the other side of the Channel – all that mattered was the answer to a simple question: when were they going to depart?

Each morning, von Gröning, the parachute captain and Eddie traipsed round to Luftwaffe HQ to press their case. The answer was always the same: 'Not today.' 'Nearly every afternoon of those cloudless May days I would bask in the sun or bathe in the Seine or another of the swimming places,' Eddie recalled. He took tourist boat rides to while away the hours. Even ordinary French citizens were openly speculating on where the Allies would land. There was a sense of inevitability, intensified by the bombing all around the country.

Early in May, he was told he would be flying out of Brussels. They went there by train, once again made aware of the damage being wrought to the rail networks. They were destined to spend three frustrating days in the Belgian capital. On the face of it,

Brussels was a revelation. 'Clothes, food and cigarettes were more plentiful, though, once more, only in the black market,' Eddie recalled. While waiting for confirmation of his flight, they watched Belgian collaborators parade through the streets with a swagger. Once again, however, it soon became clear that there was little chance of finding a crew.

They returned to Paris, dejected, where the bombing seemed to intensify even further. Batteries, flak emplacements, bridges, airfields, petrol dumps all came under bombardment. So did French civilians, in what today would be called 'collateral damage'. By the third week of May, over six thousand had been killed. Radio Paris, an official outlet for Nazi propaganda, was allowed to report that the railway system was in chaos. The reported effects chimed with Eddie's own discussions with the Parisians. 'The temper of the population, especially that of Paris, is rising because no food is available, nobody can travel and there are severe restrictions in the use of electricity,' a Radio Paris announcer had said.

Thanks to the ceaseless alerts, the atmosphere in the French capital was becoming like that of Berlin. One day Eddie watched as a couple of Flying Fortresses in a fleet of a hundred were hit as they tried to negotiate the flak barrage high above the city. Police forced the onlookers to seek refuge, for it was an offence not to take shelter. Many Parisians 'gaped and gasped', while the street urchins grinned and jeered at the occupiers as the sirens rose in fury.

By now the increasing numbers of civilian casualties caused by the bombing had begun to create feelings of hostility towards the Allies. When the British war cabinet discussed the collateral damage from the systematic destruction of rail centres, the Prime Minister had warned that it would 'build up a volume of dull hatred in France which will affect our relations with that country for many years to come'. Eddie had heard about many casualties in Nantes, where a USAAF daylight raid had coincided with a local market day. 'The French resentment against the bombing is on the increase,' it was later reported by MI5. 'They even go so far as to say that life under the Germans is preferable to having no homes.'

Despite the bombing, Eddie was still able to wander around Paris and enjoy the city. One Sunday, he and Fritz Stube were walking around the Pigalle district, taking in the exhilarating atmosphere. Young families with kids played on hurdy-gurdies and there was a curiously carefree air. 'I loved this quarter of Paris,' Eddie would recall. 'The cocottes, with their gigolos, swaggered from bar to bar.'

Suddenly, he was nudged in the back. Eddie turned to face a beaming, curly-haired, hook-nosed youth. It was Armand Amalou, the Algerian with whom he had been friendly in Romainville jail. With a German intelligence officer standing next to him, he had to think fast. Quickly, Eddie said in French, 'Don't say anything' – Stube did not speak or seem to understand the language – and asked his friend for an address. Amalou passed over a calling card.

They departed, Stube wanting to know who the fellow was and what he was after. Eddie brushed off the question, saying that he had met the lad at some club or other and he had helped him get some stuff on the black market.

Amalou's card gave his address as La Refuge, a café in Montparnasse. The next day, Eddie went there alone. Amalou said he was still in contact with Anthony Faramus, by now incarcerated in a concentration camp, adding that he had sent food parcels on to him (after the war, it was clear that they had never been received).

Amalou obviously couldn't help but wonder what Eddie was up to in Paris. When Eddie said nothing, the proprietor twinkled. 'Whatever game you are playing now?' he said. 'If you are ever in need of help or perhaps somewhere to hide, you can count on me.'*

Eddie's feeling that he might be in Paris for some time was confirmed when they took private residences. Eddie was given an exquisite flat on rue Miromesnil, which once seemed to have belonged to Marshal Pétain's doctor. One morning, the Baron took him there to meet someone whom he described as clever and

---

* Eddie said that he would come back, and indeed he did so – in the company of Betty – many times after the war. Eddie kidded his wife that when he was coming to their house in London Amalou would be wearing full kaftan and headdress. According to her, La Refuge lived up to its name, for it was 'frequented by lots of strange people from the war'. After the war, Amalou became a journalist, a part-time mercenary and, after surviving the terrors of Romainville, was shot while sitting in his car by unknown assailants.

influential. Herr Krause was slightly built and effeminate so Eddie surmised that he was homosexual. He seemed delighted to meet agent Fritzchen, whose fame had, once again, preceded him.

'I have heard and read so much about you,' he said. 'What fantastic luck you have had!' There was something about the way he said this that made Eddie uncomfortable.

Krause asked him to take some money and a camera to an Abwehr agent in England. Eddie found himself disconcerted by the way the German's eyes never left him; he didn't seem to miss a trick.

They went for a black market lunch in a restaurant improbably called the Frog, whose owner seemed to be working for the Germans. Krause bombarded Eddie with seemingly innocent questions. Eddie 'sensed that here was one who was absolutely convinced that I was not genuine'.

Indeed, at one point Eddie was sure he had been exposed. Krause mentioned a well-known man about town in London. Was this fellow working for British Intelligence? the German wanted to know. Eddie's hackles rose, and he said in some annoyance: 'I have never had the pleasure of working for the British secret service and I wouldn't want to.' Laughing sardonically, Krause apologised.

That night, Eddie attended a meal with a woman who worked at the Paris *Dienststelle* and whose husband was in the Luftwaffe. To his dismay, Krause was also there. During the meal, Eddie was asked by the cultured hostess herself about his visits to England. Krause listened with great interest, like a cat watching a mouse. 'I was not sure who was the cat,' said Eddie, 'or if there were two of them.'

By now he was very wary of Krause's obvious interest. On another occasion, the German came to dinner at the flat in rue Miromesnil, where he took an immediate interest in the expensive Chinese lacquer paintings and valuables. Eddie was very surprised to learn that Krause was an expert who had spent part of his youth in China. The material in the flat, said Krause, was probably worth £20,000; if they ever had to abandon Paris, he would take the collection away with him.

Whenever they met, Krause was unfailingly courteous. Yet Eddie could sense his underlying hostility, his conviction that Eddie was a British spy. Later, he found out that Krause had caught more British agents in Paris than any other of the counter-espionage people based at the Hotel Lutétia. With the increasing tensions caused by the imminence of the landings, Eddie was only too aware that as an Englishman in occupied territory, he might be arrested at any time. Indeed, according to his widow, Eddie knew the longer he stayed in France, the greater chance he would have of getting into trouble. It would be terrible, having come so far, to be arrested just weeks before he left for his native land.

In the last few days of May, a calm, gentle swell washed across the shores of Normandy. Paris sweltered in a heatwave. It had been the hottest Whitsun in living memory. By now, the French newspapers were openly speculating about the possibility of an Allied landing. Unlike the natives, Abwehr personnel were allowed to listen to Allied broadcasts unimpeded. For von Gröning, the wireless was a welcome treat. He listened regularly to the BBC, telling Eddie that he was a great admirer of Winston Churchill.

On the first Tuesday in June, Eddie was sitting with some Germans in von Gröning's flat when the ashen-faced Baron walked in. Without any preamble, he declared that there had been a landing in France.

'Another Dieppe?' Eddie asked.

'No,' his controller replied, 'the real thing.'

They tuned the wireless to London and heard the BBC announcement that the invasion had started. When 'God Save the King' was played, they stood up and *heiled* Hitler. Von Gröning declared that they would show the British and Americans what war really was. Yet it was clear that all the disinformation and deceptions surrounding the landing were working; the Germans had had no idea where it was going to take place or when.

Eddie decided it would be useful to gauge how the general populace was reacting. All through the capital, he found a curious calm. Most Parisians, it seemed to Eddie, were still more interested in what they were eating: his impromptu *vox populi* revealed they were more preoccupied with wanting an end to rationing than with the imminent invasion. Some were so certain the Allies would liberate Paris by the end of the month that they had already used up all their food rations.

In the days immediately after the landing, life went on very much as before apart from an extended curfew. Though the Germans expected riots and sabotage after D-Day, none happened. The Paris Commandant declared that the citizens under his orders could have one hour less of curfew conditions as they were behaving themselves. The French press, under the German censors, continued to downplay the landings as the month progressed. Pictures and reports showed German troops and tanks en route to the Normandy bridgeheads.

Eddie witnessed much transport passing through Paris on the way to the coast. The newspapers talked of heavy losses by the Allies and photographs showed wounded troops being marched to prisoner-of-war camps. 'The note was one of such sustained confidence that it seemed impossible that the invaders could carry on,' Eddie said. 'Soon they must surely be pushed back into the sea.'

One night, as the sirens wailed, Eddie was transfixed by the sight of RAF bombers caught in searchlights and flak close by the Sacré Coeur, whose bleached dome was suffused in a roseate glow. One aircraft, caught in the barrage, started to break up before his eyes. Eddie watched an airman come down, twisting to control his parachute descent. 'The glare of the searchlights showed every particle of his clothing as though made of purest white,' he recalled. 'The airman sank amid the flak fire while his body banged helplessly against a chimney pot' before he was lost to view.

Eddie wondered if he would ever get to make his own drop.

Even Stefan von Gröning had come to the conclusion that Eddie would never leave Occupied France. Just after the Normandy landings, his controller called Eddie into his office. 'The chief here considers that you understand the psychology of the British,' he said. 'He wants us to start recruiting suitable agents to remain behind in Paris to work for us should the Allies capture the city.' They wanted Eddie to penetrate the bridgeheads surrounding the landings. With Allied forces fighting in the hedgerows of Normandy there was talk that Eddie might be dropped behind enemy lines with a radio transmitter to report on the disposition of troops. After D-Day, as another MI5 report says, 'The idea was that the agent should be trained in Morse and sabotage and should be put into an evacuated town, where the transmitter should be hidden in the wall.'

Von Gröning added that he could wear any uniform he wanted. The glorious possibility of Eddie Chapman posing as a padre was briefly entertained. He could take as much money as he wanted and get help from others.

Eddie even began training a girl called Hélène with whom he had been flirting on his nights on the town. She had worked for the Germans as a typist at the *Dienststelle*. After her lover, a Luftwaffe officer, had been killed, she had already asked about the possibilities of joining in espionage operations. 'I arranged to pay her eight thousand francs a month with a proviso of ten thousand when she had finished her training,' he said. He taught her radio transmissions twice a day at his flat. 'She learned extraordinarily quickly,' he remembered. 'In three days, she had mastered the alphabet.'

Eddie and the Baron were always alert for other possible – and increasingly unlikely – recruits. Eddie wasted time and effort by asking obviously unsuitable candidates. He recalled that the friendly old porter at the Ambassador Hotel had lived in Jersey and London. He also spoke perfect English. Using illicit booze as an inducement, Eddie invited the old boy over to his flat on the rue Miromesnil. 'You, as a porter, could be of great service to us if the Allied troops decided to occupy this hotel,' he said.

The old man, worried and hesitant, replied that he was *un vieux* and well past the age for fighting. He didn't want to be a traitor, he said, particularly not at the end of his life. As a later MI5 file makes clear, Eddie also contacted 'an elderly hunch-back at the Hotel Vosges, rue Monmartre'. But neither would this man 'entertain the idea of working for the Germans'.

One evening, the Baron – probably drunk when he decided on such a course of action – announced that he wanted to pose as the owner of an antique shop. Eddie could pretend to be his assistant. In a similarly hopeless vein, von Gröning 'roped in' a German bookseller from Nantes named Hibler who was working in the Hotel Lutétia. He had lost both his foot and his business – a bookshop named Le Font – in a heavy raid on the Breton port, while his heavily pregnant French wife had been severely wounded; he 'was bitter towards the Allies'. As Hibler had lived in France for many years, he could help recruit others to spy around the Normandy bridgehead. Just before Eddie left, he also found a possible recruit in a Frau Hoffman who worked in a bookshop.

Such attempts at recruitment seem very half-hearted. Just two weeks after the invasion, it was clear which way the fighting was going. As Eddie later explained to MI5, 'the rot had set in'.

Suddenly, events accelerated. The same morning that the Führer was told about the landings in Normandy, he had issued the command for V-1 bombardment to begin, but the firing sites weren't ready. Six days after D-Day, at his daily military conference at the Berchtesgaden, he repeated the order. He was in a particularly foul mood that morning, but his eyes lit up with messianic fervour as he spoke of a rain of malignant robots that would be harder for the perfidious British to bear than the Blitz.

So it was on that first Monday after D-Day landings, 12 June, that the first 'flying bombs' landed in southern England. Two senior civil servants were strolling across St James's Park on the way to their club in Pall Mall when they heard a curious chugging noise. Suddenly it stopped and there was an ominous silence. Anticipating what it might be, the civil servants threw themselves flat on the ground. Unperturbed, two civilians nearby walked past. On hearing a distant explosion, one remarked to the other, 'I suppose that's this new secret weapon we've heard so much about.'

Adolf Hitler had made so many apocalyptic pronouncements that the arrival of the buzzbombs was hardly unexpected. Eddie's recollection of these times is instructive. While eating in the Luftwaffe restaurant in the French capital some weeks earlier, he had come across several of the experts who had briefed him in Berlin. Expressing surprise that he was still in Paris, they had told him that 'Hitler's toy' was ready to be fired at any moment. 'The German cause received a fillip a little later in June when the news came of the first use by Hitler of his long-vaunted secret weapon,' he later recalled. 'To me it was no secret.'

The Germans had also been told that everything within two hundred yards of a V-bomb impact was instantly vaporised. 'London and southern England have now been under bombardment for more than a week,' Lord Haw Haw would soon crow. 'The very term V-1 implies, of course, that Germany has other new weapons which have not as yet been employed against the enemy.'

Eddie's Abwehr controllers were certain that – much like Berlin and Hamburg – the British capital would be in ruins by the time he arrived in his native land.

The reality was very different. The BBC reported on that Monday evening that the Germans had launched their much-vaunted new weapon, but stated there were few casualties and limited damage. The next bulletin also treated the story as an after-thought, which Eddie realised was probably the best way of counteracting German propaganda. Indeed, the Baron and Krause, desperate to believe that Britain was being brought to its knees, were livid at the way the news had been reported. 'They can't write it off like that!' von Gröning snapped. 'The truth will out soon.'

Even at this late stage, there was still no word about Eddie's departure. So one night, he decided to drown his sorrows by visiting Armand Amalou's café. He was having supper there when, after closing time, a knock came at the door. Four young customers were let in. They were puzzled by his English accent and one, whom Eddie described as fiery, made a V-sign. Eddie did not respond. Though his accent was atrocious, the lad then claimed that his own mother was English. He had been with the Maquis in the Haute Savoie, he said, but had surrendered due to lack of support from the British. 'We fought to our last bullet, and many of my comrades were killed.'

He was put into a camp and offered freedom if he worked for the Germans. The young man had had little choice but to accept and he now worked for the Germans as a lorry driver. In the process, he had lost both his idealism and any interest in whether or not the Allies would liberate France. The same dejection characterised his companions. Eddie couldn't help feeling sorry for them.

He thought nothing more of this curious evening until a couple of days later when, in the company of von Gröning, he bumped into Herr Krause. The counter-espionage man invited them to dine with him and suggested they visit the Latin Quarter. Eddie hoped his poker face gave no hint of his true feelings. Had Krause been informed about his visit to Amalou's?

In the event, they spent the evening in a club very close by, where Eddie distractedly watched a belly dancer. Suddenly Krause said, with his usual deceptive conviviality, that he knew of another place nearby.

'It's called La Refuge,' he added.

Eddie blithely said he didn't wish to go there in the company of two obvious Germans. As nonchalantly as possible, he added that he had an appointment with a girl at the Lido. 'I pressed them to both come along and share a bottle of champagne,' he recalled.

Von Gröning was persuaded, but Eddie was certain he saw a knowing smile pass Krause's lips. As was later reported to MI5: 'Chapman could not refuse Krause's invitation to visit an Arab cabaret, but the invitation fortunately came to nothing.' Whatever the real reasons behind the invite, Eddie was certain that he had finally passed muster with Krause.

On the first Monday of the doodlebug barrage, only a handful got any further than the end of the launch ramp. It led some in London to conclude that these weapons were hardly harbingers of mass destruction – 'The mountain hath groaned and given forth a mouse!' said Churchill's scientific adviser.

Others within British Intelligence were less certain. The V-1s were being mass produced in increasing numbers. Made from sheet metal at a cost of roughly £200, each buzzbomb took just fifty man-hours to assemble and used ordinary gasoline with an existing engine; neither aluminium nor aviation fuel, both of which were becoming increasingly scarce in Nazi Germany, was required in their construction. In flight tests in the Baltic, the Luftwaffe firing crews had been able to launch twenty buzzbombs an hour. Why were similar numbers not landing in England?

Three days later, they did. On Thursday, 15 June, Hitler's much-vaunted retaliation began in earnest. At 10.30 p.m., the first of more than two hundred flying bombs was launched, each carrying a ton and a half of high explosive. One hundred and forty-four crossed the English coast and seventy-three reached Greater London. Within a fortnight, the Germans had launched more than two thousand V-1s. There seemed little that could be done to stop them. RAF bombers couldn't be diverted from the beaches of Normandy to pinpoint the launching sites in and around the Pas de Calais.

If such a rate of firing continued, it was clear that Hitler's vision of London in ruins might come to pass. A specially convened government committee met in secret to look at the problem, haunted by the possibility that the beleaguered population of London would panic as it became the focus for a new kind of Blitz. The Home Defence Executive, chaired by Sir Findlater Stewart, a senior adviser to Home Secretary Herbert Morrison, produced a paper on the effects of the bombing recommending that emergency measures be given the highest priority. The Home Office expected a flood of refugees and looked at establishing enormous food dumps in the wake of the missile attacks.

After two weeks of continual bombardment, at a cabinet meeting on Thursday, 27 June, the Home Secretary himself gave a grave warning. Unless the menace of the buzzbombs could be stopped, he said, more than two hundred thousand homes would be damaged or destroyed. So many millions of window panes would be shattered that an epidemic of illness from colds would result in the winter. 'After five years of war, the civil population is incapable of standing the strain of air attack,' Herbert Morrison declared. Luckily, five hours earlier, in the small hours of that same Thursday, an old friend dropped out of the sky over Cambridgeshire to make sure they would never have to.

★ ★ ★

After all his time in Paris, Eddie Chapman had never been allowed inside the Hotel Lutétia, the local headquarters of the Abwehr. Three weeks to the day after the Normandy invasion, he was told to meet Stefan von Gröning there. In the atmosphere of heightened security since D-Day, visitors required a special pass to get into the building. His controller and a pair of Abwehr officers waited for Eddie on the doorstep. Soon, they realised that their star agent Fritzchen was already in the cocktail bar.

'What the bloody hell are you doing here?' exclaimed von Gröning.

Eddie smiled. His controller was amazed: after two years of working out of the same hotel, they had never once been let in without showing their passes. Eddie explained how he had duped the guards by chatting to someone he recognised from Nantes. The guards had assumed he was a member of staff and let him pass.

There, in the hotel cocktail bar, Eddie's mission was discussed. The Baron could hardly control his excitement. 'Fritz, you are definitely going at last,' he said. 'We start tomorrow for Holland.' Because of the aerial activity around the French coast, he would be flown from there to England. Von Gröning advised him to brush up on his codes and make sure he understood every last detail about his mission.

To Eddie's chagrin, in walked Krause. When Eddie returned home, the German insisted, he should leave £1,000 and a camera for the mysterious agent whom he had mentioned before. He would be instructed by radio when to leave them. Eddie was to hide this material under a tree or in a lavatory cistern. If he didn't receive the message, then he would be free to keep the money.

The next day, a celebratory meal had been arranged on the second floor of the hotel, where the head of the Paris *Stelle* had personally sent up cognac and cigarettes. The room was thronging with people, all wanting Eddie to make sure he would record how helpful they had been to him. One colonel said that if Fritzchen was successful, his mission would have a profound effect on the outcome of the war.

'It will also,' he insisted, 'be a triumph for our secret service.'

To Eddie, the whole event seemed utterly unreal. Nevertheless, he thanked them for their kindness. Krause raised his glass, but did not drink. All of them came out to wave him goodbye. He was off – first to Brussels, then Utrecht – in a heavily armed car. Eddie couldn't help notice that everything en route was 'well and truly battered'. Near the Dutch town itself, they heard machine-gun fire, although it turned out to be German soldiers at a practice range.

Eventually – after many false turns not helped by the lack of signposts – they came to a house on the outskirts of Den Helden, hidden in woods and well camouflaged. 'In the drive stood several highly powered cars belonging to the Luftwaffe staff,' Eddie recalled. In the mess, he was introduced to the crew and the lieutenant who would fly him to England. All were young – nineteen or twenty – and one was to go on leave as soon as the mission was over. They had, it seemed, been trained in night flying. After his experiences last time around, Eddie was pleased to see a mechanic working on the trap door. 'I inspected his work carefully

Together at last: On 9 October 1947, Eddie Chapman marries Betty Farmer at the Chelsea Registry Office in a simple ceremony.

BELOW Pride and joy: The Chapman's Silver Wraith which was a post-war fixture of Belgravia. Though bought by Betty, Eddie often drove it though he had not actually passed his driving test.

Temptation: In the post-war years, Eddie had a lot of female admirers. 'It was always the women who chased him,' says his long-suffering widow Betty.

BELOW Mind how you go: After his wartime service, the authorities pardoned Eddie for his pre-war crimes. Here, his old friend Chief Inspector Bob Fabian ('Fabian of the Yard') hands him his passport back.

The Rock: Betty Chapman, in the early 1970s, when she bought an Irish castle and turned it into a health farm. Despite Eddie's manifold transgressions, friends say she was the rock on which his life was anchored.

BELOW The Baron: In September 1976, a familiar face reappears for a Chapman family wedding. Stefan von Gröning is the second from the right; Eddie is sitting below the middle painting and Betty is kneeling in front of the sofa.

Unlikely Hero: Eddie in his seventies, outside the Imperial War Museum. Despite his extraordinary bravery, he was never awarded a medal by the British government.

BELOW Eddie and Betty at Shenley Lodge, their health farm in Hertfordshire, in the 1990s. 'The Germans didn't kill Eddie,' Betty says. 'The loss of Shenley did.'

for I did not want once again to have the tricky experience of being stuck in the hole I was coming through to make my drop.'

After all the delays, Eddie still couldn't quite believe that he was about to depart. Situation reports were brought in by the commandant that all was looking good. About an hour before midnight, Eddie got dressed. Money belts were draped around his shoulders and he changed into his blue flight overalls. Soon they were driven out to the airfield itself. On the way, von Gröning told him that his flight had been timed to coincide with a Luftwaffe raid on London. The ensuing turmoil would help mask his arrival. Three days after landing, he was expected to send his first message to say he had arrived.

Somewhat diffidently, the Baron handed him a phial that contained commercial potassium cyanide in an unmarked bottle. 'Ten drops of this solution would ordinarily be fatal to man,' a later chemical analysis made clear.

They got out of the car and the crew saluted him, one of them stepping forward to strap him into his parachute. The engines roared, flames from the exhaust flickered eerily. After a final handshake, von Gröning shouted, '*Glück, viel Glück*' ('Good luck, good luck!') over the noise. Within a few seconds, Eddie was aboard.

'Three minutes later,' he recalled, 'we were airborne for England.'

CHAPTER TEN

Hard Landings

'ZIGZAG then went back to Germany and was treated royally. He reappeared over a year later with much useful information about Germany and a significant questionnaire from his German masters. Unfortunately, his successes had gone to his head and he could not stop talking of them. It became necessary to terminate his case. The Germans believed him to be moved by their promise to send him to America to start a new life after he had served them, and meanwhile by luxurious living and a supply of women when he returned to Germany.'

– Commander Ewen Montagu, Eddie's handler at the Naval Intelligence Division

IN THE EARLY HOURS of Thursday, 27 June 1944, a lone Junkers veered uncertainly over Six Mile Bottom in the Cambridge fens. Eddie Chapman couldn't help noticing the extreme nervousness of his crew. Despite Stefan von Gröning's claim, the Junkers bomber was on its own and not hidden among a larger raid, doubtless because of the overwhelming firepower of the British defences. 'My only fear was that this mastery would be so complete that the German plane [would] be shot out of the sky by my countrymen before it could reach the shores of England,' Eddie recalled.

Flying low over the North Sea, the flight was rough as the pilot purposefully 'swerved, dived and swooped up like a mad bird'.

Eddie was aware of recognition lights on the wings which signalled to the German flak gunners on whose side they belonged. Soon, they were switched off. He gained the distinct impression that the pilot was using lighthouses off the east coast of England as beacons. They flew very low over the waves to avoid radar detection and passed just above three ships. 'Then I caught sight of searchlights waving frantically,' he recalled, 'there seemed to be hundreds of them.' Eddie started to feel sick, especially when he saw a night-fighter pass maybe a hundred feet from their tail. It would soon be time to jump.

When he pulled the escape lever, the plane jolted, possibly hit by flak. Eddie fell awkwardly, protecting his face from the instrument panel in front of him. He felt his stomach drop faster than the rest of him and then, before he knew it, his parachute was open. 'I swung in the empty sky, like a pendulum in a vast clock,' he recalled. 'It was too much for my poor, rebellious stomach. I leaned over the side of my harness and spewed over England.'

Despite this, it was a perfect night for a parachute drop. It was just after 3 a.m. In the lingering midsummer twilight, there were a few wisps of cloud, and the descent was much less painful this time around. But when he was within landing distance, a gust of wind carried him past a clump of trees, over a hedge and into the middle of a narrow country road. He made a heavy landing on the tarmac and was nearly knocked unconscious. He lay still for ten minutes to regain his composure. When he tried to stand up, he was in agony.

Eddie Chapman had badly damaged a number of vertebrae. It was an injury from which he never fully recovered. 'Towards the end of his life, the pain got worse,' his widow says. 'In the end, he could hardly walk. He used to be taken out in a wheelchair.'

That warm June morning, despite the pain from his back, Eddie became aware of the brightness permeating the fenland fields. Sitting up in the dawn light, he gathered his equipment together, parcelling up his parachute by the roadside under a tree. He took off his boots, replacing them with comfortable shoes. This time he was also carrying two wireless sets – one a combined transceiver, the other a transmitter – two Leica cameras and £6,000. One of the cameras, £1,000 and the transmitter were for Herr Krause's mysterious agent.

Eddie was taking off his flight overalls and about to make his way down the country lane when he became aware of footsteps somewhere behind him. Soon he realised that there were torches flashing in the distance. A line of searchers, walking methodically through the fields, were slowly but surely making their way towards him.

'The bastard must be somewhere near here!' came a cry.

Eddie was determined to evade them and make his own contact with his MI5 handlers. Crawling on his stomach, he managed to avoid the search party by hiding under a hedge. After waiting for them to pass, he staggered a quarter of a mile down the road, in terrible pain from the injuries to his back and by now thoroughly soaked from the pre-dawn dew. How come they had been waiting for him? When he came across a row of houses in a quiet village, he was relieved. He knocked on the nearest door.

Almost immediately, a window opened above him. A woman's head appeared. 'What do you want?' she cried.

'I'm a British flyer who's had an accident. Could I use the telephone?'

The querulous female was not impressed. 'Go away, you wicked man!'

The window was slammed shut. Marvelling at the warmth of this welcome, Eddie walked down the street and came across another household which seemed to be already awake. This time a farmer was up and getting ready to head out to his fields. His bleary-eyed family welcomed Eddie in and offered him the inevitable cup of tea. He asked where the nearest police station was and was directed to use the telephone in the hallway.

A dozy-sounding policeman answered. When Eddie explained that he wanted to be picked up, the duty officer replied: 'Don't be silly. Go to bed.'

'That's exactly what they told me before,' Eddie said through gritted teeth. 'Ring up your station in Ely. They'll remember me from last time.'

He asked for transport. Now the policeman wanted to know his name and number. Eddie sighed. The policeman politely informed him that an official form had to be filled in before he could do anything. 'And, in any case, there is no transport,' he added with satisfaction.

Eddie suddenly had a brainwave. 'How far are you from Littleport?'

'About twenty miles.'

Eddie thanked the policeman and called the station there. A vaguely familiar voice answered.

'About two years ago,' Eddie said, hopefully, 'were you on duty when a man arrived in the early hours of the morning?'

'That was me,' said the proud voice.

'Well, it's me again. Could I get picked up?'

While he waited, Eddie remembered a London number he'd been given in case of emergencies. He had been told it belonged to his friend Jimmy Hunt. Keeping his voice down so that the family in the other room couldn't hear, Eddie rang the number. A surprisingly alert voice answered.

'*Joli Albert*,' was all Eddie said, hoping that there would be no repeat of the fiasco in Portugal.

It was not Jimmy who answered, but the voice asked him for more information. Eddie gained some satisfaction knowing that whoever it was, they were expecting him.

Five hours later, Eddie Chapman was lunching at the Naval and Military Club opposite Green Park accompanied by a phalanx of Security Service officers. With the change in the fortunes of the fighting, rations had improved. Eddie pronounced his lunch excellent. The MI5 team, led by his old friend Colonel Tommy Robertson, had decided on a softly, softly approach. It was almost like a reunion of old friends. Sitting discreetly in one corner, Eddie outlined his mission this time around. He was to gauge the efficiency of the onslaught of the buzzbombs and help in pinpointing their aim, reporting when and where the missiles landed. Barometric pressure reports would also help the V-1s hit their targets more effectively.

'Here I am supposed to be directing them,' Eddie said over post-prandial drinks, 'and I haven't even seen one.'

'Don't worry,' Robertson said knowingly. 'You soon will.'

At that moment, the air raid sirens sounded. For the first time, Eddie was to experience the heart-stopping noise of a doodlebug coming to the end of its flight. They went over to a large window overlooking the park. Within seconds, the engine chugged to a halt and there was a terrible silence, seemingly interminable.

In the distance, there was an explosion.

'Well, now,' Robertson said, smiling grimly. 'You have your wish.' They returned to their table. 'They are not very pleasant. You realise you have quite a spate of work to do?'

Installed in a luxurious apartment in Kensington Olympia, Eddie soon got used to the 'thick and fast' arrival of the V-1s. On his first night at Rugby Mansions, just after 2 a.m., a doodlebug crashed and detonated nearby. The explosion threw Eddie out of his bed. The next morning there was chaos in the nearby streets. A dishevelled neighbour, his night's sleep disturbed, remarked: 'That 'itler don't 'alf make a lot of noise.'

The urgency of the threat posed by the missiles – and the key role he was expected to play in combating them – meant that Eddie's reacquaintance with 'Tin Eye' Stephens was somewhat perfunctory. When he was taken to Latchmere House two days after arriving in Britain, it almost seemed as though Stephens was genuinely pleased to see him. The tenor of the interrogations shows it was akin to a pair of old friends catching up on their news after a couple of years apart.

Captain Stephens seems to have been on his best behaviour. There was much less bullying this time and the interviews took place at a more leisurely pace. That same Saturday, Eddie was even taken to lunch at a hotel in nearby Kingston-upon-Thames. The poisonous suspicions which had marred their last encounters had evaporated. In the summary to his interrogation, Stephens even goes so far as to say Eddie 'was made welcome at Camp 020'. Instinctively, 'Tin Eye' felt that Eddie was playing straight.

Eddie was allowed to make his first transmission on Sunday, 30 June, when he was let out to a nearby school with guards in attendance. This time, he was allowed to see where he was being held. Eddie used the more complex of the pair of transmitters to send a simple message: 'Hard landing. But all OK. Finding better place. Coming again Thursday.' Monitoring by the Radio Security Service revealed the Abwehr was taking him at face value. His German controllers forwarded this simple contact report to Berlin with no comment.

Though Eddie couldn't help noticing that his previously hostile interrogators were now handling him with kid gloves, behind his

back 'Tin Eye' Stephens sounded a note of caution. In the introduction to his detailed cross-examination – which was circulated to
his superiors – Stephens felt compelled to 'issue a warning about
this very strange character'. Eddie Chapman, he noted, had been
treated regally in Germany, yet here he was a fugitive from the law.
That fact alone should make them all tread very carefully.

'Where then do the loyalties of Chapman lie?' Stephens asked
with a characteristically rhetorical flourish. 'Personally I think they
are in fine balance and a few grains of irritation might well bring
down the scale on the side of England or Germany as the immediate
circumstances may dictate.'

On the first Saturday of July, Eddie was reunited with Ronnie
Reed at the RAC Club off Piccadilly. He said he was very tired, his
weariness doubtless exacerbated by the pain from his back. His
main concerns were still for his daughter, Dianne, and he wanted
to tell her mother that he had returned. For the moment, Reed
asked him not to contact them. Once again, he was using the name
Edward Simpson to avoid any complications with the police. For
a few days he was interrogated in a West End apartment block in
Hill Street close by the clubs of Green Park, where he could be
interviewed at a gentler pace. This time, he would spend a lot of
time in the company of MI5's Michael Ryde, a solicitor before the
war.

A stream of questioners from the Security Service were largely
helpful and friendly. Apart from some sharp intakes of breath when
he related the story of his revelations to Dagmar Lahlum the
summer before, there were no heavy-handed criticisms of his
actions. As Stephens would record, 'The question of how ZIGZAG
is to be handled is a delicate and highly important one.' The
security authorities had already pegged him as an egotist: now, like
the Abwehr, they were taking care to flatter him and play up to his
vanity. 'Although we do not propose to and cannot supply him with
champagne for his meals,' another MI5 man reported, 'this is the
sort of thing with which we have to compete.'

During his first week home, Eddie was keen to start making
transmissions about the impact of the buzzbombs. In particular, he
wanted to transmit details of the damage done to the Regent Palace
Hotel (which had been hit on the last day of June) and in and

around Olympia, near where he was staying. That way, the Germans would know he was being straight with them.

More than a hundred flying bombs were being launched across the Channel every day. By the end of June, there had been 2,415 recorded landings, of which nearly 30 per cent – more than seven hundred – had hit central London. The Home Defence Committee reported in its official deliberations on the V-1 menace that 'another high agent, who has recently arrived here, has been instructed to give a high priority to bomb reports'. This referred to Eddie, whose task was now to help hinder the onslaught. Soon agent Zigzag was meeting with his MI5 controllers every day to plan how they could mislead the Germans.

The effect of the buzzbombs was hard to falsify. The fake destruction of the de Havilland factory at Hatfield had been a one-off, but the V-1s were arriving one after the other, with increasing frequency. This time there was no unique action that Eddie could perform to deceive the Germans. However, it had already been noted from tracking by radar that test flights of the V-1 across the Baltic had tended to fall short of their targets. Could the agents be used to deceive the firing crews into thinking that something similar was happening in England?

Despite their propaganda claims, the way in which the Germans aimed the buzzbomb and then calibrated it in flight was remarkably crude. A small propeller at the rear mechanically recorded a number of revolutions like a milometer on a bicycle. After a certain number of turns, the fuel supply would be cut. Moreover, the buzzbombs were very much at the mercy of wind conditions. The Wehrmacht ordnance troops simply aimed the V-1 towards London and hoped for the best. A plot of the impacts since mid-June had shown that the missiles were tending to cluster near Dulwich, in south London. If the Germans could be persuaded by information from the double agents to decrease the range, then greater numbers would land in the fields of Kent. 'The back-room boys in England,' as Eddie called them, 'would have a field day altering times and locations' to make the Germans effectively shorten their aim point.

And so a plan was evolved. The double agents were to be asked to report the dates, times and places where the buzzbombs were supposedly falling. Two days after Eddie arrived home on 29 June, the Double Cross Committee agreed to begin feeding doctored information to the Germans. Juan Pujol Garcia – in his guise as Garbo – had already reported to his German controllers rumours that many of the buzzbombs were landing to the north and west of central London.

But this presented a dilemma. If genuine information was provided, it would help the enemy; yet palpably false information could be checked, particularly by photo reconnaissance (the occasional German spotter plane could still be seen in the skies above the capital). In that case the agents would be 'blown'. The whole basis of Allied deception operations would come tumbling down at the moment when it was needed the most.

Though photo reconnaissance could pinpoint exactly where the bombs had struck – it could not determine when they had impacted.

The Security Service handlers found that the double agents in their charge could easily recall the places but not the times of the bombs' arrival. '[The] important thing is to give really precise times,' one MI5 man concluded at the start of July, 'and I do not think that we can do this credibly, in view of the line taken by [the other agents] except in relation to the bombs actually seen or heard by Zigzag.' Eddie would only report those explosions which he would be reasonably expected to hear. 'These he will time exactly and then go out and find the actual locations,' it was reported. The Chiefs of Staff recommended that 'by special means we should try to recreate the impression that the bombs were appearing to overshoot the target in the hope that the range would be moved further to the East and South'. By transmitting the doctored times of impacts, it appeared that the buzzbombs had reached their targets sooner than they actually had.

Shortly after Eddie landed, Garbo was temporarily removed from circulation, supposedly arrested on the first Tuesday of July after paying too much interest in the effects of a buzzbomb blast in east London. On the last day of June, he reported, in anticipation of his supposed arrest, 'it is dangerous to ask questions in damaged areas since the public who lose their house is rather hostile'. His disappearance was reported to the Germans on 5 July.

This was another double bluff. With Patton now known to be in France, it was imperative that the Catalan go off air. That way there could be no information provided on the supposed impending landing at the Pas de Calais. Units already identified as part of the mythical FUSAG were appearing in Normandy, and soon Patton would be reported as the commander of the American Third Army.

(In the event, the delay with the imaginary forces of FUSAG would be explained by Patton's supposed demotion for insubordination by Eisenhower.)

'This development gave us precisely the break which we had tried to engineer and had so badly needed', Garbo's British handler recorded. By pretending he had been incarcerated, the Spaniard's usefulness as a double agent was not compromised. After his release on Monday, 10 July, there was good news. The Abwehr told him to 'cease all investigations of the new weapon'.

Indeed, the fictions surrounding the imaginary FUSAG now took precedence for all the double agents. Apart from Fritzchen, that is.

As the only agent not directly involved in the deceptions surrounding the Normandy landings, Eddie Chapman spent the rest of the summer traipsing around London recording details of the buzzbombs. Or rather an MI5 chauffeur, Jock Horsfall, did, taking photographs of bomb damage with the Leica which Eddie had brought with him. A pub damaged in Old Windsor. A shop damaged there, buildings destroyed. Street corners smashed up all around the capital. (Actually sending the photographs on to Lisbon was later deemed too useful for the Germans.)

Yet the Germans could still monitor BBC radio, which faithfully recorded the times of landings; maps were also printed in newspapers which showed the impact of bombs in various London boroughs. And choreographing the contributions from the different double agents was difficult. Both Eddie and the agent codenamed Brutus reported an explosion on different dates in the same area of east London. Brutus first recorded slight damage to Ilford's Park Royal on 10 July; five days later, so did Eddie. The MI5 controllers hoped the Abwehr would either think the factory had been damaged twice or else that one of them had made a genuine mistake.

As a result of the information they received, the Germans had been successfully deceived into thinking the range of the V-1 was far greater than it actually was. Within a matter of days of receiving the double agents' first doctored reports, the Wehrmacht suspected that they were overfiring and the ordnance crews took heed. British Intelligence had the satisfaction of noting that the average range of the buzzbombs was deliberately reduced for the rest of the summer. Greater numbers started falling in the southern suburbs and hopfields of Kent.

There was one final hiccup. The Prime Minister's son-in-law, Duncan Sandys, nominally in charge of all government measures mounted against the buzzbombs, made a public *faux pas* as a result of which Zigzag's cover might easily have been blown. 'In this connection, it is worth mentioning that the messages sent by ZIGZAG,' one intelligence committee noted, 'if compared in detail with the recent speech made by Duncan Sandys in the house, show very considerable discrepancies and there is a possibility that the case will be blown on these grounds.' Thankfully, the Germans didn't seem to notice. By then, most of the Abwehr staff were too busy trying to save their own skins.

Had it not been for a little dog, Betty Farmer might well have been killed by one of the buzzbombs. Indeed, she lost two homes that summer of 1944 and only escaped with her life because of a spaniel called Spitfire. At the time she was living in Nevern Square, Earls Court, but as she recalls, 'I was out in Hampshire and I wouldn't come to London that night because I couldn't leave the dog. I couldn't find anyone to look after it and I didn't want to bring it back up to town.' That evening in July 1944, the house in Nevern Square was destroyed by a V-1 missile.

After this attack, she moved into another house on the same square. Some time later, she was having tea with a friend when they became aware of a buzzbomb heading directly towards them. 'Oh my God,' Betty remembers saying, 'I hope that's not going to hit Nevern Square.' Suddenly, the engine stopped and they both stood at the window to watch it glide by. It did indeed hit their square. The only survivor was the housekeeper, who was in the basement at the time. 'Had I been in my flat,' Betty recalls, 'no doubt I wouldn't have survived it.'

Betty was still doing her bit for the war effort and that summer of 1944 was kept very busy. 'I was a firefighter,' she recalls. 'I used to go up on the roof and people used to carry buckets of water up to me.' Human chains in the form of anybody who was around – 'sailors, soldiers, anyone' – used to go up the ladder to help put out the fire. At various other times, she drove an ambulance and worked as a foreman in a factory in Earls Court Stadium that made small parts for the war effort. She was living and working less than a mile from where Eddie was based, but she never bumped into him.

As before, she was mixing with pilots whose illustrious number included Geoffrey Page of the Handley Page dynasty. That summer, he had been shot down in horrifying circumstances. 'He was very badly burned,' Betty explains, 'and I spent hours at his bedside.' And that was how she came to meet Sir Archibald McIndoe, famed for his pioneering work on wartime burns victims. By a curious coincidence, McIndoe had been treating the wife of a certain double agent, for whom Eddie was supposed to be bringing a transmitter from Herr Krause in Paris.

On Sunday, 23 July, a buzzbomb had damaged the house of the agent codenamed Brutus. His wife – herself given the codename Moustique for security purposes – suffered terrible facial injuries as a result. Brutus consulted McIndoe, for MI5 was keen to cover his expenses for any surgery that resulted. 'I believe that this gesture would be very much appreciated by Brutus who has worked valiantly for us for over a period of time without receiving any remuneration,' one of his case officers noted.

Brutus was in fact a Polish Air Force wing commander called Roman Garby-Czerniawski. Imprisoned by the Germans for running a resistance group in Occupied Europe in 1942, he had been allowed to 'escape' but revealed his mission the moment he arrived in England. The Pole 'showed himself to be a man of great daring and initiative' and he was taken on as a double agent. A pilot and an Olympic standard skier, Garby-Czerniawski had also worked for the cryptanalytical staff of the Polish General Staff before the war. Possessed of a photographic memory, he was supposedly on the Polish staff of General Patton's mythical FUSAG and was instrumental in transmitting to the Germans the fictional threat to the Pas de Calais.

Brutus's controllers had been promising him money all spring but, as usual, they had not followed through. Eddie Chapman was now to become the instrument whereby he would be paid. Before he left France, Eddie had been told that one of the cameras, £1,000 and the transmitter he was carrying were for the mysterious agent whom the sinister Krause had insisted he meet. (In his interrogation at Camp 020, Eddie had claimed he wasn't sure of this agent's identity – at one point he was told the agent was already here, then that he would arrive a month later.) He was later told by radio to leave the equipment at the Regent Palace Hotel (the same hotel where he had been hiding in the spring of 1939 before making his way to Jersey in the wake of the botched burglary in Edinburgh). Brutus had been staying there after his house had been destroyed.

Once again, Eddie was having difficulties in making and maintaining radio contact. Indeed, it appeared that his control had been changed. Monitoring by the RSS on 8 July located the radio station transmitting Eddie's orders twenty miles east of Paris. Later on, it appeared that the station was closed and had been removed directly to Hamburg where the signal was stronger. On 1 August, a 'blind' message – sent out in the forlorn hope that Eddie would receive it – suggested that the money and a camera should be delivered to 'the other man', Brutus.

This created a quandary for MI5. 'While it does not suit us to have the two agents linked,' one MI5 report makes clear, 'it is going to be very difficult to avoid it unless we close down ZIGZAG in the very near future.' If one agent was accidentally blown, so would the other be. If the agents met, there was a greater chance still that both might be compromised.

So far as possible, MI5 tried to hermetically seal the operations of agents from each other. As Brutus was now deeply involved in explaining the non-appearance of FUSAG at the Pas de Calais, he might have to be dropped (perhaps, like Garbo, by a notional 'arrest') to maintain the fiction that a second front was being planned. If the Germans learned that Brutus had been arrested, they would wonder why Eddie hadn't also been.

Thankfully, the Allied breakout into France acted as a diversion.

Eddie himself was instructed by the Abwehr to leave the money and the camera in a 'suitable' place and to tell them where. Eddie gamely replied he couldn't: his expenses were greater than he had expected and he needed to keep the money. For once, the Germans didn't quibble over finances.

In the event, Eddie would never meet Brutus. At the end of September, Eddie's controllers radioed: 'With regard to delivery of the package it is not necessary to make contact with the other person.' They expressed worries about his using a cut-out to deliver the message. 'Do you not think that the name given on the envelope may endanger you if the bearer is not quite reliable?'

Yet the Germans had no such worries about Eddie recruiting his own sub-agent to perform the other task with which he had been charged, reporting on the dispositions of Allied aircraft in air bases around southern England. The Abwehr still wanted to know 'the exact schedule' – which bombers were aiming at which cities – and to make the observations Eddie wanted to employ his pre-war criminal colleague George Darry. The Germans would be told that Darry was travelling around the country gathering details of formations and flight insignia. But MI5 was against this: they did not want to encourage Eddie's contacts with the criminal fraternity. And in the event, Eddie was able to claim that 'the friends he hoped to employ for this purpose are in prison or otherwise not available'.

On a handful of occasions, agent Fritzchen claimed that he had driven around southern England to make the reports himself; the information had actually been provided by British Intelligence. The bombing of German cities thus continued without a break.

By the end of the summer, the threat from the buzzbombs was receding. By 18 August, the Germans had already started to close down launch sites in northern France ahead of the Allied advance. Once Paris had been captured and the Allied armies were speeding through northern France, the onslaught from the V-1s tailed off. All around the Reich there was bad news: at the end of August Stefan von Gröning personally radioed to Eddie: 'My house destroyed last night.'

On Saturday, 1 September, the last of the launch sites in northern France were overrun. The day of the doodlebug was over. Approximately 5,500 people had been killed and 16,000 seriously injured in the twelve weeks since the V-1s had first been fired towards Britain – but, thanks to the efforts of the double agents, they were less devastating than they might have been. Eddie was always proud of his part in fighting the buzzbombs.

There was, however, only a week's respite. On Friday, 7 September, Duncan Sandys and Herbert Morrison held a press conference. 'Except possibly for a few last shots,' the Prime Minister's son-in-law declared, 'the Battle of London is over . . .' At twenty to seven the next evening, west London was rocketed by a huge explosion. A missile had landed near Chiswick, and it was followed by another in the Prime Minister's own constituency of Epping.

The new ballistic missiles were very different from the doodlebugs. It was impossible to divert the V-2s in the same way as the V-1s, by fooling those who fired them. Using gyroscopes to orient themselves, they could be aimed with great precision.

Militarily, they achieved very little, for their firings were at best sporadic. The Allied push into Germany meant the rockets were at the limit of their effectiveness. 'The enemy's inability to extend his range was very fortunate, but there seemed everything to be said for persuading him to shorten it still further,' records Sir Michael Howard. Psychologically, however, they were an immense success. The wonder weapons were touted by Goebbels's propaganda as a saviour of the German people. In the Third Reich, hope sprang eternal.

By now, 35 Crespigny Road was assured of its place in history. Earlier that summer, Garbo had transmitted an alert to the Abwehr about the Normandy invasion at dawn on D-Day. This had been one of the most decisive moments in the secret war. Garbo had subsequently left the property but it was still being used by MI5, particularly as a centre for radio transmissions. For the sake of continuity, Eddie was allowed to transmit from Hendon though he was living five miles to the south-west.

'I know Eddie paid all the expenses for the taxis when they went out to Hendon for their broadcasts,' Betty Chapman says. 'He used to take Michael Ryde out to eat and paid for that.' According to the files, however, the boot was on the other foot. Eddie's MI5 handlers – one of whom had spent 'the costs of a certain amount of boredom and a certain amount of money on entertaining him' – had noted that this time around he was happier and more contented. Eddie, though, was keen to return to France and help Allied counter-intelligence forces clean up the stay-behind agents left in the Germans' wake. After all, he had helped recruit them. And on 28 August, three days after the liberation of Paris, came a curious development.

'War situation need not and will not affect your return,' the Baron radioed. 'You must make suggestion in good time and you will have every support whatever happens.'

Eddie was amazed that they were even thinking about his possible return to the Continent. He would, he replied, prefer to be picked up on the north-east coast. 'Can you leave me cover address in France also radio possibility for Jimmy or myself to go there. Need French money also.' Once the fighting was finished, Eddie had said, he was keen to open a club or bar in Paris. Stefan von Gröning suggested this might provide a useful background to hide any 'stay behind' activities.

Others in British Intelligence remained keen to continue to use Eddie. MI6, via Frank Foley, who sat on the Double Cross Committee, 'had indicated that ZIGZAG may be of value [if] he could be returned to Germany' according to a report filed by MI5. The Security Service did not want Eddie to return to occupied territory. A plan was developed to arrange the pick-up off the eastern coast of Scotland, but at the last minute Eddie would radio that he wouldn't be able to leave as he couldn't find the right sort of boat to steal.

As the threat from the V-1s receded, Eddie's sense of boredom was beginning to rise. Colonel Robertson recorded that 'he is quite clearly restless and is likely to be so long as he is asked to perform the rather humdrum business of tapping a key at our instructions'. He was also complaining about the money, the £5,000 he had brought with him for his own use, though MI5 promised they would give him a 'square deal'. Eddie's career as a double agent was drawing to its end, but there was one more crucial role for him to play in the secret war.

In the closing months of the war, the Kriegsmarine wondered how so many U-boats were being sunk. Admiral Dönitz himself seems to have thought that the mounting losses may have been the result of stray emissions coming from radar warning receivers carried aboard the U-boats. The answer today is obvious: Ultra, the reading of the naval Enigma. Thanks to the work of Bletchley Park, the Royal Navy was being given the exact times and locations where submarines would surface for refuelling or replenishing air.

Nevertheless, the Führer was increasingly insisting that the 'grey wolves' would be more important than land operations. And on D-Day itself, a new set of U-boats slipped their moorings. As well as carrying the latest homing torpedoes, they were equipped with the *Schnorchel*, a tube like a periscope which allowed a submarine to run its diesel engines and recharge its batteries underwater. The grey wolves would, in theory at least, never have to surface. With the arrival of the *Schnorchel*, the British feared that opportunities to hunt down U-boats would become fewer. It became imperative on the Allied side to muddy the waters, to confuse the Germans into thinking that some other secret weapon was being used to hunt them down.

In the late summer of 1944, Eddie was introduced to a man who knew of him only by reputation from his attempt to blow up the *City of Lancaster* eighteen months earlier. The Honourable Ewen Montagu, RNVR, was one of the few naval intelligence officers ever allowed to meet double agents. So serious was the latest U-boat menace that the rules of need-to-know security were bent. A new course of action would have to be decided upon – and quickly.

The previous September, the Germans had learned of a new weapon known as the Hedgehog, which propelled depth charges to explode at ever greater depths. Agent Fritzchen now started to file reports across the airwaves that these charges were being fired forward, not aft, of the ships when they came into position. While he could give no precise details, these weapons had greater explosive force than regular depth charges and their proximity fuses greater range.

The Hedgehog was in fact an enhanced depth charge that threw a couple of dozen small projectiles several hundred feet ahead of the attacking submarine. On entering the water, each of these projectiles would be armed. They would explode on contact, either with the U-boat or when they reached the bottom of the ocean. At Montagu's bidding, agent Fritzchen was soon reporting to the Abwehr that he had broken into a naval store and photographed one of these 'Hedgehogs'.

'He now meticulously excelled himself as an ex-safebreaker,' Montagu recorded. Deliberately deceptive photographs were taken of the so-called Hedgehog; an actual device was placed next to a 36-inch rule marked as though it was a foot in length.

Eddie told his German controllers that it would be too difficult to transmit all the details via radio. He claimed he had suborned a seaman who would put the negatives of the actual photographs in a condom which would be hidden inside a tin of Epsom salts. The sailor would be under the impression that he was 'merely' smuggling drugs and would deliver them to an address in Lisbon. After his own experiences just over a year before, Eddie was glad that he wouldn't have to do this for himself. In fact the material was sent via diplomatic bag, dropped surreptitiously under cover of night at a cut-out address.

The out-of-scale photograph successfully confused the Germans. The Kriegsmarine could not understand why it was so powerful: 'The Abwehr came back to Zigzag with much praise and an insistent demand that he should get more details,' Montagu recalled. 'After they had received the photo,' another official report remarks, 'the Abwehr were avid for full details of the fuse.'

Under Montagu's direction, the Naval Intelligence Division was kept busy that summer forging a number of other items to keep the deception going. These included a letter written to a colleague by an official of the Admiralty Research Department which described the Hedgehog as a wonderful improvement on the old method of depth findings. They could, he claimed, be fired faster than the known top speed of U-boats underwater. With the help of an Admiralty scientist, the Double Cross Committee was provided with a suitably altered fuse mechanism and a letter was written on official note-paper describing how it worked. Eddie then informed the Abwehr that he had broken into a research laboratory and had photo-graphed this haul of information. The Germans inferred it was part of a greater discussion about great new strides in detecting U-boats.

By the start of September, it was clear these deceptions had been swallowed hook, line and sinker. 'Try to get the latest editions of monthly anti-submarine report issued by anti-submarine division of Admiralty staff,' Fritzchen's controllers radioed. 'Very important.' As they pondered the mysterious explosive power of the Hedgehogs, there was a resurgence in the fears about those equally enigmatic glows first mentioned to him in Norway. Eddie started to receive queries about how U-boats could be detected by a device capable of homing in on their position underwater. From determining how radio waves were reflected off the submarine's side, it was possible to discover a U-boat's exact location. Or that is what Eddie explained was happening; he claimed he was still trying to determine where this piece of kit was being manufactured.

Soon Eddie reported he had located it at a factory in Birmingham. He wasn't sure if it was the one they wanted, but, nevertheless, suggested he should perform a burglary. 'A few days later,' he recalled, 'I was obliged to send the message: "Have been unable to obtain detonator device plans."'

The message to the U-boat crews was clear. No matter how far they tried to manoeuvre out of the way, their chances of survival were slim. A near miss from one of the new weapons would suffice. A U-boat would be lucky to survive one, let alone two of these underwater barrages. Eddie Chapman had been instrumental in keeping the new U-boats at bay.

By early autumn Eddie's restlessness was becoming a problem, as MI5 had feared all along it would. Unlike the hard work and danger involved in his earlier visit to Britain, Eddie knew that in the last few months of the fighting he would have a much less important role to perform. To all intents and purposes, he was being sidelined. He started asking his MI5 handlers to be dropped. At the same time, he made it clear he wanted to make contact with the French and American governments to offer his services as an agent.

His emotions were up and down. At one point Eddie wondered if perhaps he might be able to remain in his present work after the war to 'fulfil his need for excitement'. On another occasion, he talked of opening a club in the West End, then a hotel in Southend. MI5 was sure that it didn't want any of its money – or that handed to Eddie by the Germans – used for such an enterprise. British

Intelligence's original assessment of his character had been spot on. Eddie Chapman did have an unquenchable thirst for adventure. Now that he was aware those adventures were drying up, Eddie was determined, quite literally, to go to the dogs.

The White City track in west London had always been a mecca for the criminal fraternity. And while horse racing had been severely restricted in wartime, dog racing flourished. The tracks acted as a magnet for black market activities. Money laundering, the barter of stolen identity cards and petrol coupons often took place. Dog tracks became a first port of call for military policemen looking for deserters, conscription dodgers, forgers, blackmailers and petty gangsters.

Race fixing continued apace, especially when capacity at White City grew in the last months of the war. In March 1944, for example, a mechanic rigged the totalisator to make the payout look much less than it actually was. He pocketed the difference. That December, the police caught a gang of forgers who had been carrying around false winning tickets. In later years, Eddie would say that it was so much easier in his day when the races were fixed.

Perhaps it was inevitable that Eddie would return to the tracks and get into the 'wrong' company. The first hints of his querulousness had come at the start of the month when he had asked to be let out of his service to his country. On Friday, 4 August, Eddie skipped an appointment to transmit information to the Germans as he knew he could make money on a particular race. His MI5 handlers soon became aware that he was up to no good and making 'quite large sums of money by backing the winners of races which have already been fixed'. Eddie was at pains to point out that he was not directly involved in the race fixing.

So far as MI5 were concerned, that hardly mattered. Taking 'advantage of other people's dirty work to fleece the bookmakers cannot be regarded as a desirable occupation', an MI5 report concluded. But the consequences of his being dropped were worrying for the Security Service. At a high-level review of the case by senior MI5 officers on Monday, 14 August, it was pointed out that if Eddie continued to be bored, 'he will turn his tortuous mind to working out schemes for making more money, which will almost certainly bring him to the notice of the police'.

It would, indeed, be extremely embarrassing if Eddie Chapman was arrested while still in the care of the Security Service. On this same day, Tommy Robertson had reached the end of his tether with Zigzag's antics. The chief of double-agent operations suggested that the case be closed down. The Security Service would pay him the £500 that was owed to him.

His minders reported his growing fractiousness and lack of discretion among the criminal fraternity with whom he had started to associate again. Later that month, when an MI5 case officer called at Eddie's flat in Olympia to take him up to Hendon to make a scheduled radio transmission, it was full of undesirables. One of them was Jimmy Hunt, Eddie's pre-war safecracking tutor, who loudly piped up: 'I suppose you have come to take him away on a job?'

The MI5 man wisely did not say anything in the presence of so many underworld characters. But he was left in no doubt that Hunt knew the nature of the work Eddie was doing. To his handlers, it was clear Zigzag was cockily overconfident, flush with cash. He was still on full German pay with all his living expenses paid for by the British. After the excitements of the earlier part of the war, the naval deceptions involving the Hedgehog seemed terribly tame. Eddie became restless, saying he wanted to settle down with his Norwegian girlfriend in post-war Paris.

Worse was to come later that autumn when he was overheard boasting about his activities in a Kensington pub, though to those who knew him it was Eddie just being Eddie, spinning the sorts of stories which some people dismissed as Walter Mitty-esque fantasies. 'I have on different occasions seen ZIGZAG walk up to a Norwegian and address him in Norwegian,' one MI5 man reported. 'I have seen him in the company of highly undesirable characters, speaking to a German Jewess in German, a Frenchman in French.' Even worse, he added: 'I have heard him discussing with a man with a known criminal record conditions in Paris in such a way that it must have been apparent that he has been there within the last few months.'

'I have long suspected that ZIGZAG had no regard whatever for the necessity of observing complete silence regarding his connection with us,' are the unambiguous words of virtually his last MI5 file.

'Montagu will have to decide whether in view of the inflammable situation caused by ZIGZAG's indiscretions to his very doubtful friends, he wishes us to continue this aspect of the case further.'

The end was inevitable. In early November 1944, Eddie Chapman was dropped by the Double Cross Committee for 'lack of security on the part of the agent'. 'Unfortunately, his successes had gone to his head and he could not stop talking of them,' Sir John Masterman wrote. 'It became necessary to terminate his case.'

One day the following spring, Winston Chapman was living in Cardiff after returning home from his wartime service in the mercantile marine. He received a telephone call that surprised him. 'It was from my auntie in Sunderland,' he recalls. 'She said: "Did you know your brother is still alive?"' More than a little taken aback, Winston asked Auntie Nell for Eddie's telephone number. When he reached him at the Olympia flat, Eddie was his usual excitable self.

'Drop everything!' his brother said. 'I've got plenty of money, come up to London!'

Winston was to join him on this, and many other occasions. Soon they would become near neighbours when Winston eventually settled close by Eddie's own flat. Later in 1945, the Chapman brothers spent a memorable night at White City which Eddie's old friend, Inspector Bob Fabian of Scotland Yard, always referred to as 'the great greyhound swindle'. 'We had backed this dog called Bald Truth,' Win Chapman recalls. 'It opened up on the books at 20-1.' The dog came out and won by ten lengths because all the others had been doped. 'And we took a quarter of a million pounds out of White City!'

For once, even the authorities noticed. Bookies at dog tracks all around the country had taken bets on this fixed race. 'Most of the bookies were too stunned to do anything but pay,' Fabian would write in his own memoirs. As head of the Flying Squad, it was his job to investigate the circumstances. Soon it became clear that fish soaked in chloretone had been fed to all but one of the dogs in the kennels. Despite regular security checks, one of Eddie's cronies had hidden in one particular kennel, concealed behind a pile of timber, and fed the doped food to the dogs just before the race. The police were perfectly well aware of who had done it. It was a slenderly built, athletic fellow whom Fabian called 'Johnny', though he could never pin the job on him.

After that, Eddie Chapman, so his family attest, managed to stay out of trouble – for a little while, at least.

To keep him out of harm's way, Eddie was allowed to stay in his Kensington flat over the winter of 1944–5. After he was dropped as a double agent, Betty Chapman thinks MI5 continued to pay for his accommodation. In any case, as the Allies came ever nearer to Berlin, the need for his discretion lessened. Yet as the fighting drew to a close, the authorities on both sides seemed to think he might be double-crossing them.

His contacts with the Security Service continued for a number of years, one officer noting for the record that Eddie was living 'in fashionable places in London always in the company of beautiful women of apparent culture'. One final report released from the MI5 archive states, in a comment charged with the prejudice always exhibited towards their most troublesome charge, that 'ZIGZAG is a man without any scruples who will blackmail anyone if he thinks it worth his while and he will not stop even at selling out to the opposition if he thinks there is anything to be gained out of it.'

During post-war interrogation of Abwehr personnel stationed in Paris, it became clear that those out of the immediate range of Stefan von Gröning thought Eddie might have been under the control of the British. Yet, in typical Abwehr fashion, nothing was ever done to investigate. Fritzchen's reports and supposed successes in his native land had too much valuable currency in Berlin.

Eddie's German controller knew that he was on to a good thing. By the start of 1945, nothing much had been heard from Stefan von Gröning after a very heavy raid on Bremen. Eddie recalled that there came a 'curious and rather touching message from von Gröning himself' : 'Regret delay in answering your messages, but lost my house in bombing raid.'

It was signed *Stefan*. In his autobiography published ten years later Eddie wrote: 'If he ever reads this, I hope that he will forgive me. I am sure that he will understand.'

But for now, a new world beckoned. Not for the first time, Eddie Chapman was abandoned by the British government.

Free Agent

'When war ends, it leaves a gap in one's life that is not easily filled. One has lived on a peak of anticipation, either of terror or excitement. Then comes the quiet after the storm when one realises that the chances of a sudden death have become more remote. Yet one still feels oddly insecure and afraid; afraid of the vagueness and economic instability of the future.'

– Eddie Chapman, reflecting on the challenges of peacetime

QUEEN'S GATE in South Kensington is one of the capital's more refined enclaves. Elegant Georgian townhouses vie with Victoriana – impressive museums and monuments – to produce a surfeit of gentility. At one of the more upmarket residences that hopeful summer of 1945, the old and rather pompous porter was pleased by one of the more recent residents. The demure, elegant blonde woman who rented the ground floor flat was one of his favourites. She often had a regular visitor – tall and rake thin – whom he suspected was her regular boyfriend. Normally, everything was quiet and sedate – there were one or two lords and ladies in residence – but one night, his doorbell rang close to midnight.

The porter opened the door to find the blonde girl in front of him. He was, to say the least, surprised, because she was standing there completely naked.

The porter wasn't alone in his embarrassment. Betty Farmer

didn't know where to look, or where to begin to explain. Life with Eddie Chapman in post-war London was never going to be easy.

How Eddie and Betty got together is one of the more implausible stories in a lifetime of unlikely happenings. Their life together would plumb the depths of depression and scale the heights of exhilaration. Sixty years later Betty can laugh about some of the things that went on. That she stayed with him – as Eddie faced up to his demons – is the most extraordinary thing of all.

The Eddie Chapman who strolled into the Berkeley Hotel in the spring of 1945 was perhaps a little fuller in the face than his pre-war self. He'd lost none of the self-confidence, though perhaps a little of his carefree spirit had disappeared. The war had aged him. The eyes were definitely warier.

Only just turned thirty, Eddie was too young to retire. After all the excitements of the war years, what in his life could ever replace it? The depression which he had suffered for many years seemed to have worsened. Perhaps it was simply a manifestation of war weariness. As well as the pain from his back, Eddie suffered badly from indigestion, later diagnosed as ulcers. These problems – both physical and mental – were the price agent Zigzag had paid for living a double life for so long. Eddie rarely complained, even about his back which continued to plague him for years. He knew he was luckier than some, for he had survived, against all the odds.

One thing hadn't changed. The lure of London nightlife remained irresistible. Staying at the Grosvenor House Hotel, Eddie's main interest was in going out at night for, as he later remarked, 'every plush club in town had a good customer'. Soon, though, his thoughts turned to love. He desperately wanted to find the woman from whom fate had parted him just before the outbreak of the war.

'Uppermost in my mind was the desire to find Betty,' he related in his post-war memoirs, 'my girl whom I had last seen when I dived through a hotel window before my arrest in Jersey.'

At the start of 1945, he had contacted two ex-Scotland Yard coppers who had started a private detective agency. There was a delicious irony in this; they had chased him around the country just before the war, now they were eager to take his shilling in searching for Betty Farmer. At the time of his first return to Britain, MI5 had been unable to trace her. Now the detectives had at last found traces of her. In 1943 she had been on the Isle of Man.

But they had drawn a blank after that. So they all agreed to meet up in Mayfair over lunch to work out what to do next.

And so, a week later, Eddie Chapman was now having lunch at the Berkeley Hotel with the former detective 'Doughy' Baker, and his colleague. Accompanying them was Giselle Ashley, who had been with MI5 and was keeping an eye on their most wayward wartime agent. Looking around him, Eddie thought, you could be forgiven for thinking the war had never happened. The Berkeley's dining room was full of fashionable types – debutantes, guardsmen, dapper playboys and dowagers.

The detectives had, however, turned up empty-handed. Eddie gave no sign of annoyance that they had so little to go on. After ordering their meal, Doughy asked him: 'Is there anyone here who resembles her?'

Eddie turned around and pointed to a blonde at the far end of the crowded dining room. She was in the company of an RAF officer and wrapped in conversation.

'That girl looks like her from the back,' Eddie said.

The blonde turned slightly into the sunlight.

'Jesus! It is Betty!'

Eddie walked over and tapped her on the shoulder. It was seven years since they had last set eyes on each other – also in a hotel dining room.

Betty dropped her coffee cup in her lap. 'Where have you sprung from?' she gasped.

'From over there,' Eddie said, pointing at his table.

There was an embarrassed silence as both dining companion and pre-war beau eyed each other suspiciously. 'Here's my number,' he said. 'I'm staying at the Grosvenor House, call me.'

For Betty Farmer, the victory in Europe and her reunion with Eddie Chapman were inextricably linked and remained memorable for all the wrong reasons. If Betty had any inkling that her relationship with Eddie would never be easy, it came on VE night when he ended up pushing a man through a window in Knightsbridge.

They were out on the town celebrating the ending of hostilities in Europe in a downstairs restaurant in Mayfair. Joining them were

Nye Bevan (who would shortly be responsible for establishing the National Health Service) and his wife, Jennie Lee (later a Labour arts minister), as well as Sydney Box, a noted film producer, and the Scottish writer Sir Compton Mackenzie, who would come to play an important role in their lives.

Such an eclectic mix was typical of their social life. Quite how Eddie gravitated towards the Labour left remains unclear. 'I used to call Eddie a champagne-drinking socialist,' Betty says.

The Chapmans were on their way back home to Queen's Gate when somebody ran into the back of their car in Knightsbridge. Thankfully, there was little damage and nobody was hurt. 'Why don't you go home and forget about it?' the driver said. And then, as he returned to his car, he turned to Betty and said in obvious jest, 'I wouldn't mind going home with you . . .' Whereupon Eddie suddenly flew at him and battered him against the nearest shop window.

'There was I with my handbag, bashing Eddie to stop him, who then pushed this man through a window,' Betty reflects. 'And then we drove off.'

This was one extreme example of Eddie's passionate jealousy. At other times, though, he could be romantic, spontaneous and loving. 'Eddie was always full of surprises,' Betty reflects, 'both good and bad!'

Peace brought a new world order, not least with the Labour landslide later that summer of 1945. Nobody, least of all Eddie, wanted to return to the poverty of the pre-war years and the struggle to survive. The post-war change in government was keenly felt by the Security Service whose budget was severely trimmed. The organisers of the Double Cross Committee returned to their pre-war lives, sworn to secrecy by the Official Secrets Act. John C. Masterman returned to academic life in Oxford and Colonel Tommy Robertson left MI5, not liking the new peacetime regime. Some like Ronnie Reed stayed on, later interviewing the wife of Soviet spy Donald Maclean about his disappearance in 1951. Many of the intellectuals left and most of the solicitors (like Michael Ryde, whom Eddie continued to meet) returned to practise law.

The new Prime Minister, Clement Attlee, was determined to keep the Security Service on a shorter leash. As a deliberate snub, Attlee appointed a former policeman, Sir Percy Sillitoe, as its new post-war chief. Sillitoe's regard for the institution which he had inherited was most famously captured by his disdainful comment that 'the MI should stand for Muttonhead Institute'.

Nevertheless, Eddie remained friendly with many of his security handlers. 'They all kept in touch with him,' Betty says, though perhaps it was just to keep tabs on what he was up to. Although she was aware that he had been involved in wartime intelligence operations, he was unusually reticent about his work. Despite the Security Service's fears, Eddie hardly ever told strangers his stories; his close friends learned little more. As one of them said, 'A man who is used to keeping secrets never blabs his mouth off – not even in peacetime.' Eddie was never boastful, either, though he had quite a lot to brag about. Over the years, elements of his story came out, but there was little time for reflection as Betty was always earning the money. 'Our life was full, full, full,' she says.

Eddie continued to have a love-hate relationship with the authorities, and much of the contact wasn't just for old time's sake. 'They tried to use him when they could,' Betty adds. Immediately after the war, MI5 wanted Eddie to lift some important papers from the Polish Embassy. 'We used to sit up all night absolutely mesmerised by his stories,' says Julie Cooper, a friend from the fifties. 'He told us how he cordoned off the whole of Belgrave Square to rob the Polish Embassy.' At the Security Service's behest, he roped in some of his friends to collect road signs and place them strategically around the square.

Immediately after the war, Betty Farmer went into business, selling or letting out properties after refurbishing them. 'I did a lot of property work then,' she says. 'Then I had the beauty salon, then I took a course in cosmetics.' She was never really a homemaker and was always busy with one enterprise or another. 'I loved property and I loved business,' she says.

At the end of the war, Betty had moved from Nevern Square – where she had witnessed the V-1 impacts – when her landlord came back from India. She found the property in Queen's Gate, an airy flat which opened out onto the garden. 'Eddie came and went,' she says, 'as we were courting at the time.'

Eddie was always coming and going, so much so that the porter knew him well. She still maintained a large circle of friends from the war years. 'I was always being invited somewhere by someone,' she recalls. Betty knew a lot of pilots including a wing commander called Peter Palmer, who had survived being shot down in the sea at Margate towards the end of hostilities. He now invited her to a party for RAF officers in the mess at the airfield at Hornchurch. She was delighted to attend in a full evening gown.

When Eddie visited her flat that same night, he found Betty was out. By the time she got back to Queen's Gate, she couldn't get back into the flat. Eddie had locked the door from the inside, knowing she would not be back until late.

'He opened the door and tore my clothes off, literally stripped me naked,' Betty recalls. 'I was in evening wear and he banged the door and left me outside there with nothing on.'

And that was why she had to ring the doorbell of the porter – 'Oh he was a pompous old man!' Betty recalls – for help, despite her nakedness.

Eddie Chapman was clearly a man of great passions, often erupting without warning like a bottle of his favourite champagne. The strains of the war years had not helped his emotional equanimity. Betty Farmer, by her own admission, was a little afraid of him. In the months and years to come, she would endure many nights alone, wondering when – sometimes, if – he would ever return.

'Eddie was never home,' she recalls. 'He was always out late, gadding about.'

On a number of occasions, Betty would have to pick him up when he was the worse for wear. When he was absent, she assumed he was off drinking with his buddies, for in those days he drank quite a lot. His usual drink of choice was brandy with milk, which allowed him to get drunk without hurting his ulcers. Eddie used to frequent a club called the Maisonette. 'The woman who owned it would call me,' Betty says. '"Come and get him, he's had enough."'

Even by the standards of the time, Eddie's behaviour was extreme. 'I couldn't do anything,' Betty says. 'He could do anything, but not me.' As far as possible, she tried to keep him away from the sort of ne'er-do-wells with whom he had been associating towards the end of the war years. Eddie seems to have done his best to keep on the straight and narrow. 'What I didn't know,' Betty says, 'was

jolly well hidden from me.' Many of London's criminal underworld
were in contact with him but Betty would never let them come by
the flat in Queen's Gate. Yet some time at the start of 1946, it was
raided – not by the police, but by the Security Services.

In the years after the war, Eddie would often come into contact
with the dogged and determined detective he had known during the
war years. After his wartime service in MI5, Leonard Burt would
shortly become Commander of Special Branch, the department of
the Metropolitan Police which kept an eye on saboteurs, political
troublemakers and, most famously, the atom spies who were
passing secrets to the Soviet Union.* His success and growing
reputation came from his unassuming integrity. 'No cloak and
dagger stuff, you see, and no Gestapo with special powers to
extract information,' Burt would say of his own technique within
the Branch.

It was in this role that Burt would come across Eddie Chapman
time and again; he was the man who had countersigned agent
Zigzag's signing of the Official Secrets Act. They would often go
drinking together, mainly so Burt could find out what Eddie was up
to. Indeed, Len remained friends with Eddie and Betty Chapman
for a long time. Betty remembers him as a nice man, 'a jolly fellow'.

There was more than friendship at stake. The security establishment suspected that Eddie might cause trouble. During his last few
months of work for MI5, he had blithely informed his handlers that
he was penning an autobiography. Burt had to forcefully remind
him of his obligations under the Official Secrets Act.

According to the MI5 files, Burt described Eddie as a man
without scruples who 'will not stop even at selling out to the
opposition if he thinks there is anything to be gained out of it'. He
patiently explained that it would be impossible for Eddie to disclose
any of his wartime activities for a very long time. 'Burt also advised
him that if he disclosed facts relating to his criminal past he would

---

*Many of these interrogations were carried out with his former colleagues in
MI5. In 1940 Burt had been commissioned into the anti-sabotage unit headed
by Lord Rothschild, bringing with him from the Met his deputy, Reg Spooner,
two detective inspectors and Detective Sergeant Jim Skardon. All would become
famous as interrogators in their own right.

probably render himself subject to action, if not by the police then by some of the parties whose goods he had stolen,' notes a minute from the MI5 legal advisers. 'ZIGZAG replied that he realised publication would be impossible, but that he still felt inclined to set down his recollection of what had happened to him while it was still fresh.'

And Eddie followed those very inclinations. 'He said he never signed the Official Secrets Act,' Betty explains. 'He would say: "You can't charge me, because I never signed it." They possibly made him sign something, but he didn't realise what it was. He could have signed a death warrant, and he wouldn't have known!'

Some time in 1945, Nye Bevan introduced Eddie Chapman to a man who would not only encourage his literary endeavours but put him on a collision course with the intelligence establishment. Sir Compton Mackenzie had been present at that VE night celebration in Mayfair.* Better known as a writer (soon to pen his most famous book, *Whisky Galore!*) he was also a determined poker of fun at the espionage establishment. By the end of the Second World War, Mackenzie had built a house with a magnificent library on the Isle of Barra where Eddie was invited to write about his own experiences. He started work on a manuscript in longhand. 'He went and stayed there for about six months, I think,' Betty recalls.

Another person who encouraged him in his literary endeavours had also been a thorn in the pre-war intelligence establishment's side. Wilfred Macartney, originally imprisoned for supposedly selling secrets to the Soviet Union, became a regular visitor to the Chapman home. 'Oh, he was a crazy one,' Betty remembers. 'He would stand in our flat and be looking through the window towards the Brompton Oratory and shout, '"I am God! I am God!" after he had been boozing.'

---

* Born into a theatrical family, Compton Mackenzie had served with MI6 in the eastern Mediterranean during the First World War. His four books on the subject managed to offend the establishment and, in 1932, his *Greek Memories* was banned for breaching the Official Secrets Act. Mackenzie later took revenge by writing a thinly disguised novel, *Water on the Brain*, in which the officers of MI5 and MI6 spent most of their time spying on each other.

With Macartney and Mackenzie's encouragement, some of Eddie's wartime experiences were serialised in a French newspaper in the spring of 1946. But, when the *News of the World* attempted to do the same, Eddie found himself in court in breach of the Official Secrets Act.* After being fined, he was photographed in the company of the impish Macartney on the steps of the courtroom.

'I don't remember how many thousands of copies went out before they stopped the presses,' Betty recalls. 'The story was that it was the first time ever they had stopped the print-run at the beginning of a serialisation.'

And that was why MI5 raided their flat in Queen's Gate, looking for the manuscript. They even tore their car apart in case this book had been hidden inside it. 'What upset Eddie most was they took away his new suit and his new suitcase,' Betty says. The authorities eventually found the handwritten manuscript hidden in the flat and destroyed it, hoping that would be the end of that.

On 9 October 1947, Eddie and Betty married at Chelsea Register Office – 'a simple, quiet affair' – and as he related in his own post-war reminiscences, 'we took a charming house in West Halkin Street, and, being an energetic girl, she started a beauty parlour. I did exactly nothing. I just ate, drank and made merry.'

If there was ever a prototype for someone on the edge – living fast and furious and in danger of burning out – then it was Eddie Chapman in the late 1940s. He was a heavy drinker, looking for adventure, often with women other than his wife. Much of his extraordinary behaviour was triggered by bouts of intense jealousy; the incident in Knightsbridge on VE night was not an isolated one.

'If anyone approached me in any way, Eddie would almost kill them,' Betty says. 'That was why I had to be so careful if I ever had any friendships that he never knew about, because he would have killed me and them too.'

Betty, with her platinum blonde good looks, was always the

---

*According to the diaries of Guy Liddell, the wartime director of counter-espionage, MI5 got wind that Eddie had told his story to his later ghost, the tabloid journalist Frank Owen. This apparently came from an MI6 secretary on 16 May 1945.

centre of attention, most of it innocent. She was still in touch with her wartime pilot friends, including Geoffrey de Havilland, Jr, who one day had come to tea. 'Eddie turned up unexpectedly,' she recalls, 'and because he was insanely jealous, I locked Geoffrey in the wardrobe. But Eddie managed to find him!' They had what she calls 'a bout of fisticuffs' but after that – in what proved to be the last few months of the pilot's life – he and Eddie became very good friends.

Betty Chapman was the last person to talk to de Havilland on the telephone when he attempted to break the sound barrier in September 1946. Her recollection of his last words is poignant. 'You know, Bets,' he said, 'I am getting too old for this game.' Later that day, his aircraft – a prototype jet called the Swallow – shook so violently that its airframe broke up in mid-air and he was killed. 'Eddie and I went up to Hyde Park to watch because he was going to fly over London,' Betty recalls. 'He blew up and they found his remains in the Thames.'

Just after they were married, Betty went on a trip to Paris to meet her friend Kathleen Ryan, the actress. Running over schedule on a film she was making in England with James Mason, Kathleen told Betty she would be delayed in arriving at the Hotel George Cinq. At the time, Betty was friendly with a man called Colonel Bedwell – a curious name under the circumstances – whose wealth derived from his invention of the Diner's Card.

'We went in his plane to Paris where he had booked a suite,' Betty says. 'Now the Lord is my judge, he slept on the sofa, I slept in the bed.'

All would have been well had Eddie not called the Atheneum Court and spoken to Kathleen who was obviously still in England. Straight away, he got through to the George Cinq to ask, 'Have you got a Mrs Chapman staying there?' When they said no, he made his way to Paris. Eddie was convinced she had registered under a false name. Arriving in the French capital, he contacted his friend Armand Amalou, who was working as a mercenary.

'He said to Armand, "You kill him and I'll kill her myself,"' Betty relates.

Eddie found her in Colonel Bedwell's suite but, after calming down over a bottle of champagne, she convinced him there was nothing to it, particularly when Kathleen Ryan fortuitously arrived. Soon, Eddie was chatting away with the colonel, laughing at his foolhardiness.

'Whenever I met anyone, Eddie stepped in and became their friend,' Betty says. 'And that was exit me!'

Carole Bell, a friend of the Chapmans towards the end of Eddie's life, provides an interesting perspective. 'Had Eddie been born in a different era, his behaviour would have been called dysfunctional,' she says. 'Losing his mother must have made a big impact on his young life. I think it left him angry, lonely, insecure and vulnerable. He never showed that side to his character, though. In today's society, counselling or medication would have helped him through it.'

★ ★ ★

Belgravia, in the late 1940s and 1950s, was the home of what Eddie Chapman always called his pride and joy: a Rolls-Royce Silver Wraith. With all the money that Betty was making, Eddie could afford to buy one. Her husband certainly enjoyed swanning around in it. 'He never actually passed his driving test,' his brother Winston explains, 'but Eddie always maintained that the police never pulled over the driver of a Rolls-Royce.' Sometimes he would drive up to Harrods, tip the doorman (whom he knew from the Coldstream Guards) and have the car parked for him.

'Eddie liked to show me off, too,' Betty says. And with her elegant figure and blonde hair, she did have the advantage of looking sensational. One day Eddie went out to Brook Street in Mayfair and returned with a coat that cost a bomb in those days. 'There was also a hat like a fez with a black ostrich feather down the side,' she says. 'I thought, "I can't wear that, it's too spectacular." But I did and everybody thought it was fantastic.'

It was these little touches that meant Betty would stay with him; underneath it all, she felt he had a good heart. Whatever else might happen, life would never be dull. One unexpected result of the *News of the World* serialisation was that Eddie and Betty Chapman became celebrities. They later moved to other properties around Belgravia, mixed with the elite and became friends with Hollywood stars such as Stewart Grainger, Richard Todd, Orson Welles and Burl Ives.

In 1948, together with his brother Winston, Eddie bought a steamer called the *Sir James* from a shipyard in Appledore on the north Devon coast. Ever loyal, Betty was involved with the enterprise, helping arrange the manifests. The steamer lugged coal and any cargoes they could get their hands on. By Eddie's wartime standards, it was hardly adventurous. 'During that time, Eddie was my boss,' Winston says. 'He'd bought the boat, I ran it for him.'

Later, they moved operations to Newry in Northern Ireland and ran cargo across the Irish Sea. Eddie was friendly with both the Protestants, for whom they ran the cargoes, and the Republicans, including a crewman who was a wanted IRA man. At one point, they were joined by the rebel and writer Brendan Behan as a crewmember, but how much use he was remains a moot point. In his last volume of memoirs, Behan refers to Eddie as 'the Fixer', suggesting, oddly, that he was an agent for the Italians. 'I personally think that he was an agent for himself, but Scotland Yard gave him the benefit of the doubt and freedom from all his sins, past, present and future.'

Around this time, Betty became ill. Perhaps because of the strains from Eddie's behaviour, she suffered from a nervous break-down. She remembers recuperating in a convent in Northern Ireland where the nuns looked after her. Despite the severe rationing, the nuns used to smuggle beef across the border for her to eat to build up her strength.

'The demand for business was good,' Win recalls. 'We'd liked to have had a bigger boat, but we couldn't afford it.' The authorities, however, were not so happy. The Chapman brothers upset their cosy little *status quo* – the *Sir James* provided a more convenient and cheaper service than the existing boats which were sailing out of Belfast. Vested interests meant that subsidies were made avail-able to all these other services, but not to theirs.

'We could only ferry about two hundred tons of cargo and it was too small,' Winston says. 'We couldn't make a living out of it.'

In 1949, Eddie went to Tangier where he bought an aircraft with a group of ex-RAF pilots to transport lobsters to Spanish restaurants. He was also involved in smuggling gold. Through the contacts he made in Tangier, Eddie helped construction companies with projects on the west coast of Africa. Ghana was the first country to become independent and the Chapmans became close friends of Kwame Nkrumah, the first president of the country. Yet once again, Eddie's past was used against him in an old-fashioned 'frame up' in 1953.

The British government had already let it be known that Eddie had a criminal past and accusations were made that he had bribed officials to gain a particular contract. After Betty briefly returned home to London, she wasn't allowed back to Ghana. 'The bribery scandal fell apart as they had no proof,' she says. Eddie's comment at the time, was even simpler: 'These people were my friends. I didn't have to bribe them.'

After Ghana, Eddie returned to Tangier and bought – with money provided by Betty – a yacht called the *Flamingo* which soon attracted a motley collection of his pals – including the boxer George Walker and the gangster Billy Hill. In addition to their genuine cargo work, there was smuggling of guns and cigarettes. 'I took the boat down there for them,' Winston says. 'They were supposed to go out and kidnap the Sultan of Morocco. It was a disaster though.'

When a *News of the World* reporter joined them on board the *Flamingo* in the spring of 1953, the resulting publicity was disastrous. The scheme to remove the Sultan from Madagascar – thought up in a bar in Tangier – came to naught when the French Navy got wind of it and destroyed the boat.

By the end of 1953, Eddie was finally able to publish his memoirs as *The Eddie Chapman Story*, though they were heavily censored by the British government. Instead of rewriting the manuscript from scratch after its earlier impounding, Eddie enlisted the services of a leading tabloid journalist of the day, Frank Owen. His preface to the book noted: 'This is all of Eddie Chapman's story that anyone is allowed to tell. It is only half of it: for telling the other half, Eddie was fined £50 and £35 costs at Bow Street on 29 March 1946 under the Official Secrets Act.'

The spectre of legal action overshadowed the whole enterprise. The British authorities made it clear that any reference to Eddie's work as a double agent would lead to another prosecution.

When the publishers, Allan Wingate, started pre-publication publicity in the late summer of 1953, the D-Notice Committee became interested. (This government censor vetted any material relating to intelligence matters for publication in print or broadcast.) Both Owen and the publishers were happy to show copies of the working manuscript. In September 1953, there was a 'friendly' meeting between Wingate representatives and government officials. The government position remained that Eddie should not to refer to his employment as an agent of the Security Service. Owen had already agreed to remove all references, as he still felt the story was exciting enough.

Pretty soon, though, the government realised it had shot itself in the foot. Various officials were horrified when they were sent a draft of the manuscript with all references to Eddie's 'employment' removed. One defence official termed it 'a very unsatisfactory piece of work' which paints 'Chapman as a most undesirable character'. Because all references to the Double Cross Committee had been excised, it appeared as though Eddie had been working for the Germans and had not been apprehended by the home forces. Eddie thus appeared to be 'a monster' for having witnessed the drowning of sailors in the convoy to Lisbon before blithely putting a coal bomb on the ship (the name '*City of Lancaster*' was removed) to kill more British sailors. The Security Service remained adamant that it did not wish the British public to know the real story.

When the book was published in September, a reviewer in the *Observer* reported what everybody in Fleet Street had known all along: that Eddie had been a double agent. After all, if he wasn't, how come he had never been prosecuted for treason? MI5 seems not to have considered such a possibility in the reporting.

The foreign press was a different matter. At the start of October, a story in a Sydney Sunday newspaper noted: 'British Intelligence decided to accept Chapman's story and made use of his services.' Doggedly, the government refused to budge, though the British press followed suit. 'The War Office is refusing all comment on the Eddie Chapman affair,' the *Sunday People* reported on 6 December 1953. 'Chapman, too, keeps silent. Perhaps he cannot do otherwise.'

Early the next year, the government finally admitted that Eddie Chapman had been employed as a double agent. At the time, his

publishers said, they hoped one day to tell the real story of Eddie
Chapman's wartime escapades.

Even today, Betty Chapman remains puzzled by her husband's
treatment by the Security Service. When, many years later, the
espionage writer Nigel West organised a reunion of the surviving
wartime double agents, Eddie's name was deliberately left off the
invitation. To his credit, West insisted that Eddie had to attend. A
number of wartime case officers huffily agreed.

'Any way they could undermine him, they would,' Betty says.
'The problem was MI5 didn't like any criticism.' Or, in Eddie's case,
to be made to look foolish. And though the service maintained
Eddie had been remunerated handsomely, Betty notes that they
'weren't so generous once they had finished using him'.

Lillian Verner Bonds, a writer who came to know the Chapmans
well, concurs. Her view is even more damning. 'They needed him
and boy did they resent that they needed him. If they could put him
down, they would.' According to Betty Chapman, this didn't stop
MI5 asking Eddie to continue working for them. Though they
continued to deny him the chance to explain what he had done on
their behalf, they were quite happy to send him on even more
dangerous work. They even tried to send him to Russia. 'No, I got
away with my life with the Germans,' Eddie said. 'But there is no
way I would survive in Russia.'

Eric Pleasants did, barely. Eddie's former jailmate from Jersey
had survived both the German and Soviet regimes. And telling the
horrific details of what happened became Eddie's next mission,
when he ghosted the story of Pleasants' life which came out under
the title *I Killed To Live*.

After recruitment into the Britische Freikorps, Pleasants had
been sent to a camp in Dresden in mid-November 1944 where he
taught physical exercise. He fell in love with a local girl, Annaliese
Nietscher, which led to marriage in February 1945. The timing was
unfortunate as their honeymoon coincided with one of the massive
bombing raids on the ancient and beautiful city of Dresden. The
Britische Freikorps helped dig out the survivors. By now, the
Russians had crossed the Elbe. As a precaution, Pleasants swapped
his SS uniform for a Wehrmacht one. Annaliese bandaged his head
to make it look as if he had suffered terrible injuries, and they

joined the exodus of refugees to the German capital. Pleasants and his wife took to the sewers under Berlin to try to escape from the encircled city. To survive, Pleasants' strength was used to kill two Russian soldiers with his bare hands, a fact of which he was never proud. They lay low, remaining in the Soviet zone until 1946 when they were arrested for spying. After a trial, he was sent to a camp in the Russian Arctic for seven years. He never saw Annaliese again.

In 1955, he returned to Britain. After collaborating with Eddie on his book, Pleasants settled back in his native Norfolk, remarried and became a physical education instructor and judo teacher. He would outlive Eddie by a year, dying at the age of eighty-seven close by the Broads where he had grown up.

★ ★ ★

Greater stability – for Betty, at least – came with the birth of a daughter, Suzanne, in 1954, though the passage of the pregnancy was not smooth. Betty's carrying of the baby coincided with the press interest resulting from Eddie's book and the *Flamingo* affair. 'When I was pregnant in Tangier, the press sat outside my door,' she says. 'Eddie and I had to leave in the middle of the night to avoid press interest when we came back to England.' They made their home in Coleherne Court – later made famous by the young Lady Diana Spencer when courting Prince Charles.

By the late 1950s, Eddie and Betty Chapman had gone into the antiques business. 'I had to find something for Eddie to do,' Betty says. They opened a shop on the Kings Road in Fulham whose stock came from a friend who was also an antiques dealer. Betty took out a loan, but Eddie, in his usual way, had an affair with the dealer's girlfriend, Louise. To compensate, Eddie handed him the stock of the shop. Betty can laugh about it now, though at the time there wasn't much amusement. 'No husband, no stock, a young child and a bank loan to repay,' she says.

By 1960, Eddie had moved with Louise to Shenley Lodge, a country club in Potters Bar, north of London, where he took out a lease on the property. Except that Betty gave him the money, managed the investment and oversaw many of the material improvements. It needed a lot of work, for Eddie had decided to turn Shenley into a nightclub. 'I was an honorary member and so was Ronnie Biggs,' Winston Chapman recalls. (Their younger sister, Olga, was also employed as the receptionist.)

Against all the odds, Betty managed to find the money to pay for the freehold and a full refurbishment. But Eddie's refusal to act as a police informant led to continual police raids. Friends say that their greatest memory of this time is of whistles blowing and all the lights coming on when the police raided.

Betty then made the financially astute move of transforming the club into a health farm. Close by the Elstree film studios, Shenley Lodge opened in 1961 with stars of the day regularly visiting, including Patrick Wymark, Robert Mitchum and Roger Moore, then starring on television in *The Saint*, as well as Diana Rigg, shortly to do the same in *The Avengers*.

It had struck several people that Eddie's wartime adventures would make a great film. By now, Eddie was back in contact with his former flatmate, the dapper Guards captain with whom he had last dined in 1943. In the autumn of 1961, Terence Young had been prevailed upon by two expatriate film producers based in London to adapt a thriller on which their option was about to expire.

And that was how Terence Young came to direct *Dr. No*, the first James Bond film. By his own admission, Terence became obsessed with making the film of Eddie's life. When *The Eddie Chapman Story* was first published, Young had taken out an option for six months. The security questions seemed insurmountable, as the British government was still adamant that its wartime secrets remain secret. Permission was never granted when film companies approached the War Office. 'My personal view is that Eddie has been used as an example to prevent a lot of other people writing their war memoirs,' Young would later remark.

The British government kept a wary eye on proceedings. At various times, actors as diverse as Cary Grant, Richard Burton, Laurence Harvey and Kenneth More were attached to the project. Eventually, Paramount took over the option but even Alfred Hitchcock could not get clearance from the War Office. Hitch moved on to what became one of Eddie's favourite films – *To Catch*

A Thief. The cinematic rights to Eddie's life story then bounced around various studios and became attached to directors as diverse as Darryl Zanuck and Sidney Lumet.

But the security problems remained unsurmountable. 'Twentieth Century Fox is negotiating for the rights,' the *Daily Mail* noted on 1 March 1957. 'Already, two bids to film the story have fallen through because of War Office opposition.' And by the close of the fifties, it seemed that a film of Eddie's exploits would never grace the silver screen.

★　★　★

A small fortune is hidden in a Zurich safety box. Its rightful owner – an international shipping magnate – loses the key and the code to open the safe. He suspects one of his associates has stolen them and, in a panic, hatches a plot – to fake his own kidnapping – which even the Metropolitan Police later calls 'an amazing story'. The policeman who investigates also comments, 'Truth is stranger than fiction.'

This is not the outline for a film, but the curious escapade in the early summer of 1961 in which Eddie Chapman was involved. At the time, he was living apart from Betty, which may have had a lot to do with it. 'I would meet Eddie in the Queen's Arms,' their friend Julie Cooper says, 'and he would give me money to give to Betty for the weekly groceries.' Eddie was a drinking pal of Julie's actor husband, the late Terence Cooper, who along with two other actor friends, hatched a madcap plan in the Coopers' flat one evening. Julie happened to overhear Eddie say, 'We won't wear stockings over our heads and there'll be no guns.'

Eddie's later version of the events was simple. He had been contacted by Shiv Kapoor, a wealthy Indian businessman, whom the police didn't think was spotless, either. They had known each other for a number of years. 'Although I have known Chapman,' Kapoor later told the police, 'it would be wrong to describe him as a friend.' A deal of Kapoor's involving imported coffee from Costa Rica had apparently gone wrong. Money was needed in a hurry.

In Eddie's version, it was all to do with a safety deposit box in Zurich. Kapoor wanted Eddie and some associates to pretend to kidnap him. Whoever had stolen the key would then approach the kidnappers, he reasoned. They would force the kidnap victim to write a letter of credit. That way, Kapoor would not only get the money but determine who had stolen the key. In fact, when Eddie subsequently met a number of Kapoor's associates in a Chelsea pub, they were stunned when he said he wanted £300,000 for the return of their friend.

In Kapoor's version, he claimed Eddie had some friends who could help him over the Costa Rican deal. Taken in Eddie's Rolls-Royce to a flat in Earls Court Square, he blithely said at the door, 'These secret service men want to ask you a few questions,' and disappeared. Kapoor never saw Eddie again. His trio of actor friends played their part, chaining Kapoor to the floor for a few days and giving him food. In the Indian's version, he heard a terrific row between the men and was then driven to the airport. That seems to have been true, for he departed the country in haste.

In the version told by Eddie and his pals, they panicked because the *Daily Express* ran a story headed 'Phone call riddle of rich tycoon'. Kapoor's wife, Lila, was quoted as saying, 'I'm sure this must be a very unpleasant practical joke. My husband is in Delhi or Calcutta.' According to Julie Cooper, the first she knew about it was when her husband turned up in a 'borrowed' police car one morning. Wondering what on earth he was doing with it, Julie noticed that a flat she owned at 18 Earls Court was boarded up. 'That was where Kapoor was being held,' she says. 'I was horrified. I was renting it out at the time.'

Eddie soon heard that the police were looking for him. Terence Cooper drove Kapoor to the airport and by the time the police were on to him, the businessman had left the country. The more witnesses they interviewed, the less sense an already bizarre story became. The British public had a chance to read about it the following Sunday, when the *News of the World* carried a banner headline 'Why I Kidnapped Shiv Kapoor' over a story by the 'man who did it' – Eddie Chapman, 'ex-cracksman, wartime spy and saboteur'.

The police weren't sure what happened. 'I do not believe that any of the participants in this kidnapping [have] told anything like the truth,' reports one senior policeman when writing to the

Director of Public Prosecutions. 'The reason given, however, for this false kidnapping by all four men seems quite fantastic and hard to believe.'

When the *News of the World* story broke, Julie Cooper went to pick up the estranged Mrs Chapman. 'Betty and I thought we had better leave,' she says, 'and went to hide at Shenley.' In the event, nothing came of the police investigation. Eddie was never prosecuted, but he was paid quite a lot of money by the *News of the World* for the 'inside' story of the attempted kidnapping.

The world of intelligence continued to cast a long shadow over the Chapmans' lives. By the early 1960s, Eddie Chapman was living in Rome with Mariella Novotny, one of the many women who had been embroiled in the Profumo affair. Ironically, it was Jack Profumo's task, as Secretary for War, to dissuade potential film makers from shooting any of Eddie's wartime exploits. 'I still cannot agree to allow Mr. Chapman or any person on his behalf,' Profumo wrote to one correspondent on 29 October 1962, 'in any way to recount information he acquired while in the employment of the Security Service.'

By the time of Profumo's resignation, Eddie Chapman had known Stephen Ward, the osteopath who was the one true victim of the affair, for many years. Eddie would do anything to relieve the pain of the injury he had received after his second parachute landing. In the late 1950s, when he was living with Betty in Coleherne Court, Eddie would frequent Ward's practice in Devonshire Street. 'I remember Stephen had a cat and he gave us this damned cat as a present and it used to poop in the bath,' Betty recalls. 'I remember Eddie and I had had a terrible row about it. I was in the midst of throwing his clothes out of the window when they landed on a woman who was passing by. I remember hearing her say: "Strange people live around here these days."'

Despite Ward's reputation for healing hands, Eddie's injuries intensified.

Indeed, he never received any compensation for the damage to his back though he did try to get a pension for many years. Both Eddie and Betty Chapman would grit their teeth when they saw less deserving cases awarded disability allowance. 'I can't understand it,' said one of their post-war friends, the barrister Sir Lionel

Thompson, who was in fine health. 'I've been practising since the war and I get a full disability allowance.'

On one occasion, an assessor came to their house. Betty stood and watched. She was horrified at his casual indifference. 'You've never seen such a cursory examination,' she says. 'All this fellow did was say to Eddie, "Lift up your leg."'

'We could never get anything from the authorities,' Betty Chapman says, 'except for one year before he died, we got thirty-one pounds a week. That was his pension! All those years they said they'd paid Eddie this or that, they never gave him anything.' MI5 did eventually allow him to keep the money he brought with him on his returns home during the war – a sum of around nine thousand pounds.

By the time Shenley Lodge was being refurbished, Eddie had absconded to the continent with Mariella Novotny. 'Oh, she was a madam,' says Betty of the girl with whom he eventually shacked up in Rome. Mariella was one of the more unusual participants in the Profumo affair, partly because she came under FBI investigation for having claimed to have slept with President Kennedy.

To Betty's horror, Eddie brought Mariella to the grand reopening of Shenley Lodge. 'Her mother used to ring me up,' Betty recalls, 'wondering what to do. She said: "She's got a whole trunk of whips in the basement. What shall I do?" I said, "Get rid of it." Poor woman, she was distraught.' In time, Eddie did – as he always did – return to Betty in England.

By the late 1960s, Shenley was attracting an international clientele, particularly visitors from the Middle East. It meant that Eddie Chapman was extraordinarily well placed to know what was happening in parts of the world where British Intelligence couldn't get agents in. 'I never knew whether he was still providing information when we were at Shenley,' Betty says. 'It's often been asked was he still a spy? Once a spy, always a spy, I suppose.'

Eddie returned from Rome later in the sixties and, for a while, lived with Betty in Shenley. But at some point he was off again, living with a girl in a flat in the Barbican. By now most of Betty's friends couldn't comprehend why she hadn't divorced him. Why did she never leave him? 'They just didn't understand the way it worked,' Betty says. Partly, she explains, it was because she was brought up to believe marriage vows. But one of their post-war friends articulates best why she stayed with someone like Eddie: 'Better to have lived in the light than never to have had it on at all. And that's why Betty stayed.'

Eddie always said that whenever he strayed, he would always return. Some of their friends, like Lillian Verner Bonds, saw Betty and Eddie as a double act. 'Betty was very strong,' she says. 'And Eddie always talked about her.' Indeed, despite his dalliances with other women, he always came back. She was his rock. 'That was the sad thing for the women he went off with,' Lillian says. 'Eddie could never break that bond with Betty.'

His widow agrees. 'Eddie always said, "Never resist temptation,"' Betty says. 'And I tell you it was the women who chased Eddie, not the other way around, because they knew he was soft.' He was, however, always fearful of the reaction he might provoke. She was always alert for telltale signs that he was up to no good. 'What's all this lipstick on your pants and your vest?' she recalls asking him in the laundry room. 'What do you think the judge will say when I divorce you?'

On another occasion, when he was back at Shenley Lodge with Betty, Eddie woke up around 3 a.m. in a panic. 'Hellfire!' he shouted, stumbling around in the darkness, trying to find his clothes. 'I've got to get home! I've got to get home!'

At which point Betty sat up and gently said: 'Eddie, you *are* bloody well home.'

★   ★   ★

By 1966, Eddie could finally tell *The Real Eddie Chapman Story* when his publishers released a fuller version of the text. But even after many episodes had been excised by government lawyers, his publishers were still approached by the Security Service. A mysterious spook turned up making threats and wanting to confiscate the manuscript. After further wrangles, *The Real Eddie Chapman Story* appeared in the summer of 1966. 'One of the most exciting and fantastically thrillerish stories of the war', was the opinion of the *Observer*. The publishers still had to leave out many of the details which had been cut from the 1954 version.

'We did hold up publication for a bit, but last month we brought the book out,' his publishers said in September 1966. 'We got a letter from the security man saying he noted we'd ignored his advice.'

By now, the film rights to the book had once more reverted to Terence Young. By the mid-1960s, he had become fashionable and eminently bankable, especially where espionage stories were concerned. After claiming that he had made the first Bond movie (*Dr No*), the best (*From Russia With Love*) and the most successful (*Thunderball*), Terence was looking for new challenges and thought Eddie's life story might provide it.

The year 1967 should have been a vintage one for the Chapmans with the film of his book due out. Betty Chapman knew something was wrong when she heard that the film rights to the story of her husband's life had been sold to an American who had swindled several people out of their savings. Some time in the mid-1950s, the publishers of *The Eddie Chapman Story* had – without their permission – sold the rights to this gentleman for peanuts. 'He went back to America, and sold them on for $250,000.'

When the American subsequently went bankrupt, Terence Young stepped in with a French banker to buy them. 'The man from the bank was also involved in some skulduggery over the $6 million borrowed to make the film,' Betty says. 'He set fire to the vaults and blew his brains out.'

Triple Cross was mainly filmed in France during the second half of 1966 because of continuing worries over whether the British government might attempt legal action. Location shooting took place at the Château Villascreaux, seventy kilometres south of Paris. It had been used by various Nazi intelligence services during the war and doubled for the Nantes *Stelle* where Eddie had trained for his sabotage operations.

'We still haven't got official clearance from the War Office and I don't think they'll ever give it,' Young said.

But that was nothing compared to what Terence did to his old friends. The Chapmans never received a penny for the film. 'I could never understand that,' Betty says, 'Terence and Eddie were very close. I remember going to Paris because they shot it just outside in this château. And Terence said, "I want to show you something." I came outside and in front of the hotel. There was a lovely row of

Bentleys, brand new. "The Chapman story bought me that," he said, pointing to one particular car. I was not to know that we would never see a penny.'

At first, all the omens for the film were good. With Christopher Plummer playing Eddie, Young maintained his Bond connections by casting Gert Fröbe, *Goldfinger* himself, as a corpulent German controller, and *Thunderball*'s Claudine Auger as one of Eddie's love interests. The premier of *Triple Cross* was staged at the Odeon cinema in Golders Green that its hero had robbed nearly thirty years before – at least, according to the film's publicity people (a claim which Betty disputes). 'One of the reasons that the true story of Eddie Chapman has never been told on film before', the production notes breathlessly recorded, 'is that it is so fantastic, exciting and gripping it was feared if the story weren't handled properly, movie audiences would consider it just another far-out espionage tale, the product of a writer's imagination.' Describing him as 'a cockney English safecracker', the release added: 'It's all true and Eddie Chapman runs an antique shop in London today.'

'It will make a hell of an exciting film,' Young said as he arrived at the premiere.

Alas, it didn't. When the reviews of *Triple Cross* came in they were universally hostile – 'unsatisfactory yarn' (*Sunday Mirror*); 'double-crossed by the script' (*Sunday Express*); 'a rather shoddy, anachronistic, badly directed attempt to re-create one of the most thrilling of all war adventures'. (*Observer*); 'thoroughly dull and implausible' (*New Statesman*).

Eddie, for his own part, was totally fed up with his involvement in the film industry. 'I'm in the antiques business now and it can't hurt me,' was his only recorded comment about the film. 'The only thing hurting me is the fact that those stars have been paid so much money for making my story while I've received nothing.' Betty was incensed by the portrayal of her husband which made it seem as though he was nothing more than a money-grabbing mercenary. She even used up some of her own money to try to stop the film by serving a lawsuit on the distributor, but to little avail.

In the late sixties, Betty Chapman was approached to set up a similar enterprise to Shenley in County Kildare in Eire. Kilkea Castle was an impressive building, to which she added a health farm, a function hall with its own facilities and a 21-roomed house. There were separate sections for men and women. It was, for a time, the only health club in the country.

Eddie was in his element, waxing lyrical about his 'health farm in Hertfordshire' and 'the castle I've bought in Ireland'. Eddie did his fair share of work, sometimes leading classes in the gym when his back pain wasn't too severe. 'He loved the castle, and he loved the health farm,' Betty says, 'although he didn't physically do the exercises. The women absolutely doted on him. He used to make them all work out.' (Among Shenley's more famous clientele were the boxers Frank Bruno and John Conteh, who used to train there before big matches.)

But Betty reluctantly had to leave Ireland when a bank loan was mysteriously called in. She switched her attentions back to Shenley, becoming an expert in the field of health clubs. She was consulted about establishing similar establishments in pre-revolutionary Iran and Nigeria. She received important visitors like the Shah of Iran, who also persuaded King Hussein's sister to stay. There was a certain irony that one of their last clients – who became Eddie's last mistress – was recommended by the Shah, whose country Betty visited just before the revolution at the end of 1979.

By now, at the close of the seventies, the blanket of secrecy surrounding wartime espionage had started to lift. Ironically, it was Eddie's least favourite MI5 man, Sir John Masterman, whom he had dismissed as a humourless snob, who revealed how German agents were run against the Abwehr by the British. In the immediate aftermath of the war, Masterman had written a summary of the Double Cross Committee's activities, and arranged with Yale University Press in the United States to publish it. Even today, *The Double Cross System of the War of 1939–1945* remains in print. The identity of the various agents was not revealed in the first edition, but many of them could recognise their own exploits, Eddie among them. Though he had been the first to break rank in telling his story, even he didn't realise the scale of the deceptions in which he had been so closely involved.

Throughout this time, people from his wartime past got in contact. Stefan von Gröning, in the summer of 1976, became best man at Suzanne's wedding. One day a case of Rhine wine turned up from Leo Kreusch, another of his Nantes cronies. There was no further contact with Freda White – indeed, Betty had no idea about Eddie's daughter with her until his wartime files were released in 2001. But, perhaps more surprisingly, came contact from his more exotic wartime girlfriend.

With his health failing, Eddie Chapman was spending the early 1990s in the Canary Islands. A Norwegian woman who lived in a flat next door got into conversation with him one day. As they talked, they realised that they both knew Dagmar Lahlum, his Norwegian girlfriend. And so at what proved to be the very end of their lives, they entered into a slightly stilted correspondence. 'I remember you as a kindly and charming fellow, always smiling,' Dagmar wrote in March 1992.

Though her eyesight was bad (she was by this time in her late sixties), her memory wasn't. They shared the kind of inconsequential reminiscences that old friends often do. Dagmar had recently seen a performance by a Norwegian actor called Per Aabel who was nearly ninety.* 'By the way,' she wrote in another letter, 'we saw him in Oslo. Do you remember him?'

Though she said in one letter that they were living in two separate worlds, Dagmar, it seems, visited Eddie in England just before his death in 1997.

Despite his many talents, one thing Eddie was never very good at was business. Betty and Eddie eventually decided to sell Shenley Lodge. Calamity struck when the Chapmans sold it in 1994 for £1 million. The purchaser went bankrupt and apart from a down payment they never received anything more. Receivers were called in, banks became involved, solicitors issued writs. Even today, a decade on, Betty Chapman is still trying to make sense of it all.

'Overnight, we lost everything,' she says. 'We had no home, we had nothing.' By now in his eightieth year, the loss of Shenley affected Eddie deeply. As Betty says, 'The Germans didn't kill Eddie, but the loss of Shenley did.'

---

* Aabel was one of Norway's most popular actors, admired for his elegance and wit, similar in some ways to Nöel Coward. A statue to him was unveiled outside the National Theatre in Oslo at Christmas 1999, a few days before Dagmar herself died.

The collapse of their life's work precipitated a noticeable decline in his health. Eddie's mind started to go a little. Betty recalls he would come down the stairs at night and sit quietly, obviously confused. 'Why on earth are they keeping me in this prison? Why?' he would ask, thinking he was back in Jersey. Around this time, Carole Bell came into their lives. A spirited, kindly woman from Yorkshire, she came to know Eddie and Betty Chapman well.

'Eddie was a much misunderstood soul with a brilliant mind,' she says. 'He was a character and that character was forged through hardship and adversity. Eddie and his peers are long gone, but not forgotten. There won't be anyone like him again.'

Towards the end, Eddie moved into a nursing home near St Albans. Though bedridden and often in pain, Eddie could still command an audience with his presence and charisma. 'He'd sit wearing a baseball cap, waiting for his friends to gather,' Carole says. 'On other occasions, he would lie in bed, telling his stories.'

Eddie died on 11 December 1997, the cause of death recorded as heart failure. The newspaper obituaries recognised him as a very brave man, but many trotted out the old myths, uncorrected from years of accumulated clippings. But Betty was heartened to receive a flood of letters from all over the world.

Betty didn't want a fuss, and so there was a private cremation attended only by close relatives. Over the years, the Chapman family have become wary of people trying to get close for obvious financial gain. 'It's only now that I've had time to reflect over the years that I realise how much we lost,' Betty says. 'And then, at the end of our day, to lose our home and business that was the final straw.'

Despite his unimpeachable bravery, Eddie was never awarded a pension by the British government, less still any public recognition for his bravery.* About three months after he died at the start of 1998, someone from the Ministry of Defence came to visit his widow.

'The Ministry have asked me to come and offer my condolences to you,' he said.

---

*In a revealing note held within a post-war file from the War Office, Frank Owen's original synopsis for *The Eddie Chapman Story* contains a comment about his suitability for recognition. 'Thanks no,' Eddie told Owen. 'My luck with those fellows is wearing thin. I'm not collecting gongs, and anyway, I have my Iron Cross.'

As he was leaving, he put his hand in his pocket and pulled out a piece of paper which he promptly handed to Betty. 'That might help a bit with the bills,' he said. It was a cheque for £2,500.

In the years since Eddie's death, Betty Chapman realises, her life has been 'not only different, but uneventful'. Given some of their adventures together, that is hardly surprising. Now in her ninetieth year, she is still trying to make sense of all the things that happened. She is not alone in wondering how a life like Eddie Chapman's can best be summarised. When his MI5 files were released in 2001, the press stories focused on his criminality and his womanising. Comparison of Eddie's memoirs and the official MI5 files reveals very few discrepancies, a claim which cannot be said for many wartime agents' memoirs.

Given that those files were released in the same year as the terrorist attacks on the World Trade Center, the battles Eddie fought and the world in which he lived may seem like an irrelevant anachronism. Or do they? At an address at Harvard University two years later – just before the invasion of Iraq – A. Denis Clift, president of the US Joint Military Intelligence College, discussed the problems facing the intelligence world in the fight against terror. Despite the panoply of technical aids available, Clift says, it is people, 'however varied, laudable or ugly their motives', who remain key to providing useful intelligence. And he named Eddie Chapman as just the sort of person intelligence agencies would need in the twenty-first century.

'Chapman was a complicated individual,' Clift said, 'his handling required great attention and care, not your typical laid-back Harvard graduate.' He noted that intelligence agencies would now have to deal 'with foreigners considered criminal, considered unsavoury, considered unfit for US contact'.

Perhaps this will be Eddie's greatest legacy.

At a time when the certainties of Western hegemony have crumbled, good intelligence will still have to come from unusual characters. The skills needed today in the intelligence world are the same as they were sixty years ago. But there will never be anyone quite so charming, charismatic and, at times, reckless as Eddie Chapman, for as one of his wartime handlers, Ewen Montagu, remarked, he was 'a rogue but a very brave man'.

A Note on Sources

EDDIE CHAPMAN wrote about his wartime experiences in two sets of memoirs which, as the text makes clear, were essentially disembowelled by the British government before they could be published. In July 2001, Eddie's wartime MI5 records were released into the UK National Archives in Kew where they may be found in the Security Service KV 2/ series, numbered 455 to 462. These comprise many hundreds of pages of all relevant files concerning British Intelligence's dealings with Eddie Chapman. They provide a useful chronology of events surrounding Eddie's wartime adventures.

But, though they contain a mine of useful information, there was clearly a certain amount of 'editorialising' and 'buck passing'. At times, Eddie was portrayed in the worst light possible. A number of his more remarkable adventures – such as escaping the safe house in Hendon, meeting Gerd von Rundstedt and drinking a bottle with Winston Churchill – are not mentioned in the files. Some claims, though they cannot be substantiated, do seem to have the ring of truth. Many would not be expected to be recorded in the files as his intelligence handlers would not have known about them.

As recollections from both Eddie's widow and brother make clear, much is missing from some of the reports. Though Eddie wasn't shy of exaggerating at times, what is clear is that the broad thrust of his recollections follow the record. In a subject so covered in myth, it is refreshing that his memories tally with the official files.

As his MI5 interrogators found, he was hopeless at remembering when events took place – Ronnie Reed, for example, noted in January 1943 that 'ZIGZAG is quite unable to cope with any chronology whatsoever' – and the interrogators would spend many days trying to work out the true sequence of events. Eddie, however, was rather good at recall of detail. The memories of his brother and widow have buttressed the words which appear on these pages. Though they weren't present for many of them, Eddie often talked to them about his wartime adventures.

Only later in life did Eddie realise that his wartime work fitted into a greater whole. Wherever possible I have tried to provide context. All quotes attributed to Eddie – and people with whom he was having conversations – come from verifiable sources, his own writings or recollections. As with all biographies, there are discrepancies, particularly in names of participants and sequence of events.

Throughout the text, I felt it was important to hear Eddie's voice. The primary source for many conversations are the verbatim records of his MI5 interrogations,* his own memoirs and recollections of his friends and family. Members of the Chapman family have read the manuscript and provided corrections. My thanks to Betty Chapman for opening her unique archive of correspondence, memoirs and artefacts accumulated through their time together.

Prologue: An Airman with a Suicide Pill

Eddie Chapman only ever talked briefly about the circumstances surrounding his apprehension by the British security forces in 1942. Official censorship forced him to be circumspect in Chapter 10 ('Home Sweet Home') of *The Real Eddie Chapman Story* in 1966. His MI5 personal files, particularly the first folios of KV 2/455, contain a wealth of information. Specifically file KV 2/455 67c contains the reports where Sergeants Vail and Hutchings record their meeting with Eddie for their Chief Constable in considerable detail. Additional background material comes from a letter written by Sgt Hutchings's daughter, Mrs Gwen Mills, dated 25 February 1994. The remainder of the MI5 comments about Eddie are mainly taken from the summary of interrogations – by 'Tin Eye' Stephens, KV 2/457 106xk.

1. Genesis of a Gelly Man

Detailed information about the early years and background of the Chapman family were provided by Eddie's widow, Betty, and his brother,

---

* Indeed, the 'Serials' noted below are the transcripts from four separate interrogations at Camp 020:

1	KV 2/455 56b	Serials 558–595
2	KV 2/455 62zd	597–611
3	KV 2/455 62y	612–622
4	KV 2/456 100q	635–678

Winston. Eddie himself devotes the first three chapters of *The Real Eddie Chapman* to his earliest memories. His incarceration in Jersey is dealt with in Chapter 4 'On the Inside, Looking Out'. Over the years, Eddie gave interviews to many journalists and, as is clear from the text, clearly exaggerated when it suited him – and, indeed, them.

Though Eddie implies in his memoirs that the rescue of the drowning man off Roker took place in the summer of 1930, it actually took place nearly eighteen months later. The details may be found in the story 'Roker Sea Drama' in the 2 February 1932 issue of the *Sunderland Echo and Shipping Gazette* which tells how Arnold Edward Chapman was given the award by the mayor. Details on his later, brief marriage to Vera Friedberg are sparse; it is mentioned in a couple of sentences in KV 2/455 62zd Serial 558 and on page 8, of KV 2/455 56b. Given that the visit to the family home took place seventy years ago, Winston Chapman understandably doesn't remember the date. Given the date of Eddie's wedding and the fact he was imprisoned that April, it seems likely that it took place at the start of 1936. Vera Friedberg's post-war details come from the *Jewish Chronicle* of 3 November 2000.

In his writings, Eddie changed the name of pre-war criminal associates to avoid the worst accusation of all: a grass. Most of his pre-war police files have, according to the Metropolitan Police Records Division, been lost. A later post-war investigation on another matter (the alleged kidnapping of Shiv Kapoor, MEPO 2/10461 discussed on pp. 311–313 of this book) are in the National Archives in Kew. Though Eddie's pre-war criminal record, CRO 1088/35, has been lost, its contents were summarised and cross-referenced in a handful of MI5 interrogations from December 1942 (and the Kapoor files in 1961). In his memoirs, Hugh Anson is described throughout as Phil, probably to hide his real identity. This would be the name Eddie would also assume when he travelled to Lisbon in 1943. On p. 30 of *The Real Eddie Chapman Story*, he talks of another associate called Phil who was most likely Tommy Lay. In his memoirs, Eddie just says 'one of the gang' sent the bottle of perfume and did not identify who was responsible.

When investigators tried to piece together details of his criminal past in the war years, they were hampered because the Jersey files were not available. Nevertheless, KV 2/455 53 – a letter from a Regional Security Liaison Officer in Edinburgh (where his last criminal trial on the mainland took place) – dated 16 December 1942 provides a useful summary. Details about his criminal associates are contained in note KV 2/456 127B and useful cross-reference comes from the post-war 'kidnapping' of Shiv Kapoor. Broader details may be found in Chapter 4, 'A Burglar's Life Between the Wars' of Robert Murphy's *Smash and Grab* (Faber, 1992). Eddie's pre-war career is discussed on pp. 46–47, from an interview he gave to Mr. Murphy. Eddie's appearances in the 1994 BBC series *The Underworld* were the basis for a chapter in the book of the series, written by Duncan Campbell of the *Guardian*.

Eddie also talked about some of his criminal exploits over late night drinks with his MI5 handlers at Christmas 1942. Many of these hitherto unknown stories may be found in KV 2/457 85 d through j and 88a. There are some minor discrepancies over dates, but the sequence of events is clear, culminating in the botched Edinburgh job at the end of January 1939.

Greeno of the Yard became a regular fixture of fifties tabloids. Some of Greeno's stories that had been published in *The News of the World* were gathered together under his name as *Ted Greeno's War of the Underworld*. In that book, Eddie and his gang are referred to as 'Mike S', Darry as 'Johnny the Blower' among others. Background on the legendary Greeno may be found in *The Real Sweeney* by Dick Kirby.

As regards Eddie's memories of Jersey, some of the official MI5 files are at odds with each other. This is due to Eddie getting some of the dates completely wrong. In his memoirs, for example, he puts the lunch at the De La Plage Hotel in April 1939 and his escape from the governor's house in June; the former was actually in February and the escape, July.

The dates can be checked against contemporaneous back issues of the *Jersey Evening News* which carried the stories. See, for example, 'Startling Scene at Jersey Hotel', news item, *Jersey Evening News*, Monday 13 February 1939. Further details in 'Sequel to Jersey Arrest,' JEN, 24 February 1939. In his memoirs, Eddie refers to the establishment which he burgles as the Palm Beach Casino. The contemporary press reports make it clear it was actually the West Park Pavilion, more of a large dance hall than a casino.

There was confusion when MI5 interrogated Eddie three years later about Eddie's attempted escape by plane that summer (KV 2/455 53a). 'On or about July 24 1939,' this report says, 'it came to the notice of the Edinburgh Police that Chapman had escaped from HM Prison, Jersey.' The front-page news two weeks earlier might have been the prompt! 'He was later arrested in London on a charge of safebreaking and appeared on 22 March 1939, at the London Central Criminal Court.' This is false, as even the compiler of the report couldn't quite work out how he had been arrested in London eleven days before he was known to have been in St Helier jail. According to the MI5 files, Eddie was once more sentenced at the Royal Court after his escape bid on the first Monday in September on a charge of theft and was sentenced to twelve months imprisonment (KV 2/457 85f).

In Eddie's memoirs, he says that his daring escape was attempted on the first Wednesday in July, but the contemporary issues of the *Jersey Evening*

News show that it was Thursday, 6 July (see p. 6 of that issue). Eddie says that the petty cash came to £13; the value quoted is taken from this same contemporary press report. A number of details about the punch-up the next day comes from 'Woman identifies shrimp net man as jail breaker', p. 11, *Daily Express*, Saturday, 8 July. On the back page of that same issue is a photo of Eddie under arrest which is captioned 'Police arrest man after 24 hours of freedom'.

As for his girlfriend's whereabouts that summer, the *Jersey Evening News* of 7 July reported 'Betty Farmer, who is alleged to have been associated with him, was present in court when he appeared at the Police Court and again when he was sentenced at the Royal Court, and is known to have been to Jersey to see him since his incarceration.' As noted in the text, Betty says that she had left in February 1939 and did not attend either court case.

A useful background guide to the pre-war espionage world is Jack C. Curry's *The Security Service, 1908–1945: The Official History* which was published in 1999 (by the Public Record Office). Intended only as an in-house guide, the original files have been released into the UK National Archives under the classification KV/4. A useful discussion of the state of MI5 at the start of the war may be found in Tom Bower's biography of Dick White, *The Perfect English Spy* (Heinemann, 1995).

2. Prisoners of War

Eddie Chapman's exploits on Jersey and in Romainville Prison are covered in Chapters 4 ('On The Inside, Looking Out') and Chapters 5 ('I Join the Germans') of *The Real Eddie Chapman Story*. Jersey police records from the war years are understandably patchy and, indeed, most of the official reports concerning his stay may be found in the first tranche of interviews with MI5 in late 1942/early 1943. The more vivid episodes are recalled in detail in these near contemporaneous interviews that may now be found in the UK National Archives in the KV 2/455 and KV 2/456 series. Given their proximity to the events described herein, I have used them as a guide through the many inconsistencies (mainly of names) in the various first-person accounts.

Those accounts from the main protagonists read, at times, as though they had all been incarcerated in very different prisons. In the decade immediately after the war, both Anthony Faramus and Eric Pleasants told their stories with the help of Eddie Chapman. As Eddie's 'ghost' Frank Owen records in his introduction to *The Faramus Story*, by coincidence, Tony Faramus had got in contact with their publisher about the time that the manuscript of *The Eddie Chapman Story* was completed. Frank Owen then edited Faramus's overlong memoir into publishable form. Eddie later provided the foreword in 1955. Four years later, Faramus also produced *Hands of the Devil*, a thinly disguised fictional account of some of his exploits in Occupied France (1959, Brown, Watson). Tony Faramus produced another version of his story, *Journey Into Darkness*, which appeared in 1990, the year of his death. Pointedly, Eddie Chapman's name is not mentioned and in places it is at odds with his earlier account and some of Eddie's recollections.

Eric Pleasants's membership of the *Britischer Freikorps* has often overshadowed his earlier experiences in Jersey. Adrian Weale's *Renegades* remains the standard work on that curious organisation. Individual files concerning members of the Korps may be found in the KV2 and HO45 series. Many of the files concerning Pleasants's (Internee 92153) details have been transferred to the Imperial War Museum. After his return from the Soviet gulag, Eddie ghosted *I Killed To Live* while Eric stayed with the Chapmans. It was published in 1957.

Unsurprisingly, as he had a hand in their writing, both the original Faramus story and this version of Pleasants's life are largely complimentary about Eddie Chapman. In 2003, Ian Sayer and Douglas Botting edited another version of Pleasants's memoirs, *Hitler's Bastard*, which mentions Eddie only briefly.

Though there are a number of inconsistencies in all their accounts, the overall thrust of the narrative is clear. Eddie Chapman was imprisoned in Jersey until October 1941; he was then held in Romainville from late November 1941 to April 1942. The story of Eddie and Eric's evening of larceny is taken from pp. 26–27 of *I Killed To Live*.

The British Channel Islands Under German Occupation 1940–1945 by Dr Paul Sanders (Jersey Heritage Trust, 2005) is a scholarly and evenhanded study of the occupation and covers aspects which are often misunderstood how, for example, if it had been announced the islands had been demilitarised, then it is unlikely the Luftwaffe would have killed quite so many people in the last weekend of June 1940.

Dr Sanders points out that Francois Scorret (see p. 46) was the only civilian actually executed on the island. Wehrmacht soldiers were shot for serious disciplinary offences but the native Channel Islanders were never executed on their home turf, though, as Dr Sanders notes, 'all kinds of things happened to them once they were deported'. There were two deportations of civilians, in September 1942 which included British citizens from the mainland, and, in 1943, two hundred people who were troublemakers and young people who loitered and didn't do much work. For more detailed discussion on what happened to Eric Pleasants, see Adrian Weale's *Renegades*.

Douglas Stewart, the businessman to whom Eddie confessed he wanted to work as a double agent, is referred to in KV 2/455 56b Serials 560 and 561; and also p. 2, KV 2/456 85TB which also refers to his son, whom

Eddie thought may well have been targeted as a possible hostage. As the records make clear, Stewart was never traced by the Security Service. The role of the Peace Pledge Union Scheme is taken from a review of the Abwehr's espionage activities on Jersey published by the Channel Islands Occupation Society ('Accidental Tourists: Germany, the Channel Islands and espionage, 1940–45', Mark Hull, pp. 20–28, Review No. 29, 2001).

Eddie Chapman also discussed the subject of Irish saboteurs with Lord Rothschild on two separate occasions in January 1943. The transcripts may be found in KV 2/ 456 92d and KV 2/ 458 172 B. MI5 kept tabs on islanders who escaped and a report by Major Stopford appeared at the end of June 1945 which is now in the MI5 'policy' series in the UK National Archives as: 'The Administration of the Channel Islands under the German occupation' (KV4/78, dated 30.6.45).

For background on the proposed invasion of Britain – and Admiral Canaris's role in supposedly leaking its details – see Chapter 9, 'Keeping the Empire Afloat' in Richard Bassett's masterly *Hitler's Spy Chief* (Weidenfield, 2005). This idea was first mooted by Ian Colvin on p. 118 of *Chief of Intelligence* (1951). The relocation of MI5 and the origins of the Double Cross Committee are discussed in a number of accounts; particularly useful – and detailing Dick White's crucial role – is Tom Bower's *A Perfect English Spy* (Heinemann, 1995). For more context, see Professor Christopher Andrew's *The Making of The Secret Service* and, particularly, David Stafford's *Churchill and the Secret Service*.

Sir John Masterman's own account of the double agent operations, *The Double Cross System in the War of 1939–1945*, remains the best single account. The quote from Ewen Montagu is taken from a post-war review of the double agent operations for the Director of Naval Intelligence, 'The Double Cross System' in the UK National Archives as ADM 223/794, an equally interesting document. A useful background to how the committee fitted in with other deception activities may be found in Sir Michael Howard's *Strategic Deception*, the fifth volume of the official British government history of wartime intelligence (1990).

For individual double agent cases mentioned in the text, the full story of Hermann Görtz's activities may be found in the MI5 files KV 2/1319–1323. Gösta Caroli, also known as Agent Summer to the British, may be found in the MI5 files KV 2/60. Caroli holds an unusual place in the history of double agent operations for in September 1940 for the first and only time during the war, the Security Service bartered with a captured spy. If Caroli revealed everything he knew about another spy who was about to be dispatched (Wulf Schmidt, later codenamed Tate), his friend's life would be spared. 'It was a momentous decision and it was to prove felicitous,' an official MI5 report concludes, 'for upon that promise devolved many of the most spectacular wartime successes of the British counter-espionage service.'

In Eddie's later recollection, he had actually moved to Romainville by the time his accident with the motorycle came to trial. Eddie protested his innocence but was taken before a German court in Paris. He was told that if he pleaded guilty, he would only be fined 80 marks – which he agreed to, but never actually paid (p. 7, KV 2/456 91d 'Feldgendarmerie & German Tribunals').

In his memoirs, Eddie doesn't give the date of when he and Tony Faramus were sent to mainland France. In Faramus's most recent memoirs, he suggests it is early December, while in Eddie's near contemporaneous MI5 interviews he says it occurred around the time of his birthday, 16 November. The fiery redhead is referred to as Paulette in *The Real Eddie Chapman Story*. In a later report for MI5 (KV 2/456 87f), she is referred to as Jeanette. Eddie often got names confused, particularly in the first few interrogations on his return home. Anthony Faramus refers to her as Pauline. In his more recent set of memoirs, Tony Faramus refers to one of the Belgian diamond merchants as Franz de Bruyne (p. 77, *Journey Into Darkness*).

There are also some discrepancies over dates towards the end of Eddie's stay in Romainville. According to the Ultra decrypts, Walther Thomas – using his real name of Praetorius – had come up from Nantes on 2 February, 1942 (p. 2, KV 2/456 85TA). In Eddie's memoirs, he says he left the prison on 10 April, while the log of Ultra decrypts from KV2/460 436 suggests 'he had arrived in Nantes by 11.5.42.' on 29 April, there is reference to Thomas being in Paris, but it is not clear whether this was when he was in the hotel with Eddie.

The quote from Peter Twinn is taken from p. 123, 'The Abwehr Enigma', Chapter 16 in *Codebreakers* edited by F.H. Hinsley & Alan Stripp (OUP, 1993). The role of the Radio Security Service and how its Voluntary Interceptors were used has often been overlooked. A recent study which draws together all the material is *The Secret Wireless War – The Story of MI6 Communications 1939–1945* by Geoffrey Pidgeon (USPO, 2000). Hanslope Park, a country estate in Buckinghamshire close by Milton Keynes, was originally acquired by the Foreign Office before the Second World War. More recently, it has been expanded and is now more formally known as 'Her Majesty's Government Communications Centre'.

3. House of Fun

Eddie's own recollection of the events in Nantes are described in Chapters 6 ('Training to be a Spy') and 7 ('Birth of a mission') of *The Real Eddie*

Chapman Story. When he was interrogated in December 1942, MI5 eventually worked out what the correct sequence of events was; these details may be found in KV 2/455 document 26 and the 'Summary of Interrogation' in that same file. Overall, Eddie's recall of the events was spot on though, as his case officer Ronnie Reed would later note, he 'is quite unable to cope with any chronology whatsoever' (KV 2/456 138b) and, at another stage, 'Zigzag has pointed out before that he has a very bad memory for dates' (KV 2/456 85TB). A number of salient details on his sabotage training may be found in his interviews with Lord Rothschild in January 1943 (KV 2/456 92d and KV 2/458 172B).

The various 'complications' about how all the various *Abwehrstelle* related to each other are explained in David Kahn's *Hitler's Spies*, particularly p. 239; and also in Sir Michael Howard's official history, *op cit*, p. 46. Briefly, in occupied countries, Abwehr sub-posts – *Abwehrleitstellen* or *Abwehr* – adjoining posts – were established. All would come under local *Abwehrstellens* – each subdivided where necessary into personnel who dealt with espionage, sabotage and counter-intelligence. By the spring of 1942, the Abwehr had 33 posts, 26 sub-posts and 23 outposts. Whereas there were just a dozen or so people based in Nantes, there were 382 in Paris. The suspicion that Eddie might have been a double agent is raised in a letter from Paris dated 7 November 1944 in KV2/460. This reveals that at least one Abwehr officer in Paris was very doubtful about Zigzag. His name was von Eschwege and he told a fellow officer that he thought that 'Zigzag was controlled by the British'.

The Ultra record provides useful timing on Eddie's activities in France. According to the MI5 files, Eddie started radio practice on 25 June, 'and had reached a speed of 65 letters per minute on 30.7.42' (KV 2/455 21a). The 'steaming June day' where he met the high-ups in Paris was actually that same day, 25 June (p. 2, KV 2/457112a). A certain amount of confusion exists about what language the 'funny' German controller spoke in. Eddie implies that it was English but in another part of his first MI5 interrogations (KV 2/456 100q Serial 637), Eddie states that this gentleman 'didn't speak French or English', though he obviously knew London.

In some of Eddie's recollections, Herbert Wojch is referred to as Hermann Vosch. But the near contemporary MI5 interviews show he was Herbert and his surname was spelled as in this narrative. In fairness, Eddie only ever knew of it phonetically. On 11.1.43, Eddie was shown a picture of Walther Thomas (Praetorius) by Ronnie Reed and he agreed it was his minder from Nantes (KV 2/456 121). Confirmation came of Wojch and Schmidt's real indentities from their alien registration photos which he was shown on 26 January.

Details about Operation Pastorius may be found in Kahn, *op cit*. More details on Eddie's recollections may be found on p. 89 of *The Real Eddie Chapman Story*.

4. The Man with the Golden Teeth

Eddie Chapman described the latter part of his training in Nantes and departure to Britain in Chapter 7 ('Birth of a Mission') and Chapter 8 ('In Full Service for Hitler') in his memoirs. The first few pages of Chapter 9 ('Out of the Night') deal with his flight to the fenlands in December 1942. Overall, his recall tallies with the official record though, as earlier, there were a number of inconsistencies about dates and chronology. The MI5 record KV/2 455 26 reconstructs the correct sequence of events – based on Ultra decrypts from the second half of 1942. Most of the details are taken from those transcripts. Much of the detail about his sabotage training in Nantes comes from the interviews with Lord Rothschild at the start of 1943.

The chemist in Berlin is described as 'an odd chap' on p. 86 of *The Real Eddie Chapman Story* and 'a dignified little man' on p. 26 of the first Rothschild interview KV 2/456 92d. A certain amount of confusion exists over the name of this chemist. In his near contemporary MI5 record he is referred to as Dr Bohm while in his memoirs 'Professor Karl'. Certainly Eddie's recall of people was better than names. There is, at least, consistency that he was old and grey. Professor Karl is described as scholarly and sallow-complexioned and in his late thirties (Eddie was twenty-eight at the time). 'I was just told *"Hier ist Dein Lehrer"*,' ('Here is your teacher') (by Walther Thomas) Eddie would recall (KV 2/455 56b Serial 570), and was then taught about fuses and burning materials. The 'glorious sunny morning' when he signed the contract with von Gröning is identified as in June in Eddie's memoirs. The near contemporaneous MI5 files show that it was actually August – backed up by the Abwehr Enigma decrypts relating to his case in the UK National Archives.

The work of Colonel John H. Bevan and the role of strategic deception in the Second World War could fill several books – indeed, it already has done. Formally speaking there was no 'Controller of Deception' (though everyone within Whitehall with security clearance knew that was his function) as his organisation – the London Controlling Section (LCS) – was so named to give no hint of its purpose. Unlike his immediate predecessor, Johnny Bevan was given access to Ultra. The work of the LCS was first discussed in Anthony Cave Brown's *Bodyguard of Lies*, while subsequent biographical information has come from Dennis Wheatley's *The Deception Planners* (1981) (the thriller writer was a member of the section). Most recently, Thaddeus Holt's exhaustive *The Deceivers*, discusses how the LCS worked, particularly on pp. 186–214 of Chapter 5, 'London Control'. The propaganda value of the Dieppe raid is discussed by Michael Balfour in *Propaganda In War 1939–1945* (1979). Eddie's own recollections may be found in KV 2/456 87f 'Propaganda'. All subsequent details of his time during the Vichy takeover may be found in the summaries of interrogation in KV 2/455 100y headed 'Occupation of the Free Zone', 'Limoges' and 'The Raids'. Details tally with those in *The Real Eddie Chapman Story*, pp. 98–105.

The story of the catching of Agent X is in KV 2/455 29a, a note from Dick White, then overall head of counter-intelligence within MI5. The relevant section of MI6 is identified as Section V, the counter-intelligence section of the Secret Intelligence Service. Details are discussed in KV 2/455 27a.

Though there is no mention of Eddie's meeting with von Rundstedt in the MI5 files, Eddie repeatedly told people about this event after the war. He discusses it on p.110 of *The Real Eddie Chapman Story*. The correct date for Eddie's departure from France may be found on p. 9, KV 2/ 456 85TA. In his memoirs, on p. 107, Eddie states that he left for England on the 17 December, but that was the day after he had been apprehended. Charles Whiting interviewed Oberleutnant Schlichting and his interview appears in 'Eddie with the Gelly', the seventh chapter in *Hitler's Secret War*.

The fact that Eddie was kicked out of the Junkers aircraft is discussed in KV 2/456 129b and, as another later note from MI5 investigators adds: 'his exit must have been facilitated by someone putting a foot in the back of his neck'.

5. Hendon Calling

Until fairly recently, the apprehension and subsequent interrogation of Eddie Chapman remained a closely guarded secret. In his first version of his story, published in 1954 as *The Eddie Chapman Story*, no mention is made of his contacts with British Intelligence, for reasons discussed in the epilogue to this book (pp. 302–303 and 306–309). He fell foul of the Official Secrets Act (which Eddie claimed he had never signed) because the existence of the Double Cross Committee was still a state secret. The impression in this first book is of Eddie staying in an abandoned house after he landed near Ely, taking a train to London, arriving during the rush hour, cold and starving, wondering how he could eat without having a ration book. Through underworld connections, he claimed he had stayed in a house in North London and then made his way back to Lisbon.

This broadly tallies with the cover story that he would put over to the Germans, as discussed in KV 2/459. A decade later, there were still problems in telling the real story of what happened. Even in 1966, when *The Real Eddie Chapman Story* was published, he could elaborate a little further but whole elements still had to be left out. In that book, Eddie devotes just one chapter to his interrogation and later domestic arrangements in Hendon. Tommy Robertson, for example, was identified as Colonel X. The full picture of what occurred comes from the release of the transcripts of all his interviews – firstly with 'Tin Eye' Stephens and then, later, Lord Rothschild – which may be found in KV 2/455 and 456. These various transcripts provide the narrative spine for this chapter.

For the record, they are:

Interrogation 1 17.12.42
9.30am   KV 2/455 56b
Captain Stephens
Short & Goodacre
Serials 558–595

Interrogation 2 17.12.42
15.30–17.25   KV 2/455 62zd
Captain Goodacre
Major Sampson
Serials 597–611

Interrogation 3 18.12.4
12.05–13.05   KV 2/455 62y
Major Sampson
Lieutenant Shanks
Serials 612–622

Interrogation 4 20.12.42
11.30–12.45   KV 2/456 100q
Major Sampson
Captain Goodacre
Serials 635–678

Eddie tended to concertina events in his later writings, but overall those recollections tally with the official record. 'There was one amazing thing about Eddie,' his handler Paul Backwell mentions (KV 2/458 238a) in his handwritten notes. 'He was pretty hopeless at remembering dates and times, but when it came to faces and descriptions of people he had met in France, he was good.' A useful chronology, particularly with regard to his radio transmission schedule, is a note on Valentine's Day, 1943 (KV 2/458 208b).

Eddie's sense of disorientation was acute. In the MI5 files, Eddie writes: 'I am afraid that whole thing' – he was talking about the last year since he was released from Jersey – 'has rather passed like a dream.' On New Year's Day, Eddie would explain in his first interview with Lord Rothschild that his arrival might be some sort of a trick. 'And when I landed here it was so warm that I thought "Oh my God, I'm not in England",' he said (p. 13, KV 2/456 92d). 'Really, I was quite surprised to find myself in England.' In his memoirs, Eddie says that he was first taken to a school in Kensington. It was actually a detention centre at the Royal Patriotic School in Wandsworth.

Details about Len Burt are taken from his own autobiography. The phrase 'Most formidable sleuth' comes from Lord Rothschild's Introduction (on p. ix) to that book, *Commander Burt of Scotland Yard* (Heinemann, 1959). The quote from the guard – 'I'm sure that fellow was in my guards unit' – is taken from p. 110, *Beyond Top Secret U* by Ewen Montagu (Peter Davis, 1977). The actual quote in that book says 'Irish guards' and was clearly reported second-hand to Montagu who, as examined on p. 287 of this book, was one of the few naval intelligence officers allowed to meet Zigzag. Eddie also discussed his army past with a sergeant at Ely police station.

Useful background information on how apprehended agents were handled may be found in Masterman's *The Double Cross System* and *Camp 020: MI5 and the Nazi Spies* published in 2000 by the (then) Public Record Office, now the UK National Archives. Eddie's particular case – where he is identified only as Zigzag – is examined on pp. 122–123, 131–132 and 171–173 of Masterman's book. In his own memoirs, Eddie refers to his chief interrogator as a colonel, one of many obvious obfuscations, probably imposed by the censors, to hide what happened out on Ham Common. This composite figure was most likely based on Tommy Robertson who wasn't actually based in Kew. The person who did apprehend him was the Commandant of Camp 020, 'Tin Eye' Stephens; corroboration comes from the fact that Eddie notes on p.121 of his memoirs that he 'inspected me through his monocle'.

Background details on Latchmere House are in the book *Camp 020: MI5 and the Nazi Spies*, based on Captain Stephens' original reports which have been entered into the UK National Archives. This book lists all the interrogations of captured agents and, in particular, from pp. 217–226, Eddie Chapman, whom Tin Eye dismisses as 'only war could invest with any virtue'. An amusing profile of Tin Eye comes from Oliver Hoare's introduction to that same book. Characteristically, only Captain Stephens could consider calling a post-war summary of his work at Camp 020 'A Digest of Ham'. But that is what he called it, now entered into the files KV 4/13 and 4/14 in the UK National Archives upon which the *Camp 020* book was based. The quote – 'Fiction has not....' comes from Stephens's intro to KV 2/457 106xk 'Yellow Peril', so named because it was written on bright yellow paper. This summarised the findings about Eddie for those higher in authority.

Details about Juan Pujol Garcia may be found in two standard references about the remarkable Catalan whose fictions so enthralled the Abwehr. *Garbo* by Nigel West (Weidenfield, 1983), who traced him after the war; and the original MI5 reports on his activities, written by his handler Tomas Harris, edited and collated as the book *Garbo: The Spy Who Saved D-Day* (Public Record Office, 2000). For context, see pp. 115–117, Masterman, *op cit*. The original documents in Kew may be found in KV 2/41. Other related files are KV/39, /40, /42, /64, /66 and /69. Dusko Popov's own memoirs *Spy/Counterspy* were published in 1974, while more recently, Russell Miller's *Codename Triangle* used Popov's MI5 files which may be variously found in KV 2/845 – /861.

A number of the discrepancies alluded to in Eddie's interrogations are examined in great detail in the MI5 files. In KV 2/457 112a, for example, Eddie repeatedly stated that the plane he came in on was a Focke Wulf long-distance reconnaissance plane. He told MI5 that there was special 'sound baffling equipment' which would lead to much correspondence with experts who concluded that 'some monkey business is in fact taking place' (KV 2/456 146c) and that 'something queer was taking place' in Tommy Robertson's phrase (KV 2/458 187c) on 4 February 1943.

According to his widow, Eddie thought highly of Tommy Robertson. Biographical information on Ronnie Reed was provided by Nicholas Reed to Betty Chapman. The records of Allan Tooth (KV 2/457 135b) and Paul Backwell (KV 2/458 238a) provide a fascinating insight into what happened in Hendon. They had both had been asked to record their initial opinions of Eddie, which were favourable, though they did sense that he seemed confused. Unbeknown to him at the time, Allan was assessing his character, Paul the factual side: together they would send any information back to MI5. Laurie Marshall, another member of the Security Service, recorded many interesting vignettes about Eddie's criminal past and recent training over Christmas 1942.

The details of the various Abwehr radio transmissions to 'Fritzchen' may be found throughout the MI5 files. The worries that 'they will undoubtedly get him' comes from KV 2/457 113a. In a short note, dated 10.1.43, Ronnie Reed also noted: 'It seems extraordinary that they should have such fear for ZIGZAG with this small duration of transmitting when other agents in this country are supposed to have been sending freely for about two years.' Back-ground details on the Mosquito bomber are taken from Edward Bishop, *The Wooden Wonder – The Story of the de Havilland Mosquito*(1959). Further details may be found in *Mosquito Bomber/Fighter-Bomber Units 1942–1945* by Martin Bowman (Osprey Aerospace, 1997).

6. How to Blow Up a Factory

The Hatfield job has a great symbolic significance for virtually every secret organisation was involved or used in some way. By early 1943, all the elements of the secret war – codebreaking, deception and double agent operations – had come together. Eddie Chapman himself only described the events obliquely in a handful of pages (pp. 129–134) in his memoirs. These mainly deal with the cover story and there is little detail about what actually took place to dress the factory. Only now, with the release of the relevant MI5 files, can we examine them in any detail. In particular, Volume 4 of Eddie's personal files (KV 2/458) describes the Hatfield job while Volume 5 deals with the aftermath and plans for his return home. His first interview with Lord Rothschild may be found in KV 2/ 456 92d. A useful cross-reference 'sabotage considerations' is given in KV 2/461 33a dated 12 May 1943.

The visit to Littleport was written up by both Eddie's minders. Allan Tooth's record of this visit forms KV 2/457 135b, while a slightly different perspective comes from Paul Backwell's handwritten notes – KV 2/458 238a. A far more curious event was preoccupying the police, according to these notes. The night before (15 January), enemy planes had dropped flares, evidently to use nearby dykes as a navigational aid. Had they been forewarned that Eddie had not landed there? This was a worry expressed to his handlers by the local police. There are a number of discrepancies concerning Eddie's meeting with Terence Young. Though Eddie puts this event before Christmas, the dinner actually took place on 21 January 1943. In Eddie's memoirs, the hotel is named as the Ritz. The relevant MI5 files, though, make it clear they dined at the Savoy – a place which Eddie was well acquainted with. Terence's recollections may be found in the article 'Young Romantic' by John Francis Lane, pp. 58–59, in the British Film Institute's *Film and Filming*, December 1967. Young was the son of the police commissioner in Shanghai and had been born a year after Eddie was. For some reason, he didn't mention that they had once shared a house together. Other biographical details may be found in obituaries on Terence Young; the 16 September 1994 issue of the *Independent*, 10 September the *Daily Telegraph*, and 7 September, the *Guardian*.

Reference to Sir John Turner's nickname comes from p. 141 of Dennis Wheatley's *The Deception Planners*. Colonel Turner's department was also known by its earlier name, the Starfish Organisation. Background information on camouflage may be found in Young and Stamp's *Trojan Horses* and Guy Hartcup *Camouflage*. In a number of accounts, the name of Jasper Maskelyne is mentioned as having dressed the factory. A famous pre-war magician, Maskelyne was involved in a number of tactical deception operations for various Allied services. The documentary evidence at the UK National Archives contains no mention of his name with regard to the Hatfield job.

The story of Eddie's 'visit to Barnes' appears in pages 130 and 131 of *The Real Eddie Chapman Story*. Unsurprisingly, there is no reference in the MI5 files, nor indeed to Eddie's visit to Chequers. The Prime Minister's interest in espionage is exhaustively explored in David Stafford's *Churchill and the Secret Service* (1999). Masterman's visit to Robert Barrington-Ward is mentioned in KV 2/458 173a, which *The Times* recorded when the file was declassified. See Michael Evans's story 'The Times refused to lie', p. 8, *The Times*, 5 July 2001.

7. Voyage to Lisbon

Details of Eddie's adventures in Liverpool, Lisbon and Paris are contained in Chapters 11 'The Road Back' and 12 'I Make my Report' of *The Real Eddie Chapman Story*. Detailed information comes from KV 2/461 and particularly document 29 in that series, 'Statements made by members of the crew of SS *City of Lancaster* regarding Hugh Anson'. Volume 7 of KV 2/458 has all the preparations for his voyage, particularly 'Report of Activities in Liverpool' (KV 2/458 235c). Operation Damp Squib itself is also covered in KV 2/459 Volume Six. Eddie's own recollections of these events came over a year later when he was interviewed by MI5 in July 1944. They may be found in KV 2/459 Volume Seven.

A number of accounts describe the height of the Battle of the Atlantic in March 1943 from the perspective of both sides of the fighting. The standard German account is Jürgen Rohwer's *The Critical Convoy Battles of March 1943* (Naval Institute Press, 1977); while on the British side, the three volumes of Stephen W. Roskill, *The War at Sea, 1939–1945* (HMSO, 1954–1961), from which the phrases 'The Month of the Thunderbolt' and 'torpedo alley' are taken.

Eddie's departure date is confirmed in KV 2/459 24b and KV 2/458 237a. All details about his trip which follow come from KV 2/461 passim and Chapter 11 of *The Real Eddie Chapman Story*. As noted in Chapter 1 (p. 24), Eddie referred to Anson as Phil, p. 130, *The Real Eddie Chapman Story*; p. 11 of KV 2/459 254b gives an outline of what was needed to obtain relevant documents; pp. 2 and 3 of KV 2/458 235a on what happened; while KV 2/458 235c and 226 lists all the documents. According to

KV 2/461 29 Section I, p. 1, the Chief Steward was an H. Snellgrove. Eddie clearly didn't like him: he calls him 'corpse-face'.

Background details on MI6's operations in Portugal are taken from Nigel West, (Weidenfield, 1983). According to a note in KV 2/459 278K, an MI6 source – identified as 'a reliable prostitute' – says that Eddie was 'hiding in the German Legation' on 7 April 1943. Ronnie Reed reports his side of the conversation with Ralph Jarvis in KV 2/459 264c. The details of what happened when Ronnie met Eddie comes from a biographical note supplied by Nicholas Reed to Betty Chapman

The *City of Lancaster*'s security man, J. H. Stimpson, was the source of much worry to MI5 when it appeared that he had been smuggling something off the ship when it was later moored off Gibraltar; see p. 6, KV 2/461 29. In his memoirs, Eddie says the ship docked in Portugal on 14 March (p. 140, *The Real Eddie Chapman Story*). Captain Kearon's later testimony makes it clear this was the 16th (p. 1, KV 2/459 270) and in KV 2/461 19K it is stated that the *City of Lancaster* arrived in Lisbon on 15.3.43; sailed from Lisbon on 3.4.43; arrived Huelva, 4.4.43; sailed Huelva 11.4.43; arrived Gibraltar, 12.4.43 and sailed from there 14.4.43.

The address where Eddie was sent from the embassy is not mentioned on page 142 of *The Real Eddie Chapman Story*. According to KV 2/459 269B, this was the rua de Buenos Aires. With regard to the events which followed, Eddie's memoirs have tended to compress the timescale. Rather than being handed the coal bomb and placing them on board the same day, the actual events took place over a few days, according to the MI5 files. On p. 143 of *The Real Eddie Chapman Story*, Eddie says he went out for a meal before being handed the coal. The MI5 files show this handing over took place on the following evening.

On page 144 of his memoirs, Eddie gives the text of a supposed confessional to Captain Kearon – that he was working for British Intelligence, that he had been asked to blow up his ship. This clearly didn't occur as the captain already knew. Though there is some suggestion that Eddie's fight with the 'bruiser' was staged, according to p. 2, KV 2/461 29, Section I, where O'Connor is interviewed about Eddie, there is no mention of the fight. In a later MI5 file, it is implied that the punch-up was a put-up job; but Eddie's widow says that his bruises were genuine!

According to p. 145 of Eddie's memoirs, Herr Braun asked Eddie whether both pieces of coal been placed aboard. Yes, he said. Presumably this was to avoid having to explain to the readers of *The Real Eddie Chapman Story* what had happened to the other piece of coal. In his memoirs, Eddie remembered the name on his new passport as Hans Christiansen, but the spelling of Kristiansson was recorded nearer the time.

There are two further discrepancies on his return to Europe. After his first run through of his story, the Luftwaffe crew invited him to dine at their mess but they never saw them again. A certain confusion exists because in his memoirs Eddie had claimed, 'I heard soon after that the whole crew had been shot down and killed over England: it was their sixtieth sortie.' Yet Charles Whiting interviewed Lt Schichtling after the war.

In his memoirs, Eddie claims that he told Wolfgang that he had taken two explosive cases into the boiler room at Hatfield, which contradicts the MI5 record. Eddie says that he had left one on the left boiler, the other on the right. According to the MI5 files, Eddie was 'visited by a Kapitain Müller who would travel with him to Oslo'. On p. 158 of his memoirs, Eddie makes it clear that they were going to Norway because that was where the Baron had been returned to from the Eastern Front.

8. The Oslo Connection

Eddie Chapman's recollections of his time in Norway may be found in Chapters 13 ('The Iron Cross'), 14 ('Norway Under the Terror'), 15 ('Ordered to Berlin') and 16 ('The Falling Market') of *The Real Eddie Chapman Story*. A more contemporaneous record comes from his second set of MI5 interrogations in June and July 1944 which are located in KV 2/459 and 460 at the UK National Archives. In particular, Volume 7 of KV 2/459 contains 'The Camp 020 Second Interim Report on the case of Edward Arnold Chapman' which is numbered 338a.

As is clear from the source notes which follow, Eddie's sense of chronology was still a little misplaced. After his arrival in Oslo, he tended to get the dates wrong – concerning events around the Führer's birthday and his own, for example – but only by a matter of days. His facility for faces, places and impressions remained strong. Just about the only factual inconsistency came with his visit to Trondheim at the end of 1943, which he says was Bergen. In fairness, immediately after that visit, Eddie did practise sailing in Bergen harbour.

Norway's crucial role in the secret war has been examined in a number of books. For the story of the Oslo Letter – which would cast a pall over much of Eddie's future work – the standard reference is from the late R.V. Jones, who worked in scientific intelligence for MI6, and wrote about the circumstances in his memoir *Most Secret War* (1978). An exhaustively sourced guide to the various deception operations aimed at Norway may be found in Thaddeus Holt's *The Deceivers* which had access to many of the hitherto secret papers on which the operations are based. For background to Operation Mincemeat ('The Man Who Never Was'), see Chapter 5, 'The Mediterranean Story' by Howard, *op cit*. The quote – 'It never took much to make Hitler believe in a threat to Norway' is taken from p. 82 of that work. The background to Operation Cockade is explored on pp. 71–82.

A number of authors have referred to Walter Wegener's essay which affected Adolf Hitler's thinking. See, for example, p. 17 of Ralph Erskine's *Behind the Battle, Intelligence in the War with Germany, 1939–1945* (Pimlico, 1999). The two Norwegian agents who had stayed in Hendon were codenamed Mutt and Jeff. Their files are in the KV/2 1067 and 1068 series, but have told their story in Young and Stamp, *Trojan Horses*, Chapter 20, 'The Agents' Tale', pp. 183–194.

In his autobiography, Eddie claims that Walther Thomas arrived on April 10th (p. 172, *The Real Eddie Chapman Story*). According to the MI5 files, it was actually 21 April, the day after the Führertag. In his original memoirs, Eddie claims his total financial reward was 150,000 Reichsmarks, the extra 50,000 for the sabotage of the *City of Lancaster* in Lisbon. But a near contemporaneous note from MI5 shows that the actual additional payment was only 10,000 RM. The figure in the text has been amended to make it internally consistent, taking dialogue from p. 174 of *The Real Eddie Chapman Story*.

In his memoirs, Eddie says the visit to Berlin was 'towards the end of 1943' (p. 188, *The Real Eddie Chapman Story*), though the later MI5 interrogation makes clear it was early July as this was *before* the Hamburg raids which took place at the end of that month. In his memoirs, Eddie says that he stayed at the Metropolitan Hotel on the Friedrichstrasse. A later MI5 report says it was actually the Hotel Alexandra on the Mittelstrasse. As for the delay in departure back to Oslo, in the relevant MI5 report, the reason is blamed on 'bad flying weather', after which they remained in Berlin for several days (p. 12, KV 2/459 338a).

The story of Eddie's accusation of being a spy (p. 180, *The Real Eddie Chapman Story*) does not appear in the MI5 files but there is mention of both 'Frau Arna' and Sturmbannführer Etling on p. 17 of the second 'Yellow Peril', KV 2/458 338a. The spelling of this 'Norwegian woman informer in Oslo' is 'Frue Anne' in his memoirs. The Gestapo man is referred to as Captain Etlung in Chapter 14, 'Norway Under the Terror', of Eddie's memoirs.

In the summary MI5 report, the photographer called Rotkagal is spelled Rotkegel and he is identified as a member of the Oslo *Dienststelle*. With regard to the mass arrests, Eddie says they occurred the day after his birthday (p. 184, *The Real Eddie Chapman Story*). His birthday was on the 16 November; the incidents at the university occurred on the 28th. There is, however, no doubt Eddie experienced the fallout with his near arrest. Background details on the significance of Oslo University may be found on p. 245 of *Quisling – a Study in Treachery*, Hans Fredrik Dahl (CUP, 1999).

In his memoirs, Eddie says that he went to the U-boat headquarters at Mardness Gate in Bergen (p. 204, *The Real Eddie Chapman Story*) along with 'Johann the Devil', his fellow saboteur. As noted above, the MI5 files show that it was actually Trondheim. Useful background to the final stages of the fight against the U-boats may be found in *War Beneath the Sea* by Peter Padfield (Pimlico, 1995). Chapter 5, 'Shadow and Sunlight Over the Atlantic', in Ralph Erskine's *Behind the Battle, op cit*, is a detailed look at the intelligence efforts which supported that battle.

The use of the word 'web' to describe the Icelandic agents is deliberate: their codenames were Spider, Beetle and Cobweb. Originally, they were run by Ronnie Reed – Eddie's controller – in 1942 (see footnote in the text on p. 203). The two Icelandic agents captured by the British at the start of May 1944 were only known to Eddie their spy names of Jakobsen and Bauer (p. 17, KV 2/459 338a). The mystery surrounding Eddie's 'reappearance' at the start of 1944 is explained on pp. 171–172 of Masterman, *op cit*.

9. The Long Goodbye

The penultimate phase of Eddie's work as a double agent is examined in Chapters 17 ('Berlin Under the Bombs'), 18 ('Paris on the Eve'), and 19 ('Second Front') of *The Real Eddie Chapman Story*. In the National Archives, Serials KV 2/459 and 2/460 deal with his final months as a double agent in 1944. Again, though his grasp of continuity and chronology are lacking in several places, Eddie's recall of the telling detail is astonishing. His second parachute landing and the subsequent interrogations – though more perfunctory than two years earlier – are mainly recorded in KV 2/459 Volume 7. In particular, the second 'Yellow Peril' KV 2/459 338a is a source of much useful information. A standard reference for the fight against the V-1s is R.V. Jones' *Most Secret War*, buttressed by Volume Five of the official British history, Sir Michael Howard's *Strategic Deception in the Second World War*. Frederick Lindemann's famous quote – 'The mountain hath groaned' – is taken from p. 417 of R.V. Jones, *op cit*.

The various quotes from Adolf Hitler are taken from a number of biographies. The most relevant is the second part of Ian Kershaw's magisterial biographies of Adolf Hitler, *1936–1945, Nemesis*, particularly Chapter 13, 'Hoping for a Miracle', pp. 607–652. Many excellent accounts have been written on the vast and intricate deception operation surrounding the D-Day landings. Among the most informative are Roger Hesketh's *Fortitude* (published in 1999 by St Ermin's) as well as Thaddeus Holt's *The Deceivers (op cit)*. The phrase 'musicians and choristers' comes from Sir Ronald Wingate's comment on p. 236 of *Bodyguard of Lies* by Anthony Cave Brown.

Eddie's comments about Japanese diplomats 'carrying boxes of secret and confidential papers' is intriguing. Baron Hiroshu Oshima, Japan's ambassador to the Reich, was granted unprecedented access to the Führer at this time. Bletchley Park was able to read his reports back to Tokyo which were remarkably candid in their assessments of the state of the Third Reich. See p. 128, Holt, *The Deceivers*. For background on the bombing of France before D-Day and the fate of the Luftwaffe, a useful reference is Tami Davis Biddle, *Rhetoric and Reality in Air Warfare* (Princeton, 2005), particularly Chapter 5.

It should be noted that both Garbo and Tricycle could travel freely between Britain and Iberia – and did so several times – until the ban on travel to and from Britain was imposed in April 1944. A month earlier, the airmail service to Lisbon was suspended. All diplomatic mail was subject to censorship and the use of enciphered messages therein was banned.

As regards dates and times of Eddie's various travels, according to the summary, p. 19, KV 2/459 367, the journey from Berlin to Paris is recorded as being on the 8 or 10 March. The sinister Krause is discussed on pages 225–226 of Eddie's memoirs. He claims they met in a small park off the Boulevard Raspail, though the MI5 record suggests it took place in a nearby house during their discussions. Eddie spells the name Krauser (which is how it sounds). There was some confusion whether he was the same Krause whom he had met in Oslo who worked for the S.D. (p. 2, KV 2/459 368). The answer was no: 'Furthermore Chapman had never heard of him when he was in Oslo and had only seen him in Paris.' In Eddie's autobiography, the name of the 'well-known man' about whom Krause was interested is stated to be Dennis W – which could well have been Dennis Wheatley, the thriller writer who worked for the deception staff in London. Eddie said that he had no idea whether this person was working for the British Secret Service.

As with his earlier stay in Romainville, there is some confusion over the name of the French girls Eddie and von Gröning tried to recruit. In Eddie's post-war memoirs, the French girl is called Hélène (p. 235, *The Real Eddie Chapman*). The MI5 files claim he met her at the Ambassador Hotel and that her real name was Giselle Martineiche. Whether he had changed her name to protect her from reprisals or simply forgot it, is not clear. Betty Chapman says that her husband had no further contact with her after the war. That London was expected to be devastated by the V-1s comes from p. 6 of the second 'Yellow Peril', KV 2/459 338a. In the section headed 'Goebbels Propaganda', they were certain that electricity would be in short supply because the V-1 bombings would have destroyed all the capital's power stations. If they did not hear from Eddie straight away, the *Abwehr* would assume that he had been unable to operate his transmitter due to the lack of available current.

In Eddie's memoirs, he says that his controller's birthday was 28 June. The MI5 reports make it clear that it must have been earlier: he left for England on the night of 26/27 June.

10. Hard Landings

The final phases of Eddie's work as a double agent are contained in Chapter 20 ('Journey's End') of *The Real Eddie Chapman Story*. The exact details of his work in fighting the V-1s are glossed over in that account. The MI5 files released into KV 2/459 and /460 are exhaustive. More details of Eddie's deception work – and how it fitted in with the overall scheme of things – can be found in Sir Michael Howard's *Strategic Deception*, particularly Chapter 8 (pp. 167–184) 'Crossbow: The Flying Bombs: June – December 1944'. A fuller picture of the various arguments about how to fight the vengeance weapons is discussed in both R.V. Jones and Adrian Fort, *Prof.* As well as defensive measures, a larger operation called Crossbow attempted to destroy the vengeance weapon sites. Details of the anti-submarine work are in Appendix V of Howard's book – as well as the Hon. Ewen Montagu's *Beyond Top Secret, op cit.*

The MI5 files are circumspect concerning Eddie Chapman's injuries on landing. In his memoirs, Eddie says (p. 248, *The Real Eddie Chapman Story*), 'My arm hurt but was not fractured.' There is a cursory reference to some medical examination in KV 2/459 339a: 'Dr Page examined Zigzag yesterday and said that his condition was not as bad as it might be.' It doesn't mention what the condition is. The report continues: 'He has given him some medicine and has recommended treatment, but thinks it will be necessary for a rather more concentrated treatment to be started next week. Meanwhile, he considers that ZIGZAG is well enough to be interrogated and in fact the man seems mentally quite fit though he is physically tired.'

The other main agents used against the buzzbombs were Garbo and Brutus. Relevant details about Brutus may be found in his MI5 files in KV 2/72 and 2/73.

A letter dated 5 July 1944 in KV 2/459 358a explains how Garbo and Brutus were used. The background to Garbo's supposed arrest and the issues surrounding FUSAG may be found on pp. 258–260, from *Garbo, The Spy Who Saved D-Day, op cit.* The phrase 'by special means' is a cover for the all euphemisms used to describe the double agents and their deception of their Abwehr controllers. It was a phrase that MI5 didn't like to use outside of its offices. 'Most secret sources' was how the material coming out of Bletchley was camouflaged in official reports. For a more precise definition see Holt, *op cit*, p. 129.

For background information on the V-2s, see Chapter 45 of R.V. Jones, *op cit*, The V-2. In his various interviews, Eddie seemed to think that the V-2 rockets were guided by radio control. In fact, they used an inertial guidance platform (a prototype of the one that would safely land the Apollo astronauts on the moon) involving three gyroscopes which controlled its orientation. If the missile deviated from its planned course, the gyros would correct them by altering the fins to get it back on course. After about five minutes of flight, the fuel would be cut.

For Eddie's contribution to the fight against the U-boats, see both *Naval Deceptions*, pp. 223–228, Howard and *More Naval Deceptions*, Chapter 11 in Montagu, pp. 126–127. The phrase 'gone to the dogs' is used in KV 2/460 41, a note dated 6.8.44. A useful backgroud discussion to the White City tracks may be found in Donald Thomas, *The Underground At War*. The full story of the 'the great greyhound swindle' may be found in Chapter 7, 'The Tote Double Plus' in *Fabian of the Yard*, *op cit*.

Epilogue: Free Agent

In the mid-1950s, Eddie and Betty Chapman became famous, partly as a result of Eddie's wartime exploits and also for the saga (explained in the text) of his time in the Mediterranean on the *Flamingo*. The publication of his wartime memoirs *The Eddie Chapman Story* came in 1953, followed by *Free Agent* (1955), which related the story to the end of 1954. They gave many newspaper interviews – some of which are mentioned in the text.

The saga ('Roman circus' is apt, a phrase used by one correspondent in the official files) of Eddie's post-war efforts to publish his book may be found in WO 32/15386 (1953); to turn that into a film WO 32/16232 and /17807 (1956–1963); as well as DEFE 28/187. Correspondence concerning these matters is also contained in the Treasury Solicitor's file TS 54/19. The strange case of the alleged Kapoor kidnapping is in the Metroplitan Police File, MEPO 2/10461, which uses his correct name of Arnold Edward Chapman. (All the earlier MI5 ones are labelled Edward Arnold Chapman.)

Further Reading

Christopher Andrew, *Secret Service – The Making of the British Intelligence Community* (Heinemann, 1985)

Michael Balfour, *Propaganda In War 1939–1945* (Routledge, 1979)

Richard Bassett, *Hitler's Spy Chief* (Weidenfield, 2005)

Edward Bishop, *The Wooden Wonder – The Story of the de Havilland Mosquito* (Ballantine, 1971)

Tom Bower, *A Perfect English Spy* (Heinemann, 1995)

Anthony Cave Brown, *Bodyguard of Lies* (W.H. Allen, 1976)

Leonard Burt, *Commander Burt of Scotland Yard* (Heinemann, 1959)

Duncan Campbell, *The Underworld* (BBC, 1994)

Eddie Chapman, *The Eddie Chapman Story* (Allan Wingate, 1954)

— *Free Agent* (Allan Wingate, 1955)

— *Joey Boy* (Cassell, 1959)

— *The Real Eddie Chapman Story* (Tandem, 1966)

Jack C. Curry, 'The Security Service, 1908–1945: The Official History' (Public Record Office, 1999)

Ralph Erskine, *Behind The Battle, Intelligence in the War with Germany, 1939–1945* Pimlico, 1999)

Robert Fabian, *Fabian of the Yard* (Nalchett, 1950)

Anthony Faramus, *The Faramus Story* (Allan Wingate, 1955)

— *Journey Into Darkness* (Grafton, 1990)

Adrian Fort, *Prof: The Life and Times of Frederick Lindemann* (Cape, 2003)

Edward Greeno, *War On The Underworld* (Long, 1960)

Guy Hartcup, *Camouflage* (David & Charles, 1979)

Roger Hesketh, *Fortitude: The D-Day Deception Campaign* (St. Erskine's, 1999)

Hinsley & Stipp, eds, *Codebreakers* (Oxford University Press, 1993)

Thaddeus Holt, *The Deceivers* (Weidenfield & Nicolson, 2004)

Sir Michael Howard, 'Strategic Deception in the Second World War', Volume 5 in 'British Intelligence in the Second World War' (HMSO, 1990)

R.V. Jones, *Most Secret War* (Hamish Hamilton, 1978)

Kahn, *Hitler's Spies* (Da Capo, 2000)

Dick Kirby, *The Real Sweeney* (Constable and Robinson, 2005)

Peter King, *The Channel Islands War, 1940–1945* (Hale, 1991)

John Masterman, *The Double Cross System in the war of 1939–1945* (Pimlico, 1995)

Russell Miller, *Codename Tricycle* (Secker & Warburg, 2004)

Ewen Montagu, *Beyond Top Secret U*' (Peter Davis, 1977)

Robert Murphy, *Smash and Grab* (Faber, 1992)

Geoffrey Pidgeon, *The Secret Wireless War – The Story of MI6 Communications 1939–1945* (USPO, 2000)

Eric Pleasants, *I Killed To Live* (ghosted by Eddie Chapman) (Allan Wingate, 1957)

— *Hitler's Bastard* (ed. Ian Sayer & Douglas Botting) (Mainstream, 2003)

Public Record Office, 'Camp 020: MI5 and The Nazi Spies' (2000)

— 'Garbo: The Spy Who Saved D-Day' (2000)

Paul Sanders, *The British Channel Islands Under German Occupation 1940–1945* (Jersey Heritage Trust, 2005)

David Stafford, *Churchill and Secret Service* (John Murray, 1997)

— *Ten Days To D-Day* (Little Brown, 2004)

Donald Thomas, *An Underworld at War* (John Murray, 2004)

Nigel West, *MI6 – British Secret Intelligence Operations, 1909–1945*(Weidenfield, 1983)

— *Garbo* (Weidenfield, 1985)

Dennis Wheatley, *The Deception Planners* (Hutchinson, 1981)

Charles Whiting, *Hitler's Secret War* (Leo Cooper, 1999)

Martin Young & Robin Stamp, *Trojan Horses* (The Bodley Head, 1989)

Index

Note: page numbers preceded by 'n' refer to information contained in the notes at the bottom of the page.

PORTRAIT BOOKS

If you have enjoyed reading this book, you may be interested in:

The Battle for Singapore
The True Story of the Greatest Catastrophe of World War II
978 0 7499 5099 4
£9.99

The fall of Fortress Singapore to a numerically inferior Japanese army on 15 February 1942 was one of the darkest days in the history of the Second World War. How could it have happened? Who was to blame?

Peter Thompson's gripping narrative uncovers the uncomfortable truths that have been hidden behind self-serving lies and distortions for more than 60 years. The author has interviewed numerous survivors of the tragedy – the book is packed with eye-witness accounts of the bravery, panic and self-sacrifice of Australian and British soldiers, and the trapped citizens of Singapore.

The Battle for Singapore is an enthralling and dramatic read – the fullest and most objective account yet written about one of the most fascinating and controversial episodes of the Second World War.

'An enthralling and perceptive account, which never loses sight of the human cost of the tragedy' *Yorkshire Evening Post*

'A stylishly pacy, dramatic and vivid narrative, enlivened by survivor's first-hand accounts, which will hook the most casual of readers.' *Soldier*

Available from:

Piatkus Books Ltd, c/o Bookpost, PO Box 29, Douglas, Isle of Man, IM99 1BQ

Telephone (+44) 01624 677 237
Fax (+44) 01624 670 923
Email: bookshop@enterprise.net
Free Postage and Packing in the United Kingdom
Credit Cards accepted. All Cheques payable to Bookpost

Prices and availability are subject to change without prior notice. Please allow 14 days for delivery. When placing orders, please state if you do not wish to receive any additional information.